Artificial Intelligence and Legal Evidence

This book explores AI's impact on legal evidence, with a particular focus on its use within Indian law, by identifying the key feature of an Artificial Intelligence-Driven Justice Delivery System. It seeks to bridge the gap in the literature on the intersection of AI and law, specifically the evaluation of evidence. The book focuses on AI's potential to enhance the evaluation of evidence in various legal contexts. It considers the reliability, admissibility, and standardisation of AI-generated evidence in legal proceedings.

The key features of the book are:

- Presents case studies and examples from multiple branches of law, exploring AI's use in evidence collection, analysis, and evaluation across diverse legal domains.
- Offering a unique perspective on AI and legal evidence within India, the book provides a critical look at how AI can be integrated into India's legal framework and the implications for the country's judicial system.
- Addresses the policy gaps and regulatory frameworks needed to govern AI in the legal sphere, with a focus on India's evolving stance on AI.
- Emphasises the need for ethical standards and privacy protection while using AI to evaluate legal evidence, examines the challenges in ensuring the validity and fairness of AI-generated evidence.
- Highlights the future potential of AI in transforming the legal industry, particularly in terms of improving efficiency, reducing bias, and enabling more effective evidence evaluation.

The book will be useful for academicians and scholars interested in AI's impact and use in the legal system.

Artificial Intelligence and Legal Evidence

The Indian Policy and Perspective

Edited by
Sarfaraz Ahmed Khan, Lovely Dasgupta, Saptarshi Ghosh
and Kripabandhu Ghosh

CRC Press
Taylor & Francis Group
Boca Raton London New York

CRC Press is an imprint of the
Taylor & Francis Group, an informa business

Designed cover image: Shutterstock

First edition published 2026
by CRC Press
4 Park Square, Milton Park, Abingdon, Oxon, OX14 4RN

and by CRC Press
2385 NW Executive Center Drive, Suite 320, Boca Raton FL 33431

CRC Press is an imprint of Informa UK Limited

British Library Cataloguing-in-Publication Data
A catalogue record for this book is available from the British Library

ISBN: 9781041046240 (hbk)
ISBN: 9781041046233 (pbk)
ISBN: 9781003629146 (ebk)

DOI: 10.1201/9781003629146

Typeset in Times
by Newgen Publishing UK

Contents

Preface

Artificial Intelligence and Legal Evidence: The Indian Policy and Perspective was conceived as an exercise in bringing together expertise from both law and science. This book provided a platform for the editors across the two disciplines to interact on issues concerning their field of expertise. The editors then reached out to people to find out those interested in such work. There were hurdles, doubts, and confusion; however, there was also confidence. Eventually, the chapters came in, contributors responded with enthusiasm, and finally, we have successfully put together the first of its kind book. We hope the reader learns and unlearns in the process of reading the book.

By Sarfaraz Ahmed Khan, Lovely Dasgupta,
Saptarshi Ghosh, and Kripabandhu Ghosh
Kolkata, 20/11/2025

Acknowledgement

This book would not have been possible without the support of a brilliant team of researchers. Hence, before anyone else, they need to be acknowledged. Arko Sankar Karmakar, Saurish Mukherjee, Maulimanni Jain, Abira Das, Nitya Nandan Garg, and Anirudh Sharma have tirelessly worked on this project as researchers. Without their unstinting support, it would have been impossible to finish the book on time. Rajesh Dey, Senior Commissioning Editor for Computer Science, Physics, Mathematics, and Statistics at CRC Press, Taylor and Francis Group, has, as always, been the pillar of strength, guiding us through this entire process. Last but not the least, our family members, who have endured the numerous tantrums we threw during the editing process of this book.

About the Editors

Sarfaraz Ahmed Khan is currently serving as a professor at West Bengal National University of Juridical Sciences. He previously served as Professor and Director at Symbiosis Law School, Hyderabad. He is involved in research intertwining the Criminal Justice Administration, Human Rights, and Human Trafficking. He has authored several books on these subjects, including *The Transnational Sex Trafficking: An Integrated Reparation Model* (2019) which emphasises on a human rights dimension of cross-border sex-trafficking between India and Bangladesh. He is a recipient of prestigious fellowships including the British Chevening Scholarship, Hong Kong UGC Scholarship, Michigan Grotius Research Fellowship, and the U.S. Department of State's IVLP Fellowship.

Lovely Dasgupta is currently serving as a professor at the West Bengal National University of Juridical Sciences. She has been teaching and researching Sports Law, Contract, and Legal Education. Her key publications include: *Esports and the World Anti-Doping Code* (Routledge, UK); *Online Gaming in India Technology, Policy, and Challenges*, edited By Lovely Dasgupta and Shameek Sen (); and *Sport in Contemporary India Society, Culture and Governance*, edited by Surajit C Mukhopadhyay and Lovely Dasgupta (Routledge, UK).

Saptarshi Ghosh is an associate professor at the Department of Computer Science and Engineering, Indian Institute of Technology (IIT) Kharagpur. His current research interests are in legal data analytics, AI and sustainability, and algorithmic bias and fairness. His research is inter-disciplinary and uses techniques from machine learning, natural language processing, information retrieval, and complex network theory. He received his PhD in Computer Science from IIT Kharagpur in 2013. He was a Humboldt Post-doctoral research fellow at the Max Planck Institute for Software Systems (MPI-SWS), Germany. He heads a Max Planck Partner Group at IIT Kharagpur, which focuses on algorithmic bias and fairness. He is presently an Editor-in-Chief of the journal *Artificial Intelligence and Law*, the premier journal in the domain of AI and law.

Kripabandhu Ghosh is an associate professor at Indian Institute of Science, Education and Research, Kolkata. He completed his PhD (Computer Science) at the Indian Statistical Institute, Kolkata. His research interests include information retrieval, data mining, and AI in the legal domain; information extraction from social media text in disaster situations; fairness in text summarisation; and data mining on noisy text.

Contributors

Abhivardhan
Founder, Indic Pacific Legal Research LLP, President & Managing Trustee, Indian Society of Artificial Intelligence and Law

Hiteshi Agarwal
Assistant Professor, Department of Law I, FOL, Manipal University, Jaipur

Maitreyee Apte
Researchers, www.lexres.co.in

Riya Banerjee
Faculty, JIS University, Kolkata

Supratim Bapuli
Researcher at Symbiosis Law School, Hyderabad

Abhisikta Basu
Assistant Professor, IEM's International Institute of Juridical Sciences (IIIJS)

Anik Bhattacharya
Research Scholar of Law Department, JIS University

Aayana Rai Bhojani
Agami/OpenNyAI

Akanksha Bisoyi
Professor of Law, Innovation and Legal Design, Technical University of Munich, Department of Science, Technology and Society, Munich, Germany

Atish Chakraborty
Faculty, The West Bengal National University of Juridicial Sciences, Kolkata

Subhrajit Chanda
Assistant Professor and Assistant Director, Centre for Sports Law, Business and Governance (CSLBG), Jindal Global Law School, OP Jindal Global University

Ishita Chatterjee
Professor, School of Law, SRM Institute of Science and Technology, Chennai

Debdeep Das
Faculty, The West Bengal National University of Juridicial Sciences Kolkata

Vivasvan Gautam
Research Assistant, The West Bengal National University of Juridical Sciences

Shouvik Kumar Guha
Faculty and Researcher, The West Bengal National University of Juridicial Sciences, Kolkata, India

Varun Hemachandran
OpenNyAI mission at Agami

Suman Dinesh Jain
Advocate and Founder, All About Law

Sarfaraz Ahmed Khan
Professor of Law, The West Bengal National University of Juridical Sciences

Sadqua Khatoon
Researcher, Aligarh Muslim University

Nishtha Mahapatra
Research Assistant-cum-Judicial Clerk, High Court of Orissa

Harsh Mahaseth
Faculty, Jindal Global University

Dhruv Maheshwari
Faculty, The West Bengal National University of Juridicial Sciences, Kolkata

Padmavati Manchikanti
Professor, Rajiv Gandhi School of Intellectual Property Law, IIT Kharagpur

Shreya Matilal
Assistant Professor Grade-I, Rajiv Gandhi School of Intellectual Property Law, IIT Kharagpur

Vibhav Mithal
Researchers, AI & Tech Ethics

Arjita Mukherjee
Faculty, The West Bengal National University of Juridicial Sciences Kolkata

Shtantika Mukherjee
Faculty, Manipal University, Jaipur

Keya De Mukhopadhyay
University of Engineering and Management, Kolkata

Sundaraparipurnan Narayanan
Researchers, AI & Tech Ethics

Siddharth Anand Panda
Research Assistant-cum-Judicial Clerk, High Court of Orissa

Sanjeeb K. Panigrahi
Judge of Orissa High Court

Gazala Parveen
Researcher, Rajiv Gandhi School of IP Law, IIT Kharagpur, Kharagpur, West Bengal

Pranav Patade
Independent Technology and AI Researcher
www.linkedin.com/in/pranavpatade/

Marie Potel
Researchers, AI & Tech Ethics

Monidipa Sengupta
Research Scholar at RGSOIPL, IIT Kharagpur

Harshada Shangarpawar
Researchers, www.lexres.co.in

Deevanshu Shrivastava
Professor of Law, National University of Study and Research in Law, Ranchi

Shikha Vasishta
Researcher, Bennett University, Greater Noida, Uttar Pradesh, India

Gayathri Venkatadri
Researchers, www.lexres.co.in

Daisy Verghese
Faculty, Jindal Global University

Introduction

Lovely Dasgupta

We are all besotted, scared and inquisitive about Artificial Intelligence and its impact. This book, through its various chapters, evaluates the impact of Artificial Intelligence on assets. Artificial Intelligence is gaining ground in every field. It's being recognised as both a threat and an asset. Artificial Intelligence is more than technology augmentation. It aids human intelligence and intertwines with human lives at different levels. Law, on the other hand, impacts every aspect of our lives. Every sector has to understand its compliance in different ways. From IPR to Criminal Law, from Contract Law to Labour Law, one common theme connects the diversity within this field, viz., evidence. The winning brief is the one that presents the strongest evidence. The quality of evidence determines the outcome of every case. Notably, the ability of the council to prove the veracity of the evidence used in a particular case. Thus, for instance, to establish the existence of a contract, one has to prove consensus ad idem. Similarly, evidence analysis and generating evidence are essential for success in each of the fields mentioned above.

Artificial Intelligence is a game-changer in every sense. Its interface with the law is a matter of ongoing debate and discussion. This debate includes the pros and cons of Artificial Intelligence usage within the law. The debate also involves the struggle to detect abuse of Artificial Intelligence and its impact on access to justice. A considerable amount of literature exists on this interface, along with debates about its impact across various jurisdictions globally. The primary issue concerns the admissibility and reliability of Artificial Intelligence in generating or evaluating evidence. The usage of Artificial Intelligence varies from simple to complex. Accordingly, there is a lack of standardisation as to the extent of their reliability. The uncertainty about reliability and standardisation means it's challenging for all involved.

There are no laws or regulations in India dealing with Artificial Intelligence. The Ministry of Electronics and Information Technology issued an advisory on March 15, 2024, regarding the use of Artificial Intelligence by social media platforms, content developers, and all intermediaries. Apart from that, to date, there have been no interventions from the Government of India. However, India has not been oblivious to the use of Artificial Intelligence. Across various fields, Indians are increasingly being confronted with the use of Artificial Intelligence. Artificial Intelligence in various forms is being used in Medicine, Policing, Administration, Entertainment, Media, Sports and several other industries. The point is that using Artificial Intelligence is a reality in India, regardless of the absence of laws and regulations. Like every other field, Legal education and practice in India is experiencing the growing use of Artificial Intelligence. The proposed book thus reviews the extent to which Artificial Intelligence in law has facilitated the evaluation of Evidence. Thus, the book is not about the Indian Evidence Act of 1872/Bharatiya Sakshya Adhiniyam of 2023.

It is about reviewing the extent to which Artificial Intelligence can facilitate or hinder the evaluation of Evidence in various spheres of Law. Accordingly, the book examines key areas of legal practice and their interaction with Artificial Intelligence. The areas selected are Criminal

DOI: 10.1201/9781003629146-1

Law, Corporate and Business Law, ADR, IPRs, Tax Law (Direct and Indirect), Labour Laws and Miscellaneous Soft Laws. The contributors have reviewed the extent to which Artificial Intelligence can be used to evaluate or generate evidence in each of these fields. This investigation takes them through an interdisciplinary terrain of science, tech and law. This investigation also prompts them to weigh in on concerns related to ethics, privacy and validity. The book brings together diverse positions and viewpoints on the needs or challenges faced if Artificial Intelligence is to be a legitimate tool for both evaluating and generating evidence. This book is a comprehensive compilation of Artificial Intelligence and Legal Evidence within different areas of law. The expertise and research of the contributors provide the reader with a comprehensive and reliable reference on this topic. Specifically, the book serves as the go-to reference for all matters related to Artificial Intelligence and the evaluation of legal evidence. Through the discussion of the selected areas of Legal practice, the book maps the prospects of further growth of Artificial Intelligence in the field of Legal practice in India. The book presents the Indian perspective on the use of Artificial Intelligence in Evidence evaluation in Law. Finally, the book advances the existing debate on Artificial Intelligence and Evidence evaluation in law, influencing Indian policy on this topic. Considering that the Ministry of Electronics and Information Technology is currently developing a clear roadmap for Artificial Intelligence, this book aims to make an important contribution towards that goal.

All twenty chapters are written from core interdisciplinary perspectives to ensure that both the technological aspects of AI and the legal aspects of AI are represented. The reader is guided through discussions in a format that is lucid enough to understand the nuances. The editors have put in their effort to ensure that the chapters have a logical theme. The book seeks a balance between academic discourse and a practical perspective on the challenges involved. AI is not only the normative referral in the book but also a lived reality for the authors. Authors from diverse backgrounds have thus endeavoured to present their core arguments in each of the chapters. As one of the editors of this tome, I am humbled and honoured to write the introduction to this discussion. Each chapter is unique in its contribution and tries to fill in the void in the existing literature. This book, thus, is not a mere textual formality acknowledging the reality of AI in law, but a deep dive into the debates. I hope that the reader will reflect on the debates and be inspired for future research. Importantly, this book adds to the narrative of the need for interdisciplinary collaboration and research. Law cannot be safe in its own world. It needs to venture out and mingle with all aspects of society. AI and Legal Evidence is one such interaction that will add more force to the argument for an integrated approach to policy-making. This book will surely fulfil the objective of redefining interdisciplinary scholarship.

1 Beyond Accuracy
Evaluating LLMs for Evidentiary Use in Legal Contexts

Sundaraparipurnan Narayanan, Marie Potel, and Vibhav Mithal

INTRODUCTION

Large Language Models (LLMs) are rapidly transforming the legal industry, driving a re-evaluation of traditional workflows. These AI tools are maturing for real-world deployment, revolutionizing how legal professionals approach tasks from brief writing and corporate compliance to increasing access to legal services (Nudell et al., 2023). LLMs are being applied to various legal functions, including text processing, predicting judgments, reasoning with statutes, analyzing privacy policies, and generating legal summaries (Qin & Sun, 2024).

Recent literature identifies several critical applications of large language models (LLMs) in the legal domain, including legal case retrieval, litigation strategy, question answering, document drafting, and semantic annotation. In case of retrieval, models like SAILER have achieved state-of-the-art results by structurally encoding key case components—facts, reasoning, and decisions—to improve retrieval precision (Li et al., 2023). Legal judgment prediction efforts, such as the legal domain machine learning-based SHAP values model, leverage ensemble learning and interpretable techniques like SHAP to forecast outcomes, especially in labor disputes (Guan et al., 2024). Complementary work addresses the reduction of judgment variability and supports AI's role in enhancing judicial consistency. Legal question answering models, such as Lawyer LLaMA (Zhang et al., 2023) and LLeQA (Louis et al., 2023), adopt retrieval-augmented pipelines to generate accurate and interpretable responses to complex statutory queries, demonstrating the potential of LLMs in democratizing legal information. In document drafting, models evaluated using the FOLLOWIR dataset attempt to create adherence to nuanced legal instructions (Weller et al., 2024), though challenges remain in capturing fine-grained directives. In addition, semantic annotation studies reveal that LLMs like GPT-4 can perform zero-shot identification of rhetorical roles and clause types in legal texts, enabling scalable automation of legal analysis tasks (Mohan et al., 2024).

The legal field is increasingly shifting towards functionally-aligned AI tools for legal, including developing advanced legal LLMs through continuous pre-training and supervised fine-tuning on extensive legal datasets, resulting in specialized models like LawGPT (Zhou et al., 2024), Lawyer LLaMa (Zhang et al., 2023), LexiLaw (Qin & Luo, 2024), LexGPT (Lee, 2023), ChatLaw (Chen et al., 2023), DISC-LawLLM (Li et al., 2023), and KL3M (Bommarito et al., 2025). These tailored models are designed to better understand legal terminology, apply provisions accurately, and adapt to different legal systems. Retrieval-Augmented Generation (RAG) is a key strategy employed to mitigate hallucinations and enhance factual accuracy by augmenting LLMs with external, up-to-date legal knowledge and precedents (Wang et al., 2024; Bommarito et al., 2025). Collaborative efforts between legal and AI professionals have led to the creation of specialized benchmarks like LEGALBENCH (Nudell et al., 2023) and LegalBench-RAG (Pipitone & Alami, 2024),

DOI: 10.1201/9781003629146-2

LegalAgentBench (Li et al., 2024) that support rigorous evaluation of LLMs' legal reasoning and retrieval capabilities across specific legal contexts, addressing the nuances general benchmarks often miss.

Despite their promising capabilities, both general-purpose LLMs and legal LLMs face notable limitations in the high-stakes legal domain. A primary concern is their lack of adequate specialized legal knowledge, as models trained on diverse internet data often miss crucial, up-to-date regulations, diverse jurisdictional practices, industry practices, and legal nuances (Nudell et al., 2023). LLM-based legal solutions also struggle to correct users' incorrect legal assumptions, leading to contra-factual bias (Dahl et al., 2024). They can also inadvertently create a "legal monoculture" by regurgitating information from prominent training set members, ignoring legal nuance (Dahl et al., 2024). Furthermore, some LLMs perform poorly on basic legal text handling tasks that lawyers and paralegals would expect them to manage easily (Blair-Stanek et al., 2024).

EVIDENTIARY EXPECTATIONS FROM LEGAL TECH

In the legal context, accuracy alone is not sufficient when evaluating Large Language Models (LLMs) due to several critical factors that extend beyond simple factual correctness (Lawrence et al., 2023). While LLMs show promise for legal tasks, including passing a Bar exam (Katz et al. 2023), they frequently generate factually incorrect or fabricated information, often referred to as "hallucinations," which is a significant risk in law where precision and veracity are non-negotiable (Dahl et al., 2024; Schiller, 2024; Habib Lantyer, 2025). Studies have revealed alarmingly high hallucination rates, with models like ChatGPT 3.5 and Llama 2 producing incorrect answers between 69% and 88% of the time when asked verifiable questions about federal court cases (Dahl et al., 2024). Also, in the recent past, 2 New York Lawyers were sanctioned for having used fake legal cases generated by language models without due diligence.[1] Databases now exist to track instances of when LLMs have hallucinated in Court proceedings, with at least 161 instances identified.[2] These models may also struggle to correct a user's incorrect legal assumptions, leading to counterfactual bias, and often exhibit overconfidence in their erroneous responses (Dahl et al., 2024). Furthermore, LLMs trained on general internet data often lack the specialized, up-to-date legal knowledge necessary for accurate responses, leading to an inability to grasp subtle legal nuances, rules, or judicial interpretations, or even failing to incorporate newly amended statutes (Lawrence et al., 2023; Wang et al., 2024; Blair-Stanek et al., 2024).

Beyond factual correctness, the nature of legal work demands comprehensive and nuanced outputs that simple accuracy metrics cannot fully capture. LLMs can exhibit "gaps" in their generated content, which may not be strictly "errors" but represent significant deviations or omissions compared to human-written legal analysis (Hou et al., 2024).

Evaluating LLMs in law also needs to consider their ability to provide correct legal analysis and reasoning, not just the correct conclusion, as they may struggle with explaining *how* a rule applies to facts or lack the necessary inferences (Nudell et al., 2023). This complexity necessitates human oversight, as automated metrics often fail to reflect the true quality and factual integrity of LLM-generated legal summaries and analyses (Lawrence et al., 2023).

It is also pertinent to note that use of LLMs may lead to automation bias, wherein LLM outputs may be believed even if they are incorrect (for example, instances where fake citations are cited in a legal brief), posing a particular risk to individuals without extensive legal training who might blindly trust the outputs (Dahl et al., 2024). Consequently, rigorous human oversight, comprehensible, transparent ethical frameworks that identify practical actionables, and technical and domain-specific functional evaluation are deemed indispensable for the responsible integration of AI into legal practice. While benchmarks like LegalBench support broad-based evaluations, there is a need for domain-specific and use case context-specific evaluation of these solutions. For instance, will an AI-contract generator generate a software license agreement by understanding an organization's role as a processor of personal data and the nature of processing from the data subject while drafting the data processing clause, or will the AI-contract generator leverage commonly used data processing clauses, without the necessary context of an organization? In view of these existing issues, this chapter provides a framework for the evaluation of LegalTech Tools, particularly one use case therein, i.e., "contract clause generators."

The fundamental problem lies in the baseline technology adopted by the language models designed for legal use. These language models are fine-tuned or trained versions of BERT (a language model prior to the GPT3 generation). While in many cases the training data of the models are not open sourced, but often referred as "trained on xx millions of legal corpus." Training and fine-tuning of the language model may support the performance and governance consideration to a certain extent, however, unless, such models take into account: (1) legal specific tokenizers like KL3M; (2) domain specific embedding models like Legal-BERT; (3) context enriched adaptive chunking strategy for legal; (4) multi-context synonym expansion (e.g. failure to fulfill obligations and breach of contract has contextual similarity, however, models do not consistently identify them appropriately); (5) wider multi jurisdictional training, the aforementioned failures may continue to persist.

USE CASE FOCUS: CLAUSE GENERATION IN CONTRACTS

As noted by Wang et al., 43% of corporate counsels spend at least half their time on tasks like drafting, editing, and negotiating contracts (Wang et al., 2025). The utilization of LLMs for the generation of legal contracts can facilitate the automated drafting of both standard and customized contractual clauses, based on user input or predefined templates. They enhance contract drafting and review by improving language and identifying legal issues with accuracy comparable to or exceeding human junior lawyers and Legal Process Outsourcers (LPOs) (Martin et al., 2024; Kasundra & Dhankhar, 2023). Such solutions can aid legal professionals by expediting the creation of draft contracts, ensuring consistency, and reducing the manual workload. It is particularly advantageous in high-volume contexts, such as non-disclosure agreements (NDAs), procurement agreements, or employment contracts, where the rapidity and adherence to legal standards are of paramount importance. However, as introduced above, there are key challenges associated with the contract clause generators leveraging LLMs:

Keeping pace with rapidly evolving legal landscapes across jurisdictions: LLMs often struggle to incorporate newly amended statutes and maintain up-to-date legal knowledge, leading to peak performance that lags several years behind current legal doctrine (Lawrence et al., 2023; Martin et al., 2024; Qin & Sun, 2024; Wang et al., 2024). The dynamic nature of legal systems, with continuous updates to laws and regulations, imposes higher requirements on such contract generators to remain relevant and accurate across different countries and their varying policies (Li et al., 2024; Lawrence et al., 2023). For instance, (Dahl et al., 2024) mentions that "jurisdiction and time specific" query type (especially the ones that detect circuit splits and answer unresolved questions of law within a circuit) exhibited the highest hallucination rate. Also, LLM might produce a syntactically correct clause, but it could omit essential provisions, create conflicts between two clauses, use improper terminology deviating from standard contracts, or reference inapplicable laws, leading to contracts that lack legal precision, or adaptability and could merely be void (Wang et al., 2025).

Ensuring data confidentiality, data privacy, and security in cloud-based solutions: Contract generators trained on vast datasets, especially those used in legal cases involving sensitive personal information, pose a significant risk of unintentional data exposure or leakage during content generation (Wang et al., 2024; John et al., 2025). Using LLM-based tools in legal workplaces for contract generation (including the ones that are fine-tuned on legal corpus) can lead to inadvertent disclosure of confidential client or third-party information, potentially violating NDAs or attorney-client privilege if sufficient guardrails are not maintained (NLS, 2024).

Addressing potential biases in AI-driven contract generation: LLMs can embed and perpetuate biases (e.g., racial, gender) from their diverse training data, risking unfair or discriminatory outputs that compromise legal impartiality and fairness (Qin & Sun, 2024; Nudell et al., 2023; Wang et al., 2024). Further, when insufficient context is provided, LLMs may default to generating content based on gender stereotypes and employ different writing styles for specific contracts, even amplifying these biases in "hallucinations" specifically with reference to jurisdictional biases (Garimella et al., 2023). For instance, in 2023, an attorney filed a legal brief that he had written with the help of ChatGPT, containing 6 case references that did not exist, for which he was sanctioned (Dahl et al., 2024).

Balancing automation with the necessity for human oversight and expertise: Despite LLMs' efficiency, human oversight is crucial to validate AI-generated outputs, as humans may have to deal with the consequences of these outputs in their legal practice (Qin & Sun, 2024; Lam et al., 2023). Expertise of legal professionals provides essential contextual knowledge, nuanced judgment, and ethical oversight that current AI systems cannot consistently offer, ensuring fairness and accountability in legal decision-making (Thaldar, 2025).

Standardizing contract language while maintaining flexibility for specific needs: AI tools often rely on generic templates, which may fail to account for nuanced legal requirements or the unique aspects of a business, leading to a simple oversight in language or missing clauses (Thaldar, 2025). LLM-generated contract clauses may lack the necessary legal precision and adaptability, often using "boilerplate" language or uncommon phrasing that can create inconsistencies or omit essential provisions (Wang et al., 2025). For instance, an AI-generated agreement copying boilerplate language from another country's laws could undermine enforceability in the client's home jurisdiction.

Ensuring interoperability between different contract management systems: There are challenges in converting natural language legal contracts into structured formats for smart legal contracts (SLCs) due to the complexity of legal text and the need for accurate variable extraction (Chen et al., 2023). While NLP models can aid in automating the creation of SLCs by marking up text and associating variables, significant effort from lawyers and programmers is still required for final correction and to account for complex data types and execution logic (Chen et al., 2023).

Managing the complexity of multi-jurisdictional contracts: LLMs exhibit limitations in generalizing legal tasks involving different jurisdictions, as their training data may be skewed towards specific legal systems like American law (Wang et al., 2025; Nudell et al., 2023; Pipitone & Alami, 2024; Li et al., 2024). Policy differences across countries regarding AI adoption can create compliance risks and inconveniences when LLMs are applied globally, necessitating careful consideration of the application context to avoid erroneous or inaccurately scoped outputs (Wang et al., 2024).

Addressing ethical concerns related to AI-generated legal content: The proliferation of AI-generated legal content raises significant ethical issues, including challenges in distinguishing authentic from fabricated evidence, risks of misuse, and concerns about fairness due to inherent biases (Qin & Sun, 2024; Thaldar, 2025; Nudell et al., 2023). A key ethical challenge is accountability attribution for LLM errors, as there is currently no consensus on who should be held liable for undesirable outcomes, specifically when applied to legal context (Wang et al., 2024).

A MULTI-FACETED EVALUATION FRAMEWORK

Given the above, legal contract generation solutions should be evaluated across technical, functional, and contextual dimensions. Technically, key criteria include output accuracy, hallucination detection, attribution, and robustness to ambiguous or incomplete inputs. Functionally, the system must align with legal task objectives, ensure semantic consistency with legal intent, and minimize cognitive load for legal practitioners. Contextual evaluation involves sensitivity to jurisdictional norms, potential impacts on adversarial or regulatory processes, and broader ethical and societal considerations. While LLMs offer significant potential for efficiency in contract drafting, their current shortcomings in factual reliability, comprehensive understanding, and ethical considerations mean that rigorous human-centric evaluation and oversight are indispensable for their safe and effective integration into legal practice (Lawrence et al., 2023; Dahl et al., 2024). The proposed framework, by highlighting the various dimensions to evaluate a general LLM, addresses these factors: (a) compliance and jurisdictional adaptability, (b) legal competence and reasoning, (c) accuracy, reliability, trustworthiness, (d) contextual understanding, (e) handling of structured contract elements, and (f) principles of ethics, privacy, and accountability.

The details of each of these elements and the key considerations associated with them are represented below:

Compliance and Jurisdictional Adaptability

Legal Standards

The design, development, and deployment of LLMs must adhere to strict legal standards when deployed in a legal domain context (Lawrence et al., 2023). Further, legal standards involve discerning legal conditions from facts by referencing prior cases and codified laws (Thanh & Satoh, 2024). For instance, a generic governing law and jurisdiction clause in an employment contract may contradict an employment regulation in certain jurisdictions.

Jurisdiction

Legal rules vary significantly across different jurisdictions, which LLMs must accurately account for (Pipitone & Alami, 2024; Nudell et al., 2023). LLMs' performance and hallucination rates can differ based on the specific jurisdiction (or in some cases judicial circuit as in the case of the United States of America) being queried (Dahl et al., 2024).

Regulatory Compliance

AI systems in high-risk domains like law are subject to stringent obligations and regulations, such as those anticipated by the EU AI Act (Lawrence et al., 2023). Further, inconsistencies in regulatory policies across countries may pose compliance risks for global adoption of LLMs in legal practice, specifically in contract generator AI (Wang et al., 2024). For instance, it may generate a Data protection clause anchored around GDPR or may generalize with "applicable regulations" instead of listing concrete lawful bases (like consent, legitimate interest, etc.).

Opacity

LLMs, like any other type of AI, are often considered "black boxes" due to their lack of inherent explainability, which challenges the transparency vital for judicial reasoning (Wang et al., 2024). This lack of interpretability from a technical standpoint, and lack of explainability of output, creates uncertainty for legal practitioners and raises concerns for AI-generated recommendations (John et al., 2025). Besides, transparency and explainability are both required under the EU AI Act.

Outdated Legal Knowledge

LLMs trained on general internet data may lack the up-to-date legal knowledge necessary for accurate responses, despite being fine-tuned on legal corpus, often failing to incorporate newly amended statutes (Lawrence et al., 2023). Their performance may lag behind the current state of legal doctrine, and they may struggle with both very old and very new case law as the language models are known to struggle with time series information. (Dahl et al., 2024). For example, when referring to a regulation, the model may not reflect the amendments as reference ("the most current version of the California Labor Code. ... as amended from time to time."). Similarly, the model may not misrepresent a clause in a healthcare service agreement in the United States of America, where the legal standard known as the "undue burden" test for abortion restrictions, originally established in *Planned Parenthood v. Casey* (1992), has been overturned.

Legal Competence and Reasoning

Legal Knowledge

LLMs often lack the specialized, up-to-date legal knowledge and domain nuances required for consistently accurate and reliable outputs (Lawrence et al., 2023; Martin et al., 2024). Despite their capabilities, general LLMs may not grasp the subtle legal distinctions or judicial interpretations crucial for legal tasks (Lawrence et al., 2023; Wang et al., 2024).

Legal Principles Application

LLMs are evaluated on their ability to apply specified legal rules to facts and provide explanations for their conclusions (Nudell et al., 2023). Errors in rule application can include misstatements of legal rules or facts, incorrect outcomes, and logical or arithmetic errors (Nudell et al., 2023).

Legal Reasoning

Legal reasoning demands parsing complex texts, combining various reasoning modalities, and following frameworks like IRAC (Issue, Rule, Application, Conclusion) (Nudell et al., 2023). LLMs often struggle with explaining the *how* of legal rule application and lack the ability to verbalize necessary inferences (Nudell et al., 2023). For instance, a contract generator may mutualize an indemnification clause by simply swapping the parties instead of drafting a mutual obligation, thereby exposing the failure of legal reasoning.

Nuance and Interpretation

LLMs demonstrate limitations in grasping subtle legal nuances and can misinterpret specific wordings within legal documents (Martin et al., 2024; Wang et al., 2024). Interpretation tasks require LLMs to accurately parse and understand legal texts to extract relevant information or categorize content (Pipitone & Alami, 2024; Nudell et al., 2023). For instance, in an IP clause "non-exclusive, non-transferable right to use such IP solely for the purposes set forth in this Agreement" may be an appropriate clause, but the model may not clearly understand that purpose is contextual to the contract and IP context referred, as their training on legal corpus may not necessarily link the context.

Distinguishing the Standards

LLM's capacity to understand and categorize diverse legal clauses within complex agreements, such as merger contracts, is one of the critical aspects in contract generation (Nudell et al., 2023). It tests the model's ability to interpret specialized legal language, like identifying specific limitations on consent rights within a contract (Nudell et al., 2023). For instance, the use of "reasonable efforts" or "best efforts" may be considered synonymous in some jurisdictions and may be considered different in certain other jurisdictions. The model may be generating the clause with "reasonable efforts" or "best efforts" based on the corpus and the jurisdiction of the corpus it was trained on, thereby creating complexity in outcomes.

Terminology Evolution

Lawyers use a precise, specialized language ("legalese"), which general-domain LLMs may not fully comprehend (Nudell et al., 2023). It remains unclear whether lawyers should use formalistic legal language or simpler plain-language when interacting with LLMs. It is pertinent to note that plain language contracts are indeed an emerging trend and a growing requirement in legal and commercial communications. Also, for instance, if the contract generates "personal data" for biometric-specific clauses, it may be inconsistent and can be attributed to evolving specificities in terminologies in personal data definitions. Interestingly, a 2023 experiment showed that legalese creates efficiency issues even for lawyers: they were less able to understand and recall legal contracts than equivalent content drafted in a simplified register, and they rated plain language contracts as preferable to legalese ones (Martinez et al., 2023). Writing contracts in plain language improves clarity, saves time, fosters trust, and produces better outcomes compared to traditional legalese. This approach helps ensure that contracts are more understandable and accessible to their intended audiences, which is crucial given that many consumers have limited bargaining power and may not fully comprehend complex contract terms (Schindler, 2024). Given the relevance, the International Standards Organization published a standard on plain language in 2023, primarily aiming at providing principles and guidelines for developing plain language documents (ISO 24495-1:2023 Plain language: www.iso.org/standard/78907.html), and is developing a subset of this standard specifically for legal drafting (ISO 24495-2: Plain language—Part 2: Legal communication, www.iso.org/standard/85774.html). In the absence of such conscious efforts to introduce writing contracts in plain language, LLMs' efficiency may be impacted when confronted with continuing legalese.

Time-Series Structuring

LLMs can be evaluated on their skill in identifying the function of different sections within judicial decisions, a foundational legal skill (Nudell et al., 2023). However, research also revealed that LLMs may exhibit higher hallucination rates when dealing with very old or very new case law, indicating a challenge in internalizing evolving legal history (Dahl et al., 2024).

Linguistic Conventions

LLMs can struggle to adapt to the specific linguistic styles and citation formats prevalent in legal writing (Hou et al., 2024). Such generated contract content may not consistently adhere to the precise textual conventions expected in legal documents in respective jurisdictions.

Accuracy, Reliability, and Trustworthiness

Hallucination

As previously explained, LLMs frequently generate factually incorrect or fabricated information, known as "hallucinations," a significant risk in law (Dahl et al., 2024). These legal hallucinations are alarmingly prevalent, occurring, for instance, in the United States in 69% to 88% of verifiable queries about federal court cases.

Consistency

LLMs can exhibit poor consistency, producing different outputs when processing semantically similar queries (Wang et al., 2023). The inherent stochastic nature of LLMs means that nondeterminism in their responses may persist, impacting reliability (Dahl et al., 2024).

Noise Sensitivity

Even minor, unavoidable errors in user input can cause LLMs to generate unexpected or incorrect responses (Wang et al., 2023). LLMs are susceptible to "contra-factual bias," often failing to correct a user's incorrect legal assumptions embedded in a query (Dahl et al., 2024).

Accuracy Rate

Despite their potential, LLMs frequently yield high rates of incorrect answers in legal queries, highlighting significant accuracy limitations (Dahl et al., 2024; Wang et al., 2024). Even state-of-the-art models often fail to achieve the proficiency levels of experienced legal professionals in complex legal tasks (Wang et al., 2024; Lawrence et al., 2023).

Prompt Sensitivity

LLM performance, generally across domains, is highly dependent on the precise wording of prompts and the selection of in-context demonstrations (Nudell et al., 2023). Different prompt engineering strategies can lead to substantial variations in output quality for legal tasks (Martin et al., 2024).

Parametric Knowledge Reliance

LLMs primarily rely on their latent parametric knowledge, which may be insufficient for specialized legal tasks (Asai et al., 2023). Providing explicit descriptions of legal rules in prompts can significantly boost performance compared to relying solely on the model's pre-trained knowledge (Nudell et al., 2023).

Co-Occurrence Bias

LLMs learn a co-occurrence bias from their pre-training data, favoring frequently co-occurring words over the correct answers (Kang & Choi, 2023). This bias is particularly problematic when LLMs attempt to recall rare facts and is not mitigated by increasing model size or fine-tuning.

Long-Form Factuality

Ensuring factual accuracy in long-form legal generations remains a challenge for LLMs, even with retrieval augmentation (Asai et al., 2023). While larger context windows are beneficial, including irrelevant information can still induce hallucinations in the output (Nudell et al., 2023; Pipitone & Alami, 2024).

Understanding Context

Partial Context

LLMs can produce coherent summaries but may omit critical details or generate inappropriate content due to an incomplete understanding of the broader context (Wang et al., 2024). Evaluating LLMs on short text snippets is common, but their performance can vary due to the inherent limitations of fragmented information (Savelka, 2023).

Misaligned Context

The inductive bias learned by an LLM from its training data may not align with the true distribution of real-world legal facts; it can lead to systematic errors (Dahl et al., 2024). This misalignment risks "flattening" legal nuance, causing LLMs to merely regurgitate prominent information rather than reflecting the full variation of the law.

Ambiguity Handling

LLMs struggle with legal reasoning tasks that involve degrees of correctness or situations where "reasonable minds may differ" on the outcome (Nudell et al., 2023). Current benchmarks often focus on tasks with objectively “correct” and unambiguous answers, limiting insights into LLMs’ performance on ambiguous legal problems.

Long-Form Coherence

The initial context windows of LLMs limited their ability to process and maintain coherence over longer legal documents (Nudell et al., 2023). While LLMs can generate coherent summaries, ensuring their completeness, factual integrity, and overall quality for extensive documents remains a significant challenge (Wang et al., 2024).

Structured Contract Elements Handling

Term Appropriateness

LLMs may use improper legal terminology or fail to grasp the specific context and underlying intent of contract clauses. In some research, a significant portion of inaccuracies was linked to the misinterpretation of specific wordings (Martin et al., 2024). This can result in outputs that are syntactically correct but lack the precise legal meaning required for a contract (Wang et al., 2025).

Omission of Nuance Consideration

LLMs can omit essential provisions or lack sufficient detail in critical areas of legal documents, such as data transfer agreements (Thaldar, 2025). This highlights their current inability to fully capture the intricate nuances required for legally robust and comprehensive documents.

Drafting Specificity

AI-generated contract clauses may lack the necessary legal precision and adaptability, often relying on “boilerplate” language (Wang et al., 2025). This can lead to inconsistencies or the introduction of uncommon phrasing, potentially creating conflicts between clauses. For instance, if an AI-generated software license agreement lacks a clear limitation of liability clause, that could have serious consequences for the parties to the contract.

Error Inclusion

LLM-generated clauses may not always meet strict legal requirements and can include factual inaccuracies (Lam et al., 2023). Examples of errors include invalid references to laws or precedents that do not apply to the specific situation.

Ethics, Privacy, Accountability

Training Bias

LLMs can absorb and perpetuate biases (e.g., racial, gender) present in their diverse training data, leading to potentially unfair or discriminatory outputs (Qin & Sun, 2024). This poses a critical risk to the principles of impartiality and fairness that are fundamental to the legal system (John et al., 2025) In addition, when the models are overtrained on certain jurisdictional contracts, they may be biased towards other jurisdictional requirements. For instance, research revealed that if the inductive bias that an LLM learns from its training corpus is not well-aligned with the true distribution of facts about the world, then the LLM is likely to make systematic errors when queried about those facts (Dahl et al., 2024).

Data Privacy

Legal cases often involve sensitive personal information, creating a risk of unintentional data exposure when processed by LLMs (Qin & Sun, 2024). Many current contract generator tools/solutions may not have adequate alignment to jurisdiction-specific regulatory requirements regarding privacy and thereby may pose significant challenges for evaluations involving sensitive medical or legal data (Munnangi et al., 2024).

Misuse Risk

Security vulnerabilities like "jailbreaking" and "prompt hijacking" present tangible risks of misuse for LLMs in legal contexts (Lawrence et al., 2023). These vulnerabilities could potentially be exploited to generate fraudulent legal documents or engage in other harmful activities (Martin et al., 2024).

Accountability Attribution

The clear attribution of accountability for errors or incorrect legal advice generated by LLMs remains a significant challenge, necessitating new legal frameworks (Wang et al., 2024). Despite the fact that the current legal environments are expecting humans in the loop or the human lawyers utilizing generative AI remain professionally responsible for the final outputs, it is necessary to understand what such solutions provide in terms of accountability when generating contract clauses and how they are represented to the user (Martin et al., 2024).

Misuse Transparency

Establishing robust ethical frameworks is crucial for guiding the responsible integration of contract generation AI into legal practice and addressing risks like bias and misuse (Thaldar, 2025). Human oversight is essential to demand explanations from AI systems, challenge their outputs, and promote transparency and accountability in legal decision-making (John et al., 2025).

CONCLUSION

To build trustworthy LLMs for legal applications, a multi-faceted approach focusing on a systematic and contextual evaluation, coupled with technical improvement, is essential. The aforementioned framework and guidance list the considerations to take into account prior to creating a consistent evaluation mechanism with reference to a contract generator.

Developing and deploying AI systems for legal applications (specifically a contract generator) necessitates careful attention to dataset construction (including dataset for fine-tuning), feedback integration, and ongoing safety evaluation. High-quality legal datasets should include diverse document types, annotated reasoning, and minority viewpoints, while employing domain-specific evaluation metrics. Evaluations can focus on multiple errors; some of the errors that can be explored include misstatements of the legal rule, misstatements of the fact pattern, incorrectly asserting the legal outcome, logic errors, and arithmetic errors (Nudell et al., 2023). Also, feedback systems must incorporate structured usage data and expert legal oversight (Vargas-Murillo et al., 2024) to balance specialized knowledge with broader applicability.

Further, there is a need for refining domain and use case context-specific metrics that accurately capture the nuances of legal text and reasoning (Lawrence et al., 2023; Schiller, 2024). The process should ensure transparency about the use of AI and its inherent limitations, fostering realistic expectations among users (Thaldar, 2025).

While leveraging AI for contract generation, the following actions can support, performant and governed contracts, avoiding errors and inconsistencies: (1) Use the CLAUSE framework to develop evaluation dataset aligned to the use case context and jurisdiction applicability; (2) Evaluate the contract generator using the evaluation dataset; (3) Establish a scoring mechanism for human evaluation and compile critical human evaluation outcomes for such evaluations; (4) Refine the evaluation dataset based on the human evaluation inputs and establish it as a benchmark; (5) Evaluate contract generator for every updates/fine-tuning/upgrades using the benchmark.

Continuous testing, including edge cases and adversarial prompts, alongside reliability mechanisms such as error detection, version control, and rule-based safeguards, is essential to ensure legal AI systems remain accurate, fair, and trustworthy (Eliot, 2020; Liu et al., 2022). Further, developing interpretability for LLM outputs is also vital to provide legal practitioners with the necessary transparency to trust and utilize AI recommendations effectively (Wang et al., 2024).

NOTES

1 www.reuters.com/legal/new-york-lawyers-sanctioned-using-fake-chatgpt-cases-legal-brief-20 23-06-22/
2 www.damiencharlotin.com/hallucinations/

REFERENCES

Asai, A., Sil, A., Hajishirzi, H., Wang, Y., & Wu, Z. (2023). Self-RAG: Learning to retrieve, generate, and critique through self-reflection. *arXiv*. https://doi.org/10.48550/arxiv.2310.11511

Blair-Stanek, A., Holzenberger, N., & Van Durme, B. (2024). BLT: Can large language models handle basic legal text? In *Proceedings of the 2024 North American chapter of the Association for Computational Linguistics* (pp. 216–232). https://doi.org/10.18653/v1/2024.nllp-1.18

Bommarito, M., Katz, D., & Bommarito, J. (2025). KL3M tokenizers: A family of domain-specific and character-level tokenizers for legal, financial, and preprocessing applications. *arXiv*. https://doi.org/10.48550/arxiv.2503.17247

Chen, E., Tseng, Y.-H., Roche, N., Hernandez, W., Shangguan, J., & Moore, A. (2023). Conversion of legal agreements into smart legal contracts using NLP. In *Proceedings of the 46th international ACM SIGIR conference on research and development in information retrieval* (pp. 1112–1118). ACM. https://doi.org/10.1145/3543873.3587554

Dahl, M., Ho, D. E., Magesh, V., & Suzgun, M. (2024). Large legal fictions: Profiling legal hallucinations in large language models. *Journal of Legal Analysis*, *16*(1), 64–93. https://doi.org/10.1093/jla/laae003

Eliot, L. (2020). AI and legal argumentation: Aligning the autonomous levels of AI legal reasoning. *arXiv*. https://doi.org/10.48550/arxiv.2009.11180

Garimella, A., Pu, G., Sun, J., Chang, K.-W., Peng, N., & Wan, Y. (2023). "Kelly is a warm person, Joseph is a role model": Gender biases in LLM-generated reference letters. *arXiv*. https://doi.org/10.48550/arxiv.2310.09219

Guan, ., Duan, M., Han, G., Yu, Z., Liao, Y., & Tang, R. (2024). Predicting critical path of labor dispute resolution in legal domain by machine learning models based on SHapley Additive explanations and Soft Voting Strategy. *Mathematics*, *12*(2), 272. https://doi.org/10.3390/math12020272

Habib Lantyer, V. (2025). *The phantom menace: Generative AI hallucinations and their legal implications.* Elsevier BV. https://doi.org/10.2139/ssrn.5167036

Hou, A., Jurayj, W., Holzenberger, N., Blair-Stanek, A., & Durme, B. (2024). Gaps or hallucinations? Gazing into machine-generated legal analysis for fine-grained text evaluations. *arXiv*. https://doi.org/10.48550/arxiv.2409.09947

John, A., U, A., & Panachakel, J. (2025). Ethical challenges of using artificial intelligence in judiciary. *arXiv*. https://doi.org/10.48550/arxiv.2504.19284

Kang, C., & Choi, J. (2023). Impact of co-occurrence on factual knowledge of large language models. *arXiv*. https://doi.org/10.48550/arxiv.2310.08256

Kasundra, J., & Dhankhar, S. (2023). Adapting open-source LLMs for contract drafting and analyzing multi-role vs. single-role behavior of ChatGPT for synthetic data generation. In *Proceedings of the 33rd ACM conference* (pp. 1–8). ACM. https://doi.org/10.1145/3639856.3639888

Katz, D. M., Hartung, D., Gerlach, L., Jana, A., & Bommarito, M. J., II. (2023). Natural language processing in the legal domain [Preprint]. *arXiv*. https://doi.org/10.48550/arXiv.2302.12039

Lam, K. Y., Cheng, V. C., & Yeong, Z. K. (2023, June). Applying large language models for enhancing contract drafting. In *LegalAIIA@ ICAIL* (pp. 70–80).

Lawrence, C., Hung, C.-C., Bruckner, L., Frost, L., & Rim, W. (2023). Walking a tightrope: Evaluating large language models in high-risk domains. *arXiv*. https://doi.org/10.48550/arxiv.2311.14966

Lee, J.-S. (2023). *LexGPT 0.1: Pre-trained GPT-J models with Pile of Law*. Cornell University. https://doi.org/10.48550/arxiv.2306.05431

Li, B., Shen, C., Yue, S., Liu, S., Wang, S., Yun, S., Chen, W., Huang, X., Xiao, Y., Zhou, Y., & Wei, Z. (2023). DISC-LawLLM: Fine-tuning large language models for intelligent legal services. *arXiv*. https://doi.org/10.48550/arxiv.2309.11325

Li, H., Chen, J., Yang, J., Ai, Q., Jia, W., Liu, Y., Lin, K., Wu, Y., Yuan, G., Hu, Y., Wang, W., Liu, Y., & Huang, M. (2024). LegalAgentBench: Evaluating LLM agents in legal domain. *arXiv*.. https://doi.org/10.48550/arxiv.2412.17259

Liu, H., Liu, Y., Jain, A., Jain, S., Li, Y., Tang, J., Wang, Y., Fan, W., & Liu, X. (2022). Trustworthy AI: A computational perspective. *ACM Transactions on Intelligent Systems and Technology, 14*(1), 1–59. https://doi.org/10.1145/3546872

Louis, A., Spanakis, G., & Dijck, G. (2023). Interpretable long-form legal question answering with retrieval-augmented large language models. *arXiv*. https://doi.org/10.48550/arxiv.2309.17050

Martin, L., Catterson, L., Whitehouse, N., Perera, R., & Yiu, S. (2024). Better call GPT, comparing large language models against lawyers .*arXiv*. https://doi.org/10.48550/arxiv.2401.16212

Martínez, E., Mollica, F., & Gibson, E. (2023). Even lawyers do not like legalese. *Proceedings of the National Academy of Sciences of the United States of America, 120*(23), e2302672120. https://doi.org/10.1073/pnas.2302672120

Mohan, D., Nair, L. R., Arunkumar, K., Sankar, B., Swaminathan, P., & Ramesh Kumar, D. (2024). Deep learning-based semantic segmentation for legal texts: Unveiling rhetorical roles in legal case documents. *E3S Web of Conferences, 529*, 04019. https://doi.org/10.1051/e3sconf/202452904019

Munnangi, M., Swaminathan, A., Fries, J., Jindal, J., Narayanan, S., Lopez, I., Tu, L., Chung, P., Omiye, J., Kashyap, M., & Shah, N. (2024). Assessing the limitations of large language models in clinical fact decomposition. *arXiv*. https://doi.org/10.48550/arxiv.2412.12422

National Law School of India University. (2024, September 6). *The disadvantages and limitations of using large language models in the field of law*. National Law School of India University. www.nls.ac.in/research/projects/the-disadvantages-and-limitations-of-using-large-language-models-in-the-field-of-law/

Nudell, J., Ma, M., Dickinson, G., Gao, S., Zur, T., Iyer, V., Rockmore, D., Rasumov-Rahe, N., Zambrano, D., Li, Z., Henderson, P., Kolt, N., Talisman, D., Porat, H., Guha, N., Hagan, M., Holzenberger, N., Waldon, B., Surani, F., … Gandhi, S. (2023). LegalBench: A collaboratively built benchmark for measuring legal reasoning in large language models. *arXiv*. https://doi.org/10.48550/arxiv.2308.11462

Pipitone, N., & Alami, G. (2024). LegalBench-RAG: A benchmark for retrieval-augmented generation in the legal domain. *arXiv*. https://doi.org/10.48550/arxiv.2408.10343

Qin, W., & Luo, X. (2024, December 6). A legal fact-finding model based on the T5 and LexiLaw large language models. *arXiv*. https://doi.org/10.1145/3709026.3709070

Qin, W., & Sun, Z. (2024). Exploring the nexus of large language models and legal systems: A short survey. *arXiv*. https://doi.org/10.48550/arxiv.2404.00990

Savelka, J. (2023). Unlocking practical applications in legal domain: Evaluation of GPT for zero-shot semantic annotation of legal texts. *arXiv*. https://doi.org/10.48550/arxiv.2305.04417

Schiller, C. (2024). The human factor in detecting errors of large language models: A systematic literature review and future research directions. *arXiv*. https://doi.org/10.48550/arxiv.2403.09743

Schindler, T. (2024). The making of the international standard for writing in plain language ISO 24495-1: Its usefulness, content, and how it came into existence. *AMWA Journal, 39*(1). https://doi.org/10.55752/amwa.2024.333

Thaldar, D. (2025). How effectively can ChatGPT-4 draft data transfer agreements for health research? *Humanities and Social Sciences Communications, 12*(1). https://doi.org/10.1057/s41599-025-04643-z

Thanh, N., & Satoh, K. (2024). KRAG framework for enhancing LLMs in the legal domain. *arXiv*. https://doi.org/10.48550/arxiv.2410.07551

Vargas-Murillo, A. R., Turriate-Guzman, A. M., Delgado-Chávez, C. A., Sanchez-Paucar, F., & Pari-Bedoya, I. (2024). Transforming justice: Implications of artificial intelligence in legal systems. *Academic Journal of Interdisciplinary Studies, 13*(2), 433. https://doi.org/10.36941/ajis-2024-0059

Wang, H., Li, T., Ye, W., Ou, M., Yanggong, Y., Wu, S., Chen, G., Ma, X., Zhao, J., Fu, J., & Chen, Y. (2023). Assessing hidden risks of LLMs: An empirical study on robustness, consistency, and credibility. *arXiv*. https://doi.org/10.48550/arxiv.2305.10235

Wang, J., Zhao, H., Yang, Z., Shu, P., Chen, J., Sun, H., Liang, R., Li, S., Shi, P., Ma, L., Liu, Z., Liu, Z., Zhong, T., Zhang, Y., Ma, C., Zhang, X., Zhang, T., Ding, T., Ren, Y., … Zhang, S. (2024). Legal evaluations and challenges of large language models. *arXiv*. https://doi.org/10.48550/arxiv.2411.10137

Wang, S., Zubkov, M., Fan, K., Harrell, S., Sun, Y., Chen, W., Plesner, A., & Wattenhofer, R. (2025). ACORD: An expert-annotated retrieval dataset for legal contract drafting. *arXiv*. https://doi.org/10.48550/arxiv.2501.06582

Weller, O., Chang, B., Macavaney, S., Lo, K., Cohan, A., Durme, B., Lawrie, D., & Soldaini, L. (2024). FollowIR: Evaluating and teaching information retrieval models to follow instructions. *arXiv*. https://doi.org/10.48550/arxiv.2403.15246

Zhang, C., Jiang, C., Tao, M., Huang, Q., Feng, Y., An, Z., Chen, Z., & Wu, Z. (2023). *Lawyer LLaMA technical report*. Cornell University. https://doi.org/10.48550/arxiv.2305.15062

Zhou, Z., Shi, J.-X., Song, P.-X., Yang, X.-W., Jin, Y.-X., Guo, L.-Z., & Li, Y.-F. (2024). LawGPT: A Chinese legal knowledge-enhanced large language model. *arXiv*. https://doi.org/10.48550/arxiv.2406.04614

2 From Paper Trails to Algorithms

AI's Impact on Evidence in Law

Ishita Chatterjee

INTRODUCTION

The traditional methods of evidence gathering, such as paper trails, physical records, and witness testimony, have long been the backbone of legal systems worldwide. These methods, while foundational, are often time-consuming, error-prone, and subject to human bias. Paper trails can be lost or altered, and witness testimony, though crucial, can be influenced by memory lapses, misinterpretations, or intentional deceit.[1] With the increasing complexity of modern societies, these limitations are becoming more evident, prompting the need for more efficient and reliable methods of evidence handling.

The rise of artificial intelligence (AI) is revolutionizing the legal landscape. AI-driven tools, such as predictive algorithms, natural language processing (NLP), and data analytics, are increasingly being employed in law enforcement, legal tech, and judicial decision-making.[2] AI enables faster processing of vast amounts of data, from surveillance footage and social media activity to electronic communications and digital transactions. These advancements are not only enhancing the efficiency of evidence gathering but also raising new questions about the nature of evidence itself—what constitutes valid evidence when AI can create, analyse, and even manipulate data?

This research aims to explore how AI is reshaping the concept of evidence and its legal handling. The use of AI in this domain challenges traditional notions of trustworthiness and authenticity. What happens when algorithms are used to determine the weight of evidence or influence judicial outcomes? Can AI be trusted to uphold legal standards of due process, fairness, and justice? The significance of this transformation is immense, as it has the potential to redefine legal integrity. As AI continues to evolve, its impact on legal standards will be crucial in ensuring the proper balance between technological advancement and the protection of fundamental legal principles.[3]

The evolution of evidence law has been shaped by centuries of legal traditions, emerging from common law practices and gradually adapting to societal and technological changes. Historically, the rules of evidence aimed to ensure fairness and truth in judicial proceedings, with early systems relying heavily on oral testimony and limited documentation (Thayer, 1898). Over time, statutory reforms and landmark cases, such as *Daubert v. Merrell Dow Pharmaceuticals* (1993), refined standards of admissibility, emphasizing reliability and relevance in expert testimony and scientific evidence.

In recent decades, legal technology has transformed courtroom practices. Digital databases, electronic discovery (e-discovery), and online legal research tools like Westlaw and LexisNexis have streamlined case preparation and analysis (Susskind, 2013). Courtroom technology now includes digital exhibits, virtual testimonies, and automated transcription services. Blockchain and digital evidence management platforms further enhance evidence integrity, demonstrating the increasing reliance on technological infrastructures in legal processes.[4]

 DOI: 10.1201/9781003629146-3

Artificial Intelligence (AI) in law represents a significant frontier. Case studies show AI's capacity in predictive analytics, legal research, and even decision support. For instance, ROSS Intelligence and LexisNexis' AI tools enable rapid parsing of legal texts and precedents. Predictive systems like COMPAS, used in sentencing, illustrate real-world applications but have also triggered intense academic debate over fairness and transparency (Angwin et al., 2016). Academic discourse highlights both the potential and risks of AI integration, particularly in terms of interpretability and consistency with legal principles (Surden, 2019).

Despite growing scholarship, gaps remain in the literature—particularly regarding admissibility standards for AI-generated evidence. Legal systems lack unified frameworks for assessing algorithmic reliability and transparency, creating uncertainty in evidentiary contexts. Moreover, issues of bias in AI—stemming from training data or model design—raise concerns about due process and equal treatment under the law. Legal accountability, especially in determining responsibility for erroneous or harmful AI decisions, is another underexplored area. Existing doctrines often struggle to accommodate the complex, opaque nature of machine learning systems, leaving questions of liability and recourse inadequately addressed.[5]

While historical and technological developments have propelled evidence law into the digital age, significant theoretical and practical challenges persist. Further research is needed to establish robust standards and safeguards for the admissibility and accountability of AI-generated evidence in legal proceedings.[6]

This research adopts a multi-faceted methodological approach to ensure a comprehensive understanding of the legal implications surrounding AI-driven evidence systems. Primarily, a doctrinal legal research method is employed, involving a detailed examination of existing statutes, case law, and legal principles relevant to evidentiary procedures. This helps establish a solid legal foundation and highlights how traditional rules interact with evolving technological practices.

To broaden the perspective, a comparative analysis is conducted, contrasting the legal treatment of evidence in different jurisdictions. This includes both common law and civil law systems, offering insight into how various legal frameworks accommodate or resist AI-driven innovations. Additionally, comparisons are drawn between traditional evidentiary mechanisms and those incorporating AI, assessing reliability, admissibility, and procedural fairness.

An interdisciplinary approach further enriches the study by integrating insights from computer science and ethics. Technical understanding of AI models, data integrity, and algorithmic transparency is essential to evaluating their legal robustness. Ethical considerations, such as bias, accountability, and human oversight, are examined to assess the societal implications of integrating AI into legal proceedings. Together, these methodologies create a holistic framework to critically analyse the integration of AI within the evidentiary domain.

THE NATURE OF EVIDENCE IN THE AGE OF AI

In the age of artificial intelligence, the nature of evidence is undergoing a profound transformation, particularly with the growing reliance on digital sources over traditional physical ones. Digital evidence—emails, metadata, GPS data, or surveillance footage—can be rapidly produced, replicated, and analysed. In contrast, physical evidence like fingerprints or documents requires human collection and manual analysis.[7] While digital evidence offers efficiency and breadth, its authenticity and integrity are more susceptible to tampering without robust safeguards.

AI-generated evidence introduces both powerful tools and complex challenges. Technologies such as facial recognition and predictive policing use algorithms to identify suspects or predict crime hotspots. While potentially increasing efficiency, these tools can reinforce existing biases, especially if trained on skewed datasets.[8] Deepfakes, highly convincing manipulated media, represent another AI innovation that complicates legal proceedings, as they blur the line between authentic and fabricated evidence.

Data trails—left through online activity, mobile use, and IoT devices—are continuously interpreted by AI systems. These algorithmic interpretations can infer intent, behaviour patterns, or associations, shaping narratives in legal contexts.[9] However, such interpretations depend on the algorithms' transparency and reliability, which are often proprietary and opaque.

The concept of a "chain of custody" has also evolved in digital contexts. Maintaining a verifiable log of how digital evidence is collected, transferred, and stored is critical to preserving its admissibility in court. Digital forensics must now ensure not only that evidence remains unaltered but also that its collection and processing methods meet legal and ethical standards.[10]

As AI continues to integrate with legal systems, courts and lawmakers must adapt, establishing rigorous standards for authenticity, accountability, and transparency in the use of digital and AI-generated evidence.

LEGAL CHALLENGES AND DOCTRINAL IMPLICATIONS OF AI IN THE JUSTICE SYSTEM

The increasing use of artificial intelligence (AI) in legal proceedings presents significant legal challenges and doctrinal implications that courts, legislatures, and legal practitioners must grapple with. One of the foremost concerns is the admissibility of AI-generated evidence. Courts must determine whether such evidence meets traditional evidentiary standards, such as relevance, materiality, and probative value. Questions arise regarding the foundational validity of AI tools used to analyse or generate evidence, especially when these tools function as black boxes, making it difficult for judges or juries to evaluate the reliability and objectivity of the results.[11] The use of AI in predictive policing or forensic analysis, for example, has led to debates about whether outputs from these systems can be admitted as scientific or expert evidence, particularly under standards like Daubert or Frye.

Closely related to admissibility is the issue of authentication and reliability. Legal systems require evidence to be authenticated—that is, shown to be what its proponent claims it is. With AI-generated evidence, this becomes complicated due to the lack of human oversight in its creation and the potential for tampering or misrepresentation. Moreover, reliability concerns stem from whether the AI was trained on appropriate datasets, whether it functioned correctly, and whether it consistently produces accurate outputs.[12] Legal actors must assess whether an AI system's methodology is transparent and whether its decision-making processes are replicable and verifiable, which is often not the case with proprietary or opaque AI systems.

Another major concern is the transparency and explainability of algorithms. The principle of due process demands that defendants understand the evidence and procedures used against them. However, many AI systems operate with complex algorithms that are either not fully understood by their developers or are kept secret due to intellectual property protections. This opacity can undermine a defendant's ability to challenge the evidence, violating the principle of equality of arms in legal proceedings.[13] Courts are increasingly being called upon to demand algorithmic transparency or to refuse to admit evidence derived from tools that cannot be adequately scrutinized.

The risk of bias and discrimination in AI tools is another pressing legal issue. AI systems often inherit biases present in their training data, which can lead to discriminatory outcomes in areas such as bail decisions, sentencing, or risk assessments. This raises concerns under constitutional and human rights doctrines that prohibit discrimination and guarantee equal protection under the law.[14] If an AI tool disproportionately affects individuals based on race, gender, or socioeconomic status, its use may violate statutory or constitutional rights, potentially leading to appeals or claims of systemic injustice.

Finally, the integration of AI in the justice system challenges the presumption of innocence and fair trial rights. If AI tools are used to make or influence decisions without human oversight, there is a risk that defendants may be prejudged based on algorithmic assessments rather than evidence presented and examined in court. This could erode the foundational legal doctrine that a person is innocent until proven guilty. Furthermore, a fair trial requires that defendants can confront and contest all evidence used against them.[15] The use of inscrutable AI tools undermines this right and may shift the burden of proof inappropriately, compromising the legitimacy and fairness of judicial outcomes.

In sum, while AI offers the potential to enhance efficiency and consistency in the legal system, its use must be carefully regulated to preserve core legal doctrines and protect fundamental rights. Courts and policymakers must strike a balance between embracing technological innovation and upholding the principles of justice.

COMPARATIVE CASE STUDIES: TECHNOLOGY, SURVEILLANCE, AND LEGAL FRAMEWORKS IN EVIDENCE HANDLING

The intersection of technology and law presents a growing challenge globally, particularly in how evidence is gathered, interpreted, and protected. A comparative look at four case studies—*U.S. v. Jones*, the EU's General Data Protection Regulation (GDPR), India's use of facial recognition, and China's smart courts—highlights how jurisdictions are responding to advances in surveillance and artificial intelligence (AI) in legal contexts.

In the United States, the landmark Supreme Court case *U.S. v. Jones* (2012) set a precedent for how digital surveillance is treated under the Fourth Amendment, which guards against unreasonable searches and seizures.[16] The case involved the warrantless use of a GPS tracking device on a suspect's vehicle over a period of 28 days. The Court ruled that this constituted a search, thereby requiring a warrant. The decision underscored the importance of physical trespass and signalled a broader awareness of privacy implications in the age of digital tracking. While the ruling was rooted in traditional property rights, it opened the door for more nuanced interpretations of privacy in cases involving digital surveillance technologies.

In contrast, the European Union has taken a comprehensive regulatory approach through the GDPR, which directly influences how AI and data are used in legal proceedings. The GDPR enshrines the right to data protection and sets strict rules for the processing of personal data, including data used as evidence. One of the critical implications for AI is the regulation's insistence on transparency and explainability of automated decision-making processes.[17] This presents a challenge for using AI-generated evidence in court, as parties must be able to understand and contest how conclusions are reached—an issue that can be opaque with complex AI models. The GDPR thus serves as a significant counterweight to unchecked technological encroachment on personal rights.

India represents a different set of challenges and opportunities, particularly with the use of facial recognition technology (FRT) by law enforcement. While FRT is seen as a tool to enhance public safety and streamline policing, it has raised serious concerns regarding accuracy, bias, and the lack of legislative oversight. Studies have shown a high rate of false positives, especially among marginalized communities. The absence of a comprehensive data protection law exacerbates the problem, leaving individuals vulnerable to surveillance without adequate legal recourse.[18] India's case underscores the risks of deploying powerful surveillance technologies in the absence of robust legal frameworks.

China's legal innovation through "smart courts" provides a stark contrast, with its integration of AI in judicial processes. These courts use automated evidence review, virtual hearings, and blockchain-based evidence chains to improve efficiency and consistency in rulings. While these innovations promise streamlined justice, they also raise concerns about transparency, judicial independence, and the right to a fair trial. The Chinese model reflects a top-down approach where technological efficiency is prioritized, sometimes at the cost of procedural fairness and human discretion.

CONCLUSION

This study has explored the evolving landscape of evidence within the context of an increasingly AI-integrated legal system. It has highlighted the growing use of artificial intelligence in the collection, analysis, and presentation of evidence, alongside the challenges it poses in terms of authenticity, bias, privacy, and accountability. The findings underscore that while AI offers enhanced efficiency and new capabilities for legal processes, it also introduces significant risks that must be carefully managed.

There is a clear and pressing need for comprehensive legal reforms and robust safeguards to address the implications of AI-driven evidence. These include establishing standards for the admissibility of AI-generated evidence, ensuring transparency in algorithmic processes, and reinforcing human oversight. Ethical and legal frameworks must evolve in tandem with technological advancements to maintain fairness and public trust in the justice system.

Looking ahead, the future of evidence in the legal domain will increasingly rely on a delicate balance between innovation and regulation. By embedding principles of justice, accountability, and transparency into the design and use of AI technologies, we can ensure that the integration of AI into the legal system enhances, rather than undermines, the pursuit of truth and justice.

NOTES

1 Katz, D. M., Bommarito, M. J., & Blackman, J. (2017). A general approach for predicting the behavior of the Supreme Court of the United States. *PLOS ONE*, *12*(4), e0174698. https://doi.org/10.1371/journal.pone.0174698
2 Goodman, B., & Flaxman, S. (2017). European Union regulations on algorithmic decision-making and a "right to explanation." *AI Magazine*, *38*(3), 50–57. https://doi.org/10.1609/aimag.v38i3.2741
3 McGinnis, J. O., & Wasick, R. G. (2015). Law's algorithm. *Florida Law Review*, *66*, 991–1031.
4 Eidelman, V., Ravichander, A., & Howard, N. (2018). The role of NLP in legal evidence discovery. *Proceedings of the 27th International Conference on Computational Linguistics*.
5 Završnik, A. (2019). Algorithmic justice: Algorithms and big data in criminal justice settings. *European Journal of Criminology*, *18*(5), 623–642. https://doi.org/10.1177/1477370819876762
6 Brennan-Marquez, K. (2018). Plausible cause: Explanatory standards in the age of powerful machines. *Vanderbilt Law Review*, *70*, 1249–1302.
7 Angwin, J., Larson, J., Mattu, S., & Kirchner, L. (2016). Machine bias. *ProPublica*. www.propublica.org/article/machine-bias-risk-assessments-in-criminal-sentencing
8 Binns, R. (2018). Fairness in machine learning: Lessons from political philosophy. *Proceedings of the 2018 Conference on Fairness, Accountability and Transparency*, 149–159.
9 Bornstein, B. H., & Greene, E. (2011). Jury decision making: Implications for and from psychology. *Current Directions in Psychological Science*, 20(1), 63–67.
10 Bostrom, N. (2014). *Superintelligence: Paths, dangers, strategies*. Oxford University Press.
11 Abbott, R. (2020). The reasonable computer: Disrupting the paradigm of tort liability. *Columbia Law Review*, *110*(6), 1109–1150.
12 Brennan-Marquez, K., & Henderson, S. E. (2019). The reasonable computer: Predictive policing and unreasonable searches. *University of Pennsylvania Law Review*, *167*(6), 1171–1214.
13 Burrell, J. (2016). How the machine "thinks": Understanding opacity in machine learning algorithms. *Big Data & Society*, *3*(1), 1–12. https://doi.org/10.1177/2053951715622512
14 Citron, D. K., & Pasquale, F. (2014). The scored society: Due process for automated predictions. *Washington Law Review*, *89*(1), 1–33.
15 Gless, S., Silverman, E., & Weigend, T. (2016). If robots cause harm, who is to blame? Self-driving cars and criminal liability. *New Criminal Law Review*, *19*(3), 412–436.
16 Van Brakel, R. (2016). Pre-emptive big data surveillance and its (dis)empowering consequences: The case of predictive policing. *The Surveillance Studies Reader*, 316–328.
17 Joh, E. E. (2016). The new surveillance discretion: Automated suspicion, big data, and policing. *Harvard Law & Policy Review*, *10*(1), 15–42.
18 McMullan, J. L., & Perrier, D. C. (2002). Surveillance and policing in Canada: From partisan scrutiny to database management. *Social Justice*, *29*(1/2), 144–161.

3 From Lab Bench to Legal Bench

The Role of AI in Evaluating Biological Evidence

Abhisikta Basu and Keya De Mukhopadhyay

INTRODUCTION

Biological evidence, such as samples of DNA, blood, and tissue, forms the basis of forensic science, allowing for proper identification and chronological reconstruction of events. Yet to be admissible in a court of law, the integrity of such evidence has to be unquestionable. One mechanism that provides this safeguard is the chain of custody, which carefully logs the possession of the evidence from the crime scene to trial. When procedures are not stringent or records are missing, the courts may subject the evidence to doubts regarding its validity, possibly finding it inadmissible (Badiye et al., 2023; Law 101: Legal Guide for the Forensic Expert | Chain of Custody | National Institute of Justice, n.d.).

As forensic investigations become more complex, so too should the technology utilized to examine biological evidence. Artificial Intelligence (AI), specifically machine learning algorithms, provides robust advancements in the examination of complicated datasets spanning genomic profiles to imaging data and digital trace evidence within cyber-forensic environments (Nowroozi et al., 2020). Chain of custody establishes the origin and authenticity of the evidence and guarantees that the same substance originally gathered is what is being analyzed and used in court. This includes extensive records of each person who comes in contact with the evidence, timestamps of transferal, and storage documentation under protection (Badiye et al., 2023; National Institute of Justice, n.d.; Badiye, 2023). Its integrity is so crucial that any flaw can leave the evidence almost unusable (Badiye et al., 2023). New technologies, including blockchain, are being considered to support chain-of-custody systems. Blockchain provides tamper-evident, auditable, and traceable traceability, which are crucial capabilities for improving legal defensibility, particularly with digital or multi-jurisdictional evidence (Patil et al., 2024).

In Indian judicial settings, the courts have emphasized the impact of tainted chains of custody on rendering verdicts invalid. For instance, in Prakash Nishad v. State of Maharashtra, faulty documentation regarding the handling of DNA specimens resulted in an acquittal (Indulia, 2024). Likewise, in Ashit Biswas v. State of West Bengal, chain-of-custody record gaps invalidated evidence for the seizure of drugs (Indulia, 2024).

In the U.S. federal courts, the Daubert standard requires scientific evidence to undergo stringent criteria: testability, established error rates, peer-reviewed publishing, and widespread acceptance in the pertinent scientific community. Judges act as gatekeepers in admissibility determinations (Specter, 2002; Daubert Standard, n.d.). This norm reinforced judicial control after *Daubert* v. *Merrell Dow Pharmaceuticals, Inc.* (1993) and further applied to expert testimony outside of science (e.g., expert mechanics or accident reconstruction) in *Kumho Tire Co.* v. *Carmichael* (1999) (Daubert Standard, n.d.; Kumho Tire Co. v. Carmichael, 1999).

DOI: 10.1201/9781003629146-4

AI contributes toward multiple benefits to forensic biology, specifically to improve the precision and accuracy of evidence analysis in the forensic context. The most significant of these is minimizing the rate of human error. Through techniques like pattern recognition, biometric measurement, or evidence recording, human bias brings uncertainty and misinterpretation. Artificial intelligence is transforming forensic laboratory work more and more by eliminating bias, halting human error, and making the findings more uniform and reproducible. This change not only bestows legality to the scientific worth of forensic reports but also renders expert witnesses more susceptible to being refused judicial challenges. Perhaps most critical among the benefits of AI is its capacity to detect latent patterns and clues, which underlie forensic science in this contemporary setup. Machine Learning algorithms, for instance, can handle and process incredibly complicated data sets within seconds, orders of magnitude quicker than man. This capability has been applied most notably in the areas of DNA profiling, forensic imaging, and other biometric analysis, where weak signals or latent correlations may provide unimaginably high probative value (Nowroozi et al., 2020). Both sensitivity and specificity of biological evidence analysis are thus increased, placing at the disposal of courts still firmer ground upon which to base reasonable inferences. Another advantage of AI is that it has the effective ability to handle scale variability. Contemporary labs are time and again restricted to have colossal stacks of pending cases, record-breaking crime scenes, or larger datasets. AI technology is significantly capable of sifting through all such data within a few minutes to yield comprehensive reports without compromising accuracy. This gradually becomes important in the scenario of more than one biological sample as a source of human DNA. Modern systems are increasingly being designed to produce transparent results in scientific and legal terms that are comprehensible to law enforcement professionals (Phillips & Przybocki, 2020a, 2020b). Transparency is required to attempt to meet all the admissibility criteria, for instance, those in the Daubert test. AI also has a significant impact on digital and computer forensic investigations. Computer systems today provide secure and electronic chain-of-custody to evidence that provides integrity and traceability. These technologies provide suitable solutions to the classical problems of research on cybercrime as well as transnational cooperation in cases where tracing with regular possibilities typically fails (Badiye, 2023). Since even a minute flaw in the biological evidence analysis has the potential to lead to miscarriages of justice, where accuracy and dependability cannot be compromised. AI minimizes such risks by reducing human fallibility, enhancing documentation, and bringing consistency for analyses. In addition to this, the use of blockchain for chain-of-custody protocols adds a further layer of security and accountability mechanism, such that each step in the evidence handling process is tamper-evident. Together, these technologies make different forensic processes more scientific and ensure higher probabilities of the produced evidence being of admissibility value in the court of law.

Understanding Biological Evidence

Biological evidence is becoming more and more dependent on forensic science and modern-day scientific analysis. The ability to analyze biological compounds such as DNA, RNA, and proteins can be used to give extremely specific characterization and identification of humans, infectious agents, and biological processes. The scope and variety of the biological evidence have increased due to the unrestrained progress of biotechnology and bioinformatics, necessitating research, clinical diagnosis, and criminal justice. The goal of this article is to provide the reader with a general understanding of biological evidence through its focus on definition, characteristics, data management issues, and special preservation and chain of custody issues.

Biological evidence is any material that originates from a living organism and can be analyzed at the molecular level to provide data of value for identification, diagnosis, or investigation. The best-accepted type of biological evidence is likely to be DNA, with its unique genetic information (other than identical twins) of the subject and recoverability from various sources like blood, saliva, hair roots, skin cells, and body fluids. DNA profiling is more common than forensic identification, paternity testing, and disease diagnosis. Less stable RNA evidence offers immediate information concerning gene expression at the time of sampling, offering insight into disease state, tissue condition, and cellular activity. RNA analysis has attracted particular attention in biomedical and forensic science, providing new opportunities for disease screening and evidence analysis. Widespread application is frequently hampered by the intrinsic chemical instability of RNA molecules. Proteins are more stable and have various forensic and medical roles: they can differentiate tissues, be indicators of pathological processes, and detect exposure to toxic substances. Protein-centered methods, most typically developed in the science of proteomics, allow researchers to look beyond the genetic code and investigate functional indications of biology. Such methods rely highly on sophisticated bioinformatics, as contemporary molecular research and sequencing are generating humongous amounts of data that can only be made accessible by computer use to find valid trends and useful meanings. The presence of high-throughput technologies such as proteomics, transcriptomics, and next-generation sequencing (NGS) has revolutionized the characterization of biological material. NGS, in specific, has revolutionized the field by enabling scientists to sequence RNA and DNA rapidly in high volumes. This ability has improved gene expression and genetic variation information, giving scientists unprecedented insight into molecular events. In forensic science-related issues, these advances offer significantly high effectiveness in instrumentation for the interpretation of different biological evidence with greater precision, accuracy, and reliability than conventional methods. These technologies increase the potential as well as the challenges of biological evidence analyses by generating large amounts of multivariate datasets that need to be combined and interpreted using advanced statistical tools. This chapter is intended to present a complete understanding of the biological evidence by presenting its definition, nature, challenges in data management, as well as issues that are specific and related to the chain of custody and preservation.

Scope, Objective, and Methodology of the Chapter

The primary objective of this chapter is to critically evaluate how AI is being integrated into forensic biotechnology and how this impacts evidential law. Besides confronting the ethical, legal, and procedural challenges associated with their deployment, it aims to explore how AI-based technologies are transforming the collection, preservation, and analysis of biological evidence, ranging from phenotyping to proteomics and genomes. The chapter seeks to depict the pros and cons of applying AI in forensic laboratories based on international norms, court decisions, and emerging best practices. The end goal is to propose a framework that balances constitutional safeguards with technological progress, ensuring that biological evidence facilitated by AI is both legally admissible, scientifically credible, and respectful of human rights.

Characteristics of the Biological Evidence are in Subsection 2 of this Chapter. Further "data heavy" nature of biotech outputs is discussed in Subsection 3. AI-driven forensic application in Biotechnology is dealt with under Subsection 4. Further, the rise of AI in Biotechnological Analysis is dealt with under Subsection 5, and the legal and ethical challenges are dealt with under Subsection 6.

CHARACTERISTICS OF BIOLOGICAL EVIDENCE: COLLECTING, PRESERVING, AND EXAMINING

The integrity of biological evidence is the focal point of forensic examinations, clinical diagnosis, and biomedical research, as it is the premise upon which conclusions are drawn and justice or outcomes of treatment are rendered. Biological evidence analysis is constructed around three fundamental steps: collection, preservation, and analysis. All three must be conducted according to strict procedural and scientific guidelines in order to prevent contamination, degradation, or misinterpretation.

Biological material such as blood, saliva, hair, tissue, and even cellular waste is, by nature, fragile and therefore needs to be handled with care to enable subsequent examinations to remain accurate and repeatable (Butler, 2015a, 2015b, 2015c; Budowle et al., 2019). Of all the procedures, collection is often regarded as the most important since the manner in which a sample is collected essentially determines the quality and integrity of each ensuing analysis. It is for this reason that sterilization methods, control of the environment, and resolute faithfulness to the chain of custody are crucial from the initial stages.

The sample character depends greatly on the investigative or clinical intent. In criminal investigations, forensic scientists can recover semen, blood, saliva, or epithelial cells from a crime scene, whereas in medical laboratories, healthcare providers can collect biopsies, buccal swabs, or cerebrospinal fluid to inform medical diagnosis. In all cases, swabs, tubes, gloves, and so forth must be sterilized to prevent foreign DNA or protein introduction. Of equally critical concern is evidentiary integrity: a sample contaminated at the time of collection risks being excluded from judicial proceedings. To guarantee admissibility, the U.S. National Institute of Justice (NIJ) places significant emphasis on recording every step of the collection, noting the exact location of recovery, and detailing storage conditions so the chain of custody can be verified unbroken (NIJ, 2013). To this end, forensic scientists point out that the evidence's reliability is compromised if procedures for sampling are violated since mismanagement can raise questions about the authenticity of the evidence (Houck & Siegel, 2018).

Having been collected, biological evidence is stored in ways that aim to prevent biochemical degradation. Preservation procedures are important in the sense that biological molecules vary in stability. DNA, though very stable, can still be degraded when subjected to excessive heat, water, or ultraviolet light and light. RNA and proteins are less stable and very susceptible to enzyme degradation. In order to combat such vulnerabilities, many methods are used. General methods of protein and DNA stabilization include refrigeration and freezing at −20°C or −80°C. Liquid nitrogen cryopreservation is mostly used in the case of long-term storage for the maintenance of structural and functional integrity of samples. Chemical stabilizers like RNase inhibitors or preservative buffers are widely used for preventing RNA enzymatic degradation (Chakraborty & Natarajan, 2019). The storage method is normally chosen depending on sample storage duration and molecular targets of interest. For example, forensic labs can freeze-dry blood samples for decades, while clinical laboratories working with RNA for transcriptomics must stabilize immediately to avoid loss of signal fidelity. Hence, it is not a single preservation procedure but a modified procedure that considers the specific characteristics of biomolecules and what research is designed to achieve (Alonso et al., 2018).

Following conservation, the biological sample undergoes a series of extraction, amplification, detection, and computer analysis. Extraction is the initial step in analysis, where the nucleic acids and proteins are separated from the intricate biological matrices like tissue, blood, or saliva. Methods range from the conventional extraction using phenol-chloroform to more sophisticated silica column and magnet bead automated methods. Following the extraction, amplification methods like Polymerase Chain Reaction (PCR) then become the target of amplifying the target DNA to a detectable level (Mullis & Faloona, 1987). PCR has revolutionized the field of forensic genetics as it has made it possible to analyze trace amounts as well as degraded samples and thereby provide an opportunity for the criminal justice system to utilize the reports generated from even infinitesimal traces of biological material.

Short Tandem Repeat (STR) analysis remains the well-established and validated method for generating a full genetic profile of a human individual and continues to serve as the gold standard with respect to other DNA typing techniques that are evaluated (Butler, 2015a, 2015b, 2015c). While STR is well established, the inception of high-throughput sequencing methods has extended the scope of the field of forensic genetics. Next-Generation Sequencing (NGS) allows both targeted and whole-genome sequencing, enabling the detection of single-nucleotide polymorphisms (SNPs), assessment of mitochondrial DNA variability, phenotypic features, and identification of microbial signatures that may connect an individual to a particular or multiple crime scenes (Budowle et al., 2019). These technologies deliver complex information to add more logical and informative dimensions to the conventional technique, i.e., STR-based analyses, and effectively enhance the value of DNA evidence. Proteomics also added a new dimension to the existing techniques. Based on methods such as mass spectrometry, scientists can now analyze and validate biomarkers in proteins from forensically relevant samples. These biomarkers can signal tissue type or toxic interference and allow investigation beyond DNA. Proteomics has also been shown to be of great significance in situations with problematic scenarios, i.e., small samples of DNA, degraded DNA, or absence of DNA, because it provides complementary lines of evidence to maximize the forensic utility.

Irrespective of the technique, the success of the overall instrumentation utility depends upon the robust bioinformatics support. Computational pipelines and algorithms are now common practice for the detection of genetic variation and sequence alignments. These techniques not only optimize accuracy but also facilitate in-depth insight into complex and multidimensional biological information. Without them, it will be difficult to manage huge volumes of data generated by different genetic analyzers. In all of these situations, the integrity of biological evidence and its reports are dependent on a systematic coordination of collection, preservation, and analysis in the appropriate order. Each step along the process has limitations, and a lack of control over them reduces scientific as well as court admissibility. With the frequent application of forensic practice in modern molecular biological techniques and computerized interpretation, forensic scientists are able to preserve important evidentiary values simultaneously while continuously optimizing interpretation. These steps establish forensic science as an interdisciplinary scientific discipline that collectively use medicine, molecular biology, biotechnology and bioinformatics to interpret the data obtained from biological samples correctly in a more reliable and accurate manner in recent years is.

THE "DATA HEAVY" NATURE OF BIOTECH OUTPUTS

Advancements in recent technological domains, like next-generation sequencing (NGS), proteomics, etc. have transformed the legal interpretation of biological information. The ability to process large volumes and high throughputs of data obtained from genetic material by NGS allowed legal professionals to interrogate more deeply into different gene expression patterns and different levels of genetic diversity. Advancements allow forensic experts to pose different questions on heredity and molecular function much more specifically than with older and conventional techniques. Proteomics makes these causes possible as it determines the cellular condition of working, passing information beyond genetic data. Protein interaction research allows scientists to see different activities of biological function that is inaccessible in case of DNA sequencing. While these techniques significantly extend the scope of biological evidence analysis, they give humongous and complicated datasets. The scale of such outputs demands mass bioinformatics backup with regard to interpretation, alongside data integration in an attempt to obtain valuable conclusions from the volume of output data. Biological evidence is not only analyzed scientifically but also involves a chain of custody, data handling, and long-term preservation concerns. The paper is therefore meant to provide a complete explanation of biological evidence through the study of its definition, nature, and unique issues of analysis and manipulation of it.

Chain of Custody and Preservation Issues Unique to Biotech evidence

To avoid that biological evidence is discredited or invalidated in court, it should be preserved intact. Chain of custody, under which total documentation from collection to analysis, to avoid tampering or contamination, is most crucial in avoiding that. Results are compromised by the inherent limitations placed by biological evidence, such as possible cross-contamination and molecular degradation.

The personal and intimate details in genetic information create legal and ethical concerns beyond such technical concerns. Therefore, for the safeguard of individual rights, privacy, informed consent, and data protection acts, stringent standards are that individual rights are preserved, privacy is ensured, informed consent is obtained, and data protection acts are adhered to in the correct way. Because such biological samples containing proteins or RNA are very delicate and subject to degradation, evidence analysis by biotechnologies is even more challenging. This demands strict storage and transportation protocols with traceable and controlled methods to enable reproducibility of complex tests and resist judicial scrutiny in court. Biotechnological progress and bioinformatics most commonly instigate rapid change and revolution in biological evidence analysis. Its successful collection, conservation, and interpretation require multi-disciplinary research and strict technical protection. The promptness and integrity of biological samples for scientific and legal purposes will depend on the solution of data handling and legal problems.

THE RISE OF AI IN BIOTECHNOLOGICAL ANALYSIS

Biotechnology is evolving more and more because of AI, which gives sophisticated computational power to augment the traditional experimental protocols. Such enormous data are generated by biotechnology in terms of phenotypic assays, proteomics, metabolomics, and high-throughput sequencing. As such data are typically out of reach for the analyzing capability of the traditional statistical software, artificial intelligence is becoming an integral part of biotechnological processes. AI is also accelerating the work in targeted therapy, drug design, and genetics with its ability to pinpoint sophisticated patterns, eliminate labor-intensive work, and combine unrelated sets of data. The main AI approaches, benefits, risks, and constraints of overreliance on the AI systems are all discussed in this section of the synergy of AI and biotechnology.

Sample procurement, data gathering, preparation, analysis, and interpretation are all part of a regular process in biotechnology. Through the pipeline, AI enters at a number of points to be as accurate and efficient as possible. By way of illustration, raw sequencing reads that are not yet aligned must be aligned and corrected for errors; they are aided by AI methods that can learn randomness and noise. Downstream is supplemented with phenotypic prediction, literature mining, and variation classification to inform hypotheses by AI models. AI platforms offering scientists convenient interfaces to work on complex data without substantial computational expertise are also a field where integration is needed.

TYPES OF AI TECHNIQUES USED

Genomics research thus far has greatly relied on the application of artificial intelligence techniques, specifically machine learning (ML), natural language processing (NLP), and deep learning (DL). Support vector machines, random forests, and gradient boosting models are some of the machine learning techniques that have often been used to identify genetic variants, identify biomarkers, and classify disease types. For example, using single-nucleotide polymorphism (SNP) information, machine learning (ML) models can accurately estimate disease risk, leading to earlier treatment and diagnosis. Gene expression profile clustering, which most often leads to the discovery of new disease mechanisms or subgroups of patients, is one benefit that is achieved while working with unsupervised methods. With the use of named entity recognition, topic modeling, and relation extraction, natural language processing (NLP) can assist in automating the retrieval of knowledge from large biomedical literature and patent databases.

This prohibits conventional and manual screening and enhances knowledge discovery in emerging fields, i.e., biotechnology, genetics, and genomics. Analyzing high-dimensional and complex biological information is optimally done using different deep learning (DL) models, like convolutional neural networks (CNNs), recurrent neural networks (RNNs), etc. Through more accurate phenotypic prediction and enhanced classification of samples, Deep Learning algorithms, applied on heterogeneous and multivariate data sources, like genetic, epigenetic, etc.

Advantages over Traditional Analytical Methods

In biomedicine and forensic uses, AI has proved to be an effective substitute for conventional statistical and heuristic methods. One reason AI can be effective is that it is able to process high-dimensional data, which conventional methods find challenging due to dimensionality issues in data such as whole-genome sequences or proteome profiles. Second, the nonlinearity and complexity of biological systems necessitate analytical models that can reveal subtle relationships, and artificial intelligence (AI) has proven to be superior to linear regression and basic clustering methods in extracting nonlinear interactions. Through automatic pre-processing of data, selecting features, and developing prediction models, AI not only enhances precision but also accelerates research processes by eliminating human prejudice. In addition, due to its integrative nature, scientists may integrate various types of data, including clinical data, transcriptomic data, and genomic data, to enhance systems-level understanding, which is important for systems biology and precision medicine. Finally, AI platforms allow for analysis close to real-time, which is essential in application areas where timely responses have a major bearing on the outcome, such as clinical decision-making and pathogen outbreak identification.

Limitations and Risks of Over-Reliance

While AI has shown game-changing potential in the areas of biomedicine and forensics, there are important risks and limitations that must be thoroughly assessed. Since AI models need large, high-quality data sets on which to effectively train, bias and data quality are among the most important concerns. Models that are generated where particular groups are underrepresented can generate biased or inaccurate predictions, which would even more solidify systemic disparities. Second, the interpretability problem is challenging regulatory endorsement as well as clinical adoption. It is challenging to create responsibility and trust since most AI systems, especially deep neural networks, are "black boxes" that provide little explanation of how they arrive at their judgments. Models trained on particular data will not necessarily perform well with new or unknown data because they are prone to overfitting and lack adequate generalizability, another limitation that requires rigorous validation and replication. Ethical and privacy concerns could occur in the management of sensitive clinical and genetic data, such as ownership, informed consent, and discriminatory use. Finally, overdependence on AI systems lacking adequate human control could be detrimental to the key professional and cognitive skills and overlook algorithmic failure. Overall, these considerations emphasize the importance of safe, ethical, and transparent application of AI in forensic and health care environments.

The entry of AI in biotechnological analysis has introduced a paradigm shift toward more accurate, effective, and comprehensive biological data interpretation. Researchers have now resolved complex biological queries once deemed impossible using deep learning, machine learning, and natural language processing. Solution-finding in the domains of data bias, model explainability, and ethics is imperative to make sure that AI tools are being effectively and ethically deployed. AI can greatly broaden innovation in biomedicine, biotechnology and other fields with further research and development and multidisciplinary approaches.

AI-DRIVEN FORENSIC APPLICATION IN BIOTECHNOLOGY

Though AI has immensely augmented clinical research, genetics, and personal medicine, it is not solely implemented in medicine. These techniques are increasingly being used in forensic biotechnology, where public safety and justice are concerned. AI is revolutionizing the nature of forensic investigations by making it feasible to analyze biological evidence rapidly, precisely, and comprehensively.

Forensic Genomics

The use of AI in forensic genomics has vastly improved the ability of investigators to deal with difficult genetic data sets, especially in DNA mixture resolution, missing persons identification, and pathogen source attribution. Although machine learning methods, including deep neural networks and Bayesian classifiers, have enhanced precision and scalability in DNA mixture solutions, traditional probabilistic models generally do not cope well with significantly degraded or mixed samples (Ballantyne et al., 2019).

Likewise, high-throughput AI-driven comparison methods assist in accelerating humanitarian identification processes by comparing missing persons' genetic information against reference databases (Kayser & de Knijff, 2011). One of the most fascinating case studies is the convergence of forensic and public health genetics in the 2001 US anthrax bioterrorism attacks. The source of the spores used in the letters to a specific US Army building was identified later on by following the genetic differences among Bacillus anthracis strains through AI-aided bioinformatics pipelines (Rosenberg, 2011). In microbial forensics, microbial analysis became ever more evidence-based when it was possible to trace back faint mutational fingerprints by combining AI-assisted genomic sequencing (Budowle et al., 2014). The COVID-19 pandemic's genomics tracing controversy more recently revealed the twin-use capability of forensic genomics when source attribution algorithms and contact tracing were politicized in the legal and political spheres (Maxmen & Mallapaty, 2021). These examples showcase the contentious and conceivable power of AI-based forensic genomics and the requirement for thorough validation processes to obtain admissibility in a court setting.

Forensic Phenotyping

Arguably, the most innovative applications of artificial intelligence to the examination of biological evidence are forensic phenotyping, whereby predictions of features that are visually observable can be made based on genetics. AI platforms already possess the ability to generate probabilistic predictions of face morphology and, more recently, eye, hair, and skin color from single-nucleotide polymorphisms (SNPs). Parabon NanoLabs' Snapshot DNA Phenotyping Service, its use in US criminal cases, is the ideal example of this kind of use. The technology that is AI-powered has found application in a number of well-known cold cases where other methods of investigation proved useless, such as the 2014 Heather Bogle murder in Ohio. Based entirely on DNA evidence, snapshot-created composite images yielded new leads for investigations, assisting law enforcement by minimizing the number of possible suspects (Kayser & de Knijff, 2011; Butler, 2015a, 2015b, 2015c). Furthermore, after years of futile investigation, phenotypic predictions identified Gary Hartman as the killer of Michella Welch in 1984 in Washington State (Greytak et al., 2019). These uses show the evidentiary value of AI-assisted phenotyping, but they also pose significant ethical and legal concerns about accuracy, privacy, and admissibility. Forensic phenotyping is then at the intersection of law and biotechnology, looking forward to challenges but welcoming the potential for applying AI in the criminal justice system. However, these scientific discoveries cannot be seen in a vacuum; their practical significance depends on their legal systems' admissibility and ethical validity.

LEGAL AND ETHICAL CHALLENGES

Forensic science has come a long way, with biological evidence now being utilized in criminal trials, but its use in court trials is legally and ethically problematic. The decision is on the basis of biological evidence, i.e., DNA, blood test, microbiome report, etc. But the protection of the rights of the accused and scientific integrity are two matters that should be settled by the courts. It is no longer a matter of whether or not the biological evidence is scientific but of admissibility within prevailing paradigms of evidence. There are therefore currently legislations that govern how the scientific evidence should be admitted and balanced against the quality of content on the one hand and risks of bias, misinterpretation, or abuse on the other.

The admissibility is one of the original concerns in terms of an ethical issue. The invasion of biological evidence into the body, privacy, and personhood of the individual is a constitutional issue in terms of the extent of the power vested in the government. According to Faigman (2014), courts have forever struggled between adopting scientific knowledge and skepticism regarding its use in legal inquiry. Such a balance is broken by the rising use of AI in the analysis of biological evidence, whose computational processes undermine responsibility, openness, and prejudice. Admissibility standards act as an ethical and legal filter in such a setting. Admissibility standards serve as an ethical and legal sieve in this environment.

Admissibility

Frye v. *United States* (1923) was the initial serious effort at controlling scientific evidence within the United States. New scientific evidence is required to be "sufficiently established to have gained general acceptance in the particular field in which it belongs" before the Court can deem it acceptable. For decades, this broad acceptance test was the basis for admissibility, especially in polygraph testimony. Frye established an important precedent: the judiciary should be the gatekeeper against "junk science," even though it has been criticized as too conservative and excluding the application of new scientific methods.

The restrictive Frye standard was reaffirmed in *Daubert* v. *Merrell Dow Pharmaceuticals* (1993), in which the U.S. Supreme Court enunciated a less stringent, multi-factorial standard (*Daubert* v. *Merrell Dow Pharmaceuticals*, 1993). The Court authorized judges to assess scientific reliability on factors including testability, peer review, error rates, and widespread acceptance. This decision represented a paradigm change, indicating admissibility was now dependent on methodological soundness, not merely consensus.

The following *General Electric Co.* v. *Joiner* (1997) and *Kumho Tire Co.* v. *Carmichael* (1999) decisions melded this standard into what has become known as the Daubert Trilogy. In Joiner, the Court elucidated that the admissibility decisions of the trial courts are to be reviewed under an "abuse of discretion" standard (*General Electric Co.* v. *Joiner*, 1997), allowing judges more leeway. In Kumho Tire, the Court applied Daubert principles to technology and specialized knowledge, extending them beyond "hard science" (*Kumho Tire Co.* v. *Carmichael*, 1999). Together, these decisions made judges active gatekeepers of scientific reliability, weighing legal fairness against the complexity of science (Faigman, 2014).

Prior to Daubert, courts struggled with the shortcomings of Frye. In United States v. Huber (1992), the Eighth Circuit applied Frye but emphasized its insufficiency in evaluating new forensic techniques. The ruling evidenced judicial dissatisfaction with Frye's inflexibility and presaged the Supreme Court's shift toward Daubert's liberal test.

In India, the admissibility of forensic and biological evidence has been historically controlled by the Indian Evidence Act, 1872 (IEA), a colonial piece of legislation that was not equipped to deal with the scientific subtleties of DNA profiling, toxicology, or computer forensics. Courts making reference to the IEA tended to invoke broad judicial discretion, creating uncertainty and unpredictability in the way forensic evidence was handled. For instance, in the *State of Himachal Pradesh* v. *Jai Lal* (1999) and *Selvi* v. *State of Karnataka* (2010), the Supreme Court emphasized the requirement that expert evidence must be reliable as well as legally valid, but declined to promulgate a formal framework similar to the *Frye* (1923) "general acceptance" test or Daubert (1993) standard of reliability in the United States.

The IEA's limitations were especially clear in instances of DNA evidence. In *Santosh Kumar Singh* v. *State through CBI* (2010), the Court emphasized procedural shortcomings in DNA analysis, but in *Krishna Kumar Malik* v. *State of Haryana* (2011), DNA evidence was validated as conclusive. This type of variation illustrates the existence of a disorganized admissibility doctrine, wherein the decision is not based on empirical validation but rather on the subjective interpretation of the judge. According to Faigman (2014), when a court depends on scientific evidence without a rigorous framework, the possibility for what he terms "legal alchemy," which involves converting flawed science into supposedly credible evidence, is diminished.

To forestall such complications, the Bharatiya Sakshya Adhiniyam (BSA), 2023 has been enacted to take the place of the Indian Evidence Act (IEA). It explicitly incorporates provisions regarding scientific evidence and electronic documents, recognizing the present-day reality that reliance on technological inputs for purposes of trials is increasing (Bhatia, 2023). It thereby brings Indian evidence law into closer alignment with international norms with respect to relevance and reliability. It is reflective of international trends represented by Daubert trilogy (Daubert v. Merrell Dow Pharmaceuticals, 1993; General Electric v. Joiner, 1997; Kumho Tire v. Carmichael, 1999), which mandates that the admissibility of evidence is subject to scientific validity, methodological robustness, and judicial supervision.

Skepticism also prevails regarding implementing provisions of the BSA. Furthermore, legal practitioners and judges will also have to be specially trained to grasp sophisticated forensic conclusions, with India's forensic establishment remaining plagued with delay, backlog, and non-accreditation. Unless adequately protected, the BSA would yield the same pitfalls it is meant to eliminate. More seriously is the imperative to ensure that new evidentiary norms better aligned with prevailing realities are accompanied by Institutional Reforms that rule out possibilities of abuse and restore public confidence in scientific justice.

AI in Forensic Evidence: Ethical Bridge to Transparency and Explainability

The ethical terrain of biological evidence becomes more complicated when forensic science engages artificial intelligence (AI). The traditional admissibility wars, on either the Frye (1923) or Daubert (1993) platforms, had been grappling with scientific reliability, qualified experts, and good methods. AI systems bring a new factor into the mix: the non-transparency of algorithms, which are "black boxes" (Burrell, 2015). Such opacity can have the potential to become sinister not just in science but even in the domain of due procedure and constitutional safeguard of a fair trial under Article 21 of the Indian Constitution. Procedural justice always demands that the Indian judiciary be as significant as substantive justice (Maneka Gandhi v. Union of India, 1978). Putting AI into practice on evidence should thus also be considered as subverting the constitution, and not only technology.

DNA examination and bio-evidence are already questionable in relation to abuse and miscarriage of justice unless scrutinized in the open. The Delhi High Court in Santosh Kumar Singh v. State (2010) pointed out the necessity of robust scientific examination of DNA reports prior to their being relied upon for conviction. If AI applications are superimposed on such evidence, there is a multiplication of the likelihood of error unless the algorithms behind them are open to judicial scrutiny or cross-examination by the defense (Casey et al., 2018). The lack of explainability risks denying the accused their constitutional right to contest the foundation of the case against them, a foundation stone of adversarial criminal justice systems (Parkkavi & Yadharthana, n.d.).

Courts worldwide have exercised caution in admitting forensic evidence generated by black box technologies. The American case State v. Loomis (2016) highlighted the dangers of the use of proprietary risk-assessment software unavailable to be questioned by defendants. Analogously, the UK Court of Appeal in R v. T (2010) cautioned about the risks of exaggerating scientific certainty when methods are non-transparent. Such precedents echo in Indian realities, for forensic capacity and judicial sensitization concerns are already pressing (DNA Database: A Legislative Overreach,

2021). Using AI without any certain assurance that it does not, the biases built into the system can then be embedded rather than being removed.

The moral implication is chilling: admissibility should transition from the customary standard of scientific accuracy to a global standard of justice, accountability, and transparency. And that also aligns with globe-spanning discussion about "Responsible AI" with emphasis placed upon explainability as a non-negotiable court standard (Guidotti et al., 2018). In the event an AI forensic instrument is to be used to analyze biological evidence, then it has to be measured by yardsticks that courts, attorneys, and even common jurists would be able to grasp how the outcome is determined. Or AI as a tool of evidentiary authoritarianism, where technical expertise is accorded more value than meticulous legal examination (Suresh & Guttag, 2021).

Transparency and Explainability in AI tools: Bias in AI Algorithms and Wrongful Conviction Risks

Artificial intelligence has also transformed forensic science in the analysis of biological materials such as DNA profiling, forensic genomics, and digital pathology. AI systems sift through millions of intricate data points to provide faster, more accurate, and cheaper results compared to traditional methods (Mittelstadt et al., 2016). Increasingly, however, they are underpinned by widespread concerns about transparency, explainability, and bias and wrongful convictions. While the conventional methods of forensic science and their justifications are cross-examined and peer-reviewed, AI computers are "black boxes" and unfeasible to present to judges, lawyers, or even to expert witnesses with justification inside (Goodman & Flaxman, 2017).

The Challenge of Algorithmic Bias

Bias in AI models can arise due to a variety of sources, including distorted training data, poor design, or even intrinsic social imbalances inherent in datasets. For instance, DNA mixture analysis software like STRmix and TrueAllele have been criticized for their probabilistic models, which at times yield conflicting outcomes based on algorithmic assumptions (Biedermann et al., 2017). When such tools are employed in court, defense lawyers will find it challenging to question or cross-examine results since the proprietary algorithms are kept as trade secrets, thus circumscribing transparency (Casey & Schatz, 2011)

In India, the above issues are amplified. Courts under the Indian Evidence Act, 1872, and its revised version, Bharatiya Sakshya Adhiniyam, 2023 (BSA), permit the admissibility of electronic and scientific evidence. Yet, the legislative framework remains short of firmly installing the explainability requirements demanded of AI-powered tools (Bhatia, 2023). This loophole may permit the admission of algorithmic results without adequate examination, which may violate an accused's constitutional right to a fair trial under Article 21 of the Indian Constitution.

Explainability as a Safeguard

Explainability in AI is the capacity of a system to supply reasons or explanations for its outputs in a format that is accessible to human stakeholders. This is crucial in forensic applications where evidence needs to pass cross-examination and judicial examination (Doshi-Velez & Kim, 2017). Without explainability, courts will risk replacing human judgment with non-transparent algorithmic reasoning.

One of the major issues is the "automation bias," as judges and juries tend to give excessive significance to AI-produced outcomes merely because they are considered objective or scientific in nature (Schoeman, 2020). In erroneous conviction cases across the world, like that of Cameron Todd Willingham in America, excessive dependence on defective forensic methods has been reported (*"Invalid Forensic Science Testimony and Wrongful Convictions" by Brandon L. Garrett and Peter J. Neufeld*, n.d.). With AI, this risk gets amplified because deviations would not be easily identifiable without openness in how the algorithm has been developed.

Judicial Precedents and Comparative Insights

The judicial handling of scientific and technological evidence has evolved differently in jurisdictions, but the shared concern continues to be one of reliability and equity. In the United States, the seminal case of *Daubert* v. *Merrell Dow Pharmaceuticals* (1993) set the precedent that expert evidence should be both reliable and relevant, putting trial judges in the position of "gatekeepers" who review the scientific merits of evidence prior to admitting it in court. This requirement was broadened in General *Electric Co.* v. *Joiner* (1997), where the Court ruled that judges could rule out expert evidence if the methodology did not reasonably lead to the conclusions, and again in *Kumho Tire Co.* v. *Carmichael* (1999), which applied the Daubert standard to all technical and specialized expertise, not just purely scientific evidence (Faigman et al., 2014). Together, these decisions crafted a strong model for judicial review of scientific reliability in the U.S., which may serve as an important comparative model for AI-generated evidence in criminal cases.

In India, while there is no immediate framework for algorithmic or AI-based evidence, judicial rulings reflect awareness of the threats presented by untested scientific practices. In Selvi v. State of Karnataka (2010), coercive narcoanalysis under the garb of medical science was judicially struck down by the Supreme Court both on the grounds of its doubtful scientific admissibility and violation of Article 20(3) of the Constitution, the provision against self-incrimination. It is a strong due process position, opting for the positive role of the Court in ensuring protection against invasive and faulty technology. In the same vein, in State of Bombay v. Kathi Kalu Oghad (1962), the Court asserted that it was not against Article 20(3) to require an accused person to give up his fingerprints or handwriting because evidence would be considered as physical and not testimonial. This is, however, predicated upon an attitude of acceptance of evidence on the basis of voluntariness and worthiness of trust.

Besides, in Ritesh Sinha v. State of Uttar Pradesh (2019), the Supreme Court solved the issue of admissibility of voice samples in investigation and held that courts could request individuals to provide voice samples in the interest of justice, but dwindled to only the law level. It is an expression of judicial wisdom in bringing investigation requirements and safety under the constitution together. Similarly, in Puttaswamy v. Union of India (2017), the Court's understanding of privacy as a constitutional right also meets with the constitutional fit of undercover black-box AI technology to criminal justice, especially if it involves processing genomic or biometric information.

The Indian model is far more rights-based than that of America. While the American U.S. Daubert series of cases pursues a special standard of proof in assessing the legitimacy of science, Indian law is largely operated by constitutional provisions of fair trial, privacy, and dignity. AI tools are to be implemented within the Indian criminal justice system by courts that may have to reconcile such paradigms, scientific validity, and constitutional correctness. This means that the Selvi precedent, coupled with Puttaswamy, can be the foundation of an Indian benchmark to establish AI-based forensic or biological evidence in the future.

The Risk of Wrongful Convictions

The implications of black box AI systems in criminal sentencing are stark. Erroneous convictions not only ruin individual lives but also undermine the public's trust in the justice system. Empirical research indicates that algorithmic systems can replicate racial, gender, or class-based biases present in training data (Angwin et al., 2016). For example, in predictive policing and risk assessment technology, minority groups have disproportionately been overrepresented, with fairness implications (Dirty Data, Bad Predictions: How Civil Rights Violations Impact Police Data, Predictive Policing Systems, and Justice – NYU Law Review, 2019). Similarly, when employed in AI forensic software, for example, in population genetics databases applied to DNA profiling, where the outcome can systematically rule out India's disadvantaged communities, that is, Scheduled Tribes and Dalits, who are already disproportionately represented in the criminal justice system (Singh, 2021).

A step-by-step process is employed in the application of AI for the examination of biological evidence. It shows the stages at which bias and transparency erode admissibility and fairness. The stages start from data collection to judicial decision-making. At each stage, biases of transparency and over-reliance on AI threaten scientific reliability as well as constitutional rights like the right to a fair trial. The flowchart stages—Data Collection, Algorithm Training, AI Output, Court Admissibility, and Judicial Decision—represent critical junctures where guardrails must be built.

Stage 1 is more focused on Data collection. Data quality is the cornerstone on which any AI system rests. Forensic genomics data are usually derived from DNA, pathogen genomes, or phenotypic markers. Datasets, though, might echo systemic social biases like the overrepresentation of minority populations in forensic databases. For instance, research has indicated that racial minorities are overrepresented in criminal DNA databases because of earlier policing practices (Murphy, 2013). If such biased data forms the basis for training AI models, the chances of discriminatory results skyrocket. Biased data at this point sabotages every other stage of the AI pipeline.

After being harvested, biological data is employed to train AI algorithms in stage 2. Proprietary or "black-box" models whose inner workings are not obvious are particularly problematic. Courts and defense lawyers can find it difficult to inquire how the system arrived at a particular conclusion. Researchers contend that transparency here negates Daubert's (1993) requirement of testability and peer review as admissibility requirements (Casey & Schatz, 2011). Furthermore, when algorithms are trained on biased or incomplete data, the AI will learn and reinforce these defects. For instance, AI predictive instruments in forensic analysis can systematically misidentify genetic markers of minority groups ("Gender Shades: Intersectional Accuracy Disparities in Commercial Gender Classification," 2018).

Stage 3 deals with AI Output (Biological Evidence Report). The output of the AI, usually a probability report or phenotypic prediction, serves as focal evidence in court. Outputs, though, can be unexplainable, with judges and juries having access to conclusions without realizing the rationale that generates them. This presents important due process issues, since defense counsel cannot credibly challenge evidence that is inscrutable. Further, when outputs are accepted as authoritative but uninterpreted, defendants are subjected to "epistemic injustice," being deprived of the right to credibly challenge evidence presented against them. The "black box problem" thereby immediately threatens trial fairness.

Judicial scrutiny comes into play at this point in stage 4 to determine if AI-augmented biological evidence is admissible. There is a need to look for scientific reliability, peer review, and broad acceptance. Courts, however, increasingly face proprietary AI tools, the methodology of which is protected by trade secrecy privileges, hindering disclosure. This restricts the defense from cross-examining evidence, contradicting the Sixth Amendment's Confrontation Clause in the United States (Larson, 2010). The issue is not merely technical admissibility but whether and how adversarial testing of AI-derived biological evidence is feasible in practice.

Lastly, in stage 5, the judge or jury will have to consider AI-driven biological evidence in the context of the entire trial. The danger here is overreliance on the perceived authority of AI. Evidence indicates that jurors tend to view scientific or technological evidence as more credible than it is, a result known as the "CSI effect" (Cole & Dioso-Villa, 2009). When AI outputs are presented without adequate transparency, there is a risk of fact-finders regarding them as infallible, resulting in wrongful convictions. Judicial discretion, then, must weigh the scientific potential of AI against the risk of excessive deference to black boxes.

Use of AI in analyzing biological evidence is both a technological breakthrough and an epistemological challenge to the law. As great as the promise of enhanced forensic precision is, transparency shortfalls and bias risks pose powerful threats to justice, including wrongful convictions. To forestall these dangers, courts must require explainability as an admissibility condition, similar to the requirements for reliability set out in Daubert. In India, aligning the BSA, 2023, with constitutional assurances of neutrality would translate into sharper checks upon the judiciary, mandatory disclosure of algorithmic operations, and judicial sensitization on an ongoing basis. Only thus can AI be an instrument of justice, and never a source of injustice.

Privacy and Data Protection

Artificial intelligence in forensic biotechnology and evidence law raises sophisticated issues of privacy and information security. Unlike old-fashioned evidence, AI technologies are based on vast databases of intensely personal genetic data, biometric signatures, and medical histories. The compelling parameters are between enabling justice through effective evidence and the protection of individuals' inherent rights against oppressive state incursion.

One of the first issues is genetic privacy. DNA samples, once taken, contain much more information than is necessary for identification. DNA surpasses linking criminals to crime scenes; it also reveals disease weaknesses, family ties, and heritage. Misuse or unauthorized storage of such data threatens to infringe Article 21 of the Indian Constitution, which secures the right to life and personal liberty, broadly construed to encompass informational privacy in *Justice K.S. Puttaswamy* v. *Union of India* (2017). In this seminal case, privacy was identified as an integral right by the Supreme Court through a focus on the proportionality test as a bulwark against undue state surveillance. A mandatory DNA database with insufficient protective measures would thus fall foul of the constitution, reverberating with the logic of *Selvi* v. *State of Karnataka* (2010), when the Court struck down involuntary narcoanalysis, polygraph, and brain-mapping on the counts of unreliability and breaches of dignity and autonomy.

International norms on privacy protection differ widely. The General Data Protection Regulation of the European Union stipulates requirements that are very stringent as it pertains to processing sensitive information like genetic and biometric data (Articles 9–10). Consent, purpose limitation, and data minimization by the general Datenschutzgesetzs require operational efforts in India. By comparison, the U.S. does not have a comprehensive data protection regime but utilizes sectoral legislation like the Genetic Information Nondiscrimination Act (GINA) 2008, which makes it unlawful for employers and insurers to use genetic information inappropriately. Forensic DNA privacy has also been considered by American courts. In *Maryland* v. *King* (2013), the U.S. Supreme Court upheld DNA collection from arrestees as a legitimate identification tool, sparking debate on the limits of law enforcement power versus individual privacy. Similarly, the European Court of Human Rights (ECHR) in *S. and Marper* v. *United Kingdom* (2008) ruled that indefinite storage of DNA samples of people acquitted of crimes contravened Article 8 of the European Convention on Human Rights, laying emphasis on the fact that state powers to obtain forensic evidence need to be proportionate and narrowly drawn.

India remains at a transitional point. The Digital Personal Data Protection Act, 2023 (DPDP Act) provides an overall framework for the management of personal data, but it is unclear if genetic and forensic data sets will be given special protection as "sensitive" categories. The recently withdrawn DNA Technology (Use and Application) Regulation Bill, 2019 (DNA Bill) reflects such challenges. The Bill suggested the establishment of national and regional DNA data banks and a DNA Regulatory Board on the ostensible grounds of enhancing identification in criminal, civil, and missing persons' cases. Whereas its supporters averred that it would update India's forensic strength, opponents contended that it did not have proper safeguards against abuse. Civil society organizations identified that it allowed holding on to DNA profiles of suspects, undertrials, and even acquitted persons, without provisions of express consent or regulating procedures. Moreover, it threatened genetic surveillance indiscriminately impacting marginal groups and thus triggering Article 14's guarantee of equality. All these concerns, in a strange irony, led to the withdrawal of the Bill from Parliament in July 2022. The withdrawal is an indicator of India's parliamentary lacuna concerning the regulation of genetic evidence at the very moment when AI-powered tools are increasing the efficacy and dangers of forensic science.

Statutory protection also becomes more essential when AI systems are fed forensic data. Algorithmic systems have the capability of transferring sensitive data to personal cloud providers or servers, posing threats of cross-border transfer, unauthorized use, and even commoditization of forensic datasets. Without localization controls, audit trails, or accountability controls in place, there is always a risk that genetic information leaks into non-courtroom applications, e.g., commercial research or surveillance. Further, incorporating privacy-by-design features like encryption, anonymization, and limited retention periods is crucial to ensuring that forensic AI practice is constitutional.

Comparative insights show that privacy is not merely a statutory compliance issue but a constitutional and human rights imperative. Following Puttaswamy, Indian courts have already adopted a proportionality framework for privacy restrictions, requiring state measures to meet tests of necessity, legitimacy, and least-intrusiveness. This approach resonates with S. and Marper and provides a framework for testing AI-based DNA evidence in India. As AI increases the reach of biological data analysis, courts will be required to make sure that technological efficacy does not undermine human dignity.

Finally, privacy and data protection in forensic AI are among the most urgent challenges for evidentiary law in the 21st century. The withdrawal of the DNA Bill is both a challenge and an opportunity: a challenge in that the lack of a defined statutory framework could lead to arbitrary practice, and an opportunity in that subsequent legislation can incorporate constitutional protections, AI transparency obligations, and global best practice. The way forward is through a proportionality-led, rights-based approach that balances the utility of AI in forensic biotechnology with the inviolability of privacy.

TOWARD STANDARDS AND BEST PRACTICES

To maintain accuracy, reproducibility, and credibility in legal environments, implementing robust and transparent forensic standards is very important. This section explores three significant standard-setting frameworks:

DFSS (Directorate of Forensic Science Services, India)
OSAC (Organization of Scientific Area Committees, United States)
Scientific Working Groups (SWGs) evolved into ANSI/ASB standards

DFSS—India's National Framework

The Directorate of Forensic Science Services (DFSS), under the Ministry of Home Affairs, India, is responsible for developing infrastructure and procedural norms to promote forensic capacity at the national level. The Standard List of Equipment for Establishing/Upgrading Forensic Science Laboratories (First Edition, July 2020) is a comprehensive list of equipment needed in six areas of forensics—Chemical Sciences; Biological Sciences (including DNA typing); Physical Sciences; Electronics (Cyber Forensics); Questioned Document Examination; and Forensic Investigation. Annexures 1–34 detail technical specifications for every instrument and consumable, establishing infrastructure foundational criteria (DFSS, 2020). Accompanying this, ISO/IEC 17025-aligned Quality Manuals, SOPs, and specialized procedures (crime scene management, sexual assault evidence collection) promote operational robustness (Ministry of Home Affairs, 2023). Collectively, they provide standardization in laboratory infrastructure, case management, and accreditation.

Table 3.1 shows the DFSS key guidelines, the standard document, and the purpose. India's DFSS standards provide building block infrastructure designs and operational standards essential to laboratory accreditation. The list of equipment (Annexures 1–34) ensures standardization

TABLE 3.1
DFSS Key Guidelines

Area	Standard Document	Purpose
Infrastructure	Standard List of Equipment (Annexures 1–34)	Defines lab layout and equipment eligibility
Accreditation & QA	Quality Manuals (ISO/IEC 17025–based); domain-specific SOPs and procedures	Ensures laboratory competence and procedural fidelity
Operational Protocols	Chain-of-custody, contamination control, staffing lists, case management	Promotes uniform operations and audit readiness

TABLE 3.2
Selected OSAC Standards

Standard Number	Title	Discipline
ANSI/ASB 020-18	Validation Studies of DNA Mixtures & Mixture Interpretation Protocols	DNA Forensic Biology
ANSI/ASB 018-20	Validation of Probabilistic Genotyping Systems	DNA Analytical Validation
ANSI/ASB 175-24	Guidelines for Failed Controls & Contamination Interpretation	DNA Forensic Biology
ANSI/ASB 035-20	Examination of Altered Documents	Document Examination
ANSI/ASB 056-25	Measurement Uncertainty in Forensic Toxicology	Toxicology
ANSI/ASB 128-22	Preservation/Examination of Liquid-Soaked Documents	Document Examination

among states, providing ease of consistency. Incorporating ISO-based SOPs and Quality Manuals instills global quality practices into the work routine. This framework, which is multiplexed in nature, is based on both procedure and infrastructure, and forms a strong platform for forensic reliability—most important in these times where AI-aided biological analysis is increasingly the norm.

OSAC—U.S. Forensic Science Consensus Standards

With the cooperation of the U.S. Department of Justice and implemented by NIST (2014), the Organization of Scientific Area Committees (OSAC) operates as a discipline-specific standard-setting organization for forensic practice (NIST n.d.). The OSAC Registry, as of early 2025, lists more than 220 standards—published and in development—spanning disciplines including DNA, toxicology, forensic documents, and digital evidence (NIST, 2025). Table 3.2 outlines selected standards.

OSAC standards represent a consensus-based process of forensic best practices, providing domain-specific guideline validation for increasing scientific rigor. For instance, ANSI 020-18 specifies rigorous protocols for validating the interpretation of DNA mixtures essential in complicated multi-contributor cases. Likewise, probabilistic genotyping standards provide transparency for algorithmic DNA examinations. New standards like measurement uncertainty and contamination control, introduced recently, take on challenging but far-reaching forensic issues. OSAC's formal modality, such as public comments and inter-institutional committees, enhances legitimacy and uptake across forensic institutions.

SWGs and ANSI/ASB Transition

Scientific Working Groups (SWGs) preceded OSAC, enabling forensic practitioners and academics to collaborate on discipline-specific protocols. Their legacy remains in newer ANSI/ASB standards. Table 3.3 outlines noteworthy transitions.

SWGs began standardization through inter-agency, discipline-specific collaboration, which evolved subsequently into formal ANSI/ASB documents for wider regulatory acceptance. ANSI/ASB 011 and corresponding questioned-document standards establish expertise boundaries and methodology limits, enhancing examiner credibility. SWGDE-derived standards update digital evidence protocols to accommodate cloud and IoT environments—particularly important given cyber-forensics overlap with biological data. These advancements increase legal defensibility and bring technological tools into alignment with professional responsibility.

Synthesis and Integration Strategy

Despite these rich standard ecosystems, India's forensic system faces gaps in international synchronization. The DFSS infrastructure standards are robust but can benefit from adopting OSAC and SWG-based technical rigor. Table 3.4 captures these integration vectors.

For effective forensic governance, India needs to take advantage of its DFSS base by incorporating internationally recognized discipline-specific standards. This would enhance scientific credibility, raise judicial confidence, and keep forensic services abreast and resilient in the face of evolving AI technologies.

TABLE 3.3
SWG-Derived Standards

Standard No.	Title
ANSI/ASB 011	Scope of Expertise in Document Examination
ANSI/ASB 044	Examination of Indentations
ANSI/ASB 070	Examination of Handwritten Items
ANSI/ASB 035	Examination of Alterations
ANSI/ASB 127	Charred Documents Examination
ANSI/ASB 128	Liquid-Soaked Document Examination
SWGDE 23-F-004-1.1	Cloud Evidence Acquisition Standards
SWGDE 23-F-003-1.0	IoT Seizure and Analysis Guidelines
SWGDE 17-F-002-2.0	Computer Forensic Acquisition Protocols

TABLE 3.4
Strategic Integration Recommendations

Objective	Action Plan
Validate AI-based DNA Analysis	Implement OSAC's DNA validation protocols (e.g., 020-18, 018-20) in SOPs
Strengthen Document Forensics	Adopt ANSI/ASB standards (044, 070, 035) for questioned document labs
Accreditation Alignment	Make OSAC standards compliance a criterion for DFSS/NABL accreditation
Training and Capacity Building	Create workshops and materials based on OSAC/SWG standards

Role of Interdisciplinary Validation Teams and the Case for an AI-Evidence Protocol

Assessing AI applied to biological evidence (e.g., interpretation of DNA mixtures, inference of kinship, prediction of phenotype) calls for knowledge that no single field can provide. Interdisciplinary validation groups—forensic biologists, statisticians, computer scientists/ML engineers, quality managers, legal scholars, and ethicists—can together (i) develop validation experiments, (ii) estimate uncertainty, (iii) identify data/algorithmic bias, and (iv) communicate technical performance into legally comprehensible reports. This model is consistent with international quality frameworks emphasizing competence, impartiality, and validation of the methods used in accredited laboratories (ISO/IEC 17025:2017) and forensic-specific standards that encapsulate the "scene-to-courtroom" continuum (ISO 21043 series). Operationally, the team protocol ensures method validation (design, parameters, boundaries), measurement uncertainty, control of contamination, and interpretation logic are independently cross-checked prior to casework deployment, thus complementing judicial gatekeeping and due-process measures.

International Guidelines Relevant to Forensic and AI

The incorporation of Artificial Intelligence (AI) in forensic genomics must follow internationally accepted standards to guarantee reliability, transparency, and admissibility of evidence. Some of the most impactful frameworks are those created by the International Organization for Standardization (ISO), accrediting bodies like the ANSI National Accreditation Board (ANAB) and the American Association for Laboratory Accreditation (A2LA), and direction from the OECD AI Principles. Together, these standards establish the operational, technical, and ethical boundaries within which AI-supported biological evidence needs to be analyzed. Among the core standards is ISO/IEC 17025:2017, which lays down requirements for the competence, impartiality, and consistent functioning of testing and calibration laboratories (ISO, 2017). This standard is noteworthy for forensic DNA labs using AI-supported workflows since it focuses on method validation, measurement uncertainty, traceability, and reporting structure. Accreditation bodies like ANAB and A2LA implement ISO/IEC 17025 through forensic-specific assessment matrices, allowing laboratories to align AI-augmented processes with standard clauses and show compliance (ANAB, 2022). Taken on to complement that, the ISO 21043 series is a useful standard for the forensic sciences in and of itself. Part 1 (2018, revised 2025) is a standard vocabulary, so there is uniformity across disciplines when AI technology is communicating with genomic, biometric, and digital forensic units (ISO, 2018). Part 3 (2025) specifies requirements for analysis procedures, validation, and quality assurance of new techniques, being of top priority, e.g., AI-augmented DNA mixture deconvolution or probabilistic genotyping (NIST, 2023a). Part 4 (2025) anticipates interpretation, guidelines for evaluative reasoning, and transparency being in line with the judiciary interests in explainability of AI (NIST, 2023b). ISO 18385:2016 also establishes forensic DNA-grade consumable requirements whose manufacture is controlled by manufacturers, ensuring minimal contamination of human DNA. This is particularly required where AI models, made sensitive to pick up trace signals, can be diverted by contamination in collection or storage processes (ISO, 2016a, 2016b). In the regulatory arena of AI, ISO/IEC 23894:2023 bridges forensic genomics with risk management practice. ISO 31000 standards are used to describe controls of the AI life cycle in terms of identification, evaluation, treatment, and monitoring risk and provide the forensic laboratory with a template to maintain AI registers of risks (ISO, 2023). The standard provides institutions with the capability to balance innovation in AI forensics with robust defense against bias, fault, and system failure.

These systems are also relevant at the domain level. FBI Quality Assurance Standards for Forensic DNA Testing Laboratories present operational standards that are still applicable to AI systems. Standard 9.3, for instance, requires validation of reagents of significance, and Standard 9.4 requires quantitation before amplification (Federal Bureau of Investigation, 2020). Such standards ensure the necessity of testing AI-enabled genotyping or combinations of deconvolution, such that

TABLE 3.5
Mapping Key International Standards to Forensic-AI Use in Genomics

Standard/Guideline	Core Requirements (Illustrative)	Relevance to AI on Biological Evidence
ISO/IEC 17025:2017	Method validation/verification; measurement uncertainty; traceability; competence; impartiality; reporting	Validating AI pipelines; uncertainty quantification; audit trails; competence of AI operators/ validators
ISO 21043-3:2025 (Analysis)	Analytical planning; controls; validation; quality assurance across the forensic process	Structuring AI model validation within the scene-to-court analytical stage
ISO 21043-4:2025 (Interpretation)	Evaluative vs investigative interpretation; logic, transparency, documentation	Explaining AI outputs in a way the court can interrogate
ISO 18385:2016	Manufacturer requirements to minimize **human DNA contamination** in consumables	Reducing contamination-driven false signals that can mislead AI
FBI QAS (e.g., Std. 9.3, 9.4)	Critical reagent evaluation; quantitation before amplification	Anchoring wet-lab quality that feeds AI models
ISO/IEC 23894:2023	AI risk governance across lifecycle; controls tied to ISO 31000	Lab-level AI risk registers; bias/threat modeling; monitoring
OECD AI Principles (2019)	Human-centric, fairness, transparency, robustness, accountability	Public-law safeguards for explainability, disclosure, and oversight

traditional laboratory quality control is applied to AI settings. ANAB accreditations also ensure additional impetus for harmonization of ISO/IEC 17025 and 17020 forensic laboratory practice, addressing challenges of integrating AI in routine workflows (ANAB, 2022). On the overarching governance level, OECD AI Principles (2019) is a normative framework of rules prescribing ethical and legal use of AI for forensic purposes. They are human-centered principles: transparency, resilience, responsibility, and fairness (OECD, 2019). In terms of forensic genomics, this will imply that forensic genomics will need to uphold chain-of-custody integrity, algorithmic transparency, model explainability, and due process safeguards standards. The OECD model proves helpful in the sense that it moves past technical validation to encompass societal confidence and inherent rights, so that the application of AI in forensic biotechnology has evidentiary accuracy and justice. They all establish a regime of several layers where ISO standards address technical quality and verification, QAS and accrediting bodies add forensic-specific conformance, and OECD principles define AI application on the basis of more general ethical and legal requirements. Alignment of these standards will be essential in formulating an AI evidence assessment procedure in biotech matters so that AI not only enhances evidentiary credibility but also passes judicial and constitutional tests (Table 3.5).

Operationalizing International Standards through Interdisciplinary Teams: The Case for a Dedicated AI-Evidence Evaluation Protocol in Biotechnological Forensics

Interdisciplinary validation teams are the hub of applying international forensic and AI standards when dealing with biological evidence. Every domain specialist is responsible for mapping to particular clauses of available frameworks. For example, quality managers are responsible for clause tracing according to ISO/IEC 17025:2017, guaranteeing competence, impartiality, and traceability in laboratory practice (ISO, 2017). Biologists maintain wet-lab controls and contamination safeguards in accordance with ISO 18385:2016, which governs forensic DNA-grade consumables, and the FBI's Quality Assurance Standards (QAS) 9.3 and 9.4 concerning reagent validation and DNA quantitation, respectively (ISO, 2016a, 2016b; FBI, 2020). Statisticians design validation protocols, calibration curves, and uncertainty estimates under ISO/IEC 17025 and ISO 21043-3, which outlines analytical requirements (ISO, 2017; ISO, 2025a). In contrast, machine learning engineers oversee model documentation, train/validation splits, and drift monitoring within the risk management system of ISO/IEC 23894:2023 (ISO, 2023). Scholars of law ensure disclosure, privilege, and explainability follow accountability and transparency principles sourced from the OECD AI Principles (OECD, 2019). Together, these teams perform pre-deployment validation through representative forensic cases that include low-template DNA, degraded samples, and multi-component mixtures, and document performance envelopes (e.g., detection limits, error rates) and create court-ready method summaries traceable to applicable standard clauses. Although the strength of individual forensic and AI standards, individually, is solid, there is no single tool today that sets forth an overall, court-oriented protocol specific to AI use in biological evidence. The lack of this can lead to inconsistencies in validation intensity, documentation clarity, and disclosure procedures (Phillips & Przybocki, 2020a, 2020b). In response, a stand-alone AI Evidence Evaluation Protocol (AEEP) for biotech cases can consolidate assorted standards into a single workflow, clearly cross-referencing ISO/IEC, FBI QAS, and OECD platforms.

The AEEP starts with scoping and provenance, calling for defining forensic questions, decision thresholds, and biomarkers relevant to them, as well as insistence on end-to-end registration of data lineage, including source laboratory, extraction kit, and batch identifiers, under ISO 18385 2016's contamination protection (ISO, 2016a, 2016b). This is succeeded by data governance and risk management, where model and dataset inventories are to be kept, recording balance, representativeness, and protected attributes. The risks of bias, robustness, security, and privacy need to be logged in a specific AI risk register aligned to ISO/IEC 23894 (ISO, 2023). The method validation phase incorporates both wet-lab and AI methodologies. Wet-lab validation calls for compliance with FBI QAS 9.3 and 9.4 standards for critical reagents and DNA quantitation, while audits for contamination are documented for responsibility (FBI, 2020). Validation by AI, on the other hand, requires prior-defined performance criteria like sensitivity, specificity, calibrated likelihood ratios, and stability under poor conditions (e.g., degraded or inhibited samples). These are consistent with ISO/IEC 17025 standards for method validation and ISO 21043-3 analytical rigor standards (ISO, 2017; ISO, 2025a).

Reporting and interpretation adhere to ISO 21043-4, distinguishing between investigative and evaluative opinions and demanding clear expression of assumptions, limitations, and alternative explanations (ISO, 2025b). In this case, AI outputs need to be supported with model cards and datasheets of training data, versioning, and post-hoc explainability tools (Mitchell et al., 2019). Provisions of transparency and accountability require disclosure of SOP excerpts, validation summaries, and version histories to enable discovery, as well as recording AI decision-making in line with the OECD AI Principles on human oversight and accountability (OECD, 2019). The AEEP also requires continuous monitoring, such as quarterly blind tests, proficiency testing, and updating of the AI risk register in accordance with ISO/IEC 23894 (ISO, 2023). Lastly, external review and reproducibility necessitate inter-laboratory comparisons and independent replication to guarantee objectivity and competency under ISO/IEC 17025 (ISO, 2017). By combining prevailing forensic science guidelines with AI governance regimes, the AEEP devises a court-focused protocol that explicitly tackles admissibility and weight of evidence concerns. Notably, it highlights proportionality, privacy, and fairness, so that while forensic science gains strength from the analytical capabilities of AI, constitutional and procedural rights of the individual are not sacrificed (Table 3.6).

Courts and regulatory bodies increasingly require transparent, auditable records. The artefacts above guarantee validation evidence, quality controls, and interpretive logic to be reviewable and traceable to known standards independently. Model cards and risk registers, though not yet required by forensic-specific standards, operationalize OECD principles of transparency and accountability and facilitate experts to elucidate AI limitations in cross-examination.

TABLE 3.6
Minimal Documentation Set for AI-Enabled Forensic Genomics (Cross-Walk to Standards)

Document	What It Must Contain	Standards Cross-Reference
Validation plan & report	Design, datasets, metrics, stress tests, acceptance criteria; uncertainty and limitations	ISO/IEC 17025; ISO 21043-3; ISO/IEC 23894
Contamination & QA logs	Consumables/lot numbers; controls; contamination events & corrective actions	ISO 18385; QAS 9.3–9.4
Model card & data sheet	Model versioning; training/validation sets; features; performance by subgroup; known failure modes	ISO/IEC 23894; OECD AI Principles
Interpretative statement	Evaluative vs. investigative opinion; assumptions, caveats; likelihood ratio explanation	ISO 21043-4
Governance & audit trail	Risk register; approvals; change logs; access controls; chain-of-custody for data/models	ISO/IEC 23894; ISO/IEC 17025

The incorporation of AI-based tools in forensic genomics and biotechnology requires a tough discipline of standards, transparency, and accountability to guarantee justice and scientific soundness. As one can observe from the current guidelines, whether they are national mandates such as DFSS procedures, international best practices like OSAC and SWG standards, or global frameworks like ISO and OECD principles, the position of formalized, evidence-based validation lies at the heart of enhancing forensic credibility. However, technical standards are not enough without interdisciplinary validation committees comprising legal academics, forensic experts, ethicists, and technologists to implement these standards in practice. India's DNA Technology (Use and Application) Bill, 2019 withdrawal also underscores the shortcomings in legal regulation and the imperative for context-specific protocols, especially for the assessment of AI-produced evidence in biotechnology cases. Finally, moving toward a specialized AI-proof protocol, based on interdisciplinary cooperation and international harmonization, is a necessary step to safeguard human rights, increase reliance on evidence, and secure the fairness of judicial decisions in an era of aggressive scientific development.

REFERENCES

Alonso, A., Martín, P., Albarrán, C., García, P., García, O., de Simón, L. F., ... & Sancho, M. (2018). Challenges of DNA profiling in mass disaster investigations. *Forensic Science International: Genetics Supplement Series, 6*(1), 740–742. https://doi.org/10.1016/j.fsigss.2017.09.223

American Association for Laboratory Accreditation. (n.d.). *Forensic examination accreditation program.* A2LA. Retrieved September 21, 2025, from https://a2la.org/accreditation/forensics/ANSI

Angwin et al. (2016, May 23). *Machine bias—There's software used across the country to predict future criminals. And it's biased against blacks.* ProPublica, Online Edition. – References – Scientific Research Publishing. www.scirp.org/reference/referencespapers?referenceid=3337609

Badiye et al. (2023, February 13). *Chain of custody.* StatPearls – NCBI Bookshelf. www.ncbi.nlm.nih.gov/books/NBK551677/

Ballantyne, J., Hanson, E. K., Perlin, M. W., & Baird, M. L. (2019). DNA mixture interpretation: A modern approach to an enduring challenge. *Forensic Science International: Genetics, 41*, 100–113. https://doi.org/10.1016/j.fsigen.2019.03.005

Bhatia, G. (2023). *The Bharatiya Sakshya Adhiniyam, 2023: Modernizing evidence law in India.* Indian Constitutional Law and Philosophy Blog.

Biedermann et al. (2017). Analysing and exemplifying forensic conclusion criteria in terms of Bayesian decision theory. *Science & Justice*, *58*(2), 159–165. https://doi.org/10.1016/j.scijus.2017.07.002

Budowle, B., Connell, N. D., McCall, C. E., Wilson, M. R., & Valashevsky, S. (2014). Microbial forensics and bioterrorism preparedness. *Emerging Infectious Diseases, 20*(9), e1–e8.

Budowle, B., van Daal, A., & Baechtel, F. (2019). Forensic genetics: Past, present, and future. *Forensic Science International: Genetics, 38,* 1–9. https://doi.org/10.1016/j.fsigen.2018.09.005

Burrell, J. (2015). How the machine "thinks:" Understanding opacity in machine learning algorithms. *SSRN Electronic Journal*. https://doi.org/10.2139/ssrn.2660674

Butler, J. M. (2015a). *Advanced topics in forensic DNA typing: Interpretation*. Academic Press.

Butler, J. M. (2015b). *Advanced topics in forensic DNA typing: Methodology*. Academic Press.

Butler, J. M. (2015c). *Fundamentals of forensic DNA typing*. Academic Press.

Casey, E., & Schatz, B. (2011). Digital evidence and computer crime forensic science, computers and the internet. In *Conducting digital investigations* (3rd ed., pp. 187–226). Elsevier. https://rishikeshpansare.wordpress.com/wp-content/uploads/2016/02/digital-evidence-and-computer-crime-third-edition.pdf

Casey et al. (2018). Corrigendum to 'advancing coordinated cyber-investigations and tool interoperability using a community developed specification language' [Digital Investigation 22C (2017) 14–45]. *Digital Investigation*, *28*, 183–187. https://doi.org/10.1016/j.diin.2018.10.001.

Chakraborty, R., & Natarajan, S. (2019). Preservation of forensic biological evidence: A molecular perspective. *Indian Journal of Forensic Medicine & Toxicology, 13*(4), 112–118.

Cole, S. A., & Dioso-Villa, R. (2009). Investigating the 'CSI effect' effect: Media and litigation crisis in criminal law. *Stanford Law Review*, *61*(6).

Daubert Standard. (n.d.). LII / Legal Information Institute. www.law.cornell.edu/wex/daubert_standard

Daubert v. *Merrell Dow Pharmaceuticals, Inc*., 509 U.S. 579 (1993).

DFSS. (2020). *Standard list of equipment for establishing/upgrading of forensic science laboratories* (1st ed.). Ministry of Home Affairs.

Dirty data, bad predictions: How civil rights violations impact police data, predictive policing systems, and justice – NYU Law Review. (2019, December 17). NYU Law Review. https://nyulawreview.org/online-features/dirty-data-bad-predictions-how-civil-rights-violations-impact-police-data-predictive-policing-systems-and-justice/

DNA database: A legislative overreach. (2021, August 14). Economic and Political Weekly. www.epw.in/journal/2021/32/comment/dna-database-legislative-overreach.html.

Doshi-Velez, F., & Kim, B. (2017). Towards a rigorous science of interpretable machine learning. *arXiv* (Cornell University). https://doi.org/10.48550/arxiv.1702.08608

Faigman et al., (2014). *Modern scientific evidence: The law and science of expert testimony*. Thomson Reuters.

Federal Bureau of Investigation. (2020). *Quality assurance standards for forensic DNA testing laboratories*. FBI Laboratory Division, U.S. Department of Justice.

Frye v. *United States*, 293 F. 1013 (D.C. Cir. 1923).

Garrett, B. L., & Neufeld, P. J. (n.d.). *Invalid forensic science testimony and wrongful convictions*. https://scholarship.law.duke.edu/faculty_scholarship/3861/

Gender shades: Intersectional accuracy disparities in commercial gender classification. (2018). *Proceedings of Machine Learning Research*, *81*, 1–15. https://proceedings.mlr.press/v81/buolamwini18a/buolamwini18a.pdf

General Electric Co. v. *Joiner*, 522 U.S. 136 (1997).

Goodman, B., & Flaxman, S. (2017). European Union regulations on algorithmic decision making and a "right to explanation." *AI Magazine*, *38*(3), 50–57. https://doi.org/10.1609/aimag.v38i3.2741

Greytak, E. M., Moore, C., & Armentrout, S. L. (2019). Genetic genealogy for cold case and active investigations. *Forensic Science International*, *299*, 103–113. https://doi.org/10.1016/j.forsciint.2019.03.039

Guidotti et al. (2018). A survey of methods for explaining black box models. *arXiv* (Cornell University). https://doi.org/10.48550/arxiv.1802.01933

Houck, M. M., & Siegel, J. A. (2018). *Fundamentals of forensic science* (3rd ed.). Academic Press.

Indulia, B. (2024, November 30). Securing the links: A framework for chain of custody in Indian courts. *SCC Times*.

International Organization for Standardization (ISO). (2016a). *ISO 18385:2016 Forensic DNA grade consumables*. ISO.

International Organization for Standardization (ISO). (2016b). *ISO 18385:2016 Forensic DNA grade—Minimizing the risk of human DNA contamination in products*. ISO.
International Organization for Standardization (ISO). (2017). *ISO/IEC 17025:2017 General requirements for the competence of testing and calibration laboratories*. ISO.
International Organization for Standardization (ISO). (2018). *ISO 21043-1:2018 Forensic sciences—Part 1: Vocabulary*. ISO.
International Organization for Standardization (ISO). (2023). *ISO/IEC 23894:2023 Information technology—Artificial intelligence—Guidance on risk management*. ISO.
International Organization for Standardization (ISO). (2025a). *ISO 21043-3 Forensic sciences—Analysis* (2nd ed.). ISO (in preparation, draft by NIST).
International Organization for Standardization (ISO). (2025b). *ISO 21043-4 Forensic sciences—Interpretation* (2nd ed.). ISO (in preparation, draft by NIST).
Justice K.S. Puttaswamy v. Union of India, (2017) 10 SCC 1.
Kayser, M., & de Knijff, P. (2011). Improving human forensics through advances in genetics, genomics and molecular biology. *Nature Reviews Genetics, 12*(3), 179–192. https://doi.org/10.1038/nrg2952
Kumho Tire Co. v. *Carmichael*, 526 U.S. 137 (1999).
Larson, D. (2010). Confronting the digital fingerprint: The admissibility of computer-generated DNA profiles. *University of Illinois Law Review, 2010*(2), 331–375.
Maneka Gandhi v. *Union of India*, AIR 1978 SC 597.
Mardis, E. R. (2017). DNA sequencing technologies: 2006–2016. *Nature Protocols, 12*(2), 123–128. https://doi.org/10.1038/nprot.2016.182
Marx, V. (2013). Biology: The big challenges of big data. *Nature, 498*(7453), 255–260. https://doi.org/10.1038/498255a
Maxmen, A., & Mallapaty, S. (2021). The COVID lab-leak hypothesis: What scientists do and don't know. *Nature, 594*(7863), 313–315. https://doi.org/10.1038/d41586-021-01529-3
Ministry of Home Affairs. (2023). *Quality manuals, SOPs, and collection guidelines*. Government of India. https://id.scribd.com/document/722605526/FORENSICSStandardequipmentList-25102022?
Mitchell, M., Wu, S., Zaldivar, A., Barnes, P., Vasserman, L., Hutchinson, B., … Gebru, T. (2019). Model cards for model reporting. In *Proceedings of the conference on fairness, accountability, and transparency (FAT*19)* (pp. 220–229). ACM.
Mittelstadt et al. (2016). The ethics of algorithms: Mapping the debate. *Big Data & Society, 3*(2). https://doi.org/10.1177/2053951716679679
Mullis, K., & Faloona, F. (1987). Specific synthesis of DNA in vitro via a polymerase-catalyzed chain reaction. *Methods in Enzymology, 155*, 335–350. https://doi.org/10.1016/0076-6879(87)55023-6
Murphy, E. (2013). *Inside the cell: The dark side of forensic DNA*. Nation Books.
National Accreditation Board (ANAB). (2022). *Accreditation requirements for forensic testing laboratories*. ANAB.
National Institute of Justice (NIJ). (2013). *Crime scene investigation: A guide for law enforcement.* U.S. Department of Justice.
National Institute of Justice. (2014). *Ensuring the integrity of biological evidence* (NIJ Special Report). https://nij.ojp.gov/library/publications/ensuring-integrity-biological-evidence
National Institute of Justice. (n.d.). *Law 101: Legal guide for the Forensic expert | Chain of Custody*. National Institute of Justice. https://nij.ojp.gov/nij-hosted-online-training-courses/law-101-legal-guide-forensic-expert/pretrial/pretrial-motions/chain-custody
National Institute of Standards and Technology (NIST). (2023a). *Forensic science standards development: ISO 21043-3*. U.S. Department of Commerce.
National Institute of Standards and Technology (NIST). (2023b). *Forensic interpretation standards: ISO 21043-4*. U.S. Department of Commerce.
National Institute of Standards and Technology. (2025, February). *OSAC standards bulletin: February 2025*. Organization of Scientific Area Committees for Forensic Science. www.nist.gov/magazine/osac-standards-bulletin/february-2025 NIST
National Institute of Standards and Technology. (n.d.). *The Organization of Scientific Area Committees for forensic science*. www.nist.gov/adlp/spo/organization-scientific-area-committees-forensic-science
Nowroozi et al. (2020). A survey of machine learning techniques in Adversarial image Forensics. *arXiv (Cornell University)*. https://doi.org/10.48550/arxiv.2010.09680

Organisation for Economic Co-operation and Development (OECD). (2019). *OECD principles on artificial intelligence*. OECD.

Parkkavi, E., & Yadharthana, K. (n.d.). Artificial intelligence in criminal justice: Balancing efficiency with fairness and accountability. *Indian Journal of Integrated Research in Law*, *4*(6). https://ijirl.com/wp-content/uploads/2024/11/ARTIFICIAL-INTELLIGENCE-IN-CRIMINAL-JUSTICE-BALANCING-EFFICIENCY-WITH-FAIRNESS-AND-ACCOUNTABILITY.pdf

Patil et al. (2024). Potential applicability of blockchain technology in the maintenance of chain of custody in forensic casework. *Egyptian Journal of Forensic Sciences*, *14*(1). https://doi.org/10.1186/s41935-023-00383-w

Phillips, P. J., & Przybocki, M. A. (2020a). AI and forensic science: Reliability, standards, and legal admissibility. *Journal of Law and the Biosciences*, *7*(1), 1–16.

Phillips, P. J., & Przybocki, M. A. (2020b). Four principles of explainable AI as applied to biometrics and facial forensic algorithms. *arXiv* (Cornell University). https://doi.org/10.48550/arxiv.2002.01014

R v. *T* [2010] EWCA Crim 2439.

Ritesh Sinha v. State of Uttar Pradesh, (2019) 8 SCC 1.

Rosenberg, B. H. (2011). The anthrax attacks: A forensic science case study. *Biosecurity and Bioterrorism: Biodefense Strategy, Practice, and Science, 9*(1), 7–16.

Santosh Kumar Singh v. *State*, (2010) 9 SCC 747.

Schoeman, M. (2020). Automation bias in judicial decision-making: A new challenge for justice. *Journal of Law, Technology and Policy*.

Scientific Working Group on Digital Evidence. (n.d.). *Published – Complete Listing*. Retrieved September 21, 2025, from https://www.swgde.org/documents/published-complete-listing/

Selvi v. State of Karnataka, (2010) 7 SCC 263.

Singh, A. (2021). Caste, technology, and the Indian criminal justice system: Structural bias in forensic databases. *Economic and Political Weekly, 56*(14), 45–53.

Specter, M. (2002, May 20). Do fingerprints lie? *The New Yorker*. www.newyorker.com/magazine/2002/05/27/do-fingerprints-lie

State v. *Loomis*, 881 N.W.2d 749 (Wis. 2016).

Suresh, H., & Guttag, J. (2021). A framework for understanding sources of harm throughout the machine learning life cycle. *Equity and Access in Algorithms, Mechanisms, and Optimization*, 1–9. https://doi.org/10.1145/3465416.3483305

4 Digital Justice

How Technology Can Transform Evidence in India

Aayana Rai Bhojani[1] *and Varun Hemachandran*[2]

INTRODUCTION

India stands at an extraordinary intersection of challenge and opportunity. As the world's most populous nation with 1.4 billion people, the country faces a stark access to justice gap: approximately 113 lawyers serve every 100,000 citizens, compared to the United States' 402 lawyers per 100,000 citizens.[3] India also has approximately 15 judges per million people, compared to the United States' 150 judges per million people.[4] Meanwhile, about 80% Indians qualify for free legal aid, yet existing court infrastructure has struggled to deliver meaningful access[5]. The justice system carries the weight of over 50 million pending cases across all courts, a backlog that grows annually as new cases exceed disposals. The high courts in India alone list 6.3 million pending cases[6], with evidence for each case potentially scattered across multiple formats, languages, and filing systems. In most years, the number of cases disposed of is lower than the number of cases instituted, meaning this documentary chaos compounds annually.

Yet India has already demonstrated its capacity for revolutionary digital transformation. The country processes over 16.7 billion digital transactions monthly through UPI, proving that technology can reach every corner of the nation – from metropolitan centers to remote villages. This digital revolution, however, creates its own justice challenges: even a small percentage of these billions of transactions becoming disputes would significantly increase court backlogs. India is already witnessing this with the surge in online and telephonic bank fraud cases, where digital crimes outpace the analog court system's capacity to address them.

But this challenge reveals an opportunity. The same digital infrastructure that democratized financial transactions can now democratize justice itself. Rather than viewing the mounting caseload as an insurmountable crisis, we can see it as the catalyst for reimagining courts entirely. India doesn't need to incrementally improve analog systems – it can leapfrog directly to digital-first justice delivery, using technology to bridge the access gap that traditional infrastructure has never successfully closed.

TRANSLATION AS EVIDENCE CORRUPTION

India's Constitution recognizes 22 scheduled languages, yet the country is home to over 1,000 spoken languages and dialects. Meanwhile, High Courts primarily operate in English, with some states authorized to use Hindi or their official state language in addition to English. This creates a striking mismatch: a nation of extraordinary linguistic diversity funneled through a narrow set of official court languages. High Courts publish judgments in English for cases argued in Tamil, with evidence submitted in Telugu. Court translators, when available, lack legal training and often resort to tools such as Google Translate for technical terms.[7]

DOI: 10.1201/9781003629146-5

Rather than accepting this linguistic bottleneck as inevitable, technology offers pathways to seamless multilingual justice. The World Justice Project's Global Insights on Access to Justice 2019,[8] representing the voices of more than 100,000 people in 101 countries, found that fewer than one in three people understood their legal problems, often due to language and documentation barriers. India's challenge is particularly acute: when a Punjabi oral statement must pass through translation layers before reaching a judge who works in English, the potential for meaning to shift is significant.

But this is precisely where technology can bridge what traditional infrastructure cannot. Advanced AI translation systems specifically trained on legal terminology can preserve meaning across languages far more reliably than generic tools. Court translators equipped with legal AI assistants can ensure that testimony maintains its evidentiary integrity across India's many languages, with translation becoming a bridge rather than a barrier to understanding. The same technology that enables real-time translation for global conferences can bring India's 22 scheduled languages – and eventually many more – into courtrooms, ensuring that justice is delivered in languages that citizens actually speak.

The Challenge of Enabling Digital Justice for a Digital India

Despite India recording billions of digital interactions every year, when a dispute arises from them, litigants must translate their digital evidence back into the analog world for a largely digitally disconnected justice system. For instance, an e-commerce dispute over a product purchased on Amazon, paid for through UPI, and disputed over emails must be printed out and physically submitted to the court. The primary authentication mechanism for most digital evidence remains a notary's signature on paper copies. Digital evidence in its native form contains metadata, timestamps, and verification trails that paper copies lose entirely. When courts require digital evidence to be printed, they're essentially demanding that litigants destroy the very features that make digital evidence reliable. The solution isn't to retreat from digital evidence but to embrace it fully, allowing courts to examine digital transactions in the same format they occurred, with all their inherent verification mechanisms intact.

Reaching beyond Traditional Boundaries

Courts have historically relied on evidence that requires physical presence – witness testimony, site visits, and documentation gathered by officials who must physically travel to locations. This creates fundamental limitations: legal violations that occur continuously, gradually, or in disputed timeframes become nearly impossible to prove definitively. Environmental damage unfolds over months, land encroachments happen incrementally, and labor conditions fluctuate daily, yet courts typically see only contested snapshots from single moments in time, with each party presenting conflicting accounts of what occurred when.

The 2019 Aarey Colony[9] metro shed controversy in Mumbai demonstrates how technology transforms what evidence can capture. When a court stay order prohibited land clearing in the ecologically sensitive area, activists alleged that JCBs proceeded with flattening despite the injunction. The government countered that the land was already in that condition before the stay order – a classic evidentiary deadlock where traditional methods would pit witness testimony against witness testimony, site visit against site visit, with no definitive way to establish the temporal sequence of events. Instead, satellite imagery from Google Earth provided timestamped, independently verifiable proof of the land's exact condition before and after the alleged violations, offering courts objective evidence that neither party could dispute. What once seemed unfathomable – definitive proof of land conditions across time without any physical presence – became possible through technology. This represents a fundamental expansion of what courts can know and verify, turning previously unprovable claims into documentable facts.

How Are Innovators Using Technology Such as AI to Transform Our Systems of Justice?

Technology offers targeted solutions not because it's inherently better, but because it can scale across languages, automate tedious processes, and create evidence where none existed before. A real breakthrough can come when technology amplifies India's existing networks of community organizers, local lawyers, and citizen advocates. The following initiatives demonstrate how AI and digital tools can transform each evidence barrier into an access point for justice.

Public Collective for Avoidance and Resolution of Disputes (PUCAR)[10]

In November 2024, the High Court of Kerala in collaboration with Public Collective for Avoidance and Resolution of Disputes launched India's first 24×7 online court for cheque bounce cases in Kollam district, marking a significant departure from this analog approach.[11] The online court directly addresses the mismatch between digital evidence and analog court processes – the digital court accepts native digital evidence. Bank transaction records can be submitted electronically, payment confirmations remain in their original digital format, and evidence authentication happens through digital signatures rather than physical notarization.

Adalat AI and jhana.ai: Revolutionizing Court Language and Documentation[12]

India's judicial system buckles under crushing case backlogs exacerbated by manual paperwork and an antiquated documentation processes. These systemic inefficiencies and translation problems disproportionately affect low-income and marginalized communities – including thousands of pre-trial detainees.

Adalat AI's comprehensive technological suite directly targets these problems through integrated solutions. Advanced Optical Character Recognition (OCR) technology transforms paper-based legal documents into searchable digital archives, enabling courts to instantly locate specific evidence within voluminous case files and extract key facts from witness statements. Interactive dashboards streamline case management by tracking hearing schedules, evidence deadlines, and case status updates, while multilingual chatbots provide real-time case information to litigants in their local languages – directly solving communication failures that leave citizens disconnected from their own legal proceedings. The AI system also processes complex court judgments into concise summaries highlighting crucial legal findings and evidence, enabling legal aid workers to explain outcomes clearly to clients while facilitating more efficient appellate review. Similarly, Steno by jhana[13] provides AI-powered dictation designed specifically for legal practice. The tool recognizes multiple Indian languages and legal terminology while automatically formatting text to court-ready standards, including proper citations and paragraphing.

OpenNyAI[14]: Creating Justice Collectives

Legal aid organizations, NGOs, and grassroots legal workers across India face persistent structural challenges that limit their ability to serve marginalized communities.[15] A significant portion of their time and resources is spent on manually processing large volumes of multilingual legal documents, which restricts both geographic reach and the depth of engagement with clients. These capacity constraints are compounded by the need to protect sensitive personal information within case files, an essential but time-consuming task that requires careful redaction to preserve evidentiary value. As a result, communities most in need of legal support remain underserved, not due to lack of legal knowledge, but because of infrastructural delays.

Recent collective efforts by OpenNyAI to work with legal aid practitioners, technologists, and researchers helped identify these systemic gaps. One outcome of these collaborations has been OpenNyAI's development of translation tools that expand access to legal information in 16 Indian languages, enabling more inclusive communication between legal aid providers and communities. Alongside this, redaction tools allow users to define what information needs to be anonymized and automatically detect details such as names, addresses, and identification numbers. For instance, in domestic violence cases, legal aid workers can now more easily prepare documents that protect victims' identities without compromising the legal substance required for court proceedings

Bhu Suraksha[16] and TEAL[17]: Toward Digital Land and Real Estate Files

Land records in Karnataka exist across formats – from archival paper files, cadastral maps hand-written mutation registers, to legal correspondence, survey reports, and registration deeds. Citizens requesting certified digital copies often encounter fragmented systems and language barriers, while revenue officers spend enormous effort manually verifying, locating, and cataloguing records. India's real estate sector's documents are scattered across multiple government offices, courts, and tribunals. Disputes over property boundaries, ownership history, or encumbrances often linger for years due to lost paperwork and unsynchronized databases between offices.

Karnataka launched a series of landmark digitization projects, the most recent being Bhu Suraksha, under which nearly 40 million pages of land records are being meticulously indexed, scanned, catalogued, and converted into digital formats. This project builds on earlier efforts like Bhoomi – the state's pioneering Land Records Management System – and integrates geospatial surveys (including drone mapping in urban local bodies), linking Aadhaar numbers with land ownership databases, and setting up phased digital access points. The initiative began with pilot scanning in one taluk office per district (eventually expanding to all 236 taluks), and has now moved to same-day digital issuance of records for documents already digitized. The focus is on certified "A" category records (permanent retention) and "B" category records (30-year retention), which are now accessible at nadakacheris and gram panchayat digital kiosks, minimizing the need for repeated government office visits. Geospatial and drone surveys help resolve boundary disputes by creating modern, high-resolution digital cadastral maps. Previously, parties had to present physical documents during property litigation. Now, digitally signed RTC (Record of Rights, Tenancy and Crops) and other land records in Karnataka are considered legally valid evidence in courts for ownership, inheritance, boundary disputes, and fraud investigations. The records download options and Aadhaar-linked ownership make evidence verifiable for legal proceedings.

Teal India uses AI and big data to aggregate, standardize, and deliver real estate records from hundreds of public sources across 50+ million addresses. Their Application Programming Interface (API)s and dashboards enable users to instantly check ownership status, title risks, disputes, and regulatory compliance, transforming months of manual research into real-time digital queries.

University of Nottingham: The Evidence Crisis in Hidden Crime

India's brick kiln industry operates through widespread labor exploitation, including bonded labor, child labor, and conditions that constitute human trafficking.[18] With tens of thousands of kilns across remote rural areas – many unregistered or non-compliant – regulators cannot effectively track or enforce standards. Manual monitoring is slow, expensive, and inadequate for the scale of the problem. Ground-based investigations face safety risks and often rely on unreliable testimony from coerced victims, creating evidence gaps that allow abuses to continue.

Technology can now fundamentally reshape how this legal evidence is gathered, validated, and presented in India, expanding not just the volume but the type and quality of evidence that courts and authorities can rely on. In recent years, researchers and activists have deployed satellite imagery to detect, document, and fight forced labor – particularly in hard-to-reach rural locations like India's brick kilns. For example, analysts use high-resolution satellite images to pinpoint locations operating at suspicious hours and with physical layouts typical of slave labor, thereby providing precise geospatial evidence that supplements or even replaces unreliable ground testimony. This kind of remote sensing data has begun to play an increasingly accepted role in courts and government investigations, offering timestamped, location-specific, and independently verifiable proof. Satellite images provide fact-based, time-stamped records that cannot be easily manipulated. The use of satellite and AI-driven imagery shifts the justice system's lens from slow, manual, and localized survey-based approaches to far-reaching, scalable data-driven ones.

ATREE: Walk for Evidence[19]

Indigenous and tribal communities in India have lived on their traditional lands for generations, but they couldn't legally prove ownership. The problem was that government land records were often wrong, incomplete, or deliberately altered. Even though India passed the Forest Rights Act in 2006 to help secure tribal land rights, the implementation was plagued with problems. Traditional government surveys were inaccurate and biased, bureaucratic processes were complex and corrupt, and many legitimate land claims were rejected because families couldn't provide the type of evidence officials demanded.

ATREE found a simple but powerful solution by giving GPS devices directly to community members. Instead of relying on government surveyors, tribal families could walk their own land boundaries and record exact coordinates using handheld GPS devices. This created accurate digital maps based on the communities' own traditional knowledge of their territory. These community-generated maps were then overlaid on satellite images from Google Earth, providing clear visual proof of land boundaries and forest use patterns.

These digital maps became strong legal evidence that courts and officials could easily understand and verify. For the first time, tribal communities had precise, defensible proof of their continuous occupation and use of ancestral lands. The technology bypassed corrupt bureaucrats and empowered communities to create their own documentation. Many families who had been fighting legal battles for years finally secured official land titles, enabling them to protect their forests, access government benefits, and improve their livelihoods with confidence.

CONCLUSION

India is teetering on the edge of a pivotal moment where technological innovation can transform evidence processing from being a barrier to an enabler of justice, but only if every Indian can access and leverage AI and technology tools. As pilot projects scale nationwide, success requires concerted community efforts and collaboration – from courts opening up data to legal tech innovators building tools for communities no one has serviced yet. Ultimate success will be measured when a Tamil farmer in rural Karnataka can access the same evidence-based justice as an English-speaking litigant in metropolitan Delhi.

NOTES

1 Adalat AI. (n.d.). *End-to-end justice tech stack*. https://www.adalat.ai
2 Varun Hemachandran. (n.d.). *LinkedIn profile*. www.linkedin.com/in/varunh/
3 World Population Review. (2025). *Lawyers per capita by country 2025*. https://worldpopulationreview.com/country-rankings/lawyers-per-capita-by-country
4 New Indian Express. (2025, April 15). *Only 15 judges per million population in the country: 2025 India Justice Report*. www.newindianexpress.com/nation/2025/Apr/15/only-15-judges-per-million-population-in-the-country-2025-india-justice-report-3
5 Times of India. (n.d.). *Only 0.5% of population gets legal aid in India: Justice Bobde*. https://timesofindia.indiatimes.com/city/nagpur/only-0-5-of-population-gets-legal-aid-in-india-justice-bobde/articleshow/70716754.cms

6 National Judicial Data Grid. (n.d.). https://njdg.ecourts.gov.in
7 Mishra, R. (2025). Language and the Indian judiciary: Constitutional challenges in addressing linguistic conflicts. *Indian Journal of Law & Social Sciences.*
8 World Justice Project. (2019). *Global insights on access to justice 2019: Findings from the World Justice Project general population poll in 101 countries.* https://worldjusticeproject.org/sites/default/files/documents/WJP-A2J-2019.pdf.
9 Business Standard. (2022, July 28). *SC to hear plea against construction of metro car shed in Aarey forest area.* www.business-standard.com/article/current-affairs/sc-to-hear-plea-against-construction-of-metro-car-shed-in-aarey-forest-area-122072800804_1.html
10 PUCAR. (n.d.). *Public collective for avoidance and resolution of disputes.* https://pucar.org
11 Bar & Bench. (2024, November 19). *India's first 24x7 online court launched in Kollam, Kerala.* www.barandbench.com/news/indias-first-24x7-online-court-launched-in-kollam-kerala
12 Adalat AI, *End-to-End Justice Tech Stack*, https://www.adalat.ai (last visited Sept. 24, 2025).
13 jhana.ai, *India's First AI Paralegal*, https://jhana.ai (last visited Sept. 24, 2025).
14 OpenNyAI, https://opennyai.org (last visited Sept. 24, 2025).
15 Chien, C. V., & Kim, M. (2024). Generative AI and Legal Aid: Results from a Field Study and 100 Use Cases to Bridge the Access to Justice Gap. *UC Berkeley Public Law Research Paper, Loyola of Los Angeles Law Review.*
16 Karnataka Government, *Record Room Services*, https://recordroom.karnataka.gov.in/service4 (last visited Sept. 24, 2025).
17 TEAL India, *Technology for Equitable Access to Land Records*, https://www.tealindia.in (last visited Sept. 24, 2025).
18 Anti-Slavery International & Partners. (2024, August 12). *Slavery in India's brick kilns & the payment system: Way forward in the fight for fair wages, decent work and eradication of slavery.* www.antislavery.org/latest/report-slavery-india-brick-kilns/
19 Ashoka Trust for Research in Ecology and the Environment (ATREE), *ATREE*, https://www.atree.org (last visited Sept. 24, 2025).

5 Recreating Reality

Testing the Admissibility of AI-Powered Cyber Crime Scene Reconstruction

Debdeep Das and Arjita Mukherjee

INTRODUCTION

The Internet has been a messianic liberator to a world plagued by territorial barricades, bearing the potential to revolutionize the paradigm. In its relatively short history, the internet grew from threads of bits to evolving into the fabric of cyberspace, resulting in the creation of an alternate realm unshackled from physical constraints. This led to individual and collective efforts of capitalizing on its immense potential. The words, crime results partly from the opportunities presented by physical environment (Clarke, 1985), can be squarely applied to cyberspace with the omission of the term "physical" to highlight that these opportunities are not limited to bona fide exploitation, but can be a trove for cybercriminals. When conceptualized in the backdrop of the routine activity theory (Felson & Cohen, 1979), criminal activity can be regarded as a reactionary phenomenon to the emergence of opportunity. When applied to cyberspace, the motivated offender is a deviant with adequate technical knowledge willing to commit the crime, either due to the presence of strain (Agnew, 1992) or learned criminal behavior (Bandura, 1977). The suitability of the target is based on technological or psychological vulnerabilities, and the lack of adequate legal guardianship, coupled with the added presence of dissociative anonymity and identity flexibility (Jaishankar, 2007). Unlike physical crimes, cybercrimes are often transnational (Podgor, 2004), with different geographic locations of origin and effect, which leads to blurry determination of substantive and procedural jurisdiction, due to differences in law, uncertainty in evidence collection and discontent in sharing investigative information due to security and sovereign concern, and erosion of due process. The tussle between subjective and objective jurisdiction is plagued with considerations of a lack of physical crime scene, data being held in different jurisdictions, and the need for consent of the country possessing the data. Though mutual legal assistance arrangements exist, they are faced with technical limitations and fear of self-incrimination by the provider state or its subjects. Parallel to the development of cyberspace, humans marvelled at the idea of an alternative consciousness replicating their intelligence, which led to the conception of multiple theoretically possible AI models. However, only Reactive Machine AI and Limited Memory AI are actualized realities at the time of writing this paper. Though there has been ample discourse on the utilization of AI for crime scene reconstruction and evidence generation, most exploratory or application-based studies are restricted to the physical realm, and thus necessitate the exploration of the potential of AI-powered cybercrime scene reconstruction.

AI-POWERED CYBER CRIME SCENE RECONSTRUCTION

Before delving any further into the discussion, the technology used and its potential applicability need demystification.

DOI: 10.1201/9781003629146-6

The Technology behind the Reconstruction Process

Crime scene reconstruction is perceived as a tedious process requiring the assistance and expertise of specialists, which costs dearly without the surety of precision. Crime scene reconstruction is the systematic, sequential reconstruction of events relating to the beforemath, occurrence, and aftermath of a crime. In general parlance, it is limited to the reconstruction of physical evidence, based on scientific experimentation and records (Shenoy et al., 2023). AI streamlines this process and makes it more efficient, accurate, and cost-effective. A combination of predictive, i.e., algorithms blending statistical analysis and machine learning to detect patterns and forecast future outcomes, and Generative AI, i.e., algorithms using prompts to synthesize training data to create something new, like realistic and interactive scaled spatial environments (Microsoft, 2024), needs to be utilized for different aspects of the reconstruction process. Additionally, when coupled with NLPs, the AI could decipher human speech or text, like witness testimonies, police records, historic crime scene data, and other ancillary data. The data can be tailored to the concerned incident (Anjajala & Pullagura, 2024). These AI models are coupled with VR, AR, computer-generated 3D animation, or a combination thereof to enhance their reliability and interactivity.

Cyber Crime Scene Reconstruction

Although cybercrime scenes are transient and intangible, resulting in the notion that they lack a crime scene, they do possess characteristics that are vital for the commission of a crime. For instance, ***preparation***, which can be subdivided into *reconnaissance*, i.e., collection of information on the target and its vulnerability, and *weaponisation*, i.e., selection of an exploitation agent, ***intrusion,*** i.e., the *delivery* of the payload, the *exploitation* of the target, and the *installation* of the malicious program. Finally, ***execution,*** which involves *command* and *control* of the malware for realizing the offender's objective.

In order to contextualize the offense, two hypothetical situations have been framed. ***Scene 1***, where the computer is the target, and *Scene 2*-where the computer is a tool.

Scene 1 – *An online e-commerce website, about to have its yearly sale, started offering discounts on its products, which would be enhanced if reviews were submitted by users on their previous purchases. A group of cybercriminals detected vulnerabilities on the public-facing servers running on Apache software for accepting reviews. They collect information about the IT support personnel and send them a Trojan malware through email, disguised and delivered in the form of a security update patch. Once delivered, the malware prompts a request to update the security system and install the patch. After installation, the malware creates a backdoor into the main network, gaining access to customer credentials, including encrypted payment details. The malware creates a secure channel for remote command between the server and the offender. The malware automatically deletes the payload delivery email and sends a ransom note for the removal of the malware from the affected server.*

Application of AI – *First,* the technical nuances might not be understandable by the victims, or at times, the investigating agency, thus, resulting in the non-detection of missing links in the timeline. Here, AI can be utilized for log file correlation and timeline reconstruction based on server logs. Predictive AI can chronologically map the event while detecting abnormalities in the server. The time of occurrence and the duration of exfiltration and external communication can be recreated, along with the detection of abnormal activities like backdoor creation and unauthorized remote control *Second,* after timeline re-creation, GenAI can reconstruct the payload delivery email. *Third* based on the recreated email, the AI can mimic the behavior of the payload, in this case, the Trojan, in a sandbox environment, aiding the reconstruction of the internal navigation of the malware. *Fourth,* generating visual attack maps can aid the investigators understand the nature, scope and virtual structure of the attack. Additionally, a generative model could potentially simulate the entire attack.

Scene 2 *– A social media influencer, known for her traveling blogs, was approached by an individual through the direct messaging function of the platform. The individual proposed to her and threatened to harm himself if denied. The influencer expressed her disinterest. However, the individual pestered her with repeated and similarly tuned messages, after which he blocked her profile. The individual started creating new profiles with different user names and continued to threaten her. She continued to block his profiles. However, since the influencer's profile was available for public viewership, the individual used a profile of his acquaintance and started analysing the tagged locations, stories, and captions to track her travel itinerary, identifying her posting habits, preferred destinations, and upcoming schedule. Upon tracking her location, he found her outside one of her shoot locations and assaulted her.*

Application of AI – *First,* the AI's NLP can create a linkage between the messages sent from different accounts, detecting the emotional tone, escalation of aggression, writing style, time zone consistency, and frequency, alongside detecting an influx in post reactions, comments, and story views from new accounts. IP clustering, device IDs, and browser fingerprints can relate seemingly unrelated accounts. *Second,* though repeated blocking would lead to scarce information, the AI can reconstruct the timeline, create threat maps, and behavioral summaries. *Third,* in the absence of payload delivery, unauthorized surveillance is the intrusion, and location history and surge in activity from a similar IP address can utilized for detecting the motive and intention by the Predictive AI. *Fourth,* a Generative AI can create a visual representation of the perpetrator's activities.

JURISDICTIONAL ISSUES IN CYBERSPACE

Though a laissez-faire approach was adopted in the beginning (Lessig, 1999), the tide gently shifted toward a regulated environment in consonance with neo-jurisprudential thought (Reed, 2018). However, the lack of definitive boundaries made jurisdictional issues a persistent and predominant challenge due to the emergence of transnational crimes. Due to the need for a single jurisdiction for enforcement and adjudication (*Hartford Fire Insurance Co. v California*, 1993), principles from other disciplines were borrowed (Shelke & Gurpur, 2019). Traditionally, subjective jurisdiction, i.e., jurisdiction in the place of conduct, seemed appropriate due to the presence of evidence in the location of the crime, knowledge of law for the offender, and the Foucauldian concept of expression of criminal will. However, technical difficulty in locating the criminal due to IP masking and the possible involvement of multiple conduct jurisdictions posed significant hindrances. Thus, Objective jurisdiction, i.e., jurisdiction in the place of effect, was deemed an alternative. Nonetheless, it came with the added requirement of establishing minimum contact between the offender and forum state (*International Shoe Co. v Washington*, 1945), satisfaction of purposeful availment of the benefits and protection of the forum state (*Asahi Metal Industry Co. v Superior Court*, 1987), establishment of interactivity in the forum state (*Zippo Manufacturing Co. v Zippo Dot Com,* Inc., 1997), and the fulfilment of the test of knowledge of injury and actual effect on the forum state or an entity therein (*Calder v Jones*, 1984). Given the abovementioned requisites are satisfied, issues have arisen regarding to lack of mutual assistance between the states.

While Mutual Legal Assistance Arrangement, allow prosecutors to request assistance from foreign jurisdictions for investigation and collection of evidence, these mechanisms are hindered by need of bilateral/multilateral arrangements, complex procedural requirements, and possible refusal on grounds of sovereignty, security, public order and essential public interest of the requested state. Additionally, MLAT are requested at the instance of the Investigating Officer, thus lacking judicial authority. Letter Rogatory is an agreement-independent alternative, issued by a competent criminal court based on the assurance of reciprocity (Bharatiya Nagarik Suraksha Sanhita, 2023, §112), but they are often ineffective due to the discretion available to the requested state (MHA, 2019). Thus, making AI-powered reconstruction tools a practical and effective alternative.

ADMISSIBILITY OF AI-POWERED CYBER SCENE RECONSTRUCTION

Digital Forensics under the New Criminal Laws (BNS, BNSS, and BSA)

The advent of digital technologies has drastically revolutionized the criminal justice landscape, and necessitated the revisitation of legal provisions to accommodate the emerging catena of scientific and technology-driven evidencing mechanisms, laying down procedures for collection, preservation, and admissibility. The challenges are heightened in cybercrimes due to the over-reliance on digital evidence, making it extremely crucial in the adjudication process. The enactment of the Bharatiya Nyaya Sanhita (BNS), 2023, the Bharatiya Nagarik Suraksha Sanhita (BNSS), 2023, and the Bharatiya Sakshya Adhiniyam (BSA), 2023, focused on integrating science and technology, thereby transforming the Indian Criminal Justice System while accommodating the exigencies of cybercrime and digital evidence to a great extent. The substantive aspects have been included in the BNS along with the already existing provisions in the Information Technology Act, 2000 (Bharatiya Nyaya Sanhita, 2023, §111). The BNSS has integrated technology in almost every procedural aspect of the criminal justice system (Bharatiya Nagarik Suraksha Sanhita, 2023, §105, 520).

The growing nature of cybercrimes and digital evidence created a legal vacuum in the governance of such crimes and evidence. This vacuum has been filled by the BSA, which laid down a comprehensive framework for the admissibility of electronic evidence. The definition of "documents" has been expanded to include electronic and digital records (Bharatiya Sakshya Adhiniyam, 2023, § 2(1)(d)). Electronic record has been defined under the IT Act (Information Technology Act, 2000, § 2(1)(t)). The definition of "evidence" has been expanded to include statements given electronically (Bharatiya Sakshya Adhiniyam, 2023, § 2(1)(e)). This permits the appearance of witnesses, accused, experts, and victims to depose their evidence through electronic means. The scope of an expert has been expanded to include persons skilled in 'any other field' along with the previously defined skills under the Indian Evidence Act (IEA) (Bharatiya Sakshya Adhiniyam, 2023, § 39). The ambit of Primary Evidence has been expanded to include

> digital electronic records created or stored simultaneously or sequentially in multiple files, electronic records produced from proper custody if not disputed, video recording simultaneously stored, broadcasted and transmitted to another device, and electronic records automatically stored in a multiple storage space in a computer resource.
>
> (Bharatiya Sakshya Adhiniyam, 2023, § 57)

The ambit of Secondary evidence has been expanded to include "oral admissions, written admissions, and evidence provided by a person who is skilled in examining certain documents, which, being technical or voluminous, cannot be conveniently examined" (Bharatiya Sakshya Adhiniyam, 2023, § 58). Digital or Electronic records have the same legal effect, validity, and enforceability as any other document (Bharatiya Sakshya Adhiniyam, 2023, § 61). The BSA also enlarges the ambit of the provision by covering electronic records produced by any communication device or otherwise stored, recorded or copied in any electronic form (e.g., DVR, Flash Drive, CD/ DVD, Server, Cloud, etc.), and not produced by a computer only, as was the case in the IEA. It outlines the requirements for submitting certificates, which have been appended in "THE SCHEDULE." Earlier, a certificate signed by a person in charge of the computer or management of relevant activities was sufficient. Now, in addition to a certificate signed by the person in charge of the computer or communication device, another certificate duly signed by an expert must be submitted (Bharatiya Sakshya Adhiniyam, 2023, § 63, The Schedule). The certificate shall contain details such as the kind of device, model, serial number, color, hash value, etc. The expert's certificate ensures the authenticity of electronic records admitted in evidence.

This legal framework has become even more complex with the introduction of Artificial Intelligence (AI) into digital forensics. Though AI greatly aids in digital forensic and cybercrime investigations, it would greatly benefit from its applications, its admissibility and procedural position have not been expressly covered under the existing framework, necessitating urgent appraisal (Ma, 2024).

Admissibility of Digital Evidence

The evidentiary value of digital evidence depends on the circumstances of collection, preservation, and presentation, and not just the content. The unique nature of digital evidence has necessitated special standards to ensure authenticity and prevent its manipulation. The Supreme Court held that electronic records can be proved only as per the procedure prescribed under Section 65B of the IEA (now replaced by Section 63 BSA) (*Anvar P.V. v. P.K. Basheer,* 2014). The Court decided that for electronic evidence to be admitted, it must be accompanied by a certificate confirming its legitimacy and describing the device from which it was obtained, as well as the steps taken to retrieve it. This stance was later reaffirmed by the Supreme Court (*Arjun P. Khotkar v. Kailash Kushanrao Gorantyal*, 2020). Procedural rigor is crucial for protecting against the dangers of data manipulation. These rules provide a strong foundation for the admissibility of digital evidence, but they do not adequately handle the problems presented by evidence that is created or augmented by AI. The lack of standardized validation procedures, the dynamic and opaque character of unexplainable AI algorithms, lead to evidentiary challenges that are not taken into account by the current legal framework.

Admissibility of AI-Generated Digital Evidence

Due to the lack of a physical crime scene, cybercrime investigations must rely on scattered and inconsistent digital evidence. According to the BSA (Bharatiya Sakshya Adhiniyam, 2023, § 2(1)(d) & 2(1)(e)), such AI-generated reconstructions would be considered "electronic records" and be admissible (Bharatiya Sakshya Adhiniyam, 2023, § 61 & 63). Electronic records on emails, server logs, documents on computers, laptops, or smartphones, messages, websites, locational evidence, and voice mail messages stored on digital devices can all be considered documents. However, the BSA assumes human custodianship as reflected in the mandate of certificates in the Schedule, which is difficult when reconstructions are produced automatically by AI systems.

Internationally, courts have carefully accepted AI-assisted forensic evidence, even though no case has yet explicitly addressed AI-reconstructed cybercrime scenes. Recently, a U.S. federal judicial panel advanced a draft proposal to regulate the admissibility of AI-generated evidence in court proceedings. The proposal recommends subjecting AI-generated outputs to the same admissibility standards as expert testimony under Federal Rule of Evidence 702, reflecting growing judicial concern regarding the evidentiary reliability of generative AI tools. The measure is currently open for public comment and awaits final consideration by the Judicial Conference's Rules Committee (Raymond, 2025). A Washington appellate court rejected AI-enhanced video evidence, citing a lack of peer-reviewed methodology and opacity in AI processes (*State v. Puloka,* 2024). This suggests that admissibility should be contingent upon (a)*documented procedures*, (b)*independent expert validation*, (c)*methodological transparency*, and (d)*acknowledged limitations of the AI system*. In the absence of such safeguards, reliance on AI-generated reconstructions risks compromising evidentiary reliability and procedural fairness in criminal proceedings.

CONCLUSION

There are no spots without the evidence, and there is no flawless cloak.

Similar to the physical realm, crimes in the cyberspace leave behind certain traces, which might not be entirely visible to the human eye. This highlights the advantages of using AI in the investigative and evidencing process. However, its lack of authenticity as first-hand evidence strips away its substantive status, rendering it merely corroborative. Additionally, ethical issues related to the authenticity, completeness, and integrity of the data are critical to the evidentiary value of the reconstruction (Phillip et al., 2021). Further, reconstruction bias due to the potentially skewed datasets may result in misleading narratives or misattributed blame (Mittelstadt et al, 2016), and the opacity of the AI systems deters their use in the legal sphere (Cary Coglianese & David Lehr, 2019), undermining adversarial safeguards. Privacy issues arise with the bulk processing of the data, which bears the potential of encroaching on unrelated individuals' privacy. Thus, for ethically integrating AI-reconstructed cybercrime scenes as evidence in the Indian regime, the incorporation of procedural safeguards based on transparency, explainability, and accountability is imperative (OECD, 2024). Further, independent validation and peer-reviewed scrutiny before being used in courts for evidence analysis, authentication by experts in the field, and mandatory prosecutor disclosure of error rates, limitations, and methodological assumptions (U.S. Judicial Conference Advisory Committee on Evidence Rules, 2025), while maintaining the established legal standard of privacy, are vital considerations for a seamless integration.

REFERENCES

Advisory Committee on Evidence Rules. (2025, May 2). *Agenda book: Advisory Committee on Evidence Rules meeting.* U.S. Courts. www.uscourts.gov/sites/default/files/document/2025-05_evidence_rules_committee_agenda_book_final.pdf

Agnew, R. (1992). Foundation for a general strain theory of crime and delinquency. *Criminology, 30*(1), 47–88. https://doi.org/10.1111/j.1745-9125.1992.tb01093.x

Angajala, S. R., & Pullagura, S. (2024). Crime scene reconstruction and evidence generation: AI paints the picture of the past [Crime scene reconstruction]. *International Journal of All Research Education and Scientific Methods (IJARESM), 13*(5), 849–852. www.ijaresm.com/uploaded_files/document_file/Dr._Srinivasa_Rao_Angajala_Ncbf.pdf

Anvar P.V. v. P.K. Basheer, (2014) 10 SCC 473.

Arjun P. Khotkar v. Kailash Kushanrao Gorantyal, (2020) 7 SCC 1.

Asahi Metal Industry Co. v. Superior Court, 480 U.S. 102 (1987).

Bandura, A. (1977). Self-efficacy: Toward a unifying theory of behavioral change. *Psychological Review, 84*(2), 191–215. https://doi.org/10.1037/0033-295X.84.2.191

Bharatiya Nagarik Suraksha Sanhita, No. 46 of 2023, Acts of Parliament, 2023 (India).

Bharatiya Nyaya Sanhita, No. 45 of 2023, Acts of Parliament, 2023 (India).

Bharatiya Sakshya Adhiniyam, No. 47 of 2023, Acts of Parliament, 2023 (India)

Calder v. Jones, 465 U.S. 783 (1984)

Clarke, R. V. G. (1985). Delinquency, environment and intervention [Jack Tizard Memorial Lecture]. *Journal of Child Psychology and Psychiatry, 26*(4), 505–523. https://doi.org/10.1111/j.1469-7610.1985.tb01639.x

Coglianese, C., & Lehr, D. (2019). Transparency and algorithmic governance. *Penn Carey Law- Legal Scholarship Repository.* https://scholarship.law.upenn.edu/faculty_scholarship/2123/

Cohen, L. E., & Felson, M. (2010). Social change and crime rate trends: A routine activity approach (1979). In *Routledge eBooks* (pp. 203–232). https://doi.org/10.4324/9781439817803-12.

Hartford Fire Ins. Co. v. California, 509 U.S. 764 (1993).

Information Technology Act, No. 21 of 2000, Acts of Parliament, 2000 (India).

International Shoe Co. v. Washington, 326 U.S. 310 (1945).

Jaishankar, K. J. (2007). Establishing a theory of cyber crimes. *Cyber Crime Journal, 1*(2). www.cybercrimejournal.com/pdf/Editoriaijccjuly.pdf

Lessig, L. (1999). *Code and other laws of cyberspace* (p. 87). Basic Books. https://lessig.org/images/resources/1999-Code.pdf

Ma, J. (2024). Smart tech meets forensics: Enhancing crime scene investigation with digital simulations. *Forensic Science International, 365,* 112296. https://doi.org/10.1016/j.forsciint.2024.112296

Microsoft Corporation. (2024). *Introduction to AI* [White paper]. Microsoft. https://cdn-dynmedia-1.microsoft.com/is/content/microsoftcorp/microsoft/final/en-us/microsoft-brand/documents/2024-wttc-introduction-to-ai.pdf

Ministry of Home Affairs. (2019, December 17). *Integrated Secured Intelligence Initiative: Comprehensive guidelines.* Government of India. www.mha.gov.in/sites/default/files/2022-08/ISII_ComprehensiveGuidelines_17122019%5B1%5D.pdf

Mittelstadt, B. D., Allo, P., Taddeo, M., Wachter, S., & Floridi, L. (2016). The ethics of algorithms: Mapping the debate. *Big Data & Society, 3*(2), 1–21. https://doi.org/10.1177/2053951716679679

OECD (2024). *AI principles*. OECD. www.oecd.org/en/topics/sub-issues/ai-principles.html

Phillips, P. J., Hahn, C. A., Fontana, P. C., Yates, A. N., Greene, K., Broniatowski, D. A., & Przybocki, M. A. (2021). Four principles of explainable artificial intelligence. *National Institute of Standards and Technology Interagency or Internal Report 8312*. https://doi.org/10.6028/nist.ir.8312

Podgor, E. P. (2004). Cybercrime: National, transnational, or international? *Reading Room*. https://readingroom.law.gsu.edu/cgi/viewcontent.cgi?article=1414&context=faculty_pub

Raymond, N. (2025, May 2). US judicial panel advances proposal to regulate AI-generated evidence. *Reuters*. www.reuters.com/legal/government/us-judicial-panel-advances-proposal-regulate-ai-generated-evidence-2025-05-02/

Reed, C., & Murray, A. (2018). *Rethinking the jurisprudence of cyberspace*. Edward Elgar Publishing.

Shelke, A., & Gurpur, S. (2019). Problem of jurisdiction in cyberspace and its impact on International and Domestic Laws. *SSRN Electronic Journal*. https://doi.org/10.2139/ssrn.3500049

Shenoy, S. U., Nagar, V., & Akhith. (2023). *Artificial intelligence-based techniques for crime scene reconstruction and investigation: An overview*. www.hilarispublisher.com; https://doi.org/10.37421/2157-7145.2023.14.563

State of Washington v. Puloka, No. 21-1-04851-2, King Cnty. Super. Ct. Wash., Mar. 29, 2024.

Zippo Manufacturing Co. v Zippo Dot Com, Inc., 952 F. Supp. 1119.

6 The Dual Role of Artificial Intelligence in Anti-Money Laundering

Challenges in Evidence Admissibility and Governance in India

Harsh Mahaseth and Daisy Verghese

INTRODUCTION

In today's technologically advanced world, financial crimes like money laundering and fraud are becoming increasingly sophisticated. Financial systems are often exploited by criminals who disguise the origins of illicitly obtained funds to make them appear legitimate, posing significant risks to the integrity of global markets and institutions (Han et al., 2020). These illicit crimes have transformed from simple fraud and rudimentary laundering schemes to a multifaceted challenge for financial institutions. This transformation is driven largely by the convergence of rapid technological development, globalization, and sophisticated criminal networks (Ibitola, 2025). In this regard, generative AI has been hailed as a cure-all for AML compliance, thus emerging as a modern panacea in response to evolving financial crime risks.

A nuanced understanding of the transformative role of AI necessitates an examination of its evolution and the capacities it brings to the financial sector. Its application in the domain dates several decades ago to the use of rules-based AML mechanisms, primarily designed to flag fraudulent transactions. However, these traditional methods, characterized by manual process and reactive strategies, often led to inefficiencies, such as a high rate of false positives and missed illicit activities (Ibitola, 2025). Financial institutions were ultimately burdened with the task of monitoring vast volumes of transactions and reporting suspicious activities (Alabi et al., 2025). Moreover, the limitations of these traditional rules-based mechanisms were further exposed as financial sectors embraced modern digital transformations. Rooted in static assessments and a rigid rules-based framework, they proved inadequate in responding to the continuously evolving threat landscape. Consequently, there emerged a critical need to move beyond these conventional methods and adopt dynamic and proactive solutions capable of revolutionizing AML practices.

The integration of AI and predictive analytics represents a paradigm shift in the modernization of AML practices. Generative AI, with its advanced capabilities, has significantly enhanced the effectiveness of AML by offering several operational benefits. The most critical advantage of AI integration is the ability to analyze vast volumes of financial data at speeds far beyond human capability (Tsolakis, 2022). By monitoring millions of transactions made every day within seconds, it can detect complex patterns and anomalies that would be difficult to identify through conventional methods (Tsolakis, 2022). Thus, contrary to traditional methods, AI-powered systems can adapt to emerging money laundering strategies, making them more effective in deterring financial crimes. In addition to their improved detection capabilities, AI plays a pivotal role in reducing the high number of false positives through the application of its advanced algorithms (Ricadela, 2024). By accurately

DOI: 10.1201/9781003629146-7

distinguishing between legitimate and illicit activities, it enhances the overall effectiveness of AML initiatives, enabling human analysts to allocate their attention to high-profile cases.

A key strength of AI's utility lies in its predictive analysis capability. Predictive models rely on historical data and current trends to forecast potential risks, thereby enabling financial institutions to implement proactive measures and strategically adjust their compliance measures accordingly. As a result, these models significantly enhance the proactiveness of AML interventions by anticipating emerging threats and identifying high-risk before they completely materialize (Tiwari, 2024).

The integration of AI and predictive analytics into AML systems has significantly enhanced transaction monitoring and the nuanced risk assessment process, bolstering the integrity of financial systems. However, despite its several benefits, this advanced technology introduces a labyrinth of risks and regulatory complexities, evidencing its inherent dichotomous nature (Menz, 2024). One critical barrier is the opaque or "black box" nature of AI algorithms, which threatens transparency and accountability of financial sectors (Barocas, 2018). The opaque nature of AI models fails to clarify how models flag a particular transaction as suspicious. Consequently, developers find it difficult to justify their compliance decisions, which may conflict with legal requirements in the highly regulated finance sectors.

AI models thus act as a double-edged sword in AML initiatives, offering both transformative potential and regulatory complications. Against this backdrop, the current paper aims to explore the evidentiary value and challenges associated with the integration of AI in India's financial sectors. Initially delving into the evolution of India's AML framework, the paper analyzes the increasing reliance on AI models in enhancing fraud detection and compliance mechanisms. A paradigm shift from the Indian Evidence Act, 1872, to the Bharatiya Sakshya Adhiniyam, 2023, is then examined to access the statutory provisions governing the legal admissibility of AI-generated evidence in judicial proceedings. The evidentiary challenges posed by the opaque nature of AI systems are further addressed, setting the premise for a comparative analysis with global jurisdictions from which India can draw strategic insights. The paper then concludes by proposing a recommended framework tailored to India's socio-economic landscape, aimed at bridging regulatory gaps and loopholes in its existing legal framework.

AI-INTEGRATED AML FRAMEWORKS IN INDIA

India's AML regulatory trajectory has been shaped by a series of legislative changes and amendments. The pre-AML era was characterized by unethical practices such as forged instruments, manipulated financial records, and inflated asset valuations (AML Regulations in India [AML in India], 2025). These practices not only tarnished the credibility of financial institutions but also created systemic vulnerabilities for potential money laundering activities. Recognizing the urgency of countering these evolving threats, India made a significant step in 2002 with the enactment of the Prevention of Money Laundering Act (PMLA) (Harikumar, 2023). This Act, designed to align with international AML standards such as the Financial Action Task Force (FATF) recommendations, formed the bedrock of the country's AML regulatory framework (Bag, 2024). It set the premise for a stringent regulation of financial crimes in India, emphasizing particularly identifying and curbing money laundering schemes and the funding of illicit activities (Bag, 2024). The enforcement of the PMLA picked up momentum since 2014, witnessing a total of 5,297 cases registered under its provisions, with a notable surge in prosecutions following the enactment of more stringent amendments in 2019 (Yashawardhana, 2024).

One of the key provisions of this Act is the creation of its specialized enforcement agencies, namely the Enforcement Directorate (ED) and the Financial Intelligence Unit (FIU) (AML Regulations in India [AML in India], 2025). While the ED is tasked with the investigation and prosecution of money laundering crimes, the FIU operates as a repository for receiving cash and suspicious transaction reports (STRs) from financial institutions (Srivastava, 2024). These agencies, along with the Reserve Bank of India (RBI), played a pivotal role in shaping India's AML framework. However, the growing sophistication of money laundering techniques employed by criminals necessitates modernized regulatory frameworks. The case of *Nirav Modi v. Enforcement Directorate* where over ₹11,400 crore was siphoned through fraudulent Letters of Undertaking exemplified the limitations of traditional modes of inspections (Nirav Modi v. Enforcement Directorate, 2019). Given the sheer volume of financial activity processed daily, conventional modes of inspection, which involve manual scrutiny of transactions, prove to be time-consuming (Marwala, 2024). In addition, these methods are more susceptible to errors and omissions. The ICICI Bank Fraud case of 2018 further underscored these limitations, where conventional internal controls failed to detect and prevent the occurrence of fraudulent financial activities for years (Goyal, 2024).

In response to these systemic vulnerabilities, financial sectors in India have increasingly adopted AI models to improve the parameters of fraud detection in the country. A notable example is the AI-automated fraud detection model installed in HDFC Bank of India. Unlike traditional mechanisms, this model leverages self-learning algorithms to analyze real-time credit card transactions and flag anomalous behaviors based on patterns of fraud (Goyal, 2024). Similarly, the State Bank of India (SBI) incorporated machine learning algorithms in compliance with the provisions of PMLA to detect and report high-risk transaction cases to the appropriate regulatory authorities. Furthermore, the FIU recently launched its upgraded IT system (Version 2.0), equipped with AI and machine learning tools. This technologically advanced model has significantly enhanced the unit's capacity to efficiently process and analyze the increasing volume of suspicious transaction reports submitted by financial institutions (India, 2024).

EVALUATING THE ADMISSIBILITY OF AI-DRIVEN EVIDENCE IN INDIA

With the increasing integration of AI into the financial sectors of India, a critical issue arises regarding the admissibility of AI-generated evidence in legal proceedings. The Indian Evidence Act, 1872 (IEA) has long served as the cornerstone of India's legal framework, governing the admissibility of evidence in both civil and criminal cases. However, the original framework of the Act did not account for digital evidence, thereby falling short of addressing the evidentiary needs of technologically driven contemporary India. To address this lacuna, the Information Technology Act, 2000 (IT Act) was enacted, which introduced key amendments to the IEA pertaining to the admissibility of digital evidence.

Most notably, Section 65B of the amended Act permitted the admissibility of electronic records, provided it is accompanied by a certificate that authenticates the source as well as ensures the reliability and integrity of the data. This provision was upheld in the landmark judgement of *Anvar P.V. v. P.K. Basheer* (2014), where the Supreme Court mandated the valid certificate prerequisite, underscoring the importance of untampered and authentic digital evidence (Anvar P.V. v. P.K. Basheer, 2014). While the Act marked a turning point in the regulation of digital evidence in Indian courts, it failed to address modern-day concerns arising from advanced technologies such as AI and blockchain. In this regard, the Bharatiya Sakshya Adhiniyam (BSA) was introduced to replace the Indian Evidence Act with the intent to modernize the judicial system. Conversely to the IEA, the BSA adopted a technologically inclusive interpretation for the term "document" which encompasses digital and electronic records. This includes electronic records stored on computers, laptops, smartphones, and other digital platforms (Bharatiya Sakshya Adhiniyam, 2023). A crucial question that arises is whether this definition is sufficiently broad to encompass AI-generated evidence. While the BSA does not explicitly refer to artificial intelligence, the position of the writer is that an output generated from AI would fall within the category of "document" and thus be classified as "digital" or "electronic evidence."

The rationale for this position is grounded in BSA's provision that any communication device or otherwise stored, recorded, or copied in any electronic form shall be deemed to be a document

(Bharatiya Sakshya Adhiniyam, 2023). By implication, this includes AI systems that perform similar functions of storing and processing information, irrespective of operational differences. This stance is further reinforced by the illustrations to the statutory definition of "document" provided within the BSA, which recognizes a wide range of electronically stored information as evidence, admissible in judicial processes. Another significant development was the replacement of Section 65B of the IEA with a more flexible Section 63 (Changing scope of Certificate as per BSA 2023 for admissibility of Electronic Evidence, 2025). While mandating the certificate requirement, it permits courts to consider digital evidence even in the absence of a certificate under exceptional circumstances (Shafhi Mohammad vs The State Of Himachal Pradesh, 2018). Complementing this flexibility, the BSA emphasizes proper custody for ensuring procedural integrity. By ensuring that all electronic records are preserved, handled, and presented in accordance with standard legal norms, the Act enhances the probative value of digital evidence (Decoding Bharatiya Sakshya Adhiniyam, 2023: Comparative Insights & Study with Indian Evidence Act, 1872, 2025).

AI UNDER SCRUTINY: EVIDENTIARY COMPLEXITIES AND LEGAL PITFALLS

The BSA classifies digital records as primary evidence within its framework (The Bharatiya Sakshya Adhiniyam, 2023). While this categorization grants the highest probative value, it simultaneously brings forth inherent evidentiary challenges.

A fundamental issue that arises is the black box nature of AI systems, wherein the internal decision-making process remains opaque and non-identifiable. For instance, financial institutions are often tasked with identifying and explaining suspicious transactions. However, the deep learning algorithms embedded within AI models often make it difficult for them to justify the rationale behind specific detection outcomes. This lack of transparency presents challenges to stakeholders in determining whether AI-driven decisions are fair or biased. Although the seemingly neutral and mechanical look of AI may create an illusion of reliability and objectivity, it is crucial to "open the black box" to ensure a fair and just verdict.

Hallucinated outputs, algorithmic biases, and data-driven inaccuracies further escalate this concern, questioning the overall credibility of digital evidence. In consonance with the principle that AI acts only on the basis of data fed into the software, a successful AI output is inextricably linked to the accuracy, completeness, and representativeness of its historical data (Gill, 2020). On the other hand, feeding incomplete or biased data can lead to erroneous outputs, potentially reinforcing existing systemic biases. When left unaddressed, they run the risk of exacerbating social disparities by producing discriminatory outputs, potentially resulting in flawed judicial decisions. In parallel, the right to privacy enshrined in the Indian Constitution further complicates the admissibility of digital evidence (*Justice K. S. Puttaswamy (Retd.) vs. Union of India*, 2017). This issue is of relevance when personal or sensitive information, submitted under a cloak of privacy, is used for AI training, potentially amounting to a breach of confidentiality. Courts must therefore strike a balance between the admissibility of AI-generated outputs, especially those derived from personal data, and the privacy rights of individuals.

CROSS-JURISDICTIONAL ANALYSIS OF AI MODELS

India currently lacks a dedicated legislation exclusively governing the ethical use of AI, making it a grey area for financial institutions relying on AI-driven systems (Singh, 2025). Although the recently enacted Digital Personal Data Protection Act addresses data privacy concerns, it remains silent on AI-specific concerns such as algorithmic accountability and bias. For instance, in cases of erroneous outputs, the existing framework fails to specify who will be held liable, and the question of accountability thus remains unresolved. These regulatory loopholes present a major conundrum for finance regulators. To combat these problems, it is imperative for India to enact a comprehensive framework that regulates the transparent and accountable use of AI through clear and enforceable provisions. While a notable step was taken by the Securities and Exchange Board of India (SEBI) in mandating the disclosure of AI/ML applications used by market participants, such efforts still remain at its infant stage, lacking any regulatory backing (Chatterjee, 2020).

In this regard, the European Union's AI Act is cited as a textbook example for the regulation of trustworthy AI. Passed in 2024, this Act mandates stringent obligations on AI developers and deployers in ensuring that the AI systems are transparent, safe, and secure and do not violate any personal or sensitive information (Global Lessons for India's AI Regulation, 2025). A critical component of the Act is its "provider accountability" concept, which ensures that any negligent handling of AI systems is clearly attributed, thereby strengthening institutional accountability. The AI Act classifies AI applications into 4 tiers of risk, i.e., minimal, limited, high, and unacceptable risk, and increases the level of human oversight based on the risk type. For instance, AI integrated in the financial sectors will fall within the high-risk category, subject to a greater level of scrutiny and governance. It thus adopts a risk-based, human-centric approach, aligning with the protection of fundamental rights.

The United Kingdom has also made significant strides through its context-sensitive approach in AI governance. Although it lacks a central AI regulatory framework, the country's 2023 White Paper elucidates a pro-innovation framework anchored with cross-sectoral principles such as responsible innovation, proportionality, and stakeholder clarity (AI Watch: Global regulatory tracker – United Kingdom, 2025). This nuanced approach prioritizes responsible AI proliferation based on their contextual development rather than imposing any rigid regulations that risk impeding AI adoption. Similarly, Canada's AI and Data Act (AIDA) represents an important milestone in the jurisdiction's existing AI regulatory landscape. Akin to the EU, the AIDA adopts a risk-based approach that emphasizes protecting human rights while mitigating systemic biases that infiltrate AI systems (Canada, 2022).

PROPOSED AI REGULATORY FRAMEWORK IN INDIA

While India's heterogeneous populace and kaleidoscopic diversity might render the wholesale adoption of these global paradigms unfeasible, they nonetheless offer strategic insights. Drawing from these models, the authors aim to provide an agile, inclusive, and human-centric framework, tailored to the ethical governance of AI in the country.

The guidelines provided herein seek to accommodate international legal standards without overriding the existing national regulations on AI. The main intent is to promote transparency, accountability, and rigorous oversight, while remaining adaptable to developing technological advancements.

Inclusion of a Statutory Definition for AI

Akin to the EU AI Act, where a concise definition of AI is provided under Article 3(1), India must also include a statutory definition for AI and its subcategories. Such a statutory definition will establish the scope of regulatory authority, avoiding ambiguity in enforcement or interpretation.

Preserving Human Responsibility

The fundamental factor setting apart AI and human decision-making lies in consciousness. No machine, by definition, possesses mental awareness of its decision. Moreover, while human decisions are shaped by nuanced reasoning and ethical considerations, AI arrives at its decisions purely through computational analysis. This contrasting nature underscores a necessity for imposing limitations on the use of AI. In this regard, the framework sets out the following recommendations.

Firstly, an independent and personal analysis of the AI-generated output must be conducted to ensure its credibility. *Secondly*, training programs, integrated with ethical guidelines, must be implemented to equip the concerned person on AI's capabilities and limitations.

Risk-Based Classification

A risk-tiered classification, inspired by the EU's AI Act, must be adopted by India in categorizing AI systems. India must categorically ban any AI systems that manipulate, discriminate, and violate fundamental rights of the citizens. Furthermore, AI systems employed in critical sectors such as healthcare or finance must be subject to rigorous human oversight, while lenient transparency requirements may be adopted for low-risk systems. However, disclosure policies must be mandated to ensure transparency.

Ethical Data Governance

Grounded in Article 15 of the Constitution, the proposed framework mandates that AI systems should be designed to mitigate biases and protect the rights of marginalized communities. Implementing India's DPDP Act, data protection protocols must be clearly established with strict guidelines on how the data is used, collected, and stored. Personal and sensitive data must be handled lawfully, with informed consent, and with robust security mechanisms. Clear lines of accountability must also be established where each stakeholder in the AI lifecycle is held liable for the system's performance, particularly when it comes to high-risk applications.

Establishment of a Central Regulatory AI Authority

Similar to the EU AI Office, the framework proposes that India should either create a dedicated regulatory authority or extend the jurisdiction of the **Data Protection Board of India (DPBI)** to include AI oversight. This is essential to monitor AI deployments in various sectors, investigate incidents of algorithmic malfunction, and ensure compliance with AI regulations. Additionally, the establishment of such a body will provide a formal reporting mechanism for individuals adversely affected by AI-related errors or malfunctions.

Ensuring Compliance by Imposing Penalties

Stringent penalties must also be imposed for non-compliance or gross violation of AI regulations embedded in the framework. Penalties must remain proportional to the scale and impact of the violating entity, effectively deterring both large tech firms and smaller enterprises from unethical or negligent AI practices.

CONCLUSION

The integration of AI in India's AML Framework marks a watershed moment in the nation's battle against complex and large-scale financial crimes. Although these advanced models bring forth unparalleled advantages, particularly through its predictive analytics and enhanced detection capabilities, it simultaneously introduces complexities that require urgent addressal. India's existing DPDP Act, while progressive in nature, remains silent on core concerns regarding transparency, algorithmic bias, and institutional accountability. These gaps, if left unaddressed, pose significant barriers to the overall credibility of AI-generated evidence.

The transformative shift from the Indian Evidence Act to the Bharatiya Sakshya Adhiniyam marks a commendable moment in modernizing the nation's evidentiary standards. However, the lack of a dedicated AI-specific regulatory statute exacerbates the existing hurdles in responsible AI deployment, particularly in crucial sectors such as finance. A comparative analysis of AI models in cross-border jurisdictions, especially those adopted by the European Union, United Kingdom, and Canada necessities the imperative need for India to adopt a risk-based, human-centric approach. In response, the authors propose a comprehensive framework, aligned with EU's AI Act, that is tailored to India's socio-economic landscape. The proposed framework emphasizes four critical pillars for the ethical use of AI; statutory clarity, human oversight, ethical data governance, and institutional accountability. Pivotal to this framework is the establishment of a centralized authority with regulatory and enforcement powers to monitor the responsible deployment of AI across sectors.

Ultimately, this paper advocates for a balanced and agile regulatory paradigm that not only fosters innovation but also mitigates risks associated with AI. Only then can India fortify the integrity of its evidentiary system and position itself as a global leader in ethical AI governance.

BIBLIOGRAPHY

AI watch: Global regulatory tracker – United Kingdom. (2025, March 23). Retrieved from White & Case: www.whitecase.com/insight-our-thinking/ai-watch-global-regulatory-tracker-united-kingdom

Alabi et al. (2025). *Enhancing anti-money laundering (AML) efforts through AI- driven transaction monitoring.* ResearchGate.

AML Regulations in India [AML in India]. (2025). Retrieved from KYCHub: www.kychub.com/blog/aml-regulations-in-india/

Anvar P.V. v. P.K. Basheer, 473 (Supreme Court september 18, 2014).

Bag, S. (2024, August 19). *The use of AI in arresting financial crime.* Retrieved from Observer Research Foundation: www.orfonline.org/research/the-use-of-ai-in-arresting-financial-crime

Barocas, S. (2018). *Fairness and machine learning: Limitations and opportunities.* MIT Press.

Bharatiya Sakshya Adhiniyam, Act No. 47 of 2023, §2(d) (2023). Retrieved from www.mha.gov.in/sites/default/files/2024-04/250882_english_01042024_0.pdf

Bharatiya Sakshya Adhiniyam, Act No. 47 of 2023, §57 (2023). Retrieved from www.mha.gov.in/sites/default/files/2024-04/250882_english_01042024_0.pdf

Bharatiya Sakshya Adhiniyam, Act No. 47 of 2023, §63(1)(2023). Retrieved from www.mha.gov.in/sites/default/files/2024-04/250882_english_01042024_0.pdf

Canada, G. o. (2022, July 22). *Pan-Canadian artificial intelligence strategy.* Retrieved from Canada.ca: ised-isde.canada.ca/site/ai-strategy/en

Changing scope of Certificate as per BSA 2023 for admissibility of Electronic Evidence. (2025, January 7). Retrieved from Corporate and Technology Legal: https://corpotechlegal.com/certificate-bsa-2023-for-admissibility-of-electronic-evidence/

Chatterjee, S. (2020). AI strategy of India: Policy framework, adoption challenges and actions for government. *Transforming Government: People, Process and Policy, 14*, 757–775.

Decoding Bharatiya Sakshya Adhiniyam, 2023: Comparative Insights & Study with Indian Evidence Act, 1872. (2025, March 24). Retrieved from LexisNexis: www.lexisnexis.in/blogs/decoding-bharatiya-sakshya-adhiniyam-2023-comparative-insights-study-with-indian-evidence-act-1872/

Gill, K. S. (2020). Prediction paradigm: the human price of instrumentalism. *AI & Society, 35*, 509–517.

Global lessons for India's AI regulation. (2025, January 13). Retrieved from National Economic Forum.

Goyal, D. (2024). The role of AI in combating corporate fraud in the financial sectors: Legal framework and regulatory challenges. *International Journal of Research Publication and Review, 5*, 1877–1885.

Han et al. (2020). Artificial intelligence for anti-money laundering – A review and extension. *Digital Finance 2*, 211–239.

Harikumar, P. (2023). An overview of anti-money laundering practice in the indian financial system. *Journal on Economics & Commerce, 3*, 33.

Ibitola, J. (2025, January 22). *Embracing AI to shape the future of AML compliance.* Retrieved from Flagright: www.flagright.com/post/ai-and-the-future-of-aml-compliance

India, P. T. (2024, May 5). Financial Intelligence Unit arms itself with AI to check money laundering. *Business Standard.*

Justice K. S. Puttaswamy (Retd.) vs. Union of India, 494 (Supreme Court 2017).

Marwala, T. (2024). *Artificial intelligence and the law*. Palgrave Macmillan.

Menz, M. (2024, February). *The pros and cons of generative AI in AML compliance*. Retrieved from International Compliance Association: www.int-comp.org/insight/the-pros-and-cons-of-generative-ai-in-aml-compliance/

Nirav Modi v. Enforcement Directorate, Criminal Application No.126 of 2019 (April 10, 2019).

Ricadela, A. (2024, August 28). *Anti–money laundering AI explained*. Retrieved from Oracle: www.oracle.com/qa/financial-services/aml-ai/

Secretariat, R. S. (2023). *Two hundred forty eighth report on the Bharatiya Sakshya Bill, 2023*. Delhi.

Shafhi Mohammad vs The State Of Himachal Pradesh, 2302 (Supreme Court January 30, 2018).

Singh, A. (2025, February 26). *The AI regulatory landscape in India: What to know*. Retrieved from AZO Robotics: www.azorobotics.com/Article.aspx?ArticleID=742#:~:text=The%20Current%20AI%20Regulatory%20Landscape,different%20aspects%20of%20AI%20deployment

Srivastava, N. (2024, May 5). Financial Intelligence Unit arms itself with AI, ML tools to check money laundering. *Press Trust of India*.

Tiwari, P. (2024). Finance's AI revolution: Transforming banking and investments for tomorrow. *International Conference on Emerging Systems and Intelligent Computing*.

Tsolakis, N. (2022). Artificial intelligence and blockchain implementation in supply chains: A pathway to sustainability and data monetisation. *Annals of Operation Research*, *327*, 157–210.

Yashawardhana. (2024, August 25). AI boosts Money Laundering Prevention Act's effectiveness. *The Sunday Guardian*.

7 Evolving Role of AI in Precedent Search

Harshada Shangarpawar, Gayathri Venkatadri, and Maitreyee Apte

WHY IS PRECEDENT IMPORTANT

While Gram Nyayalayas are not bound to follow the rules of the Bharatiya Sakshya Adhiniyam, all other courts – district courts, high court benches, and the Supreme Court are bound to do so. The Bharatiya Sakshya Adhiniyam, 2023, has several sections, dealing specifically with judgments, orders, or decrees as evidence. The objective is to ensure case precedents used as evidence are relevant to the issues in dispute and authenticated according to legal standards. This maintains the integrity of judicial processes and aligns with the doctrine of 'stare decisis.' This doctrine is a fundamental feature of many judicial systems – the UK, the USA, and India, to name a few.

In India, lower courts are required to follow the Supreme Court's rulings, but there is a degree of flexibility in how precedents are applied in light of evolving interpretations and the need to address new legal issues (Sharma, 2025). Given the persuasive strength of properly cited precedent, it will come as no surprise that almost all cases argued in High Courts and Supreme Courts cite previous judgments, orders, and decrees.

PRECEDENT IN THE SUPREME COURT OF INDIA

In the two-year period from July 2023 to July 2025, the Supreme Court disposed of approximately 1.2 lakh cases in total. This includes roughly 80,000 civil matters and 40,000 criminal matters (Kashyap, 2025). The Supreme Court's final rulings routinely invoke relevant past decisions as binding authority or persuasive guidance. We can judge from the cases; ~6,549 regular hearing matters in 2023 that led to full judgments (Supreme Court of India, n.d.); that 100% of them cited one or more judicial precedents.

It is a common practice for lawyers in the Supreme Court to bolster their oral arguments with citations to past judgments, especially in appellate and constitutional cases. Written pleadings also contain extensive case-law references. While there is no quantitative data published on the number of cases where oral arguments or written pleadings cited precedent, because the court does not track this, anecdotal evidence holds that this is the norm.

PRECEDENT IN THE HIGH COURTS

High Court judgments, especially in civil appeals, writ petitions, and criminal appeals, routinely cite judicial precedents. Judges at the High Courts are bound by Supreme Court case law and often refer to prior High Court rulings (including Full Bench decisions) for consistency. While there is no formal count of how many of the ~2 lakh disposed cases of the Bombay High Court, to take one

DOI: 10.1201/9781003629146-8

example, involved precedent citation, we can infer that every final reasoned judgment delivered by the High Court cites relevant case law. Many High Court orders (like simple interim orders, bail orders, etc.) are short and may not quote precedents, but any substantive judgment on law will.

PRECEDENT IN DISTRICT COURTS

District Courts are the workhorses of India's judiciary. Maharashtra's district courts, for example, disposed of 15.3 lakh cases in 2022 (Govt. of India, Ministry of Law C Justice, 2023) and a similar number in the years since. Unlike the appellate courts, trial court judgments seldom contain extensive precedent citations, relying instead on codified statutes of law. In day-to-day practice, oral arguments are fact-focused and brief, and while binding precedents are cited where necessary, the necessity remains rare. It must be noted that District Courts typically function in the language of the State, unlike the Supreme Court and the High Courts, which use English. So, while routine matters that dominate the courts' roster do not require precedent, the language barrier also serves as a deterrent to the use of precedent in District Courts.

CURRENT PRACTICE IN PRECEDENT SEARCH

Indian legal professionals today have a range of digital tools for case law research, but their choices and habits vary widely by seniority and court level. Platforms like SCC Online, Manupatra, Indian Kanoon, and the judiciary's eCourts portals dominate the landscape. Surveys and commentary suggest that while top advocates often leverage multiple databases, many lawyers – especially in lower courts – still rely on free resources or traditional libraries. One Supreme Court lawyer posts about the wide range of tools, national and international, that he accesses. (Singh, 2024)

While the landscape of using paid, digital resources is similar for high court lawyers or those employed by larger firms, smaller firms, or those who operate independently continue to depend on e-libraries or free resources.

Lawyers also differ on 'how' they search for cases. Senior lawyers tend to remember cases by dates and judge names; if not they prefer to search by subject and relevant act/law within that subject to find applicable precedents. e.g., Conveyance can be a subject, and under this subject, multiple acts like the Transfer of Property Act, Registration Act, Maharashtra Ownership Flats Act, etc. would be applicable. More junior lawyers, though, spend some time (between 10 and 20 minutes) scanning the judgment text to decide whether there is any applicability either of the Provision of Law related to the case or one of the less prominent aspects. In addition, during the search process, lawyers look for easy identification of the party who won the case, citations used in the case itself, and whether the judgment in the case has been overruled by newer judgments.

THE ROLE OF AI AND TECHNOLOGY

Precedent retrieval as a 'push-button' task enabled by computer technology is not new to India. By the mid-1990s JUDIS (Judgement Information System) enabled a computerized search of all reported Supreme Court Decisions since 1950. (Department of Justice, n.d.). High Courts soon followed, and by the 2000s all 21 High Courts and their 10 benches were also fully computerized (Awadesh Kumar Patel, 2008). While the push has now moved to scan and preserve legacy records of High Courts and also district courts, there is still some way to go.

Alongside record digitization, a suite of tools has emerged to help lawyers and judges search and analyze legal precedent. While the court-run databases like JUDIS and the e-courts portal (ecourts.gov.in) provide information for free to the public, legal information startups like Indian Kanoon, Manupatra, SCC Online, etc., have provided access to more than 1.4 million laws and judgments from the Supreme Court and High Courts. (Sinha, 2011).

Lawyers across India can now instantly query vast digital libraries of judgments, a task that once required laborious manual perusal of physical books and files. The only catch – the district courts and many of their regional language judgments are not included.

CHALLENGES OF USING AI IN OUR DISTRICT COURTS

AI systems face significant challenges in handling Indian languages due to the country's linguistic diversity. India has over 121 languages and numerous dialects, each with unique grammar, vocabulary, and contexts. This diversity complicates AI model development. Indian languages often use affixes to modify words, requiring AI to handle a wide range of word forms, a challenge for systems primarily trained in less morphologically complex languages like English. In English, for example, the sentence, 'Amita reads a book' would stay the same irrespective of Amita's gender. In Hindi, however, it would change from 'Amita kitaab padhta hai' to 'Amita kitaab padhti hai' depending on Amita's gender. There are many other significant differences between

English, on which a majority of the world's Large Language Models are trained and Indian languages.

There is also script variability. Indian languages use scripts like Devanagari, Tamil, and Bengali, each with unique characters and rules. This makes it difficult for universal AI tools to process text across scripts. Many Indian scripts follow an abugida format where consonants carry inherent vowels, challenging tokenization and text processing.

Regional dialects within a single language vary significantly in pronunciation, vocabulary, and syntax. AI systems must adapt to these variations to function effectively (Divyanshu Kakwani, 2021). In addition, multilingual speakers often switch between languages (code-switching), complicating AI's ability to understand and generate text.

Even supposing that the more powerful NLP algorithms available to us today could overcome the challenges described above, we have a paucity of training data. Many Indian languages lack digital resources and annotated datasets, limiting effective natural language processing (NLP) applications (Madanapalle, 2024).

For our purposes, we need to understand that solutions in Indian languages are contingent on the success of foundational solutions. Efforts in data collection, model development tailored to linguistic features, and investment in research to enhance the digital presence of Indian languages. Initiatives like Bhashini aim to create open-source datasets and improve language processing capabilities, enhancing AI applications in India.

THE LEX RES EXPERIENCE

Two of the authors of this study come from a background in AI / ML usage, and through the development of Lex Res, an application that will provide voice search and result capabilities for precedent search, we have some findings to share on the state of AI usage in the space.

DIGITIZED DOES NOT MEAN AI-READY

As described previously, while the Supreme Court of India and all the High Courts have put up judgments on their websites, they are not easily downloadable or accessible for an AI. The Supreme Court site, for example, uses CAPTCHA codes[1] that make access more difficult. The formats used across high court sites are not standard for acquisition, e.g., some high courts follow a PDF/A standard while others have regular PDFs uploaded. The judgment itself can be directly accessed in some cases, whereas it comes with an HTML, XML, or document wrapper in certain sites.

The data is also not standardized for analysis. The Allahabad High Court, for example, lists cases dating from even the 1930s on its site with more recent timestamps. AI systems, which depend on the accuracy of input data, would be led astray in such situations.

INDIA-SPECIFIC NEEDS

Across the spectrum, whether it is the acquisition of data, analysis, or delivering results via Text to Speech, models built on non-Indian languages and accents do not yield completely viable results. We tried standard Google Text to Speech and other open-source text-to-speech models, but they do not recognize or render Indian accents very well. Bhashini, an India-specific model, did provide better results, but the lack of customer support makes it difficult for a commercial entity to use their services. Sarvam, PARAM, and other India-specific LLM's are currently being explored. This does seem to be the way forward (Pandey, 2025).

THE GROUND IS MOVING BENEATH OUR FEET

When we began working on the problem in 2022, the best option was to build near foundational models, collect and annotate case data for information on case type, hearing court, timeline, winner, evidence, etc. Base models like T5, BERT and domain-specific models like LAWBERT were used to augment metadata and drive the search. While there were international examples of success, these were mostly in geographies like the USA, where standard judgment contents and formats were available. With the challenges of India's data described above, the results were not very positive.

With the arrival of LLM's like ChatGPT, we have been testing it and other open-source models like Huggingface for summarization tasks. However, besides the higher cost implication, the results are still not commercially viable. What is clear, though: base models like T5/BERT, which are less than 8 years old, are already outdated or subsumed within a more sophisticated solution.

CONCLUSION

Precedent search in India is evolving from manual research in law libraries to AI-enabled tools. Despite digitization efforts, inconsistency in formats, limited machine-readability, and language diversity pose significant hurdles. AI remains constrained by poor-quality data and the under-representation of Indian languages in model training.

Platforms like Lex Res show what's possible, but widespread adoption will require India-specific innovation, better infrastructure, and robust public datasets. As courts and practitioners increasingly rely on technology, the shift from digitized to intelligent precedent search is sure to happen. The only question is whether Indian participation will genuinely drive this or whether we will wait for global giants currently driving the AI revolution to get there first.

NOTE

1 CAPTCHA stands for the Completely Automated Public Turing test to tell Computers and Humans Apart. It typically features tasks like identifying distorted numbers etc. that are easy for humans but harder for computers.

REFERENCES

Awadesh Kumar Patel, B. K. (2008, March 1). *International CALIBER 2008.* Retrieved July 2025, from Application of ICT in Judicial Library System: https://ir.inflibnet.ac.in/server/api/core/bitstreams/7375db77-4d22-4c33-85bb-5e6861b6ac22/content

Department of Justice. (n.d.). *Department of Justice*. Retrieved July 2025, from doj.gov.in: https://doj.gov.in/judgment-search-portal/#:~:text=Image%3A%20Judgment%20Search%20Portal%20A,text%20search%20engine%2C%20which%20finds

Divyanshu Kakwani, A. K. (2021, February 10). *Levelling up NLP for Indian languages*. Retrieved July 2025, from RBC DSAI: https://rbcdsai.iitm.ac.in/blogs/leveling-up-nlp4-indian-langs/

Govt. of India, Ministry of Law C Justice. (2023, July 21). *Sabrang India*. Retrieved July 2025, from sabrangindia.in: https://sabrangindia.in/wp-content/uploads/2023/07/Settlement-of-Cases-in-Courts.pdf#:~:text=2%20Maharashtra%20256229%201188934%201553069,Rajasthan%20453978%20723598%201048909%20525877

Kashyap, G. (2025, January 7). *Supreme court observer*. Retrieved from www.scobserver.in: www.scobserver.in/journal/supreme-court-review-2024-a-steady-recovery-in-pendency-after-the-pandemic-years/#:~:text=2023%20and%203316%20cases%20in,cases%20in%20total%20 in%202024

Madanapalle, A. (2024, December 09). *Challenges with developing AI applications in Indic languages*. Retrieved from news9live.com: www.news9live.com/science/challenges-with-developing-ai- applications-in-indic-languages-2768894

Pandey, J. (2025, June 11). *Param-1 and the rise of BharatGen: India's AI voice roars into the global arena*. Retrieved July 2025, from Techequityindia.com: www.techquityindia.com/param-1-and-the-rise-of-bharatgen-indias-ai- voice-roars-into-the-global-arena/

Sharma, D. N. (2025, July 17). *Journal of Emerging Technologies and Innovative Research*. Retrieved from www.jetir.org: www.jetir.org/papers/JETIR2408733.pdf

Singh, N. (2024, August 30). *My go to databases for Indian legal research*. Retrieved July 2025, from linkedin.com: www.linkedin.com/pulse/my-go-to-databases-indian-legal-research-major-nirvikar-singh--cnd7c#:~:text=1

Sinha, S. (2011, April 22). *Indian Kanoon – The genesis and the legal thirst*. Retrieved July 2025, from Cornell University Law School Blog: https://blog.law.cornell.edu/voxpop/2011/04/22/indian-kanoon-the-genesis-and-the-legal-thirst/#:~:text=Image%3A%20Supreme%20Court%20Building%2C%20IndiaIndian,and%20a%20few%20law%20journals

Supreme Court of India. (n.d.). *Bar and bench*. Retrieved July 2025, from https://images.assettype.com/: https://images.assettype.com/https://images.assettype.com/: https://images.assettype.com/barandbench/2023-12/54b6f79e-31a8-421d-b520-d11bc76a4e6b/Supreme_Court_case_disposal_press_release_2023_Dec_pdf.pdf#:~:text=In%20another%20achievement%2C%20the%20Supreme,registered%20during%20the%20said%20period

8 Artificial Intelligence-Driven Evidence in Arbitral Proceedings

A Panacea or an Anathema?

Atish Chakraborty and Dhruv Maheshwari

INTRODUCTION

Man and machine in the present are slowly and steadily becoming intertwined in a manner that it is often extremely difficult to separate one from the other. The luxuries of the past have come up to become the necessities of the present. It won't be wrong for one to infer that advanced technologies like Artificial Intelligence (hereinafter referred to as "AI") are having a consequential role in our day-to-day lives. AI today is reshaping the contours of dispute resolution mechanisms, having profound implications for the production and evaluation of evidence (Giacalone, 2025). In arbitration, where party autonomy forms the key tenet of an arbitral proceeding, it allows both the parties and tribunals to craft bespoke rules that best satisfy the interests of the parties. The introduction of AI-generated or AI-analyzed evidence tends to raise important questions with regard to laying down standards for admissibility, authenticity, integrity, and fairness. The newly enacted Bharatiya Sakshya Adhiniyam (hereinafter referred to as "BSA"), 2023, replacing the Indian Evidence Act, 1872, takes an ambitious step toward modernizing the evidence law and takes into account the challenges brought in by the digital era. Its provisions recognizing digital records and documents are a testimony to the acknowledgement of emerging technologies in the Indian legal system, thereby making it timely to explore how AI-generated or analyzed evidence can be integrated, assessed, and regulated in arbitral proceedings that are located within or seated in India.

Historically, AI-based evidentiary tools have ranged from computer-aided transcription to machine learning algorithms, which are capable of identifying patterns across vast datasets (Rashidi, H. H., et al., 2025). While forums like ICC or SIAC have accommodated these processes pragmatically, their use is guided by overarching principles of confidentiality, proportionality, and procedural fairness. In India, the Arbitration and Conciliation Act, 1996, empowers tribunals to determine their own procedure (§ 19), creating room to admit AI-derived and generated evidence subject to party agreement and tribunal discretion. However, the standards governing admissibility are enshrined in the BSA, thereby underscoring its importance to recognize AI's role in arbitration.

The BSA actively embraces digital technology, expanding the definitions of terms like documents (§57) (Section 57 of BSA), criteria for admissibility (§63) (Section 63 of BSA), and authorizes electronic evidence, which can be interpreted to include AI-generated outputs. Section 57 treats electronic records, emails, server logs, audio, and video, as primary or secondary documentary evidence, eliminating procedural hurdles that previously complicated outcomes under Section 65B of the Indian Evidence Act. Section 63 further, through sub-section (2) sets reliability criteria, such as consistent use, proper functioning, and fidelity to original input, while sub-sections (3–5) merge complex computing systems into a unified "computer," requiring dual-party certificates (responsible

DOI: 10.1201/9781003629146-9

officer and expert), and mandate cryptographic hash values. Such provisions modernize technological authenticity requirements as well as fortify the digital chain-of-custody safeguards.

However, for AI-generated outputs, there lie certain challenges. AI systems, operating on opaque deep-learning models, often act as "black-boxes." The Indian courts have often addressed concerns like Justice Prathiba M. Singh of the Delhi High Court remarked that the *"accuracy and reliability of AI-generated data are still in the grey area"* having evaluated ChatGPT-style responses (*Christian Louboutin SAS v. The Shoe Boutique*, CS(COMM) 582 of 2023). The BSA anticipates potential issues by requiring expert validation in certificates; however, it remains silent on defining "expert" or outlining the standards for AI-specific auditing. This dilemma is acute in arbitration, and tribunals must determine whether evidence given by AI is transparent, unbiased, and secure to be admitted without impinging upon fairness and equity.

Contextualizing India within the global panorama reveals that jurisdictions such as the United States and the UK approach AI-evidence under benchmarks of relevance and reliability, closely scrutinizing probabilistic outputs and system transparency. In the arbitration domain, institutional guidelines, from the IBA Rules of Evidence to SVAMC principles, advocate for disclosure of AI use, confidentiality assurances, and human oversight (Eftekhar, R., 2025). Although these are soft laws and are not binding in India, the Arbitration Act's procedural autonomy allows tribunals to apply them. AI-generated evidence, therefore, must navigate a dual test of meeting BSA's statutory admissibility safeguards while conforming to international standards of procedural fairness, especially in cross-border disputes.

Thus, while the BSA significantly streamlines the acceptance of digital evidence, it does not resolve how AI's complexity and automation affect authenticity and expert certification. Further, arbitration tribunals face a choice to strictly apply BSA's framework, potentially excluding complex AI outputs, or adopt a more flexible approach, integrating global best practices to maintain both legal validity and procedural efficiency.

This chapter seeks to address these questions in a three-pronged manner. First, it will map the statutory regime which allows for the use of AI-generated evidence under the BSA, especially in the context of arbitration. Second, it will dissect the cross-jurisdictional jurisprudence, both Indian and international, to assess how courts and tribunals evaluate AI-based evidence under standards such as explainability, bias testing, data security, and expert certification. Third, it will propose a calibrated framework for arbitral tribunals that harnesses AI's prospects while ensuring compliance with evidentiary norms.

APPLICATION OF AI EVIDENCE IN ARBITRAL PROCEEDINGS UNDER BSA

The integration of AI into evidence production within arbitral proceedings marks a significant departure from traditional modes of documentary and oral evidence. Under BSA, 2023, the admissibility of AI-generated or analyzed evidence and their evidentiary value becomes a concern for arbitrators and practitioners. This section examines how AI-generated or analyzed evidence fits within the BSA's new statutory framework, under Sections 57, 61, and 63, and considers how tribunals might adapt procedural norms to accommodate, scrutinize, and evaluate AI-generated or analyzed evidence.

Electronic Records as Primary and Secondary Evidence

One of the most transformative features of the BSA is its expanded conception of "document." Section 57 redefines primary evidence to include electronic records stored in multiple formats and locations. For instance, Explanation 5 expressly allows any electronic or digital record *"produced from proper custody"* to be deemed primary evidence unless its authenticity is disputed. This establishes a presumption favoring admission of electronic content, transcripts, logs, or AI-generated outputs, provided the chain of custody is maintained. Given these provisions, AI-analyzed documents, such as predictive coding outputs, when extracted from secured systems and certified under Section 63, should qualify as primary evidence and not just secondary exhibits. Nevertheless, the BSA clearly demarcates requirements, particularly in Explanation 4 of Section 57, that recordings and files stored in multiple locations are each to be treated as original, reinforcing the federal weight of digital content. In arbitration, this means each node, whether a cloud copy, local archive, or cached file, may be regarded as equally authentic unless the opposing party can demonstrate tampering or inconsistency. Despite these advances, the lines between primary and secondary evidence remain significant. Section 58 (Section 58 of BSA), now permits admissions and expert testimony to validate inaccessible originals, a provision that can support AI use when an AI expert explains obscure algorithmic logic, filling gaps when raw system traces are unavailable for tribunal inspection. Where predictive coding systems produce clusters or algorithmic relevance scores, expert evidence may serve as secondary support to primary electronic outputs, especially when tribunals require human intermediaries to interpret AI's logic (Bell et al., 2023).

Authentication and Certification under Section 63

Section 63 of the BSA streamlines the process for admitting electronic records, effectively replacing the rigid rules under the old Section 65B of the Indian Evidence Act. It sets out a clear two-step certificate requirement. Sub-section (2) lists reliability criteria, usage in ordinary course, system maintenance, accurate reproduction, and (4) mandates a dual certificate signed by the "person in charge" of the device and an "expert," detailing record origin, device, integrity measures, and hash values. This construct is particularly pertinent to AI-generated materials like predictive annotations, AI-enabled summaries, or metadata reports: properly signed certificates affirming data integrity and cryptographic fingerprinting will be essential.

The hash value requirement is notably modern. Under section 63(4), the certificate must include a hash of the electronic record to allow verification of its exact content. In arbitration, this implies that when a party seeks to introduce AI-generated documents, like a relevancy-ranked list, those outputs must be accompanied by a verifiable cryptographic hash and without such certification, tribunals may regard the evidence inadmissible.

The BSA, however, does not define "expert" or analytics standards required in the context of an AI. This gap may lead tribunals to adopt ad hoc criteria such as qualifications, forensic accreditation, and audit trails for AI systems. Some institutions may require AIS-specific technical audits confirming that training data sets were unbiased, the model versions remain stable, and the logs document every algorithmic transition (Pyrrho Investments Ltd v MWB Property Ltd, [2016] EWHC 256 (Ch), ¶31) (Praštalo, 2024). Such protocols would enhance the statutory certificate without contravening its broad language.

Modeling AI Evidence in Arbitration Procedure

Arbitral tribunals, under section 19 of the Arbitration and Conciliation Act, have discretion over procedure. They can adopt or develop specific protocols for AI-evidence handling within the electronic evidence framework contained in the BSA. For example, tribunals might require parties to disclose their use of Technology Assisted Review (TAR) systems at the outset (Larkin et al., 2024), accompanied by expert reports explaining model training and relevance thresholds. The party introducing AI-evidence would provide the necessary section 63 certificates, hash values, system documentation, metadata indicating tool version, date of processing, and logs, thus satisfying the dual-person and expert certification requirement.

Opposing parties may then question the validity, pointing to concerns such as bias, recall or precision rates, or the correctness of the training data (Kattnig et al., 2024). The tribunals may allow cross-examination of experts or parties on these metrics; request production of error rates, validation tests, or peer-reviewed audits. These processes occur within BSA's flexible structure: the AI outputs are primary evidence (per section 57) and properly certified (section 63), but their weight is adjusted based on adversarial scrutiny. Global arbitration institutions have embraced such frameworks (Bennett Moses et al., 2023). For instance, the ICC's 2023 guidelines suggest parties to disclose the use of predictive coding, accompanied by audit credentials and human review logs. If Indian-seated arbitrations adopt such processes, they can remain aligned with both statutory requirements and evolving best practices, exhibiting procedural efficiency without sacrificing evidentiary standards.

Admissibility Standards: Reliability, Relevance, Fairness

The BSA emphasizes relevance and probative value, requiring authentication and permitting dispute (Rath, 2025). AI-generated or analyzed material may meet formal criteria but still be excluded if it risks unfair prejudice or distortion. Issues such as model bias, e.g., disregarding certain document types, or over-reliance on algorithmic ranking can raise due-process concerns grounded in the Arbitration Act's requirement for equality of arms.

Indian courts have already flagged such concerns, and this ambiguity echoes in arbitration proceedings. The tribunals must adopt adversarial testing of AI outputs through randomized sampling and manual review, similar to US Da Silva Moore-style methodologies (*Da Silva Moore v. Publicis Groupe & MSL Group*, 287 F.R.D. 182 (S.D.N.Y. 2012)), or UK High Court-endorsed rigor as in Pyrrho Investments (*Pyrrho Investments Ltd. v. MWB Property Ltd. & Ors.*, [2016] EWHC (Ch)). In essence, AI-evidence must be shown to be sufficiently reliable and fair, else the tribunals may disregard it, regardless of the BSA compliance.

USE OF AI IN DISCOVERY AND PRODUCTION OF EVIDENCE IN ARBITRAL PROCEEDINGS

The discovery and production of evidence are instrumental in arbitration, particularly when disputes involve voluminous electronic documents. AI tools, ranging from basic metadata filters to sophisticated predictive coding systems, have begun to reshape these stages by offering enhanced speed, efficiency, and accuracy. Yet, their integration raises critical legal and procedural questions, especially within the framework of BSA. This section critically examines AI's utility and limitations in evidence discovery, explores how different jurisdictions and institutions regulate its use, evaluates reliability and admissibility criteria, and draws upon cross-jurisdictional jurisprudence to elucidate best practices and potential hiccups in using AI for document production.

Mechanisms and Efficacy of AI in E-Discovery

At its core, AI-powered e-discovery relies on machine learning (hereinafter referred to as "ML") and natural language processing (hereinafter referred to as "NLP") to sift vast datasets – emails, digital communications, contracts, and more – for relevance. Techniques such as Technology Assisted Review (hereinafter referred to as "TAR") and predictive coding use supervised learning: legal professionals manually tag a subset of documents, and the AI system extrapolates this classification to the remainder (Nagineni, 2024). This reduces human effort by prioritizing high-salience content. According to DLA Piper, tools like "RelativityOne" and "Jus-AI" (GPT-based) can create concise evidence bases or summaries in a fraction of traditional times. Additionally, the White & Case global survey further confirms that 54 percent of arbitration practitioners anticipate AI driving time savings and cost-efficiency, though concerns about bias and confidentiality persist (White & Case LLP, 2025).

In India, the BSA does not prescribe or proscribe AI discovery tools but implicitly permits their use under sections 57 and 63. The accountability for authentication now rests with parties using section 63 certificates supported by hash values and expert sign-off. However, because AI-generated outputs may lack human-readable audit trails, tribunals may require additional expert scrutiny to meet reliability standards, especially where algorithms function as opaque "black-boxes."

Institutional and Jurisdictional Approaches

Globally, arbitral institutions and courts have begun interpreting best practices for AI-assisted discovery. In the United States and United Kingdom courts, cases like *Da Silva Moore* and *Pyrrho Investments* have emphasized that AI tools like predictive coding software for e-disclosure can be used if the results produced thereof exhibit precision and the science behind the black-box of the software need not be given much importance. These decisions assert that AI tools can generate admissible evidence when properly sampled and tested (Bennett Moses et al., 2023). Further, Australian and New Zealand tribunals provide for procedural discretion under UNCITRAL Article 17, which allows tribunals to sanction AI use, provided the usage denotes equality among the parties and fairness. These jurisdictions suggest leveraging formal procedural orders or agreements, which can be adopted in advanced cases (Supreme Court of New South Wales, 2024); (Courts of New Zealand, 2023). Finally, the recently enacted SVAMC draft guidelines of 2023 emphasize transparency, party consent, confidentiality safeguards, and human oversight when AI is used (Eftekhar, R., 2025). This exhibits that AI-enabled discovery is globally accepted, so long as parties disclose usage, ensure system explainability, and apply adversarial testing.

Reliability, Admissibility, and BSA Considerations

AI-generated evidence must satisfy BSA's relevance, authentication, and integrity requirements. An AI-generated or analyzed document list or summary would qualify as a "document" under BSA section 57 and can be admitted as primary evidence if the certificate under section 63 is in order. However, mere compliance may not suffice, and the tribunal must evaluate probative value and fairness of the evidence so produced. While Indian courts have questioned the accuracy and reliability of AI-generated or analyzed data, leaving the tribunals to navigate this ambiguity through additional scrutiny. Foreign courts in cases like *Da Silva Moore* and *Pyrrho Investments* have identified the need for statistical validation to avoid sampling error and recall/carry out precision testing, algorithmic audits demonstrating that the training data is unbiased, human review protocols to prevent hallucination and displaying metadata logs showing when, how and by whom the documents were reviewed and altered.

The section 63(4) certificate in India must include a hash for each dataset or output, authenticated by a "person-in-charge" and an "expert." While BSA lacks a definition of *"expert,"* existing SOPs. like the forensic specialists under section 39(2)(c) of the Information Technology Act, 2000, could act as such experts.

DECONSTRUCTING THE PROMISE: CHALLENGES, LIMITATIONS, AND STRATEGIC ROADMAP

While the potential prospects of leveraging AI into arbitral discovery and evidence production are significant, they are shadowed by challenges that lie at the intersection of technological complexity, legal legitimacy, procedural fairness, and institutional adoption. Drawing from statutes, case law, institutional practices, and international standards, this section systematically deconstructs key limitations and proposes strategic pathways to ensure that the adoption of AI in Indian arbitral proceedings under the auspices of the BSA is both responsible and resilient.

The Explainability Gap and Evidentiary Transparency

One of the most persistent challenges in AI systems, particularly those based on deep learning models, is their "black-box" nature of operation. They often deliver outputs without transparent reasoning, posing a problem when used in a legal proceeding that demands evidentiary traceability. Under the BSA, while section 63 mandates certification, it does not require submission of underlying algorithms, training data, and the decision-making rationale. This creates scenarios that make it difficult to challenge or verify the AI's conclusions. Comparatively, jurisdictions like the EU have begun embedding "explainability" requirements into AI regulation through the EU AI Act. By adapting these principles, arbitral tribunals can condition admissibility upon the disclosure of decision-making protocols, transparency reports, or model interpretability metrics. Instituting minimal technical disclosure, such as feature importance insights from model outputs, would enable adversarial review and would thereby promote fairness, without requiring full open-sourcing of AI systems.

Bias, Representativeness, and Algorithmic Fairness

AI systems are trained on datasets, and consequently, they tend to inherit or perpetuate biases linguistic, cultural, or contextual. In arbitration, this might manifest as an under-representation of documents with non-English content, atypical file types, or documents from individuals outside the dominant stakeholder's demographic data, posing a lack of fairness. Given the objective to uphold fair trial as embedded in Articles 14 and 21 of the Indian Constitution, tribunals must proactively counteract such bias.

In jurisdictions like the United States, in the case of *Da Silva Moore* and subsequent cases, they insisted on setting recall thresholds of 75–80%, combined with random sampling, to verify TAR output reliability. The UK High Court in *Pyrrho Investments* also insisted on precision metrics and human review loops. A similar approach could be adopted by the Indian tribunals for statistical validations, which require parties to submit error rates, test sample results, and explanations of how the AI was trained on representative data. This statistical transparency becomes a cornerstone of procedural fairness, ensuring that AI does not inadvertently suppress critical evidence.

Chain-of-Custody Integrity and Cybersecurity

While the BSA requires authentication via hash values and expert certification (§ 63), chain-of-custody extends beyond simple file integrity. AI systems often involve third-party infrastructure cloud service providers, offshored databases, or shared computational environments. Each layer introduces potential vulnerability: unauthorized access, tampering, or accidental data leaks. This risk is magnified in international arbitration, where data may traverse multiple jurisdictions, invoking GDPR, India's Digital Personal Data Protection Act, and local banking secrecy laws potentially generating legal friction.

To mitigate such risks, arbitration panels should require parties to: maintain encrypted data at rest and in transit; provide system logs; implement secure audit trails; and ensure that providers adhere to ISO 27001 or equivalent standards. Indian law could take a leaf from the IBA's cybersecurity provisions for arbitration and the ICCA-NY Bar-CPR Rule-making Project, which suggests mandatory cybersecurity baselines for digital proceedings. Integrating technical accreditation into section 63 certification, indicating not only hash values but secure custody, would align statutory and functional integrity.

Accountability and Ethical Liability

If AI-assisted processes misclassify or omit crucial documents, the question arises as to who shall bear the responsibility. Traditional legal ethics place an onus on the counsel to conduct due diligence.

But when AI tools make final decisions regarding document production, accountability becomes murky, with liability being attributable to parties or the counsel or the AI or the service provider. The United States has allowed courts to hold parties accountable for TAR failures, and European Data Protection Boards have held controllers responsible for algorithmic mistakes. A similar approach could be adopted by Indian arbitral tribunals. While AI systems streamline discovery, the final responsibility should vest with parties and their counsel. This can be built into procedural orders and ethics codes, reinforcing that AI is an expansion of human agency, and not a shield from accountability.

CONCLUSION AND STRATEGIC ROADMAP FOR RESPONSIBLE AI INTEGRATION

While AI is transforming every walk of life in the present day and can reform the working of legal proceedings, it still continues to be at a nascent stage and requires further attention and development to tap the complete potential which such technology brings. When looking at the potential of AI from the vantage point of it being used as a tool for discovery and evidencing in Indian arbitral processes, it definitely prompts that while we have made strides toward transformation, there still remains a significant path that we still need to take in order to realize the complete potential of such technology. This, in our opinion, could be achieved through following a systematic roadmap, which we shall highlight hereinafter. Firstly, similar to global arbitral institutions like ICC, SIAC, and IIAC, which have developed their "AI protocols" for discovery in arbitral proceedings, a similar framework needs to be incorporated under the BSA to guide the parties on certification, explainability, validation, and audit standards. Secondly, BSA could formulate amendments by providing adequate clarity on terms like "expert," "hashing algorithms" and "AI transparency data" and introducing a legal framework for admissibility of AI-based evidence, thereby streamlining the practice and reducing procedural friction. Thirdly, academic and institutional training programs should include modules on AI literacy, covering hash functions, model risk indicators, cybersecurity, and AI forensics to apprise and develop the knowledge of such modern technology to encourage adoption of such technology in the long run. Fourthly, educational institutions and arbitration centers can incubate open-source AI tools tailored for discovery and evidence, akin to "ArbLab" initiatives in the United Kingdom, ensuring access for parties without resources. Fifthly, ethics codes must clarify that parties and counsel remain responsible for AI outcomes, while arbitrators should have powers to exclude evidence or impose adverse inferences when certifications are lacking, audit logs are missing, or there is insufficient transparency, even if the AI system is compliant under BSA. Finally, tribunals should add AI-specific annexes to procedural orders, defining use-cases, responsibilities, and validation schedules. These orders will bridge statutory gaps and suit case-specific needs. This will, in turn, help us bridge the current scenario, wherein we are at a crossroads, wherein we can devise a definitive legal framework and harness this technology to not only reform the arbitral system but also join in the government's strive to make India a hub of arbitration in the days to come.

REFERENCES

Bell, F., Bennett Moses, L., Legg, M., Silove, J., & Zalnieriute, M. (2023, December 22). *AI decision-making and the courts: A guide for judges, tribunal members and court administrators*. Australasian Institute of Judicial Administration. https://ssrn.com/abstract=4162985

Bennett Moses, L., Legg, M., Silove, J., & Zalnieriute, M. (2023, December 22). *AI decision-making and the courts: A guide for judges, tribunal members and court administrators* [with research assistance from S. Mahmood]. Australasian Institute of Judicial Administration. https://doi.org/10.2139/ssrn.4162985

Bharatiya Sakshya Adhiniyam, 2023 Act of Parliament (Act No 47 of 2023).

Christian Louboutin SAS v. The Shoe Boutique, CS(COMM) 582 of 2023 (India).

Courts of New Zealand. (2023, December 7). *Generative AI guidelines for judicial proceedings [Practice guidelines].* www.courtsofnz.govt.nz/assets/6-Going-to-Court/practice-directions/practice-guidelines/all-benches/20231207-GenAI-Guidelines-Judicial.pdf

Da Silva Moore v. Publicis Groupe & MSL Group, 287 F.R.D. 182 (S.D.N.Y. 2012).

Eftekhar, R. (2025, March). *The legal framework applicable to using AI by an arbitral tribunal.* Daily Jus. https://dailyjus.com/legal-tech/2025/03/the-legal-framework-applicable-to-using-ai-by-an-arbitral-tribunal

Giacalone, M. (2025, January 2). *AI and the future of private dispute resolution mechanisms (Draft chapter).* SSRN. https://doi.org/10.2139/ssrn.5083207.

Kattnig, M., Angerschmid, A., Reichel, T., & Kern, R. (2024). Assessing trustworthy AI: Technical and legal perspectives of fairness in AI. *Computer Law and Security Review, 55*, 106053. https://doi.org/10.1016/j.clsr.2024.106053

Larkin, K., Sherman, J., & Patel, A. (2024). Using technology and e-disclosure. In *The guide to evidence in international arbitration* (2nd ed.). Global Arbitration Review. https://globalarbitrationreview.com/guide/the-guide-evidence-in-international-arbitration/2nd-edition/article/using-technology-and-e-disclosure

Nagineni, P. (2024). The rise of AI in e-discovery: How machine learning is revolutionizing legal data processing. *International Journal of Computer Engineering and Technology (IJCET), 15*(5), 329–341. https://iaeme.com/MasterAdmin/Journal_uploads/IJCET/VOLUME_15_ISSUE_5/IJCET_15_05_031.pdf

Praštalo, B. (2024, August 23). *Arbitration Tech Toolbox: AI as an arbitrator: Overcoming the "black box" challenge*? Kluwer Arbitration Blog. https://arbitrationblog.kluwerarbitration.com/2024/08/23/arbitration-tech-toolbox-ai-as-an-arbitrator-overcoming-the-black-box-challenge/

Pyrrho Investments Ltd v MWB Property Ltd [2016] EWHC 256 (Ch).

Pyrrho Investments Ltd. v. MWB Property Ltd. & Ors., [2016] EWHC (Ch).

Rashidi, H. H., Pantanowitz, L., Dash, R., Harrison, J. H., Deebaja, M., Pantanowitz, J., & Hanna, M. G. (2025). Introduction to artificial intelligence and machine learning in pathology and medicine: Generative and nongenerative artificial intelligence basics. *Modern Pathology, 38*(4), 100705. https://doi.org/10.1016/j.modpathol.2025.01.001

Rath, A. (2025, January 14). Electronic evidence under Bharatiya Sakshya Adhiniyam. *The Legal Voice.* Supreme Court of New South Wales. (2024, November 21). *Practice note: Generative AI* [Practice note]. https://supremecourt.nsw.gov.au/documents/Practice-and-Procedure/Practice-Notes/general/current/PN_Generative_AI_21112024.pdf

White & Case LLP. (2025,June). *The 2025 international arbitration survey: Arbitration and AI.* www.whitecase.com/insight-our-thinking/2025-international-arbitration-survey-arbitration-and-ai

9 Pioneering AI in Indian Sports

Legal and Evidentiary Foundations for Tomorrow's Innovations

Subhrajit Chanda[1] *and Deevanshu Shrivastava*[2]

INTRODUCTION

Overview of AI in Sports

From player selection to performance analysis and even strategic decision-making, artificial intelligence (AI) is revolutionizing the entire sports sphere. Data intelligence through AI tools like machine learning and predictive modelling helps to augment on and off-field results through data-driven insights. In addition to talent scouting, game-enhancing applications have spread and empowered innovation and efficiency (Brady, 1985).

A major field in AI is injury prevention. Liverpool FC has adopted AI to monitor the fitness of players, predict when one might suffer injuries, and optimize training. AI helps in making real-time decisions to improve the well-being of athletes by analysing data such as biometrics and performance metrics (*KS Puttaswamy v. Union of India, 2017*). Even for strategic planning, AI is helping; an instance is basketball teams which employ a machine learning algorithm to analyze footage from past games in order to come up with counter-strategies (Cath, 2018).

AI is transforming fan engagement and broadcasting. Algorithms tailor experiences for fans, recommend content, and simulate situations. Virtual Reality (VR), AI and Natural Language Processing (NLP) can provide immersive visualization along with tracking the accurate commentary and analytics (Chatterjee, 2020). Through robotics and predictive modelling, we see further innovation in training, game outcome predictions, and decision-making, which underlines the transformative impact of AI in sports (Brady, 1985).

Contextualizing AI in Indian Sports

While AI has disrupted the world at large, AI sports adoption has been slow in India. Incorporated because of structural and regulatory reasons. Cohesive policies to integrate AI remain elusive due to governance issues, as exemplified in the case of *BCCI v. Cricket Association of Bihar* (2015). Count in ethical questions, like data privacy and algorithmic bias, and you make things more complicated. *The KS Puttaswamy v. Union of India* (2017) ruling, however, highlights the imperative of creating protective measures for athlete data and addressing other ethical risks (Cath, 2018).

Indian sports also suffer from technical expertise gaps and a reliance on traditional methods, which can delay the adoption of AI. On the contrary, global organizations are investing heavily in AI while Indian associations continue to play catch-up, constraining their competitive position on the global landscape (Chatterjee, 2020).

DOI: 10.1201/9781003629146-10

Progress is evident, despite these hurdles. There are sports-specific AI collaborations being fostered because of India's tech innovation ecosystem. In cricket, particularly the IPL, AI is being used by the umpires and for ball-tracking as well as the Hawk-Eye system (Cath, 2018).

Hence, policymakers must guide the AI adoption framework to facilitate section-level implementations. Regulatory frameworks, such as the EU's GDPR, could be useful in India in balancing innovation and data protection. Workshops can help solve the skill gap for professionals to train them in using AI (Chatterjee, 2020).

But AI will also democratize sports access in India. Data analysis can help identify talent and recommend personalized training at both school and college levels, bridging urban-rural divides (Brady, 1985). In addition, the public health impact of sports initiatives can be measured using predictive analytics, strengthening policymakers to align sports with larger developmental ambitions (Cath, 2018; Chatterjee, 2020).

GLOBAL APPLICATIONS OF AI IN SPORTS

From performance analytics and talent acquisition to strategy design and fan engagement – AI has changed the course of the global sport business by bringing in innovations. For example, Liverpool FC uses AI to predict and prevent injuries using fatigue, biomechanics and stress markers, and machine learning to optimize tactical strategies (Gawande et al., 2020). In line with this, AI-powered tools are used by Barcelona FC for scouting and acquiring talent, where they analyze video footage and statistical information to pinpoint emerging players with high potential ability, thus supporting recruitment as well as training decisions (Maity, 2019).

The Chicago Cubs, for example, use AI analytics to optimize their player rotations and game-day decisions. Combining historical data, individual metrics, and real-time factors, they find optimal player utilization assisted by wearables that emit injury risk alerts (Jha et al., 2023). From a fan engagement perspective, Getafe CF is leveraging AI to process data directly relating to the audience, ultimately facilitating engagement via personalized promotions, matchday activities, and practices that foster and build brand loyalty amongst their fans, leading to increased revenue (La Source, n.d.; SPORTFIVE, n.d.).

From biomechanical modelling and real-time game strategy adjustments to automated data visualization, innovation has continued to shape sports. Biomechanical modelling alongside wearable technology now tracks athlete movement and exposes injury risk to ensure athlete longevity (*Naruto v. Slater*, 2018). Game data is examined, and tools like real-time strategy analyze it to identify your opponent's weaknesses before providing a counter strategy for improved game outcomes. Automated visualization tools (heat maps and tactical simulations), such as, help to make complex performance data more accessible, thereby facilitating training and strategic planning (Cath, 2018).

Nor are these innovations limited to elite organizations in Europe and North America. However, the approaches taken by Liverpool FC in England, Barcelona FC in Spain and the Chicago Cubs in the US can be adapted to Indian sports teams too. With India now embracing sports science, AI-driven performance analysis and injury prevention tools can facilitate athlete development and training across disciplines.

The fortunes of organizations such as Liverpool FC, Barcelona FC, and Getafe CF show the transformative power of AI and how it can help construct a system of processes to help them become more efficient and competitive, while also enhancing fan engagement, making it omnipresent in the modern sports industry (Fierens & De Bruyne, 2020).

THE STATUS OF AI INTEGRATION IN INDIAN SPORTS

With initiatives like the National AI Strategy and other supportive programs, India's nascent AI industry can make a real impact in changing the way we play and watch sports. With AI, talent in sports can easily identify players' performance statistics, biometrics, and even behavioral patterns, and provide insights unmatched by human analysis (Chatterjee & Dohan, 2021). AI-powered tools even allow for tailored training regimens, collecting data from wearable sensors and video tracking systems to evaluate performance strengths and weaknesses. Analysis of speed, agility, endurance, etc., is available in real-time for comprehensive performance analysis (Maity, 2019).

The predictive capacities of AI greatly contribute to injury prevention, allowing for analysis of biomechanics & workload to individualize training/recovery schedules (Musat et al., 2024). These not only help players record, review, and improve their innings but also provide actionable feedback on their footwork in cricket, kicking technique in football and several other sports using video analysis tools (Kaya, 2023; Naik et al., 2022). Even AI-driven tailored nutrition plans optimize athletes' overall fitness and health management; for instance, HealthifyMe is currently transforming how people manage their health (Sharma, 2023; The Times of India, 2021). Also, performance simulations help athletes to manage high-pressure situations, enhancing decision making and competition preparedness (Richlan et al., 2023). AI further increases fan engagement via chatbots and recommendation engines, providing tailored content and strengthening loyalty.

Amidst these challenges, there are several barriers to AI adoption in Indian sports. For people without university access, this movement is hindered by limited infrastructure, especially at the grassroots level, which impairs access to motion sensors, cameras, and wearables and creates a growing divide between elite and amateur sports. High-end AI software tools remain unattainable for most semi-professional organizations. Coaches, analysts, and administrators lacking the knowledge to encourage innovative practices and use AI systems also inhibit this (Xu & Baghaei, 2025).

Digital learning is made more complicated by legal and privacy challenges surrounding AI. There is no overarching legal framework for data ownership and athlete privacy in India, similar to EU's GDPR. The uncertainty as to who rightfully owns predictive models created through AI the athletes, the teams or the developers creates further complications, especially in a cross-border context (Chatterjee, 2020).

The regulation of AI in the sports sector in India is still in its infancy. And questions about intellectual property, liability, and athlete consent are hindering large-scale adoption. For example, accountability is unclear when an AI tool wrongly predicts whether a player is fit to play or how long it will take for him to recover. Dishonesty Ethics, mistrust, and the black-box nature of AI decision processes, from player selection to injury diagnostics, feed trust issues. Addressing these concerns is critical in deriving confidence and ensuring responsible and ethical adoption of AI in Indian sports (Xu & Baghaei, 2025).

LEGAL AND REGULATORY FRAMEWORK IN INDIA

In terms of digital technology, India's legal framework, with the Information Technology Act, 2000 as its foundation, is vital in addressing issues of cybersecurity, along with electronic contracts and digital data protection. In contrast, the Act fails to adequately address the more sophisticated issues raised by AI in sport, such as what we do with real-time performance analytics or data from wearables. For example, sensitive information relating to biometric and performance-oriented data will be harvested by AI systems, demanding regulations that may include provisions to verify compliance with remaining ethical and privacy-upheld boundaries. To realistically ascertain the level of privacy available to Indians, it is essential to first note the Supreme Court's ruling in *KS Puttaswamy v. Union of India* (2017) as it laid down the law by ruling that the right to privacy was a fundamental right under Article 21 of the Constitution (Marda, 2018).

The Digital Personal Data Protection Act, 2023, updates India's data privacy laws, laying more emphasis on user consent in the processing of data, data accountability, and creating safeguards for the processing of personal data (Ebers, M., & Sein, K. (Eds.),2024; Häuselmann, A. N, 2024). However, it is silent on subtleties like who owns insights derived from AI – a challenging issue documented in Feist Publications, *Inc. v. Rural Telephone Service Co.* (1991). There are also gaps, such as absence of guidelines for monetizing AI analytics in sports, for example, in developing predictive models to evaluate players, which are increasingly becoming part of the sports ecosystem or measures to prevent algorithmic bias in AI systems for talent identification or to improve audience engagement. This highlights the importance of adopting sector-specific policies based on international best practices.

The data is up to date as of October 2023. Over the years, Indian case law has rendered pertinent insights for regulation related to AI, especially in sports. In *Star India Pvt. In the case of Ltd. v. Society of Indian Record Manufacturers* (2019), the significance of intellectual property rights in protecting proprietary content was emphasized by the court. This applies especially to AI-generated insights such as player performance predictions or fan behavior analyses that are considered intellectual property, and thus require protection through copyright laws to foster innovation and prevent misuse (WIPO, 2020). Similarly, *KS Puttaswamy v. Union of India* (2017) entrenched privacy rights and had significant implications for the governance of personal and biometric data collected via AI-led technologies. Marda argues that wearables and analytics collecting sensitive data in relation to heart rate, sleep, and calorie intake should abide by principles of legality, necessity, proportionality and informed consent (Marda, 2018). Also related to the above, in *BCCI v. Cricket Association of Bihar* (2015), the court emphasized the primacy of governance and accountability in sports administration. This precedent is especially applicable for AI applications in decision-making domains like team selection or umpiring; any oversight is a necessity for transparency and fairness (Rai, 2016).

Although the General Data Protection Regulation (GDPR) has become a gold standard of data protection internationally, and provides learning opportunities for Indian policymakers. The key GDPR principles pertaining to AI in sports include data minimization, purpose limitation, informed consent, and data subject rights (e.g. access, rectification, and erasure of personal data) (Pesapane et al., 2021; Wachter et al., 2020). They have lessons for Indian policy-makers also, such as the need to define terms like "biometric data" and "algorithmic outcomes" to avoid ambiguity create accountability mechanisms for sports organizations and AI developers, and formulate rules for safe cross-border data transfers, especially in global sports events (Scholz, 2022).

EVIDENTIARY AND ETHICAL CONSIDERATIONS: OWNERSHIP AND INTELLECTUAL PROPERTY

As sports organizations increasingly adopt AI, the issue of who owns AI-generated scouting reports, analytics, and other types of data has emerged as a pressing one. Existing intellectual property (IP) law does not sufficiently account for the complexity surrounding authorship, originality, and ownership of AI-generated content. This legal uncertainty impacts teams, tech providers, and athletes alike, highlighting the necessity for updated regulations. As Chanda observes in From Pixel to Podium, AI governance frameworks should include ethical, psychological, and legal considerations to ensure the stakeholders' rights are squarely balanced against promoting innovation (Chanda, 2024)

Key Legal Precedents

However, legal precedents can clue us into the ownership and authorship complexities at play when it comes to AI-generated works. In a different case, *Naruto v. Slater* (2018), the court decided that copyright could not be assigned to a non-human author. This brings the authorship of AI-generated content into question. When it comes to AI-driven sports analytics, who owns it: the AI's developer, the organization that employs its models, or the contributors of the training data? Adding to the complexity, originality became a requirement for copyright when *Feist Publications, Inc. v. Rural Telephone Service Co.* (1991) established the notion, and this must be determined based on creativity, which is not an easy task when dealing with machine-generated outputs.

Evidence Law is also applicable here, in terms of admissibility and especially authenticity of AI-generated content. The admissibility of electronic records is covered under sections 65A and 65B of the Indian Evidence Act (amended), and it must be proved that the system was reliable. In the context of sports, AI-generated reports or analytics would have to be shown to be free of bias or manipulation before they could serve as evidence in legal or contractual disputes. The credibility of AI systems is critical to resolving claims of ownership and liability.

Consent, Data Privacy, and Reporting Requirements

With the integration of AI technology into sports-based systems, massive volumes of sensitive athlete data, including biometrics and performance statistics, are processed and analysed, resulting in serious privacy issues. Informed consent for data collection was emphasized in the *KS Puttaswamy v. Union of India* (2017) judgment that recognized privacy as a fundamental right. Athletes need to know how their data is being collected, processed, and used.

While the Draft Digital Personal Data Protection Bill (2022) is a positive starting point, the respective Act does not provide specific considerations for the entry of AI into the world of sports, especially when it comes to cross-border data sharing during international tournaments and storage of biometric data. Informed consent mechanisms, transparent data policies, and reporting requirements should be part of robust governance frameworks, protecting the mental as well as the legal well-being of athletes (Chatterjee, 2020). Principles underlying Evidence Law emphasize the importance of keeping direct, well-understood records of consent and contracts of usage of data, such that the records can withstand challenge.

Algorithmic Bias and Transparency

AI systems can suffer from algorithmic biases that compromise talent scouting, player evaluations, and game strategies. For example, biases may be widely spread on information that favors certain physical traits, resulting in unfair outcomes. To prevent this from happening, we must conduct regular audits of AI algorithms and ensure that they have transparent decision-making processes. Principles of Evidence Law are at work validating the objectivity of AI-powered determinations, in which stakeholders can dispute biased or opaque algorithms.

The decision of the court in *White v. Samsung Electronics America, Inc.* (1993) stressed that clear ownership and rights were particularly important with new technologies. This principle is not different for any AI systems, including those used in sports, where biases in algorithms and opacity can erode trust. To be accepted, however, AI systems must be developed with fairness, accountability, and explainability at their focus; their outputs must be ethical, trustworthy, and legally justifiable.

PROPOSING A FUTURE-FOCUSED FRAMEWORK

A well-defined governance framework is critical for the effective and ethical deployment of AI within the domain of Indian sports. It must also be designed to promote fairness, transparency, and privacy while also encouraging innovation. Indian sports administration will form its own pillars for AI governance.

Data Ownership and Rights

As AI players continue to thrive, one of the major challenges will be who owns these AI-generated insights and data, and the absence of regulations on ownership can lead to unnecessary friction between the primary stakeholders in the sporting ecosystem, including the players, team owners, and AI technology providers. We need to resolve the ambiguities around whether data belongs to athletes (the source of data), to teams (the primary users) or to developers of AI-based technology (the creators of insights). There must be implementing legislation establishing ownership of data generated by AI things. Hoping to align with Article 20 of GDPR (portability), Indian governance frameworks should advocate for throwing the keys to the kingdom for an athlete, putting them in charge of their own data points. As Marda points out, data rights must remain at the forefront of decision-making for athletes (Marda, 2018).

Informed Consent

The procedures through which consents are taken must be standardized; this is a must to help athletes know how their data is collected, processed, and utilized (Khan et al. (Eds.), 2024). Initially developed in the context of medical practice, the principle of informed consent, entrenched in global privacy laws and the landmark case *KS Puttaswamy v. Union of India (*2017), dictates that consent should be given voluntarily, be specific, and based on sufficient information (Brady, 1985). Create digital consent forms and dashboards for athletes to observe, approve, or request their data permission settings (similar to credit reports). Finally, consent mechanisms should be re-evaluated regularly for their validity.

Privacy Safeguards

Strong data protection policies will be crucial to prevent sensitive athlete data from being abused, including biomechanical and performance metrics. Based on the GDPR, Indian sports organizations can adopt pseudonymization, encryption, and shortened data retention periods, furthering their mission to establish a unique identity for their sports. Additionally, India's promised Digital Personal Data Protection Bill (2022) lays down robust legislative levers that can be appropriately drafted to delineate sports-specific data privacy precepts.

Algorithmic Transparency

AI methodologies thus, should be transparent to ensure trust by all stakeholders and fairness. AI models tend to be "black boxes" that aren't easily interpreted, making it difficult to understand the mechanics behind decisions, be it player scouting or predicting injury risk. In order to tackle this problem, AI developers must share methodologies, decision-making processes and data sources. Transparency is crucial in preventing biases and ensuring accountability. Zaufal also cited FIFA's AI and Technology Regulations (2023), which insist on transparency by the providers of AI tools used for match analysis, setting a standard for the world.

Ethical Oversight

Nonetheless, in order to avoid athletes getting hurt and to preserve equity, the introduction of AI in sports ought to be codified by ethics. Plus, to avoid misalignment with moral codes and international standards (Jha et al., 2023), independent ethical oversight committees must be created to assess AI implementations in sports. Such committees could be centered around algorithmic fairness, player privacy, and the mental health of players impacted by decisions driven by AI technologies, for example. Ethics training must be included in AI-specific programs for sports professionals to make them aware of ethical dilemmas.

Policy Implications and Recommendations

The logic presented in the previous paragraph establishes a need for comprehensive legislation that properly addresses AI in the sporting world, and in order to operationalize the framework provided. Laws must establish data ownership, athlete rights, and ethical data practices, and be harmonized with international practices such as the General Data Protection Regulation (GDPR), while addressing India-specific challenges. Public Private Partnerships (PPP) can also be paramount in providing funds for AI sports infrastructure, which demonstrates the role of PPPs as an accelerator in AI adoption by, for instance, pooling resources and expertise. In addition to this, we should subsidize new & cutting-edge AI hardware for grassroots sports, & build multiple innovation hubs for AI Research & development specifically for Indian challenges to solve.

Such programs should aim to upskill sports professionals, including coaches, analysts, and administrators, on the technology and the ethical considerations surrounding AI technologies. The curriculum should address themes of AI-powered performance analysis, injury prediction, and the ethical use of data, which should be grounded in global reference points such as UEFA's Centre of Excellence for AI in Football. In addition, Indian sports bodies could draw on FIFA's AI and Technology Regulations (2023) that emphasize transparency, data security, and athlete well-being as local guidelines mirroring global best practices.

CONCLUSION

How AI Could Reshape (or Ruin) Sports Forever

AI has the potential to transform sports to optimize performance management, injury prevention, and talent acquisition. These advancements offer methods for data-driven conclusions with a much more capable and productive preparation and technique improvement. AI tools can monitor athletes and their modus operandi, schedule optimum recovery, analyze data patterns of player data globally, offer insights for both talent and performance, and suggest feedback in real-time. But with these opportunities come significant legal, ethical, and technological challenges. These issues, such as data ownership, privacy, system bias, and transparency, can destroy trust in AI systems and result in key issues of accountability and fairness. This duality of AI in sports illustrates that the euphoria around newer technologies must be matched with strong governance. Without any clear frameworks, the potential exists for AI misuse, inequity, and marginalization for athletes, particularly at the grassroots level. Addressing these challenges is of paramount importance not only for generating trust and fairness across the sports ecosystem but also for ensuring that AI works to distribute its benefits across the damages horizontal.

Bridging the Gap of Law, Ethics, and Technology

But for this potential to be realized, urgent measures are needed to plug deep deficits in law, ethics, and technology to enable India to lead the way in the ethical and responsible integration of AI in sports. It is ineffective to regulate the nuances of AI in sports through intellectual property rights and existing data protection laws. Big questions remain about the ownership of a scouting report or other information generated by AI that an athlete would typically garner as a product of good scouting, opening the door for disputes among athletes, teams, and AI developers. To ensure the protection of an athlete's interests, determine data ownership, and instill accountability in AI-driven decisions, strong AI-specific regulations are required. On the ethical front, algorithmic bias and athletes' mental health from intrusive monitoring represent significant challenges. For example, biases in talent scouting systems can disadvantage athletes from marginalized geographic areas or economic backgrounds. Integrating ethical oversight such as independent review boards will guarantee the fairness, transparency, and inclusivity of AI adoption. On the tech side, poor access to AI infrastructure at the grassroots level is perpetuating the divide between elite and amateur sports. Public-private partnerships (PPPs) thrive in this domain where AI technologies require funding for research and development; education solutions need to be established for the industry alongside affordable solutions for the organizations in the area.

What It Means for India to Be a Leader in the World

India stands on the cusp of a watershed moment as far as AI in sports is concerned. Under this prescient governance model, the nation will be a model for global sport. Such framework must not only align with the global best practices in data protection and security (such as the GDPR) or the FIFA's AI and Technology Regulations (2023) but also should address the peculiar challenges faced by the Indian sports ecosystem (Ebers & Sein, 2024). To achieve this, sports policymaking, stakeholder organizations, private tech companies, and academic institutions need to work together like a think-tank to devise a sustainable framework for AI governance within the industry. Focusing on athletes, transparency, and using cutting-edge practices can make India not just a follower, but a leader in this exciting new frontier.

Call to Action

Sports are not just a tech play for AI; it is also a social and moral issue. By working together, stakeholders of all types have the opportunity to build a holistic yet equitable and transparent system that grows the sports ecosystem but does so without compromising the rights or welfare of athletes. As these disparate strands of law, ethics, and technology weave together, India stands at the threshold of leading this transformative paradigm. By the judicious use of the double-edged sword of AI, India may raise the future of the governance of sports to a level never reached in the developed world, and offer the world transformation, using the nascent but powerful tools of AI integration and the innovative, but judicious, use of AI penetration in sports management.

NOTES

1 Assistant Professor and Assistant Director, Centre for Sports Law, Business and Governance (CSLBG), Jindal Global Law School, OP Jindal Global University, Sonipat, India; **Email ID:** schanda@jgu.edu.in

2 Associate Dean & Associate Professor, School of Law, GD Goenka University, Gate No 3, GD Goenka Educational City, Sohna, Sohna Rural, India. **Email ID:** deevanshu.shrivastava@gmail.com.

REFERENCES

BCCI v. Cricket Association of Bihar, (2015) 3 SCC 251.

Brady, M. (1985). Artificial intelligence and robotics. *Artificial Intelligence, 26*(1), 79. https://doi.org/10.1016/0004-3702(85)90013-x

Cath, C. (2018). Governing artificial intelligence: Ethical, legal and technical opportunities and challenges. *Philosophical Transactions of the Royal Society A: Mathematical, Physical and Engineering Sciences, 376*(2133), 20180080. https://doi.org/10.1098/rsta.2018.0080

Chanda, M. S. (2024). From pixel to podium: AI's impact on sports governance and psychological well-being. *Education and Society शि± ण आणि समाज, 47*(1).

Chatterjee, S. (2020). AI strategy of India: Policy framework, adoption challenges and actions for government. *Transforming Government: People, Process and Policy, 14*(5), 757–775. https://doi.org/10.1108/tg-05-2019-0031

Chatterjee, S., & Dohan, M. S. (2021). Artificial intelligence for healthcare in India. *International Journal of Healthcare Information Systems and Informatics, 16*(4), 1. www.researchgate.net/publication/354999164_Artificial_Intelligence_for_Healthcare_in_India_Policy_Initiatives_Challenges_and_Recommendations

Ebers, M., & Sein, K. (Eds.). (2024). *Privacy, data protection and data-driven technologies* (1st ed.). Routledge. https://doi.org/10.4324/9781003502791

Feist Publications, Inc. v. Rural Telephone Service Co., 499 U.S. 340 (1991).

Fierens, M., & De Bruyne, J. (2020, August 21). *Artificial intelligence in sports – The legal and ethical issues at play*. LawInSport. Retrieved January 27, 2025, from www.lawinsport.com/topics/item/artificial-intelligence-in-sports-the-legal-and-ethical-issues-at-play

FIFA. (2023). *AI and technology regulations*. Federation Internationale de Football Association.

Gawande, V., Badi, H. A., & Makharoumi, K. A. (2020). An empirical study on emerging trends in artificial intelligence and its impact on higher education. *International Journal of Computer Applications, 175*(12), 43. https://doi.org/10.5120/ijca2020920642

Häuselmann, A. N. (2024). *EU privacy and data protection law applied to AI: Unveiling the legal problems for individuals* (Doctoral thesis). Universiteit Leiden. Retrieved from https://scholarlypublications.universiteitleiden.nl/handle/1887/3747996

Jha, D., et al. (2023). Ensuring trustworthy medical artificial intelligence through ethical and philosophical principles. *arXiv*. https://doi.org/10.48550/arxiv.2304.11530

Kaya, F. (2023). Artificial intelligence and its use in sports. In *Spor Bilimleri ve Egzersizde Bütünsel Yaklaşımlar* (pp. 121–129). Gazi Kitapevi. https://orcid.org/0000-0003-4007-9561. Retrieved from www.researchgate.net

Khan, I. U., Ouaissa, M., Ouaissa, M., Fayaz, M., & Ullah, R. (Eds.). (2024). *Artificial intelligence for intelligent systems: Fundamentals, challenges, and applications* (1st ed.). CRC Press. https://doi.org/10.1201/9781003496410

KS Puttaswamy v. Union of India, (2017) 10 SCC 1.

La Source. (n.d.). *Digital transformation at Getafe CF*. Retrieved January 27, 2025, from www.lasource.io/news/digital-transformation-getafe-cf

Maity, S. (2019). Identifying opportunities for artificial intelligence in the evolution of training and development practices. *Journal of Management Development, 38*(8), 651–663. https://doi.org/10.1108/jmd-03-2019-0069

Marda, V. (2018). Artificial intelligence policy in India: A framework for engaging the limits of data-driven decision-making. *Philosophical Transactions of the Royal Society A: Mathematical, Physical and Engineering Sciences, 376*(2133), 20180087. https://doi.org/10.1098/rsta.2018.0087

Ministry of Electronics and Information Technology, India. (2022). *Draft Digital Personal Data Protection Bill*. Government of India.

Musat, C. L., Mereuta, C., Nechita, A., Tutunaru, D., Voipan, A. E., Voipan, D., Mereuta, E., Gurau, T. V., Gurău, G., & Nechita, L. C. (2024). Diagnostic applications of AI in sports: A comprehensive review of injury risk prediction methods. *Diagnostics*, 14(22), 2516. https://doi.org/10.3390/diagnostics14222516

Naik, B. T., Hashmi, M. F., & Bokde, N. D. (2022). A comprehensive review of computer vision in sports: Open issues, future trends and research directions. *Applied Sciences, 12*(9), 4429.

Naruto v. Slater, 2018 WL 1902414 (9th Cir. 2018).

Pesapane, F., Volonté, C., Codari, M., et al. (2018). Artificial intelligence as a medical device in radiology: Ethical and regulatory issues in Europe and the United States. *Insights Imaging* **9**, 745–753 (2018). https://doi.org/10.1007/s13244-018-0645-y

Rai, A. (2016). Governance in Indian sports: The impact of judicial intervention. *Indian Journal of Sports Law.* Retrieved from https://journals.sagepub.com

Richlan, F., Weiß, M., Kastner, P., & Braid, J. (2023). Virtual training, real effects: A narrative review on sports performance enhancement through interventions in virtual reality. *Frontiers in Psychology, 14*, 1240790. https://pmc.ncbi.nlm.nih.gov/articles/PMC10622803/

Scholz, T. (2022). Regulating cross-border data flows in sports: Lessons from GDPR. *International Review of Law, Computers & Technology.* Retrieved from www.researchgate.net

Sharma, D. (2023, August 23). *HealthifyMe: The life-changing magic of tidying up your fitness habits with an AI coach.* ConsumerTech & Healthcare Commentary. Retrieved January 28, 2025, from https://blume.vc/commentaries/healthifyme-the-life-changing-magic-of-tidying-up-your-fitness-habits-with-an-ai-coach

SPORTFIVE. (n.d.). *Artificial intelligence: Digital support for fan experience.* Beyond the Match. Retrieved January 27, 2025, from https://sportfive.com/beyond-the-match/insights/artificial-intelligence-digital-support-for-fan-experience

Star India Pvt. Ltd. v. Society of Indian Record Manufacturers, (2019) SCC OnLine SC 746.

The Times of India. (2021, July 5). *Decoding how HealthifyMe is empowering people to pursue fitness from their homes.* Retrieved January 28, 2025, from https://timesofindia.indiatimes.com/spotlight/decoding-how-healthifyme-is-empowering-people-to-pursue-fitness-from-their-homes/articleshow/84057186.cms

Wachter, S., Mittelstadt, B., & Floridi, L. (2020). Why a right to explanation of automated decision-making does not exist in the General Data Protection Regulation. *International Data Privacy Law, 7*(2), 76–99. Retrieved from https://journals.sagepub.com

White v. Samsung Electronics America, Inc., 971 F.2d 1395 (9th Cir. 1993*).*

WIPO. (2020). Intellectual property and artificial intelligence: Key issues and challenges. *World Intellectual Property Organization.* Retrieved from www.wipo.int

Xu, T., & Baghaei, S. (2025). Reshaping the future of sports with artificial intelligence: Challenges and opportunities in performance enhancement, fan engagement, and strategic decision-making. *Engineering Applications of Artificial Intelligence*, *142*, 109912. https://doi.org/10.1016/j.engappai.2024.109912

10 Predictive Policing Meets Procedural Law

Crafting Admissibility Standards for AI-Driven Forensic Tools in Indian Criminal Justice

Abhivardhan[1] and Supratim Bapuli[2]

THE CURRENT LANDSCAPE OF AI IN INDIAN CRIMINAL JUSTICE

The evolution of Artificial Intelligence ("AI") began with Alan Turing's 1950 question, "Can machines think?," followed by Herbert Simon's work on overcoming human cognitive limits. Although no universal definition exists, AI is broadly understood as machine-based systems that perceive environments, model inputs, and produce outcomes like recommendations and decisions and has been defined as an umbrella term. AI goals vary: the engineering perspective focuses on task performance, while the cognitive view aims to replicate human cognition. AI systems may be either rule-based (using logical commands) or learning-based (employing algorithms like neural networks). Now, Big Data-enabled AI's expansion beyond research into private and government sectors. AI assists or replaces human decisions in sectors including finance, military, and law. While the use of automation and AI supplements various means of dispute resolutions, the technology's lack of explainability and vendor-related issues still make AI adoption complicated. Despite international law's slow adaptability, courts might pivot to early adoption of AI (*Dimitropoulos, 2023*).

The rise of AI research in legal technology may offer possibilities to India's criminal justice system for precision and expedience, as a spectrum of institutional limitations and ethical quandaries is unveiled. Despite global advances in AI research, India's integration of AI remains uneven and largely experimental. This contrast is shaped by deep structural imbalances between urban judicial bodies and rural or lower-tiered courts, which include infrastructural deficiencies, especially in district courts, struggling with outdated record-keeping systems and overburdened caseloads. Nevertheless, according to the Supreme Court of India, AI and ML have been utilized for case management and transcription of oral arguments in Constitution Bench matters under a competent authority in cooperation with the apex court's registry *(Ministry of Law and Justice, 2025b).*

The Indian judiciary is undergoing a transformative shift through the integration of AI to address longstanding issues like case backlogs, language barriers, and procedural inefficiencies. In law enforcement, predictive policing models, drone surveillance, facial recognition, and AI-based forensic tools are reshaping investigation methods. Platforms such as CCTNS, e-Prisons, and e-Forensics are being strengthened with AI-driven analytics for improved crime tracking. The Vimarsh 2023 Hackathon, organised by the DoT and BPR&D, showcased innovations including AI-assisted FIR systems and AR-based crime scene analysis. These initiatives collectively reflect a strategic push toward a more efficient, transparent, and technologically empowered justice system in India *(Ministry of Law and Justice, 2025a).*

DOI: 10.1201/9781003629146-11

In 2022, the United States led globally in private AI investments at $47.4 billion—about 3.5 times China's amount. While Europe, for instance, lags behind China and North America in AI development, the European Union is actively working to boost AI adoption and has adopted a stringent Artificial Intelligence Act *(Marti, 2024)*.

Country	Regulatory Model	Key Laws/Initiatives	Focus Areas
United States	Decentralized, sector-specific regulation with no comprehensive federal AI law	FTC guidelines, NHTSA rules, California Consumer Privacy Act (CCPA)	Consumer protection, autonomous vehicle safety, state-level data governance
European Union	Proactive and rights-based centralized model	General Data Protection Regulation (GDPR), Proposed Artificial Intelligence Act	Privacy, ethical AI, transparency, accountability
China	Centralized, government-led strategy integrating ethics and national goals	Cybersecurity Law, New Generation AI Development Plan	AI dominance by 2030, ethical use, cybersecurity, data protection
Canada	Balanced regulatory model supporting innovation and ethics	Pan-Canadian AI Strategy, Canadian AI Ethics Council, PIPEDA	Ethical AI development, privacy protection, responsible innovation
Australia	Principle-based ethical regulation with sectoral enforcement	National AI Ethics Framework, enforced by ACCC	Ethical design, competition compliance, consumer protection

[1.1] This table presents a comparative overview of AI regulatory frameworks across five major jurisdictions.

EVIDENCE FRAMEWORK UNDER THE BHARATIYA SAKSHYA ADHINIYAM: A LITERATURE REVIEW

The journey from the Indian Evidence Act, 1872 ("**IEA**") to the Bharatiya Sakshya Sanhita, 2023 ("**BSS**") is pivotal in India's legal history, since such a rich legacy of evolution of Indian evidence law espouses the need to strengthen and modernize evidence law in the digital age. The IEA, drafted by Sir James Fitzjames Stephen during British Rule, was a unifying statute that standardized evidentiary principles across Indian courts. Rooted in English common law, it codified rules on oral and documentary evidence, burden of proof, and witness examination—offering a revolutionary legal framework for its time. However, it was deeply reliant on physical forms of proof and became increasingly inadequate in the face of digitalization (Ganguli, 2024).

However, the Supreme Court had reaffirmed that a certificate under Section 65B(4) of the IEA is mandatory for the admissibility of electronic records. This ruling resolved inconsistencies from earlier decisions in *Tomaso Bruno (Tomaso Bruno & Anr. v. State of U.P., 2015)* and *Shafhi Mohammad (Shafhi Mohammad v. State of Himachal Pradesh, 2018)*, which had diluted the requirement. The Court emphasised that Section 65B is a complete code, and compliance with both Sections 65(B)(2) and 65(B)(4) is essential. It had overruled the earlier *Navjot Sandhu* judgment and upheld *Anvar P.V. v. P.K. Basheer (Anvar P.V. v. P.K. Basheer & Ors, 2014)*, clarifying that oral evidence cannot replace the mandatory certificate. However, where the original device is presented, the certificate is not required. In networked systems, the certificate must accompany the reproduced copy. If the concerned authority fails to issue a certificate, courts can compel production through procedural laws. Importantly, the certificate can be filed at any time before the trial concludes. The

Court directed telecom and internet service providers to securely retain call records to ensure proper authentication during trials. It also called for new Information Technology Act ("**IT**") rules covering data retention, metadata preservation, chain of custody, and stamping protocols to avoid evidence loss or corruption during extended litigation (Mehta et al., 2020).

As India progressed, the limitations of the IEA became evident. The emergence of electronic communication, cybercrime and online transactions posed challenges that the IEA—despite amendments via the IT Act, 2000—could not fully resolve. The Act also struggled to reflect evolving societal and constitutional values. Moreover, its rigid procedures contributed to juridical backlogs, exposing the need for a flexible and efficient framework. In response, the BSS was enacted in 2023, as part of a comprehensive overhaul of criminal laws. It integrates mechanisms for collecting, preserving, and admitting digital evidence, expands the definition of admissibility to include digital signatures and forensic data, and aligns closely with privacy and liberty under constitutional mandates. By simplifying procedures and enabling speedy trials, the BSS addresses both technological and procedural deficiencies, marking a shift from colonial rigidity to a forward-looking, rights-based evidentiary regime.

Under the Bharatiya Sakshya Adhiniyam ("BSA"), AI-generated content might be classified as digital or electronic evidence, aligning with the broader definition of documents to include emails, server logs, and files on digital devices. While this appears to formalize existing practices from the IEA, it does not represent a substantive legal shift. Digital evidence may be primary or secondary, but AI outputs struggle to qualify as primary due to the lack of AI explainability, i.e., in explaining how AI systems reach decisions. Justice Pratibha M. Singh had also noted the unreliability of such evidence, citing issues like hallucinations (Jha, 2023). Even classifying AI-generated outputs as secondary evidence is problematic, as authentication under Section 63 requires a certificate from someone in charge of the system, which is difficult due to the multi-layered development of AI. Moreover, the evolving, complicated, and often self-learning nature of AI challenges the applicability of Section 63, which was originally designed for simpler digital technologies (Pol & Karthik, 2024).

Aspect	Indian Evidence Act, 1872	Bharatiya Sakshya Sanhita, 2023
Digital Evidence Recognition	Introduced via IT Act, 2000; Section 65B mandates strict certification	Simplifies admission; focuses on authenticity and reliability over procedural formalities
Authentication Methods	Relies on Section 65B certificate	Accepts digital signatures, cryptographic keys, and tech-based validation
Evidentiary Standards	Prefers primary evidence; digital records often treated as secondary	Recognizes duplicability; values integrity over form
Chain of Custody	No specific legal framework	Explicit mandates on maintaining chain of custody for digital records
Privacy & Data Protection	Limited protections	Aligns with modern data protection norms; respects personal data rights
Presumptions on Digital Records	Narrow (e.g., Sec. 85A on digital contracts)	Broader presumptions on emails, metadata, and blockchain records

[2.1] This table outlines the key differences between the IEA, 1872, and the BSS, 2023, with a focus on the treatment and admissibility of digital evidence.

DISSECTING AI FORENSIC TOOLS: TECHNICAL FRAMEWORK FOR ADMISSIBILITY

The admissibility of AI-generated forensic evidence in Indian courts remains mired in procedural uncertainty due to the absence of domestic validation protocols. As of now, the Bureau of Indian Standards ("**BIS**") has not issued AI-specific testing frameworks. Consequently, forensic agencies rely on international protocols, notably the National Institute of Standards and Technology's ("**NIST**") Computer Forensic Tool Testing Program ("**CFTT**"). The CFTT standardizes the testing of digital forensic tools through defined functions, test environments, and reproducibility mechanisms to ensure credibility and consistency. Complementing this, NIST's Digital Forensics Program and the National Software Reference Library ("**NSRL**") allow Indian agencies to benchmark tools against established hash datasets, reducing the risk of misidentification or software anomalies (National Institute of Standards and Technology, n.d.).

Standard / Framework / Case	Key Points	Application/Impact
ISO/IEC 27037:2012 *(International Organization for Standardization, 2012)*	Outlines best practices for handling digital evidence; invoked in absence of BIS regulations	Not tailored to India's linguistic, technical, or legal peculiarities
Beckett-Slay-Guo Framework	Functionality-oriented validation framework; mapping core EE functions (searching, preservation) into testable subcategories; modular model	Enables precise, scalable validation; individual EE tool functions tested independently; enhancing forensic reliability and ISO accreditation readiness; streamline tool certification; bolster admissibility arguments under Section 65(B) BSA *(Guo et al., 2009)*
DNA Evidence	Backed by probabilistic models; scientific precision and adherence to chain of custody protocols; meets Section 65(B) standards through detailed certification under Sections 61–64 Bharatiya Sakshya Adhiniyam, 2023 *(Chetty & Ali, 2024)*	**Cases:** State of Maharashtra v. Prakash Mangal Gopal; Karnataka High Court relied on DNA profiling in Machindra v. Sajjan Galfa Rankhamb and Ors.
AI forensic tools in India	Lack standardised error metrics; operate without uniform admissibility standards	Given India's linguistic and demographic diversity, developing documented error rates and validation protocols essential; ensure AI–generated evidence meets admissibility threshold and maintains judicial credibility
Daubert v. Merrell Dow (1993)	Establishing criteria for scientific evidence admissibility; key factors: testability, peer review, known error rates, general acceptance *(Daubert v. Merrell Dow Pharmaceuticals, Inc., 1993)*	Error rates as critical—principle Indian courts should adopt to assess reliability of AI forensic tools and ensure evidentiary integrity
Anvar P.V. v. P.K. Basheer (2014)	Electronic evidence inadmissible without certificate under Section 65(B) IEA, issued at time of acquisition; electronic records must meet four conditions under Section 65(B) *(Anvar P.V. v. P.K. Basheer & Ors, 2014)*	Including being produced by computer in regular course of activity and maintaining data continuity

[3.1] This table outlines certain Indian and international admissibility requirements around digital evidence.

AI systems often transform raw digital data—such as CCTV footage, audio recordings, or text inputs—into derivative outputs using algorithms. For instance, AI may enhance video quality, convert speech-to-text, or detect patterns. These transformations are not mere reproductions but involve interpretive computation, which may affect the evidentiary value. As a result, courts may require step-by-step documentation of each processing stage to verify the reliability of the final output. This includes logging algorithmic inputs, transformation logic, system versioning, and any human intervention. To align with the principles of *Anvar*, the BSA must incorporate AI-specific chain of custody protocols that ensure transparency, reproducibility, and judicial confidence in AI-derived evidence.

CONSTITUTIONAL IMPLICATIONS AND RIGHTS PROTECTION

The lack of explainability in AI systems presents a fundamental challenge to the principles of transparency and due process enshrined under Article 21 of the Indian Constitution. This concept refers to situations where the internal decision-making logic of AI systems remains opaque, even to the individuals affected by their outcomes which can have serious implications, with regard to criminal justice. The table below summarizes keys constitutional law implications under Article 21, which might be adequately related to AI explainability in the context of evidence laws.

Legal Provision/Case	Key Points
Maneka Gandhi v. Union of India	Article 21 expanded: Fairness, procedural integrity in criminal trials *(Maneka Gandhi v. Union of India, 1978).*
Shiv Kumar v. Hukam Chand	Emphasized prosecutorial transparency *(Shiv Kumar v. Hukam Chand & Anr, 1999).*
State of Madhya Pradesh v. Chintaman Sadashiva Waishampayan	Right to cross-examination intrinsic to natural justice *(State of Madhya Pradesh v. Chintaman Sadashiva Waishampayan, 1960).*
Article 20(3) of the Constitution of India, 1949	Protects against self-incrimination; accused cannot be compelled to testify against themselves.
Selvi v. State of Karnataka	Involuntary narco/polygraph tests violate Articles 20(3) & 21; unreliable, risks false outcomes, undermines "beyond reasonable doubt." Voluntary test results admissible under Section 27, IEA *(Selvi & Ors v. State of Karnataka & Anr, 2010).*

[4.1] This table depicts key constitutional law provisions and case laws around Article 21 of the Indian Constitution.

A LEGAL FRAMEWORK FOR AI EVIDENCE ADMISSIBILITY: STANDARDS AND SAFEGUARDS

With the enactment of the Bharatiya Sakshya Adhiniyam, 2023, effective from 1st July 2024, Section 65B of the old Evidence Act has been replaced by Section 63, refining the legal regime for electronic evidence. The historical relevance of *State of Tamil Nadu v. Suhas Katti (State of Tamil Nadu v. Suhas Katti, 2004)*, where Naavi submitted the first 65B certificate for internet-based evidence, highlights the judiciary's early engagement with digital proof.

- o Section 63(1)–(5) now codifies stringent admissibility standards, treating computer output as documentary evidence subject to specific operational conditions under Section 63(2), and recognizing networks and intermediaries as a unified evidentiary source under Section 63(3).

- o Section 63(4) requires a certificate detailing device use, data handling, and compliance, signed by an unauthorized person or expert.
- o This framework remedies inconsistencies arising from *Afzal Guru (State (NCT of Delhi) v. Navjot Sandhu @ Afzal Guru, 2005)* and *Shafi Mohammed (Shafhi Mohammad v. State of Himachal Pradesh, 2018)*, which were later clarified in *Arjun Panditrao Khotkar (Arjun Panditrao Khotkar v. Kailash Kushanrao Gorantyal & Ors, 2020)*. The prescribed certificate format under Section 63(4)(c) further institutionalizes procedural uniformity. CEAC now transitions to issuing "Section 63 BSA Certificates," aligning with contemporary mandates, including those under Digital Personal Data Protection Act, 2023.

The admissibility of expert testimony under Sections 39 and 40 of the BSA represents a critical evolution in evidentiary law, particularly in light of growing reliance on scientific and technical inputs in judicial proceedings.

Legal Provision / Case	Key Points
Section 39	Expert opinions admissible only for matters beyond court's understanding, must be scientifically grounded and judicially robust *(Selvi & Ors v. State of Karnataka & Anr, 2010).*
Section 40	Expert opinions require recognized expertise and independent corroboration; forensic testimony is probative but not conclusive *(Murari Lal S/O Ram Singh v. State of Madhya Pradesh, 1979)*; opinions inferential, not substantive *(S. Gopal Reddy v. State of Andhra Pradesh, 1996).*

[5.1] This table summarises the conceptual aspects of expert testimony admissibility under Sections 39 and 40 of the BSA.

Now, in patent law, as per the latest revised draft Computer-Related Inventions Guidelines Version 2.0 by the Indian Patent Office, while AI-related inventions are categorized into AI-generated and AI-assisted inventions *(Indian Patent Office, 2025)*, the proposed legal understanding differs in both categories:

- o AI-generated inventions may not be regarded as "patentable" since the assumption is that there is quite limited to zero human intervention, which is why AI systems cannot be designated as a "Person" claiming to be the true and first inventor of an invention under Section 6 of the Patents Act, 1970 *(Indian Patent Office, 2025).*
- o AI-assisted inventions, however, involving AI as an inventive tool in building something is regarded by the Patent Office as an add-on, which is why they believe that such kinds of inventions are not categorically non-patentable under Section 3(k) of the Patents Act, 1970 *(Indian Patent Office, 2025).*

Developers and corporations have turned to trade secret protection as a primary safeguard. Proprietary algorithms, like those behind ChatGPT and Google Gemini, are closely guarded, with usage governed by restrictive contractual clauses to prevent reverse engineering.

Case/Concept	Core Understanding to Be Inferred from these Cases and Concepts
Golikari v. Century Spinning	Confidential manufacturing methods are protected via injunctive relief.
Daljit Titus & Burlington Home Shopping	Courts uphold protection of commercial secrecy, including client lists.

Case/Concept	Core Understanding to Be Inferred from these Cases and Concepts
Levandowski Case (U.S.)	Misappropriation of trade secrets can lead to criminal consequences *(United States v. Levandowski, 2020).*

[5.2] This table depicts certain case laws on invoking trade secret protections as a primary safeguard for proprietary algorithms.

A set of standards is therefore proposed in line with the Prayagraj Principles on Responsible and Accessible Legal Automation Technologies proposed by the Indian Society of Artificial Intelligence and Law *(Indian Society of Artificial Intelligence and Law, 2025)*, and existing Indian evidence law instruments, i.e., *Evidentiary Standards on Automation and Explainability*. The table below outlines the set of proposed standards, as summarized.

Standard Proposed	Context
Algorithmic Processing Transparency	o **Court-Accessible Explanations**: AI evidence inadmissible unless reasoning explained in plain language accessible to legal professionals without technical expertise
Evidentiary Chain Integrity	o **Authority Classification**: Clear distinction between binding precedent, persuasive authority, and non-authoritative sources in AI training data should be made o **Source Verification Protocol**: Comprehensive documentation and accuracy verification of all sources relied upon
Training Dataset Transparency	o **Source Attribution Framework**: AI systems must reveal training data sources with forensic methods for tracing outputs to original sources o **Open-Source Verification**: Make attribution methods open-source for independent validation
Human Engagement and Testimony Integrity	o **Comprehensive AI Disclosure**: All witnesses must reveal AI assistance in testimony preparation, analysis, or live proceedings with specific tools, versions, and confidence levels to gain no-objection to their testimonies submitted o **Cross-Examination AI Literacy**: Opposing counsel entitled to question witnesses about AI tools, limitations, and biases o **Documentation Protocol**: Clear chain of custody for human vs. AI contributions with sworn certification

[5.3] Proposed Evidentiary Standards on Automation and Explainability.

CONCLUSION AND POLICY RECOMMENDATIONS

India's transition from Section 65B to Section 63 BSA represents a foundational shift, yet AI evidence challenges the demand targeted interventions beyond traditional electronic evidence frameworks. The constitutional tension between Article 21's due process guarantees and AI systems' inherent opacity requires careful legislative and judicial attention. In line with the evidentiary standards proposed, the following recommendations are put forth:

1. Transition CEAC from basic certificate issuance to AI evidence validation authority
2. Develop AI-specific certification protocols under Section 63(4) BSA framework
3. Create specialized "AI Evidence Certificates" with algorithmic transparency requirements

4. Mandate technical training for judicial officers to handle AI-related evidentiary challenges
5. Develop "AI Miranda Rights" requiring disclosure of AI assistance in testimony preparation
6. Establish minimum explainability thresholds for AI evidence in criminal cases
7. Create appellate review protocols for AI evidence admissibility disputes

NOTES

1 Abhivardhan is a Technology Law Specialist and an AI Governance Consultant. He is additionally, the President & Managing Trustee of the Indian Society of Artificial Intelligence and Law & the Managing Partner of Indic Pacific Legal Research. The author may be reached at connect@abhivardhan.com.

2 Supratim Bapuli is a Student at Symbiosis Law School, Hyderabad. The author may be reached at 21010323131@student.slsh.edu.in.

References

Anvar P.V. v. P.K. Basheer & Ors, (2014) 10 SCC 473 (India).

Arjun Panditrao Khotkar v. Kailash Kushanrao Gorantyal & Ors, Civil Appeal Nos. 20825-20826 of 2017 (India 2020).

Chetty, S. M. M., & Ali, H. (2024, May 12). Evaluating the role of DNA evidence in criminal trials: Analyzing admissibility, reliability, and judicial impact in Karnataka. *Educational Administration: Theory and Practice*, *30*(5), 15572–15583. https://doi.org/10.53555/kuey.v30i5.9924

Daubert v. Merrell Dow Pharmaceuticals, Inc., 509 U.S. 579 (1993).

Dimitropoulos, G. (2023, March). Artificial intelligence and international adjudication. In *The Max Planck encyclopedia of international procedural law*. Oxford University Press. https://opil.ouplaw.com/display/10.1093/law-mpeipro/e3888.013.3888/law-mpeipro-e3888?d=/10.1093/law-mpeipro/e3888.013.3888/law-mpeipro-e3888&p=emailAg75i6yMPF2s

Ganguli, P. (2024, October 6). *Admissibility of digital evidence under Bharatiya Sakshya Sanhita: A comparative study with the Indian Evidence Act*. SSRN. https://ssrn.com/abstract=4977238

Guo, Y., Slay, J., & Beckett, J. (2009). Validation and verification of computer forensic software tools—Searching function. *Digital Investigation*, *6*(Supplement), S12–S22. https://doi.org/10.1016/j.diin.2009.06.015

Indian Patent Office. (2025). *Guidelines for examination of computer related inventions (CRIs): Draft version 2.0*.

Indian Society of Artificial Intelligence and Law. (2025, April 30). *The Prayagraj principles on responsible and accessible legal automation technologies [The Prayagraj AI Principles]* (Version 1). www.isail.in/the-bharat-pacific-principles/prayagraj

International Organization for Standardization. (2012). *ISO/IEC 27037:2012 Information technology — Security techniques — Guidelines for identification, collection, acquisition and preservation of digital evidence*. www.iso.org/standard/44381.html

Jha, P. (2023, August 28). *Responses from AI chatbots like ChatGPT cannot be the basis to decide issues in court: Delhi High Court*. Bar and Bench. www.barandbench.com/news/responses-ai-chatbots-chatgpt-cannot-basis-decide-issues-court-delhi-high-court

Maneka Gandhi v. Union of India, AIR 1978 SC 597 (1978).

Marti, L. (2024). *Cross-country comparison of the use of artificial intelligence in European companies and its determinants*. Qeios. https://doi.org/10.32388/TDJRJ0

Mehta, A., Sreenivas, A., & Ghosh, S. (2020, July 27). *Section 65B of the Indian Evidence Act, 1872: Requirements for admissibility of electronic evidence revisited by the Supreme Court*. India Corporate Law. https://corporate.cyrilamarchandblogs.com/2020/07/section-65b-of-the-indian-evidence-act-1872-requirements-for-admissibility-of-electronic-evidence-revisited-by-the-supreme-court/

Ministry of Law and Justice. (2025a, February 25). *Digital transformation of justice: Integrating AI in India's judiciary and law enforcement* [Press release]. Press Information Bureau of India. www.pib.gov.in/PressReleasePage.aspx?PRID=2106239

Ministry of Law and Justice. (2025b, March 20). *Use of AI in Supreme Court case management* [Press release]. Press Information Bureau of India. www.pib.gov.in/PressReleasePage.aspx?PRID=2113224

Murari Lal S/O Ram Singh v. State of Madhya Pradesh, AIR 1980 SC 531 (1979).
National Institute of Standards and Technology. (n.d.). *Computer forensics tool testing program (CFTT)*. www.nist.gov/itl/ssd/software-quality-group/computer-forensics-tool-testing-program-cftt
Pol, R., & Karthik, A. (2024, January 10). Can India's new evidence act address the challenges posed by artificial intelligence? *The Secretariat*. https://thesecretariat.in/article/can-india-s-new-evidence-act-address-the-challenges-posed-by-artificial-intelligence
S. Gopal Reddy v. State of Andhra Pradesh, (1996) 4 SCC 596 (India).
Selvi & Ors v. State of Karnataka & Anr, AIR 2010 SC 1974 (India).
Shafhi Mohammad v. State of Himachal Pradesh, (2018) 5 SCC 311 (India).
Shiv Kumar v. Hukam Chand & Anr, (1999) 7 SCC 467 (India).
State (NCT of Delhi) v. Navjot Sandhu @ Afzal Guru, (2005) 11 SCC 600 (India).
State of Madhya Pradesh v. Chintaman Sadashiva Waishampayan, AIR 1961 SC 1923 (1960).
State of Tamil Nadu v. Suhas Katti, CC No. 4680 of 2004 (Metropolitan Magistrate, Egmore 2004).
Tomaso Bruno & Anr. v. State of U.P., (2015) 7 SCC 178 (India).
United States v. Levandowski, No. CR 19-377 WHA (N.D. Cal. 2020).

11 Telemedicine Platforms and AI
Legal Challenges in India

Gazala Parveen and Padmavati Manchikanti

INTRODUCTION

The Indian healthcare system has changed considerably in the last few years, predominantly due to the implementation of digital technology and artificial intelligence (AI). Telemedicine uses information and communication technology to provide healthcare services from a distance. Though it has existed for some time, its significance increased dramatically during the COVID-19 pandemic, which revealed the shortcomings of in-person consultations and underscored the critical need for accessible healthcare across India's vast and diverse population.

In March 2020, the Ministry of Health and Family Welfare announced the Telemedicine Practice Guidelines, which made it official that remote healthcare delivery was legal in India. At the same time, more and more AI-powered apps, such as diagnostic chatbots and clinical decision support systems, have been added to telemedicine platforms to improve the accuracy of diagnoses, lighten the strain, and tailor treatment to each patient.[1] AI-enabled telemedicine can bridge this gap by expanding access to clinical expertise without the need for physical proximity. Platforms such as Practo,[2] 1mg,[3] and Tata Health[4] already utilise AI to assist with symptom checking, triage, and follow-up consultations.[5]

The increasing reliance on AI-powered telemedicine raises legal concerns that have not yet been comprehensively addressed by Indian law. The current regulatory framework is fragmented, consisting primarily of the *Information Technology Act*, 2000 (IT Act), the *Indian Medical Council (Professional Conduct, Etiquette and Ethics) Regulations*, 2002 (IMC Regulation), and the *Telemedicine Practice Guidelines,* 2020 (TPG). While these instruments provide a foundational structure for digital healthcare, they are largely silent on the specificities of AI, including issues such as model accountability and the explainability of machine learning outputs.[6] AI systems often operate as "black boxes," making it difficult to trace how decisions are made and an opacity that complicates the attribution of liability in medical negligence or misdiagnosis cases.

One of the most urgent legal issues in AI-driven telemedicine is data privacy. AI systems require vast patient data to train and refine their algorithms. This dependence raises concerns about how sensitive health data is collected, stored, processed, and shared. The Digital Personal Data Protection Act of 2023 (DPDP) is pivotal in protecting individual privacy. However, significant shortcomings persist within the legislation, which may undermine its overall effectiveness. For instance, the law lacks explicit guidance on anonymising health data for AI training and the governance of cross-border data transfers, a critical concern given that many telemedicine platforms use cloud servers outside India.[7] Patients often lack awareness of how their data is being used, which undermines the principle of informed consent, a cornerstone of medical ethics.

DOI: 10.1201/9781003629146-12

This chapter explores the legal challenges associated with deploying AI in telemedicine platforms in India. It critically analyses existing legal provisions and identifies regulatory gaps concerning data privacy, liability, and intellectual property. The scope of the chapter includes a detailed discussion of the TPG, the DPDP, and other applicable statutes. Additionally, the chapter considers emerging global best practices and proposes recommendations for a comprehensive legal framework that can guide India towards a robust, patient-centric AI-healthcare ecosystem.

TRADITIONAL TELEMEDICINE VS. AI-INTEGRATED SYSTEMS

Traditional telemedicine platforms function primarily as digital replicas of conventional doctor-patient interactions. These systems typically facilitate appointment scheduling, video consultations, and basic documentation. They are instrumental in expanding access to healthcare in underserved rural and semi-urban regions, but lack sophisticated capabilities such as intelligent triage or clinical decision support. Some platforms rely on largely manual workflows, often structured around digital question-and-answer formats and audio/video consultations. These systems operate on rule-based logic with minimal AI integration and depend heavily on human medical expertise. As a result, they are constrained by the availability of physicians, slower response times, and a reliance on manual input for decision-making.

On the other hand, AI-assisted telemedicine platforms are transforming digital healthcare delivery by incorporating advanced functionalities such as symptom checkers, triage bots, predictive analytics, and personalised health recommendations. For example, some platforms use AI to assess symptoms through camera-based vital monitoring and natural language processing chat interfaces, enabling rapid pre-diagnosis and reducing reliance on real-time doctor input. Others employ AI to generate preventive care suggestions based on user history and diagnostics, enhancing continuity and personalisation of care. AI optimises backend processes, for instance, by routing patients to appropriate specialists based on symptoms and availability, or supporting physicians through symptom-based assessments and differential diagnosis tools.

A representative list of telemedicine platforms operating in India, spanning both government-led and private initiatives, is provided in Table 11.1. It outlines key features such as the year of platform launch, introduction of AI, types of services offered, platform access modes (web or app), and links for further reference. Web platforms refer to browser-based portals accessible via computers or mobile devices, while apps are downloadable software programs available on smartphones or tablets, typically through the Android or iOS app stores. Both interfaces allow users to schedule consultations, access prescriptions or lab results, and communicate with healthcare providers. Whether AI is integrated into the platform, what are the specific applications, such as symptom checkers, risk prediction models, or triaging systems are enlisted. This comparative overview helps illustrate the growing digital health ecosystem in India, emphasising the role of AI in enhancing efficiency, personalisation, and accessibility in healthcare delivery.

Telemedicine in India was formally introduced through government initiatives, with *eSanjeevani* launched in 2019 as the first large-scale, central government-supported teleconsultation platform under the Ministry of Health and Family Welfare. Its early success in doctor-to-patient and doctor-to-doctor consultations set a precedent for digital health delivery. However, the first private-sector telemedicine service was pioneered much earlier by Apollo Hospitals through its Apollo Telemedicine Networking Foundation in March 2000, connecting the rural Aragonda village hospital to Apollo Hospital in Chennai, marking the inception of private telemedicine in India.[8] The integration of AI has since transformed private telemedicine by enabling AI-based symptom checkers, predictive diagnostics, and automated triage, enhancing scalability and personalisation. The earliest known AI-integrated telemedicine platform in India was *mfine*, founded in 2017, whose app incorporated an AI-driven triage and symptom-analysis engine from its inception in September 2017.[9] While public

TABLE 11.1
Representative Telemedicine Platforms in India

Platform Name	Type	AI Usage	Launch Year and AI Introduction Year	Platforms Used	AI Functionality (if Present)	Website Link
eSanjeevani OPD	Government	No AI at present	2020; No AI introduced	Web, Android App	General OPD consults; No AI involved	https://esanjeevani.mohfw.gov.in/#/
eSanjeevani AB-HWC	Government	No AI at present	2019 (pilot); No AI introduced	Web	Hub-and-spoke D2D model for primary to secondary referrals; No AI	https://esanjeevani.mohfw.gov.in/#/
National Telemedicine Service (NTS)	Government	No AI; future possible	2020 (as umbrella); AI planned (no launch yet)	Web, Integrated Platforms	Integrated digital health services; Potential future AI integration under ABDM ecosystem	https://services.india.gov.in/service/detail/esanjeevani-national-telemedicine-service
Practo	Private	Yes	2008; AI around 2016–2018	App (iOS/Android), Website	Symptom checking, doctor recommendation, NLP-based EHR input, predictive analytics	www.practo.com/
Apollo 24/7	Private	Yes	2020; AI from launch phase	App, Website	AI-powered triaging, health monitoring insights, chronic condition risk analysis	www.apollo247.com/specialties
Tata Health	Private	Yes	2019; AI from 2020–2021	App, Web	AI for early disease risk prediction, health assessments, symptom analysis	https://tmckolkata.com/in/tele-consultation/
mfine	Private	Yes	2017; AI from 2018	App, Website	AI symptom checker, predictive diagnostics, decision support tools for doctors	www.mfine.co/
DocsApp (MediBuddy)	Private	Yes	2015 (DocsApp); AI from 2017–2018	App, Web	AI-driven chatbot triage, symptom-to-specialist mapping	www.docsapp.in/
1mg (Tata 1mg)	Private	Yes	2015; AI from 2020 (post-Tata acquisition)	App, Web	Medication reminders, personalised recommendations, AI-driven symptom evaluation	www.1mg.com

Lybrate	Private	Mostly rule-based	2013; Basic rule-based systems from early phase	App, Web	Basic AI/chatbot interface for FAQ routing, symptom-based triage (mostly rule-based, not ML-driven)	https://doctor.lybrate.com/
CallHealth	Private	No	2013; No AI introduced	App, Web	Human-led care, sample collection & diagnostics; No AI declared	www.callhealth.com/doctor-consultation/mode/online?srsltid=AfmBOoq3wCYHEBP0dXmp-Rbah-OCQT_LS5wO-N-sXQVmqn8eVTN6vx8X
Meddo	Private	No dedicated AI	2018–2019; No AI introduced	App, Web	Hybrid model connecting clinics to digital care; No announced AI features	https://meddo.in/info-for-doctors
CureBay	Private (Hybrid)	No	2021; No AI introduced	Hybrid: Field agents + Web app	Assisted human interface for remote populations; human mediators handle tech; no AI functionality	https://patients-preprod.curebay.in/

Source: Compiled by the author.

platforms like *eSanjeevani* currently lack AI, collaborations are emerging, such as ABDM-linked pilots' future integration.[10] The private sector offers technological agility and patient-centric innovation, whereas the public sector ensures scale, affordability, and trust. Cross-sectoral learning can enhance the ecosystem: the public sector can adopt adaptable AI models from private entities, while private platforms can benefit from public infrastructure and regulatory support to improve equity and governance in AI-driven telehealth.

LEGAL LANDSCAPE OF TELEMEDICINE IN INDIA

India's legal framework governing telemedicine has evolved significantly, especially after the COVID-19 pandemic underscored the necessity of remote healthcare. The TPG, issued in March 2020, marked a historic move towards formalising telemedicine in India. However, while these guidelines, along with existing statutes such as the IT Act and IMC Regulation, provide a foundational legal scaffold, they largely overlook the unique complexities introduced by AI. This section critically evaluates the current legal landscape and argues that it is primarily tailored for traditional telemedicine models rather than AI-integrated systems (Table 11.2).

TABLE 11.2
Laws Regulating Telemedicine Platforms in India

Name of the Legislation/ Regulation/Guideline	Effective Date	Relevant Clauses
Information Technology Act, 2000	9 June 2000	• Section 43A – Compensation for failure to protect sensitive personal data • Section 66C – Identity theft • Section 66D – Cheating by personation using computer resources • Section 72 – Breach of confidentiality and privacy
Indian Medical Council Regulations, 2002	11 March 2002	• Regulation 1.3 – Maintenance of medical records • Regulation 2.1.1 – Patient confidentiality • Regulation 7.14 – Informed consent • Regulation 7.16 – Professional misconduct in telemedicine (contextual relevance)
Telemedicine Practice Guidelines, 2020	25 March 2020	• Guideline 3 – Telemedicine applications (types of consultation) • Guideline 4 – Patient consent • Guideline 5 – Duties and responsibilities of RMPs • Guideline 6 – Guidelines for prescribing medicines
Digital Personal Data Protection Act, 2023 (DPDP Act)	18 November 2022	• Section 2(g) – Definition of "Personal Data" • Section 2(i) – Definition of "Data Fiduciary" • Section 6 – Consent Framework • Section 7 – Purpose Limitation • Section 8 – Data Minimisation & Notice Requirements • Section 14 – Grievance Redressal Mechanism • Section 11 – Consent Manager
DPDP Rules, 2025 (Draft)	3 January 2025 (draft released)	• **Rule 3**: Clear notice of data usage to users on apps/web • **Rule 6**: Obligations for strong security measures (anonymisation, masking) • **Rule 7**: Breach notification to user within 72 hours • **Rule 10**: Verifiable parental consent for minors

Source: Compiled by the author

Role of the Information Technology Act, 2000

The Information Technology Act, 2000 (IT Act), lays down the essential legal framework for India's electronic governance, data security, and cybercrime oversight. A key component, Section 43A, is essential for telemedicine as it requires compensation if sensitive personal data, including health information, is mishandled, something that's crucial for digital health platforms. Moreover, Sections 66C and 66D talk about issues like identity theft and impersonation through computer resources, which are pressing concerns for AI-driven and remote healthcare services. Section 72 also plays a vital role in protecting privacy by imposing penalties for unauthorised data disclosures during service delivery. These legal provisions set up fundamental privacy and security responsibilities for telemedicine platforms. However, some critics point out that the IT Act's framework lags behind the rapid changes in digital health technologies and AI.[11]

The Indian Medical Council Regulations, 2002

Regarding ethics, the Indian Medical Council's regulations, 2002 on Professional Conduct, Etiquette, and Ethics guide how medicine is practised in India. Although these rules were established before telemedicine and AI started integrating into medical practice, they still highlight crucial aspects like patient confidentiality, informed consent, and professional accountability, which are key principles for virtual healthcare. Without clear guidelines on algorithmic decision-making and remote diagnostics, healthcare providers and regulators[12] are challenged.

The Telemedicine Practice Guidelines, 2020

The TPG, 2020,[13] formally recognises the use of technology platforms for healthcare delivery and provides a regulatory framework for their operation. These guidelines require platforms to ensure that only Registered Medical Practitioners (RMPs), duly verified and compliant with ethical and legal standards, can consult patients. Platforms must display RMP credentials, facilitate secure data exchange, and maintain privacy.[14] Regarding the usage of AI in telemedicine, as per section 5.4 of the guidelines, AI and digital tools may support RMPs, but they cannot independently prescribe or counsel patients.

"While new technologies such as Artificial Intelligence, Internet of Things, advanced data science-based decision support systems, etc. could assist and support an RMP on patient evaluation, diagnosis or management, the final prescription or counselling has to be directly delivered by the RMP."

The Digital Personal Data Protection Act, 2023

To keep up with the changing digital landscape, the DPDP Act, 20,23 has been introduced to oversee how digital personal data is handled, ensuring that individuals' privacy rights are respected. The Act defines "personal data" as any information that can identify an individual. The "data fiduciary" is the organisation that decides how personal data is processed, similar to a data controller in other global privacy frameworks. Telemedicine platforms usually take on the role of data fiduciaries and must ensure their data processing aligns with principles like purpose limitation, data minimisation, and consent-based processing.[15] The Act also introduces the idea of "consent managers" and requires mechanisms for notice and grievance redressal, providing stronger and more modern protections than the previous IT Act.[16] While these legal frameworks lay the groundwork for telemedicine in India, there are still gaps, especially regarding AI transparency, accountability for algorithmic mistakes, and cross-border data sharing, which call for further reforms and specific guidelines.

The Digital Personal Data Protection Rules, 2025

The Draft Digital Personal Data Protection (DPDP) Rules, 2025, are based on the DPDP Act of 2023 and introduce crucial provisions for digital health and telemedicine in India. Rule 3 requires data fiduciaries, including telemedicine platforms, to provide users with clear and accessible notices about the personal data being collected and the purposes for its collection. This ensures that users can give informed consent. Rule 6 establishes strict data security obligations, such as encryption, masking, and access controls, to protect sensitive health data. Rule 7 mandates that in the event of a personal data breach, affected users and the Data Protection Board must be notified promptly, ideally within 72 hours. Rule 10 emphasises the protection of minors, requiring verifiable parental consent before processing any data related to children. Together, these provisions enhance transparency, accountability, and user control in digital health services. Telemedicine platforms must align their operations with these rules to ensure the lawful and ethical handling of patients' personal and health-related information.

While recent legal reforms have significantly strengthened India's telemedicine governance, the integration of AI into clinical workflows exposes critical blind spots in the existing legal apparatus. The DPDP Act, 2023, and its accompanying Draft Rules, 2025, underscore the importance of consent, transparency, and security in personal data handling. These laws primarily focus on data protection and professional ethics, offering limited clarity on AI-specific risks such as algorithmic accountability, auditability, or bias mitigation.[17] The regulatory focus remains procedural rather than anticipatory, failing to address the structural shifts AI introduces to clinical judgment and medico-legal liability. While the legal framework has matured post-pandemic, it remains rooted in traditional models of telemedicine, struggling to accommodate the evolving complexity of AI-enabled care systems. This gap sets the stage for unresolved regulatory challenges.

THE CHALLENGES OF THE CURRENT LEGAL FRAMEWORK

Despite regulatory advancements like the TPG, 2020, and the DPDP Act, 2023, India's current legal infrastructure remains ill-equipped to handle the unique challenges AI-enabled telemedicine presents. Certain functions of AI in the health care system remain unanswered. For example, there is liability in medical negligence, where AI-based telemedicine tools are involved, and health-related data, where the server is in an offshore location, raises critical concerns regarding accountability, cross-border data transfer, and enforceability of patients' and RMPs' rights.

The TPG permits AI and digital tools to assist RMPs but explicitly prohibits them from independently prescribing or counselling. This binary framing fails to account for the nuanced reality where AI algorithms, while not directly issuing prescriptions, significantly influence diagnosis and treatment decisions. For instance, in the case of *Deepa Sanjeev Pawaskar v. State of Maharashtra*[18] before the Bombay High Court, a physician was denied bail for giving remote instructions over the phone that led to a patient's death. The court emphasised the duty of care even in indirect forms of medical communication. This precedent raises complex liability questions when AI-generated clinical suggestions are involved, particularly if an RMP acts based on flawed algorithmic advice.

Current Indian jurisprudence and legislation provide no clear mechanism for attributing liability in the event of harm caused by algorithmic bias or malfunction. Unlike the U.S. FDA's Software as a Medical Device (SaMD) framework, India lacks a dedicated authority to evaluate and certify AI-based clinical tools.[19] The absence of such regulation results in uncertainty over liability, should it rest with the physician, the software developer, or the platform operator? The Supreme Court in *Indian Medical Association v. Union of India*[20] has expressed concern over non-licensed entities offering medical services online, implicitly questioning the legitimacy of algorithm-based triage and consultation tools. This accountability vacuum hampers redress for patients and creates a chilling effect on responsible AI innovation.

To address liability arising from AI-generated clinical suggestions, India could adopt a tiered or shared liability model, drawing on principles of vicarious liability, where responsibility is attributed to the human or institutional actors deploying the AI.[21] If an RMP acts on flawed AI-generated advice, liability could be distributed among the physician, the healthcare institution, and the developers, depending on whether due diligence, validation, and disclosure norms were followed. This approach mirrors emerging legal principles in authorship and copyright law. For instance, in the U.S. Copyright Office's decision on *Zarya of the Dawn*,[22] copyright was granted only to the human author who provided the textual prompts to an AI, not the AI itself. This precedent supports a framework where the person giving direction to the AI bears primary legal responsibility. Mandating certified AI tools, audit trails of AI decisions, and clear disclaimers can further ensure accountability while enabling innovation.

AI systems require vast datasets to function effectively. While the DPDP Act introduces robust principles like purpose limitation and data minimisation, it remains silent on the use of personal health data for AI model training and lacks mandates for de-anonymisation risk assessments or federated learning protocols. Many platforms rely on click-wrap consent agreements, standard form contracts where users accept terms by ticking a box, without meaningful disclosure of data usage, retention, or third-party sharing.[23] Under Indian contract law, particularly Section 10 of the Indian Contract Act, 1872, valid consent requires free and informed agreement, which is often absent in such digital contexts, especially for non-English speakers or low-literacy users. Courts have shown reluctance to enforce click-wrap contracts in the absence of real choice or comprehension, as said in the case of *Trimex International v. Vedanta Aluminium.*[24] The resulting consent framework fails to meet even basic standards of informed consent, undermining the legitimacy of data processing under both contract law and emerging privacy jurisprudence post-*Justice K.S. Puttaswamy v. Union of India.*[25] Without stricter regulation of consent formats and AI-specific data safeguards, patient privacy remains vulnerable, especially when data is routed through offshore servers, as highlighted in the ongoing case of *Zara Healthcare Pvt. Ltd. v. Union of India.*[26]

Numerous studies have shown that AI models trained on skewed datasets may yield racially or socioeconomically biased outputs. Yet, Indian law imposes no statutory obligation for algorithmic audits or health equity impact assessments. The lack of these checks can reinforce structural inequities, disproportionately affecting women and rural populations. Without a mandate akin to the "Right to Explanation" under the EU GDPR, patients in India have no means to challenge or even understand decisions made by AI systems, particularly dangerous in matters involving diagnostics or prioritised care.[27]

Although the TPG requires that only verified RMPs provide teleconsultations, enforcement is limited to platform self-certification, with no independent audit mechanism. This regulatory vacuum raises concerns under Section 79 of the IT Act, which grants intermediary liability exemption only if due diligence is observed. If platforms allow AI-generated advice to influence diagnoses or prescriptions without clear disclosure, they risk losing this protection. In *Shreya Singhal v. Union of India,*[28] the Supreme Court clarified that intermediaries must act upon actual knowledge of illegal content, an analogy relevant for health misinformation or unauthorised AI usage. The platforms may incur third-party liability if they knowingly facilitate unlicensed advice, especially when algorithmic prompts mimic prescriptions. The absence of a central authority to oversee such violations leaves patients vulnerable and limits redress mechanisms.

CONCLUSION

India's healthcare landscape stands at a pivotal juncture where both public and private telemedicine systems play crucial roles. While government initiatives like eSanjeevani enhance rural accessibility, private AI-integrated platforms deliver personalised and scalable healthcare services. However, the legal and regulatory frameworks remain largely outdated, leaving significant gaps in addressing AI-related issues such as liability, data privacy, and algorithmic transparency. In the interim, India must strengthen enforcement of existing guidelines, mandate AI audit trails, and enhance data protection through stricter consent frameworks. Public platforms should also explore responsible AI integration to boost efficiency.

In the long run, India requires a comprehensive regulatory overhaul. This includes establishing an independent digital health authority, adopting AI-specific liability models, and enforcing algorithmic fairness audits. Clear standards for AI explainability and cross-border data governance are essential to foster patient trust, ensure accountability, and create an inclusive, resilient digital healthcare ecosystem.

NOTES

1 Naik et al. (2022). Legal and ethical consideration in artificial intelligence in healthcare: Who takes responsibility? *Frontiers in Surgery, 9*, 862322. https://doi.org/10.3389/fsurg.2022.862322
2 *Practo* www.practo.com/. Retrieved July 7, 2025
3 **1mg.** www.1mg.com/. Retrieved July 7, 2025
4 **Tata Medical Center** https://tmckolkata.com/in/tele-consultation/ Retrieved July 7, 2025, from
5 IndiaAI. (n.d.). *The role of AI in telemedicine developments in India.* https://indiaai.gov.in/article/the-role-of-ai-in-telemedicine-developments-in-india
6 Mathur et al.(2022, February). *Artificial intelligence in healthcare: 2021 year in review.* ResearchGate. https://doi.org/10.13140/RG.2.2.25350.24645/1
7 Desai, A., & Dutta, B. (2024). DPDP challenges on healthcare data security. *International Journal of Engineering Research in Computer Science and Engineering (IJERCSE), 11*(12). www.ijercse.com
8 eHealth Magazine. (n.d.). *Apollo Hospitals: A Pioneer in Telemedicine in India.*
9 Inc42. (n.d.). *How mfine Is Using AI To Transform India's Telemedicine Sector.*
10 NASSCOM. (2022, December 15). *Digital doctors: Smart systems transforming India's healthcare.* NASSCOM Community. https://community.nasscom.in/communities/digital-transformation/digital-doctors-smart-systems-transforming-indias-healthcare
11 Parthasarathi et al. (2024). Exploring the potential of telemedicine for improved primary healthcare in India: a comprehensive review. *The Lancet regional health. Southeast Asia, 27*, 100431. https://doi.org/10.1016/ j.lansea.2024.100431
12 Aneja, J., & Arora, S. (2021). Telemedicine and ethics: Opportunities in India. *Indian Journal of Medical Ethics, 6*(4). https://doi.org/10.20529/IJME.2021.042
13 TPG 2020, MoHFW, 2020.
14 Jain, D. (2023). Regulation of digital healthcare in India: Ethical and legal challenges. *Healthcare (Basel), 11*(6), 911. https://doi.org/10.3390/healthcare11060911
15 Sood et al. (2025). Challenges and recommendations for enhancing digital data protection in Indian Medical Research and Healthcare Sector. *NPJ digital medicine, 8*(1), 48. https://doi.org/10.1038/s41746-025-01448-x
16 Chettri et al., S. K., Deka, R. K., & Saikia, M. J. (2025). Bridging the Gap in the Adoption of Trustworthy AI in Indian Healthcare: Challenges and Opportunities. *AI, 6*(1), 10. https://doi.org/10.3390/ai6010010
17 Das et al., (2024). AI in Indian healthcare: From roadmap to reality. *Intelligent Pharmacy, 2*(3), 329–334. https://doi.org/10.1016/j.ipha.2024.02.005
18 *Deepa Sanjeev Pawaskar v. State of Maharashtra*, Cr. Bail Appl. No. 1227 of 2018 (Bom. HC 2018).
19 Chauhan et al., (2025). Artificial Intelligence Driven insights for Regulatory Intelligence in Medical Devices: Evaluating EMA, FDA and CDSCO Frameworks. *Global Clinical Engineering Journal, 7*(2), 11–24. https://doi.org/ 10.31354/globalce.v7i2.210
20 *Indian Medical Ass'n v. Union of India*, (2011) 7 SCC 179 (SC).
21 Sahoo, D. K. (2024). Vicarious liability: A solution to a problem of AI responsibility. *Journal of Informatics Education and Research, 4*(3), 1808. http://jier.org
22 U.S. Copyright Office. (2023). *Zarya of the Dawn: Decision on copyrightability of AI-generated works.* Retrieved from www.copyright.gov/rulings-filings/
23 Utz et al., (2019). (Un)informed consent: Studying GDPR consent notices in the field. In *Proceedings of the 2019 ACM SIGSAC Conference on Computer and Communications Security (CCS '19)* (pp. 973–990). Association for Computing Machinery. https://doi.org/10.1145/3319535.3354212
24 *Trimex Int'l FZE Ltd. v. Vedanta Aluminium Ltd.*, (2010) 3 SCC 1 (SC).
25 K.*S. Puttaswamy (Retd.) v. Union of India*, (2017) 10 SCC 1 (SC).
26 *Zara Healthcare Pvt. Ltd. v. Union of India*, W.P. (C) 10384/2019 (Del. HC 2019).
27 European Parliament & Council. (2016). *General Data Protection Regulation (EU 2016/679): Right to explanation and automated decision-making.* Official Journal of the European Union. Retrieved from https://eur-lex.europa.eu/legal-content/EN/TXT/?uri=CELEX:32016R0679
28 Shreya Singhal v. Union of India, (2015) 5 SCC 1 (SC).

12 Navigating AI in Insurance

Legal Perspectives on Evidence, Fraud, and Risk Evaluation

Pranav Patade

INTRODUCTION

The integration of artificial intelligence (AI) into the insurance sector marks a profound shift not only in operational efficiency but also in the evidentiary standards and legal doctrines that underpin contractual and regulatory adjudication. From underwriting to fraud detection, AI systems are no longer peripheral aids but central actors in determining risk, liability, and eligibility. This transformation, however, presents complex legal ramifications, especially when algorithmic outputs are presented as evidence or when automated decisions materially affect policyholder rights. In a country like India, where the insurance landscape is rapidly digitizing under the gaze of both market forces and public welfare obligations, the convergence of AI and legal evidence demands urgent scrutiny.

This paper interrogates the interface between AI-generated evidence and the legal frameworks governing insurance disputes in India. It explores the evolving evidentiary challenges that emerge when machine learning models influence or substitute human decision-making, often without the transparency or explainability demanded by the rule of law. Drawing from comparative practices in jurisdictions such as the United States, European Union, Singapore, Japan, and Australia, the analysis seeks to highlight both the possibilities and perils of algorithmic adjudication in insurance contexts. The Indian regulatory regime, notably the Evidence Act, the Code of Civil Procedure, and emerging data protection laws, is evaluated through the lens of procedural fairness, substantive justice and constitutional values. The paper concludes with a set of structured recommendations for legal reform, institutional preparedness, and regulatory design geared towards building an AI-insurance ecosystem that is not only innovative but also lawful, fair, and accountable.

APPLICATION OF AI IN INSURANCE SECTOR

AI has made a profound impact across the insurance industry, not only in streamlining core operational workflows but also in enhancing customer service, fraud detection, and strategic planning. Below is a categorization of AI applications across major functional areas:

A. **Core Insurance Operations:** AI plays a vital role in streamlining fundamental operations like risk evaluation, pricing, and claims management. Risk assessment is significantly enhanced through telematics data from vehicle sensors, which monitor driving patterns and behaviour to predict future risk exposure (Chan et al., 2024). Satellite and geospatial imaging assist in assessing environmental risks, particularly in marine and property insurance (AXA XL, 2021). Climate risk modelling uses long-term data to forecast weather-based hazards (Axios Media Inc., 2021). In health and life insurance, AI evaluates biometric data to predict potential

DOI: 10.1201/9781003629146-13

medical issues, though ethical and legal implications must be considered (SmartDev, n.d.). Reinsurance modelling also benefits from AI, enabling accurate analysis and the design of efficient risk-sharing arrangements (The Insurance Universe, 2024a, 2024b).

B. **Underwriting:** AI-powered underwriting automates and improves decision-making by analysing real-time data and behavioural trends. Automated engines, often combining machine learning with rule-based systems, allow for swift underwriting decisions (Inaza, 2025). Integration of IoT and wearable devices provides ongoing health or usage data, particularly relevant for health and motor insurance (Kosa, 2024). This enables dynamic premium pricing based on actual behaviour. Behavioural risk modelling further supports insurers in developing customized, fair policies (Rahul N., 2025).

C. **Claims Management:** Claims processing is significantly optimized through AI-driven systems. The automation of First Notice of Loss (FNOL) allows immediate incident reporting (Blue Prism, 2023). Image and video recognition tools assist in damage assessment from user-submitted media (Altaworld, 2024). NLP technologies streamline document handling and data extraction, enhancing efficiency. AI also plays a critical role in detecting fraudulent claims by identifying suspicious patterns. In parametric insurance, smart contracts execute claim settlements automatically when predefined criteria are met (Scoble & Cronin, 2025).

D. **Customer-Facing Functions:** AI revolutionizes customer interaction by providing constant, personalized support. Chatbots and voice assistants offer 24/7 help, addressing common queries and guiding users through services (BotInsight, n.d.). AI tools analyse customer data to recommend tailored insurance policies. Sentiment analysis of interactions helps resolve complaints effectively, while multilingual capabilities enhance accessibility (Parasrampuria et al., 2021). These tools collectively increase satisfaction and policyholder retention.

E. **Product Design and Customization:** AI facilitates the creation of innovative, customer-centric insurance products. Microinsurance models and parametric products offer targeted solutions for underserved demographics (The Insurance Universe, 2024a, 2024b). Usage-based insurance adjusts coverage according to actual behaviour, such as driving frequency or health habits (So. et al., 2020). AI also enables granular market segmentation, allowing insurers to identify niche customer bases and refine their offerings to suit evolving needs (Visionet, 2024).

F. **Risk and Fraud Monitoring:** Proactive fraud prevention is another crucial area where AI excels. Anomaly detection systems identify outliers in claims or behaviour, prompting deeper scrutiny. Behavioural analytics assess location and time-based patterns, which can expose irregularities (LeewayHertz, n.d.). Social network analysis identifies links between claimants and service providers that could suggest organized fraud. Red-flag systems provide early warnings to insurers, enhancing overall operational security (Óskarsdóttir et al., 2020).

G. **Cyber Insurance and Digital Risk Scoring:** In the digital age, AI enables insurers to underwrite cyber risks and digital assets effectively. It evaluates cybersecurity readiness and monitors real-time threat intelligence. Premiums can be dynamically priced based on current risk profiles (Zurier, 2020). For digital assets such as NFTs and cryptocurrencies, AI assesses volatility and exposure to propose suitable coverage strategies (Insider Inc., 2025).

H. **Strategic and Back-Office Functions:** AI also supports internal operations and compliance (Alston, 2024). Regulatory tools ensure adherence to local and global norms, such as IRDAI guidelines or data protection laws. Contract analysis powered by AI reviews clauses for consistency and legal validity. Workflow automation increases staff efficiency, while AI tools help monitor employee well-being and performance (Smith, 2025). These back-end enhancements lead to leaner, more adaptive organizations.

I. **Market Intelligence and Future-Readiness:** Insurers leverage AI for strategic insights and planning. Churn prediction tools forecast customer attrition, enabling timely intervention

(Financial Times, 2024). AI scans public sources and internal data to evaluate competitor activity and pricing. Market expansion forecasting helps identify areas with unmet demand. AI also supports scenario modelling for events like pandemics, aiding in risk preparedness and business continuity planning.

J. **Emerging Domains of Explainability and Blockchain:** Ethical deployment and accountability are becoming increasingly important. Explainable AI ensures decisions in underwriting and claims can be understood and justified (Longo et al., 2024). Tools for bias detection and fairness auditing promote transparent practices. Blockchain integration supports secure and automated operations through smart contracts, facilitating trust and efficiency in premium payments and claims processing (Scoble & Cronin, 2025).

TYPES OF AI-GENERATED EVIDENCE IN INSURANCE

As AI becomes increasingly integral to insurance workflows, it generates new forms of evidentiary material that go beyond traditional documentation, each presenting unique implications for legal scrutiny and admissibility.

A. **Direct Digital Evidence:** This form of evidence involves raw data generated and captured by AI-powered systems without modification. Examples include telematics data from connected vehicles, timestamped GPS logs, IoT sensor data, or security camera footage integrated with AI systems. These data sets serve as objective digital records and are often used to verify factual claims such as location, time of an event, or health parameters in usage-based insurance models.

B. **AI-Interpreted Evidence:** In this category, the AI system processes raw data and outputs conclusions or summaries that hold evidentiary value. This includes image recognition results for damage estimation, NLP-based document assessments, or diagnostic analytics. While based on direct digital inputs, this evidence involves algorithmic inference, making the explainability and reliability of the underlying model crucial.

C. **Scored or Predicted Evidence:** Scoring systems, such as credit or risk scores, and prediction models for fraud, claims likelihood, or customer churn fall under this group. These scores are the result of AI's probabilistic assessments derived from large datasets. Their admissibility and probative value in legal settings depend on transparency, consistency, and the avoidance of algorithmic bias.

D. **Pattern-Based or Anomalous Behaviour Evidence:** AI excels in detecting unusual patterns across claims, policyholder behaviour, or transactions. Evidence generated in this manner includes flagged anomalies in timing or geolocation, links in social network behaviour indicating fraud, or deviation from established norms. Though powerful in fraud detection, such evidence may require human corroboration for admissibility.

E. **Procedural and Smart Contractual Evidence:** This refers to automated processes and transactions recorded through AI-enabled smart contracts. For example, auto-triggered claim settlements in parametric insurance or contractual fulfilment logs backed by blockchain. These records provide verifiable, tamper-proof digital trails that validate compliance with insurance terms.

F. **Derived or Secondary Inferences:** These are conclusions drawn from multiple layers of AI processing, often involving combined sources like telematics plus medical history or market behaviour plus credit history. They support underwriting or risk profiling decisions. The challenge lies in tracing the inferential chain and ensuring the data integrity at each step to satisfy evidentiary standards.

ADMISSIBILITY UNDER INDIAN EVIDENCE LAW

The admissibility of evidence in legal proceedings is governed by specific statutory provisions and judicial interpretations, which are particularly significant in the context of emerging technologies such as AI. While this section refers to the Indian Evidence Act, 1872 (IEA) (Government of India, 2023a), it is pertinent to note that the Act has recently been replaced by the Bharatiya Sakshya Adhiniyam, 2023 (BSA) (Government of India, 2023b). However, since most judicial precedents, academic commentary, and interpretive frameworks are still grounded in the IEA, this paper continues to refer to the IEA to maintain coherence with established case law, procedural interpretations, and academic discourse, while noting corresponding provisions under the BSA where applicable.

INDIAN EVIDENCE ACT: SECTIONS ON DIGITAL EVIDENCE

The Indian Evidence Act, 1872 (Government of India, 2023a), has evolved to accommodate the dynamic nature of digital technology, and this includes AI-generated outputs. Section 3[1] of the Act now recognizes "electronic records" as a form of evidence, thereby allowing AI-generated content, such as telematics data, chatbot transcripts, or predictive analytics reports, to be presented before courts. This is crucial in insurance contexts where a large part of the decision-making is either based on or supported by algorithmic outputs.

Section 65B[2] stands as the statutory bedrock for admitting electronic evidence. For AI-generated data, whether structured logs or AI-interpreted summaries, to be admissible, a certificate under Section 65B (4) must accompany it. This certificate must detail the manner in which the data was produced, affirm the integrity of the source device, and identify the person in control of the data-generation process. The absence of such a certificate often renders otherwise vital AI-derived insights legally irrelevant.

Additionally, Section 45A[3] authorizes the court to consider expert opinions from examiners of electronic evidence. Since AI systems frequently function as complex, "black-box" tools, the need for technical experts to explain the logic, reliability, and operational standards of these systems becomes indispensable. For instance, an insurance company relying on a fraud score produced by an AI engine must substantiate its reliability through a qualified expert's certification. In some cases, Section 67A[4] becomes relevant when disputes involve AI-generated documents authenticated using digital or electronic signatures, particularly in online insurance contract execution.

JUDICIAL PRECEDENTS, IRDAI STANCE, AND INSURANCE RELEVANCE

Indian courts have laid down strict procedural norms for digital evidence, which directly affect how AI-generated outputs must be treated. In *Anvar P.V. v. P.K. Basheer* (2014) (Supreme Court of India, 2014), the Supreme Court ruled that any electronic record presented as evidence must be accompanied by a certificate under Section 65B (4). This landmark decision marked a departure from earlier interpretations and imposed stricter compliance requirements. Later, in *Arjun Panditrao Khotkar v. Kailash Kushanrao Gorantyal* (Supreme Court of India, 2020), the apex court reiterated this mandate, emphasizing that even if the original device is available, the procedural certificate remains mandatory unless the evidence is produced by a person in lawful control of the device.

More recently, *Christian Louboutin SAS v. Nakul Bajaj & Ors.* (Delhi High Court, 2018) in the Delhi High Court highlighted the limitations of relying solely on AI-generated outputs. The court expressed reservations about using chatbot transcripts or algorithm-generated responses without human oversight, signalling the judiciary's cautious approach towards opaque or unverified AI evidence. These precedents collectively underscore that AI-generated data, though technologically advanced, must meet traditional legal thresholds to be admissible.

From a regulatory standpoint, the Insurance Regulatory and Development Authority of India (IRDAI) has actively promoted digital innovation while emphasizing compliance. The 2021 InsurTech Working Group recommended adopting AI for fraud detection, underwriting, and customer engagement. However, it also urged insurers to comply with data protection laws, ensure transparency, and document model assumptions. The IRDAI Chairperson, in public speeches, has reinforced that while AI and ML offer unprecedented operational leverage, they must function within a framework that ensures fairness, accountability, and traceability.

Further, the 2023 IRDAI Information & Cyber Security Guidelines (Insurance Regulatory and Development Authority of India, 2023) require insurers to implement strong encryption, tamper-detection mechanisms, and maintain detailed logs, elements that are critical in establishing data credibility and legal reliability. AI-generated evidence that fails to meet these safeguards may be legally vulnerable, no matter how technologically sound.

CHAIN OF CUSTODY, INTEGRITY, AND RELIABILITY

Courts have increasingly stressed the importance of establishing a clear and tamper-proof chain of custody for digital and AI-generated evidence. This requirement applies to insurance scenarios where data is captured via telematics devices, IoT sensors, or AI-assisted claim assessments. Maintaining an audit trail that captures every stage, from data generation and transmission to storage and eventual presentation, is critical to demonstrate that the evidence has not been altered or compromised. Timestamps, access logs, and cryptographic hash functions can help support claims of data authenticity. In high-value insurance disputes, blockchain-enabled logs (Bonomi et al., 2018) offer an additional layer of verifiability by rendering transactional data immutable.

Beyond custody, data integrity is non-negotiable. Insurers must implement rigorous internal data governance protocols, including end-to-end encryption, digital access controls, and multi-level authorization systems. The IRDAI's ICSP framework (Insurance Regulatory and Development Authority of India, 2024) mandates these standards, which, if ignored, could result in the exclusion of key digital evidence from judicial proceedings. Moreover, maintaining detailed documentation on the AI model's development lifecycle, such as training data used, updates applied, and decision thresholds, is critical to ensure traceability.

As for reliability, Indian courts are increasingly insisting on model validation and explainability, especially when proprietary algorithms are used. The admissibility of AI-generated outputs often hinges on the presence of accuracy benchmarks, testing reports, and error-rate disclosures. Explainable AI (XAI) documentation helps bridge the understanding gap between technical and legal domains by demystifying the logic behind the AI's conclusions. Where such clarity is lacking, courts may call upon expert witnesses under Section 45A to interpret the technology. In such instances, models that are overly opaque, highly subjective, or proprietary without adequate transparency may face rejection or diminished evidentiary weight.

PROCEDURAL AND SUBSTANTIVE CHALLENGES

As AI becomes embedded within insurance workflows, from underwriting and pricing to claims management and fraud detection, it introduces a host of procedural and substantive legal challenges. These challenges are not merely theoretical but arise in real-world contexts where AI-generated evidence is tendered before adjudicatory bodies or forms the basis of critical contractual decisions.

Expert Testimony vs. Algorithmic Inference

Under the Indian Evidence Act, Section 45A, expert testimony is permitted for electronic records; however, this provision assumes the expert can comprehend and explain the logic of the system producing the evidence. When it comes to AI systems, especially deep learning models, the inference process is often non-linear, probabilistic, and computationally opaque. This presents a problem: Can a human expert meaningfully testify about an AI system they did not design or cannot fully interpret? (Pol & Karthik, 2024)

When AI-generated outputs such as fraud scores or damage assessments are introduced in insurance litigation, it is not sufficient to merely present the result. Courts increasingly expect a clear explanation of the methodology used, accompanied by expert testimony capable of translating technical outcomes into legally comprehensible terms. In practical terms, this may require a layered approach, drawing upon data scientists, software engineers, and forensic auditors to bridge the interpretative gap between algorithmic inference and judicial scrutiny.

Moreover, in projects like LexPredict's Contract Analytics (Arbel & Hoffman, 2023), legal professionals have encountered situations where AI tools flagged clauses for risk without clear criteria. Presenting such algorithmic results in a courtroom without a transparent basis invites judicial resistance, particularly when these models influence high-stakes decisions like denial of insurance claims or fraud prosecution.

Role of Explainability and Proprietary AI Models

Explainability (or the lack thereof) sits at the intersection of technological capability and constitutional due process. An insured party denied coverage due to an AI-determined "high-risk score" must be afforded an opportunity to challenge the basis of that decision. But if the insurer relies on proprietary AI systems, such as closed-source risk engines developed by third-party vendors, the underlying decision logic may be inaccessible to the litigant or even the insurer itself.

This raises serious questions of accountability. Courts are unlikely to defer to outcomes from systems that function as black boxes. In *State v. Loomis* (Wisconsin Supreme Court, 2016), the court upheld the use of the proprietary COMPAS algorithm in sentencing decisions but emphasized that such tools cannot replace judicial discretion. This logic applies equally to insurance contexts: AI may inform, but not dictate, decisions, especially where legal liability or entitlements are involved.

To mitigate this, insurers should adopt explainable AI (XAI) practices, including using interpretable models (e.g., decision trees or regression-based systems) for high-impact decisions or supplementing complex models with post-hoc explanation tools like LIME (Local Interpretable Model-agnostic Explanations) (Lima et al., 2022). Additionally, model audit trails and change logs must be maintained to reconstruct how and why a particular inference was made.

Bias, Opacity, and Due Process Concerns

AI systems learn from historical data, which can reflect entrenched biases, be it socio-economic, geographic, or behavioural. In insurance, this could manifest as disproportionately higher premiums for applicants from certain ZIP codes or claim denials based on behavioural scoring systems that are indirectly correlated with caste, religion, or income.

For instance, a 2022 review of AI use in auto insurance in the U.S. by ProPublica found racial disparities in premium pricing when algorithms factored in zip code and credit score (Angwin et al., 2017). If similar systems are deployed in India, it may violate Article 14 of the Constitution, which guarantees equality before law, and also run afoul of data protection norms under the DPDP Act, 2023.

Opacity also compounds due process violations. If a customer is denied a claim based on a "suspicious activity" score generated by an AI engine, they must be allowed to challenge the inference. This includes knowing what variables were considered, whether there was human oversight, and how similar cases were treated. The right to a fair hearing is rendered meaningless if the basis for an adverse decision is neither disclosed nor contestable (Consumer Federation of America, 2021).

From a procedural standpoint, failure to disclose AI model specifications or audit logs could breach disclosure norms under the Code of Civil Procedure or violate evidentiary standards under the Indian Evidence Act. Furthermore, institutions may need to establish algorithmic accountability frameworks, akin to those outlined in the OECD's AI Principles or the European Union's AI Act, to safeguard legal process and protect individual rights (Organization for Economic Co-operation and Development [OECD], 2019).

The tension between innovation and due process is stark in AI-powered insurance systems. While AI can enhance efficiency, reduce fraud, and personalize services, its integration must not circumvent procedural safeguards or substantive fairness. Courts, regulators, and insurers must collectively evolve mechanisms to ensure that algorithmic evidence is not only technically robust but also legally sound, constitutionally compliant, and transparent enough to withstand judicial scrutiny.

GLOBAL APPROACHES

As the integration of AI into insurance accelerates worldwide, jurisdictions have begun establishing distinct legal and regulatory postures regarding the treatment of AI-generated evidence, especially in high-stakes matters such as claims, underwriting decisions, and fraud investigations. These approaches offer critical insights for India as it shapes its regulatory and evidentiary landscape.

United States: Evidentiary Standards and Sector-Specific AI Regulation

In the U.S., the legal system evaluates AI-generated evidence primarily through the lens of *relevance, reliability, and foundation*, guided by Federal Rules of Evidence (FRE) (Administrative Office of the U.S. Courts, 2023). FRE Rule 702 governs the admissibility of expert testimony, allowing AI outputs if an expert can explain their reliability based on tested methodology. AI-driven tools like AI-powered damage estimators used by State Farm or Lemonade's fraud detection algorithms are admissible if a qualified expert demonstrates their scientific credibility and the system has undergone peer validation.

The *Daubert standard*, established in *Daubert v. Merrell Dow Pharmaceuticals* (U.S. Supreme Court, 1993), mandates that courts assess the scientific reliability of such tools, including peer review, known error rates, and general acceptance in the field. For AI-generated insurance evidence (like predictive fraud scores), this means insurers must be prepared to show testing results, audit trails, and expert interpretability.

Additionally, the National Association of Insurance Commissioners (NAIC) has issued Model AI Governance Principles (2020) (National Association of Insurance Commissioners, 2020) emphasizing accountability, fairness, and consumer transparency. These principles urge insurers to document algorithmic decisions and ensure internal review processes, providing a model India can adapt for regulatory oversight of AI usage in claim adjudication and pricing.

Singapore: Proactive Legal-Tech Integration with Explainability Mandate

Singapore is globally recognized for its proactive legal-tech ecosystem. The Personal Data Protection Commission (PDPC) has published Model AI Governance Frameworks (2019) (Personal Data Protection Commission [PDPC], 2019), which, while voluntary, set de facto standards for responsible AI deployment in regulated industries including insurance.

In the insurance sector, companies like NTUC Income and Great Eastern have implemented AI-based customer service and claims tools under strict explainability and auditability mandates (Olano, 2017). Notably, the Monetary Authority of Singapore (MAS) promotes FEAT Principles, Fairness, Ethics, Accountability, and Transparency, which demand that insurers document the logic behind every AI-based decision, especially those affecting coverage or liability (Monetary Authority of Singapore, 2018).

Singaporean courts have yet to rule extensively on AI evidence in insurance, but administrative tribunals are increasingly accepting AI-based documents and outputs as long as they are accompanied by metadata, human oversight, and model documentation. India's regulators can draw from MAS's industry-led governance with a government oversight model to strike a balance between innovation and accountability.

European Union: AI Act and the Risk-Based Framework

The European Union has introduced the Artificial Intelligence Act (European Parliament and Council, 2024), which categorizes AI systems by risk. High-risk systems, including those used in finance and insurance, must comply with strict transparency, documentation, and human-in-the-loop requirements.

In jurisdictions like Germany and France, courts follow GDPR-compliant standards requiring that any automated decision with legal or significant effect on individuals (such as denial of insurance claims) must be explainable and subject to appeal. Moreover, under Article 22 of the GDPR (European Parliament and Council, 2016), data subjects have the right not to be subject to decisions based solely on automated processing. This directly impacts the use of AI in underwriting and claims, requiring insurers to offer explanations and human recourse, a standard India could adapt to protect policyholder rights.

Japan: Algorithmic Transparency and Sectoral Codes

Japan's AI Utilization Guidelines (Ministry of Economy, Trade and Industry [METI], 2024) emphasize explainability and consumer trust, especially in sectors like insurance. Leading Japanese insurers such as Sompo Holdings have integrated AI in claims review with legally mandated explainability and post-decision consumer feedback mechanisms (Sompo Japan, 2023).

Japanese regulators encourage sectoral self-regulation, backed by a public-private framework where AI guidelines are enforced not just through legal mandates but an industry code of conduct. This approach fosters innovation while ensuring accountability, especially for algorithmic risk scoring and fraud prediction tools.

Australia: Probative Weight and Admissibility through Digital Evidence Rules

Australian courts have begun evaluating AI evidence under the Uniform Evidence Law, which permits digital records if they are reliable, contemporaneous, and accompanied by an explanation of their source and integrity (Australian Law Reform Commission, 2010).

In the Suncorp Group's implementation of AI for customer verification and policy recommendations, auditability and transparency are considered integral (Suncorp Group, 2025). The Australian Prudential Regulation Authority (APRA) also guides insurers to validate models periodically and ensure human oversight, practices which courts use as indicia of reliability (Australian Prudential Regulation Authority, 2025).

BEST PRACTICES INDIA CAN ADAPT

Based on comparative legal trends, India can proactively incorporate the following practices into its regulatory and judicial ecosystem to ensure trustworthy adoption of AI-generated insurance evidence:

1. **Adopt a Risk-Based Regulatory Framework:** Inspired by the EU AI Act, categorize AI applications by legal risk (e.g., high-risk for fraud detection, medium for underwriting), with proportional oversight and documentation requirements.

2. **Mandate Explainability and Human Oversight:** Drawing from Singapore's FEAT principles and GDPR standards, mandate that AI-based decisions affecting policyholders, such as claim denial or premium adjustments, must be subject to human validation and explainability reports.
3. **Introduce Sector-Specific AI Governance:** Like the NAIC in the U.S., India's IRDAI could issue AI deployment guidelines specific to insurance, requiring internal governance, model validation, periodic audits, and consumer communication protocols.
4. **Evidentiary Certification Protocols:** Modify Section 65B certifications under the Indian Evidence Act to include model validation summaries, AI logs, and expert endorsements, aligning legal documentation with the technical realities of AI-generated evidence.
5. **Build an Algorithm Accountability Registry:** Create a national registry for high-risk AI models used in financial services, including insurance, wherein each registered system must include details of purpose, dataset origin, validation results, and redress mechanisms.
6. **Facilitate Cross-Border Judicial Learning:** Judicial academies in India could study global precedents like *Loomis (U.S.)* or GDPR enforcement cases to shape jurisprudence that treats AI evidence with informed scrutiny.

India's journey into AI-regulated insurance is still nascent, but global models offer a roadmap. By combining constitutional safeguards with adaptive regulation, India can build a legal architecture that fosters innovation while upholding justice and procedural fairness.

RECOMMENDATIONS AND REFORMS

As India prepares to fully integrate AI into insurance governance and evidentiary law, it must balance technological advancement with constitutional guarantees, consumer protection, and institutional readiness. Based on comparative international approaches and current gaps in the Indian legal infrastructure, the following reforms are proposed.

Proposed Legal Tests for Admissibility and Evidentiary Value

To bridge the gap between algorithmic outputs and procedural law, Indian courts and lawmakers can adopt a set of formal legal tests designed to assess the validity and probative value of AI-generated insurance evidence:

1. **The "Traceability & Chain-of-Custody" Test:** Evidence must show an uninterrupted, secure chain from data capture (e.g., telematics, IoT devices) to final algorithmic inference. Blockchain-anchored logs and secure timestamps can establish integrity.
2. **The "Model Reliability & Validity" Test:** Judges may require model documentation, such as accuracy rates, false positive/negative ratios, and third-party validation reports, especially for predictive tools in underwriting and fraud detection. A parallel can be drawn with forensic tools, which must undergo Frye or Daubert[5]-type reliability assessment.
3. **The "Human-Involvement & Accountability" Test:** AI decisions affecting policyholders must involve human oversight at critical decision points. This ensures alignment with principles of Article 14 (equality before the law) and Article 21 (protection of life & personal liberty) of the Indian Constitution.
4. **The "Explainability & Contestability" Test:** Only AI decisions accompanied by a reasonable explanation of their logic, parameters, and input data should be admitted as prima facie evidence. This aligns with European GDPR Article 22 and the FEAT Principles from Singapore.

Regulatory Clarity from IRDAI

The Insurance Regulatory and Development Authority of India (IRDAI) should take the lead in formalizing AI governance within the insurance ecosystem through sector-specific guidelines and enforceable rules:

1. **AI Certification and Risk Profiling Framework:** IRDAI should create a tiered certification regime, where AI systems are classified as *low, moderate, or high risk*, based on their influence on policyholder rights. High-risk systems, such as those involved in fraud scoring or premium risk modelling, must undergo periodic third-party audits.
2. **Mandatory Disclosure and Auditability Requirements:** Insurance providers using AI for material decisions must disclose the nature of the algorithm, key risk factors, and appeal mechanisms to consumers. These disclosures can be modelled after Section 11 of the EU AI Act and should be made part of the IRDAI's consumer protection charter.
3. **Data Protection Harmonization:** AI deployment must be harmonized with India's Digital Personal Data Protection Act, 2023 (Government of India, 2023c), requiring insurers to obtain informed consent before using personal data for AI training. IRDAI could issue detailed guidance on "data minimization" and "purpose limitation" in algorithmic underwriting and claims handling.
4. **Dynamic Sandbox and RegTech Integration:** IRDAI should expand its Regulatory Sandbox Framework (originally notified in 2019) to include AI-specific innovations, where insurers can pilot new technologies under real-time supervision and legal guardrails. This enables safe experimentation and scalable innovation.

Institutional Capacity-Building

Technological evidence poses interpretive challenges even for seasoned legal professionals. For AI-generated evidence to be meaningfully assessed, India must invest in multi-tier institutional capacity development:

1. **Judicial Training Programmes:** Judges, particularly those in civil, commercial, and insurance litigation, should undergo continuous legal-technical education in AI models, algorithmic reasoning, and data integrity. These programmes can be spearheaded by the National Judicial Academy (Bhopal) and regional academies in partnership with NITI Aayog's AI for All Initiative.
2. **AI-Law Clinics and Technical Advisors:** Insurance tribunals and consumer courts should be supplemented by independent AI-technical advisors, similar to the amicus curiae model, who can assist in interpreting algorithmic logic, error margins, and model documentation. Additionally, top law schools (NLUs) can be encouraged to set up AI-Law Clinics, offering technical-legal support in real cases involving contested AI outputs.
3. **Sector-Specific Bench Formation:** High Courts and NCDRC may consider setting up Technology-Insurance Benches, staffed with judges trained in digital evidence. These can help create early jurisprudence around explainability, fairness, and due process in AI-insurance disputes.
4. **Bar Council Reforms for Tech-Legal Literacy:** The Bar Council of India (BCI) must mandate inclusion of "Law and Emerging Technologies" as part of continuing legal education (CLE). Modules should include algorithmic ethics, AI-generated evidence, and insurance applications to prepare future advocates.

Consumer Rights and Procedural Safeguards

A technologically progressive yet equitable framework must centre around policyholder rights and access to redress:

1. **Right to Explanation:** Policyholders should be entitled to an intelligible explanation if their claim is denied or premium raised due to AI assessment.
2. **Right to Appeal:** All AI-based insurance decisions should include a built-in mechanism for human review, to comply with constitutional and administrative law norms.
3. **Right to Algorithmic Audit:** Consumers must be empowered, either directly or through regulatory bodies, to demand a fairness or bias audit of systems affecting them.

National AI Registry and Public Audit Platform

India should consider developing a centralized AI Registry, a publicly accessible platform where high-risk AI models used by insurance companies must be disclosed, alongside their audit results, performance metrics, and intended use cases. A similar registry exists in the EU AI sandbox and has been recommended by the OECD.

This registry can be jointly administered by IRDAI and MeitY, with cross-sectoral enforcement capabilities.

Collaborative Regulatory Ecosystem

Finally, India must not regulate AI in insurance in isolation. A coordinated governance model involving IRDAI, MeitY, MoLJ (Ministry of Law and Justice), and the Data Protection Board is essential to address intersecting challenges involving algorithmic legality, data privacy, consumer welfare, and evidentiary fairness.

Joint workshops, shared enforcement infrastructure, and cross-reporting protocols will help create a unified approach that recognizes the multidimensional nature of AI.

India stands at a pivotal juncture where AI is poised to redefine the insurance industry, from actuarial science to courtroom evidence. Legal and regulatory reforms must not merely react to disruption but pre-emptively shape it. By embedding transparency, accountability, and human dignity into the technological core of insurance systems, India can become a model jurisdiction that protects innovation and individual rights with equal vigour.

CONCLUSION

AI has steadily worked its way into the core of insurance processes, often doing its job quietly, behind the scenes. For most people, the benefits look clear: quicker settlements, fewer loopholes for fraud, and better ways to measure risk. But if we pause for a moment, it's hard to ignore the legal and ethical dilemmas that this silent shift brings with it.

In India, the legal structure is still adapting to the pace at which technology is advancing. When a claim is denied based on AI analysis or an automated decision alters someone's entitlement, we're faced with a hard question, how do we challenge something that doesn't "think" in the way humans do? And how do we ensure fairness if a person isn't even aware of what data was used or how it was interpreted?

There is clearly a legal gap, not just in terms of statutes, but in procedural safeguards. And that gap can leave ordinary citizens vulnerable, especially when decisions seem arbitrary or unexplainable.

In the long run, the lack of transparency can do more harm than good, not only in legal outcomes but in public trust.

This paper doesn't aim to resolve everything, but it tries to shine a light on a space that's becoming harder to ignore. If the law stays passive, people will be left at the mercy of systems they don't understand. But if it evolves with awareness and compassion, then we stand a chance of building a system where innovation and justice go hand in hand.

NOTES

1 Under the Bharatiya Sakshya Adhiniyam, 2023, the equivalent provision is Section 2(1)(d), which continues to recognize electronic records as evidence.
2 Now mirrored in Sections 61 and 63 of the Bharatiya Sakshya Adhiniyam, 2023, which retain the requirements for electronic records and the certificate mechanism.
3 Corresponds to Section 39 of the Bharatiya Sakshya Adhiniyam, 2023, allowing expert opinion on electronic evidence.
4 Corresponds to Section 71 of the Bharatiya Sakshya Adhiniyam, 2023, relating to authentication of electronic signatures.
5 The *Frye* standard permits scientific evidence only if it has gained general acceptance in its field, whereas the *Daubert* standard used in U.S. federal courts considers a broader set of factors including testability, peer review, error rates, and general acceptance (Frye v. United States, 1923; Daubert v. Merrell Dow Pharmaceuticals, Inc., 1993).

REFERENCES

Administrative Office of the U.S. Courts. (2023). *Federal rules of evidence (Effective December 1, 2023).* www.uscourts.gov/file/78325/download

Alston, G. (2024, November). Meet the specialists digitising companies' legal teams. *Financial Times.* Retrieved June 12, 2025, from www.ft.com/content/6deada48-5b30-41b2-86a5-3ed7c567119c

Altaworld. (2024, January 9). The role of AI & machine learning in insurance innovation. *Altaworld.* https://altaworld.tech/the-role-of-ai-machine-learning-in-insurance-innovation/

Angwin, J., Larson, J., Kirchner, L., & Mattu, S. (2017, April 5). *Minority neighborhoods pay higher car insurance premiums than white areas with the same risk* [Investigative report]. ProPublica.

Arbel, Y. A., & Hoffman, D. (2023, August 14). Generative interpretation. *arXiv.* https://arxiv.org/abs/2308.06907

Australian Law Reform Commission. (2010). *Uniform Evidence Law: Documentary evidence (ALRC Report 102).* www.alrc.gov.au/publication/uniform-evidence-law-alrc-report-102/6-documentary-evidence/reliability-and-accuracy-of-computer-produced-evidence/

Australian Prudential Regulation Authority. (2025). *APRA's AI transparency statement.* www.apra.gov.au/apras-ai-transparency-statement

AXA XL. (2021, May 12). *Space data: How satellites are changing insurance.* AXA XL. https://axaxl.com/fast-fast-forward/articles/space-data-how-satellites-are-changing-insurance

Axios Media Inc. (2021, August 14). Using AI to better price wildfire insurance. Axios. www.axios.com/2021/08/14/artificial-intelligence-predict-wildfire-insurance

Blue Prism. (2023, March 15). *AI in insurance claims processing.* Blue Prism. www.blueprism.com/resources/blog/ai-insurance-claims-processing/

Bonomi, S., Casini, M., & Ciccotelli, C. (2018). B-CoC: A blockchain-based chain of custody for evidences management in digital forensics [Preprint]. *arXiv.* https://arxiv.org/abs/1807.10359

BotInsight. (n.d.). *Conversational AI in insurance industry: Use cases and benefits.* ChatInsight.ai.

Chan, I. W., Tseung, S. C., Badescu, A. L., & Lin, X. S. (2024, April 16). Data mining of telematics data: Unveiling the hidden patterns in driving behaviour. *arXiv.* https://arxiv.org/abs/2304.10591

Consumer Federation of America. (2021, April 9). *Insurance Commissioners: Address the racially discriminatory use of credit-based insurance scores* [Letter]. Dēmos. www.demos.org/testimony-and-public-comment/insurance-commissioners-address-racially-discriminatory-use-credit

Delhi High Court. (2018). *Christian Louboutin SAS v. Nakul Bajaj & Ors., Delhi High Court, Nov. 2, 2018.*

European Parliament and Council. (2016). *Regulation (EU) 2016/679 of the European Parliament and of the Council of 27 April 2016 on the protection of natural persons with regard to the processing of personal data and on the free movement of such data (General Data Protection Regulation).* Official Journal of the European Union. https://eur-lex.europa.eu/eli/reg/2016/679/oj

European Parliament and Council. (2024). *Regulation (EU) 2024/1689 of the European Parliament and of the Council of 13 March 2024 laying down harmonised rules on artificial intelligence (Artificial Intelligence Act) and amending certain Union legislative acts*. Official Journal of the European Union. https://eur-lex.europa.eu/legal-content/EN/TXT/?uri=CELEX:32024R1689

Financial Times. (2024, March 26). Financial services counting on AI for a productivity boost. *Financial Times*. www.ft.com/content/9ffe888e-2f78-4f59-9536-2e31f5bde8b7

Government of India. (2023a). *The Indian Evidence Act, 1872 (as amended)*. Ministry of Law and Justice. https://legislative.gov.in

Government of India. (2023b). *Bhartiya Sakshya Adhiniyam, 2023*. Ministry of Law and Justice. https://legislative.gov.in

Government of India. (2023c). *Digital Personal Data Protection Act, 2023*. Ministry of Law and Justice. https://legislative.gov.in

Inaza. (2025, February 12). AI-powered underwriting: The future of risk assessment. *Inaza*. www.inaza.com/blog/ai-powered-underwriting-the-future-of-risk-assessment

Insider Inc. (2025, May 12). At Mastercard, AI is helping to power fraud-detection systems. *Business Insider*. www.businessinsider.com/mastercard-ai-credit-card-fraud-detection-protects-consumers-2025-5

Insurance Regulatory and Development Authority of India. (2023). *Information & cyber security guidelines*. IRDAI. https://irdai.gov.in/documents/3314780/

Insurance Regulatory and Development Authority of India. (2024). *Insurance Cyber Security Policy (ICSP) framework*. https://irdai.gov.in/documents/37343/366029/IRDAI+CS+Guidelines+2023.pdf/81730785-f51-977b-5a92-d9cfd7eb2cd6?version=1.0&t=1682401978542&download=true

LeewayHertz. (n.d.). *AI in fraud detection: Use cases, benefits, solution and implementation*. LeewayHertz. www.leewayhertz.com/ai-in-fraud-detection/

Lima, G., Grgić-Hlača, N., Jeong, J. K., & Cha, M. (2022, May 11). The conflict between explainable and accountable decision-making algorithms. *arXiv*. https://arxiv.org/abs/2205.05306

Longo, L., Brcic, M., Cabitza, F., Choi, J., Confalonieri, R., Del Ser, J., Guidotti, R., Hayashi, Y., Herrera, F., Holzinger, A., Jiang, R., Khosravi, H., Lecue, F., Malgieri, G., Páez, A., Samek, W., Schneider, J., Speith, T., & Stumpf, S. (2024). Explainable Artificial Intelligence (XAI) 2.0: A manifesto of open challenges and interdisciplinary research directions. *Information Fusion*, 106, 102301. https://doi.org/10.1016/j.inffus.2024.102301

Ministry of Economy, Trade and Industry (METI). (2024, April 19). *AI guidelines for business ver. 1.0 compiled* [Press release]. www.meti.go.jp/english/press/2024/0419_002.html

Monetary Authority of Singapore. (2018, June). *Principles to promote fairness, ethics, accountability and transparency (FEAT principles)*. www.mas.gov.sg/-/media/MAS/News-and-Publications/Monographs-and-Information-Papers/FEAT%20Principles%20Final.pdf

National Association of Insurance Commissioners. (2020, August). *Principles on artificial intelligence as adopted by the task force*. https://content.naic.org/sites/default/files/inline-files/AI%20principles%20as%20Adopted%20by%20the%20TF_0807.pdf

Olano, G. (2017, June 4). NTUC income, IBM announce Singapore AI partnership. *Insurance Business Asia*. www.insurancebusinessmag.com/asia/news/breaking-news/ntuc-income-ibm-announce-singapore-ai-partnership-69665.aspx

Organization for Economic Co-operation and Development. (2019). *OECD principles on artificial intelligence*. OECD Publishing. www.oecd.org/going-digital/ai/principles/

Óskarsdóttir, M., Ahmed, W., Antonio, K., Baesens, B., Dendievel, R., Donas, T., & Reynkens, T. (2020, September 15). Social network analytics for supervised fraud detection in insurance [Preprint]. *arXiv*. https://arxiv.org/abs/2009.08313

Parasrampuria, R., Ghosh, A., Dutta, S., & Sarkar, D. (2021, August 5). Recommending Insurance products by using Users' Sentiments [Preprint]. *arXiv*. https://arxiv.org/abs/2108.06210

Personal Data Protection Commission (PDPC). (2019, January 23). *Model AI governance framework* (1st ed.). PDPC. www.pdpc.gov.sg/help-and-resources/2020/01/model-ai-governance-framework

Pol, R. & Karthik, A. (2024, January 10). Can India's new Evidence Act address the challenges posed by artificial intelligence? *The Secretariat*. https://thesecretariat.in/article/can-india-s-new-evidence-act-address-the-challenges-posed-by-artificial-intelligence

Rahul, N. (2025, June 9). *Precision underwriting: How AI is reshaping risk assessment and pricing in P&C insurance.* Medium. https://medium.com/@niveditarahul91/precision-underwriting-how-ai-is-reshaping-risk-assessment-and-pricing-in-p-c-insurance-db2fa9871077

Scoble, R., & Cronin, I. (2025, March 4). The impact of AI on the insurance industry. *Unaligned Newsletter.* www.unaligned.io/p/the-impact-of-ai-on-the-insurance-industry

SmartDev. (n.d.). *Underwriting and risk assessment in AI revolution.* SmartDev. https://smartdev.com/underwriting-and-risk-assessment-in-ai-revolution/

Smith, J. (2025, January). AI can take the slog out of compliance work, but executives not ready to fully trust it. *The Wall Street Journal.* www.wsj.com/articles/ai-can-take-the-slog-out-of-compliance-work-but-executives-not-ready-to-fully-trust-it-7cd60a16

So, B., Boucher, J.-P., & Valdez, E. A. (2020, July 6). Cost-sensitive multi-class AdaBoost for understanding driving behavior with telematics. *arXiv.* https://arxiv.org/abs/2007.03100

Sompo Japan. (2023). *Digital technology in products and services: Fully automated claims service using digital technology.* Sompo Holdings. www.sompo-hd.com/en/csr/action/customer/content4/

Suncorp Group. (2025, April 23). *Adam Bennett on Suncorp's AI journey: "It's about responsible and fair automation*". Suncorp Group. www.suncorpgroup.com.au/news/features/adam-bennett-ai

Supreme Court of India. (2014). *Anvar P. V. v. P. K. Basheer & Ors., Civil Appeal No. 4226 of 2012, 10 SCC 473.*

Supreme Court of India. (2020). *Arjun Panditrao Khotkar v. Kailash Kushanrao Gorantyal & Ors., Civil Appeal Nos. 20825–20826 of 2017, 7 SCC 1.*

The Insurance Universe. (2024a, June 27). *The impact of AI on reinsurance: Transforming the landscape.* The Insurance Universe. https://theinsuranceuniverse.com/the-impact-of-ai-on-reinsurance/

The Insurance Universe. (2024b). *Innovations in microinsurance technology: Transforming access and affordability.* The Insurance Universe. https://theinsuranceuniverse.com/innovations-in-microinsurance-technology/

United States Court of Appeals, D.C. Circuit. (1923). *Frye v. United States, 293 F. 1013.*

United States Supreme Court. (1993). *Daubert v. Merrell Dow Pharmaceuticals, Inc., 509 U.S. 579 (1993)*

Visionet. (2024, January 19). Rediscovering insurance target market segmentation with artificial intelligence. *Visionet.* www.visionet.com/blog/rediscovering-insurance-target-market-segmentation-with-artificial-intelligence

Wisconsin Supreme Court. (2016). *State v. Loomis, 881 N.W.2d 749 (Wis. 2016).*

Zurier, S. (2020, October 31). *Anomali* [Product review]. SC Media. www.scworld.com/product-test/anomali-platform

13 Regulating AI-Driven Facial Recognition in Policing

Legal and Ethical Imperatives for India

[1]Shtantika Mukherjee and [2]Hiteshi Agarwal

INTRODUCTION

The march of technology has enabled us to do things at scale efficiently and sophisticatedly. To name a few, CCTVs locate individuals, sophisticated cameras unlock phones, fingerprints reveal an individual's identity, and robots become human assistants. Every challenge that we face today has a technological solution; however, this solution-oriented approach has its own consequences. With the help of these technological successes, surveillance (Bureau of Police Research & Development, 2024) becomes more pervasive, and communication of information about how individuals act or transact in their daily lives becomes more accessible. The previous decade saw an increased deployment of Facial Recognition Technology ("FRT") in the Indian police sector. FRT, much like fingerprint and iris scan, captures the facial features of an individual and creates a mathematical sequence called a face template. The technology (Sinha, 2024) can broadly perform two functions; *first,* it can capture an unknown face and match it to the existing database fed through various public and private agencies, *second* it can verify a known face against a known template. FRT, as compared to other biometric identification techniques, has several advantages. *"Besides being natural and non-intrusive, the most important advantage of it is that it can be captured from a distance in a covert manner"*. Based on its use, FRT applications can be divided into two categories – security and non-security. The non-security use of FRT serves the purpose of identification and verification of the identity of an individual. It usually involves 1:1 use of FRT in cases where the individual either seeks access to a certain facility or derives certain benefits from a service provider. For example, its use in airports or educational institutions generates unique IDs for college courses. It is the security use of FRT that is garnering much scepticism among privacy advocates, researchers and academics. In this context, FRT is generally used for law-and-order considerations, identifying missing persons, investigations and screening of public spaces for violations of protocols. Within these use cases, it is the live and post facto use of FRT which is being increasingly debated from ethical and legal standpoints. A prime example of automated or live use of FRT is Surat and Delhi where video surveillance systems were integrated with a watchlist of suspects for the purpose of crowd control, identifying violations, and absconding violators.

An uptick in the adoption of FRT in India came in with the National Crime Records Bureau (NCRB) inviting tenders for the creation of a National Automated Face Recognition System (NAFRS). Thereafter, Delhi Police pioneered law enforcement through FRT, followed by other states such as Chennai, Telangana and Punjab (Common Cause & Lok Niti, 2023).

In this background, the paper seeks to analyse the existing legal framework around the use of FRT. The analysis wishes to initiate discussion around the key risks posed by FRT, and through a doctrinal analysis of the existing scholarship, provides certain proposals on its regulation within the Indian context.

DOI: 10.1201/9781003629146-14

RELATED WORK

Monique Mann and Marcus Smith (2017) argue on the legal and regulatory front, pointing out the concerns associated with FRT. *First*, that the privacy impacts in the case of FRT are never assessed prematurely by government agencies. *Second*, privacy legislation lacks a balancing approach between individual rights and state interests. Exemptions often override the individual's right to privacy and other interests. *Third*, biometric information must be classified as *sensitive personal data* and must be collected only when reasonably necessary with the consent of the individual concerned. Lastly, the literature lists certain suggestions to counter the privacy challenges associated with FRT.

Similarly, Leslie D (2020), concerned and critical of the proliferation of such systems, argues that the existence of technologies like facial recognition has been taken for granted and is regarded as a necessary means for securing public safety without any focus on remediation of the most basic ethical concerns surrounding its justifiability and ethical permissibility.

Busting the most popular assumptions associated with FRT, argues that there exists an erroneous assumption that the technology essentially bolsters human efficacy in surveillance and monitoring, criminal detection and overall law and security. *Second*, the technology is speedier and more accurate in crime detection and prevention as compared to human police forces. However, it is pertinent to note that FRTs have usually been registered to have an accuracy of only close to 70-80% (Hindustan Times, 2018). Roughly, the technology can misidentify up to 2-3 lakh people for every one million. It is argued that accuracy and ideal conditions are co-dependents in the case of FRT.

Smriti Parsheera (2019), citing transparency as one of the concerns in the use of FRT, argues that the data principals do not have enough access to the information regarding the contexts in which the FRTs will be used and adopted. Similarly, they know very little about the bodies storing and collecting the data. In her viewpoint, transparency is a critical factor, especially when the data is used in the context of criminal investigations, because of the omnipresent principle of natural justice.

Marda and Narayan (2020), critiquing the Delhi Police's predictive policing initiative Crime Mapping, Analytics and Predictive System (CMAPS), argue that bias and discrimination are deeply embodied.

LEGAL IMPERATIVES – INDIA'S GOVERNANCE FRAMEWORK FOR FRT

In its landmark judgement of *K.S. Puttaswamy v. Union of India (2019)* ("Aadhaar judgement"), the Apex Court recognised right to privacy as an "intrinsic part of right to life and personal liberty under Art. 21 and Part-III of the Indian Constitution". The judgement changed the legal landscape on two fronts: *first,* it teased out privacy rights and the concerns surrounding it, *second,* it established a tiered test of proportionality to mitigate the ill effects of surveillance by the State in various forms and shapes. As per the proportionality test, interventions that result in violation of privacy rights must be supported by a legitimate law, sponsored by a state interest and necessarily balance the purpose of the restriction with the nature of the right. In essence, the judgement lays down a four-prong test of *Legitimacy, Suitability, Necessity & Balancing* that helps us construct a clear picture of the scenario where the right to privacy cannot be endangered. Every state intervention, limiting or restricting the right to privacy, must discharge the affirmative burden of establishing that the intervention is proportionate, and that other societal interests have been taken care of. Moving forward, the enquiry proceeds to examine FRT against the test one by one.

Is It Supported by a Legitimate Aim?

FRT helps police personnel digitise criminal records and criminal searches at the ground level. Features like facial recognition also happen to retrieve information of criminals in real-time and are seen as smart law enforcement, enabling a 360-degree view of the citizens. Theoretically, the measure is deemed to achieve legitimate aims such as public safety, crime prevention and national security.

Does It Balance Individual Rights with State Interests?

FRT profiles people on a large scale in publicly accessible spaces. The adoption of this measure not only cultivates a fear of prosecution but also jeopardises the anonymity aspect, which is a key component of a functioning democracy. Moreover, it amplifies the profiling of certain underrepresented groups in the context of gender, colour, caste, class and religion. The use of such infrastructure attracts assessment under Art. 14, 15 and 21 of the Indian Constitution since it contributes to the disadvantage and discrimination of a certain group of individuals.

Is It the Least Intrusive Alternative Measure?

Surveillance in the guise of law enforcement and national security becomes a highly intrusive act when it interferes with the right to decisional autonomy and privacy of an individual. Art. 21's use of the phrase *"procedure established by law"* has been read inclusive of both substantive and procedural due process elements. Procedural due process ensures that even if the procedures regarding deprivation of liberty are supported by a substantive law, the procedure itself contained in the law must be *"fair, just and reasonable"*.

The present deployment of a technology like facial recognition vitiates this very standard for more than one reason. FRT collates and processes data in the most invisible and dubious manner. The data holder has absolutely no security in terms of the data being kept anonymous and its use only being restricted to authorised purposes. This also goes directly in conflict with the Aadhaar judgement that emphasised, *"principles of transparency, accountability, disclosure supplemented with informed consent are foundational concepts of informational privacy, the state must ensure that information is not used without the consent of users and that it is used for the purpose and to the extent it was disclosed"*. All of which to say, that the State today continues to deploy CCTVs and FRT machines without discharging the burden of proof that there was no other less intrusive alternative measure or a more transparent formulation that would achieve the objectives of the State effectively.

LEGAL FRAMEWORK IN THE EUROPEAN UNION (EU)

Within the EU, the regulation of biometric data processing via FRTs is governed by the *General Data Protection Regulation 2016* (EU) ("GDPR") and the *Artificial Intelligence Act 2024* (EU) ("AIA"). The GDPR is primarily concerned with ensuring that personal data, including biometric identifiers, is processed in a lawful and accountable manner. The AIA seeks to create a framework for the expansion and deployment of trustworthy AI systems. Under Art. 9 of the GDPR, biometric information is categorised as a distinct class of personal data, and its processing is permissible only under narrowly defined exceptions, such as for safeguarding public security. Art. 5(1)(h) of the AIA designates technologies involving biometric data as high-risk AI systems, thereby subjecting their market deployment to stringent regulatory requirements applicable in instances like terrorism or human trafficking. Moreover, under Art. 5(1)(e), the AIA explicitly prohibits the use of AI systems that construct or broaden facial recognition databases by indiscriminately collecting facial images from sources such as the internet or CCTVs (Simmler & Canova, 2025). A notable example that would be proscribed under this is the U.S.-based private company Clearview AI software, which offers advanced FRT primarily to law enforcement, military, and government agencies. Its web-based platform draws on a vast database of over 60 billion facial images sourced from publicly available online content like social media, news, and mugshots.

While the AIA prohibits the indiscriminate scraping of facial images, it remains largely silent on the broader regulation of data collection processes. What is required is a framework that delineates the permissible types and sources of biometric data, the demographic groups impacted, the transparency of the data-gathering measures, and the specific purposes for which such data is collected (Simmler & Canova, 2025). The deployment of automated FRTs raises complex legal, technical, and operational challenges that may infringe upon data protection rights, undermine the uniform enforcement of the GDPR and the AIA, and result in fragmented implementation. Consequently, human rights advocates have expressed strong concern over the removal of a proposed general ban on real-time FRT in both the June 2023 draft and the final version of the AIA, citing the inadequacy of restrictions and the threat of mass surveillance.

LEGAL FRAMEWORK IN INDIA

In *Anivar Aravind v. Ministry of Home Affairs* (2020), the Karnataka High Court raised significant concerns about the legal validity of FRT, emphasising the need for a comprehensive regulatory framework governing the use of AI in policing. While statutes such as the *Information Technology Act 2000* (Ind), *Aadhaar Act 2016* (Ind), *Bharatiya Nagarik Suraksha Sanhita 2023* (Ind), and particularly the *Criminal Procedure (Identification) Act 2022* (Ind) ("CPA"), and *Digital Personal Data Protection Act 2023* (Ind) ("DPDPA"), touch upon related issues, none provide robust oversight. S. 29 of AA prohibits the disclosure of biometric data without consent. However, S. 33 allows disclosure of data in the interest of national security, which is vaguely defined (Parsheera, 2019).

The CPA broadens state powers to collect biometric data, including iris and retina scans, with S. 3 permitting retention for up to 75 years. This poses serious privacy risks and contravenes Art. 21 as articulated in the Aadhaar judgement. It also goes against *Selvi v. State of Karnataka* (2010), where the Supreme Court recognised that involuntary biometric collection infringes the right against self-incrimination under Art. 20.

The DPDPA mentions about Data Fiduciaries, which as per S. 2(i) refers to any person who alone or in conjunction with other persons determine the purpose and means of processing of personal data. This encompasses the State, corporations, digital platforms, juristic entities, and individuals. Although the DPDPA obligates Data Fiduciaries to ensure data accuracy, security, and timely deletion once its purpose has been met under S. 8, the broader legal framework must place stronger emphasis on safeguarding sensitive personal information, particularly in the context of AI use within the criminal justice system.

FRT enables continuous and covert surveillance in public spaces, potentially granting governments and corporations the ability to monitor people's actions, movements, and interactions (Naren & Mishra, 2025). This raises serious concerns about consent and autonomy, especially considering S. 6 of the DPDPA, which sets conditions for consent for lawful data processing to be unconditional and unambiguous. S. 4(1)(b) can be seen as an exception to consent as it allows processing personal data of a Data Principal (the concerned individual) for *"certain legitimate uses"*. The GDPR's version of this section, as a *"legitimate interest"* ground, is mentioned in Art. 6(1)(f). The key difference is that the GDPR requires compliance with a three-part test when invoking this exception: purpose test, necessity test and balancing test. This is similar to what was held in the Aadhaar judgement. However, under the DPDPA, such kind of a mechanism is unfortunately missing.

Under S. 17(2), DPDPA also significantly limits individual rights by permitting broad exemptions for government agencies and authorising the Central Government to exclude certain data processing activities from its scope. In deploying AI, it is imperative to adhere to core ethical principles, including respect for individual autonomy, harm prevention, fairness, and transparency (Centre for AI and Digital Policy, 2023).

PROPOSED REGULATORY MEASURES

NITI Aayog's policy document *Responsible AI for All* (2022) outlines a vision for AI governance that emphasises the benefits of AI while advocating for a careful balance between innovation and risk. The report promotes a primarily self-regulatory, non-interventionist approach, acknowledging potential threats to rights but characterising them as remote or speculative issues to be addressed only when they actualise (NITI Aayog, 2022). However, any move towards formalising the use of automated FRTs must be heralded by a transparent and participatory policy-making process. This entails a clear articulation by the government of the objectives sought, a rigorous evaluation of alternative measures, and a justification of automated FRTs as necessary and proportionate. Importantly, such a process must allow for genuine public and stakeholder engagement, with a corresponding duty on the part of the State to respond meaningfully to the feedback received.

As a starting point, the law must clearly and narrowly delineate the permissible scope of automated FRT, specifying both the purposes for its use and the categories of individuals whose images may be included in gallery databases. One approach to ensuring such narrow tailoring would be to mandate that automated FRT deployment occur solely pursuant to a judicial order, and only in the context of investigations involving serious criminal offences, specifically, those classified as cognizable and non-bailable (Parsheera, 2019).

Moreover, the legal framework should strictly limit the sources from which images may be drawn for inclusion in the gallery database, rather than permitting indiscriminate inclusion of images from the general public. It should specify that only individuals with a prior record of conviction, accusation, or reasonable suspicion of involvement in an offence may be included. Nonetheless, the law may allow for judicial authorisation to expand the scope in exceptional cases, where the facts and circumstances warrant the use of alternative image sources for matching purposes.

Finally, the architecture of the automated FRT system must incorporate a robust audit mechanism to monitor and record its use. This should include detailed logs documenting each instance of deployment, the outcomes produced, the officials responsible for reviewing the results, the decisions taken based on those outcomes, and the subsequent consequences. Such a system of traceability is essential for enabling independent audits and ensuring the accountability of those who operate and oversee the application of such a technology.

CONCLUSION

A foundational aspect of any theory of privacy must involve characterising the intrinsic value of freedom from specific forms of intrusion. In this regard, the Indian state bears a duty to ensure complete transparency in its use of automated FRTs. At a minimum, it should take active consent of individuals, disclose aggregate data on the number of authorisations granted and denied, further broken down by service provider, investigative purpose, and category of request. Moreover, independent oversight bodies must be established to guarantee accountability and transparency in such surveillance practices. Drawing on Rawls (1971) *A Theory of Justice*, which postulates that institutions must safeguard equal liberties and fair opportunities, especially for the least advantaged, it follows that AI-based crime prevention tools must be designed and deployed in ways that do not perpetuate systemic inequalities or disproportionately impact marginalised populations.

From a Rawlsian perspective, the ethical use of AI in law enforcement demands that such systems be structured to reduce inequality, uphold justice, and reinforce civil liberties. In the Indian context, administrative agencies have traditionally operated with considerable discretion in policymaking and implementation, a latitude often justified by the imperatives of a welfare-oriented state. However, this broad administrative leeway, coupled with an evolving legislative framework that permits AI integration, is now facilitating the incorporation of privately developed surveillance technologies into governmental functions. As these systems become embedded in administrative and legal processes, transparency and explainability are essential to uphold the integrity of AI-driven evidence in judicial proceedings, thereby safeguarding the legitimacy and fairness of the justice system.

NOTES

1 Assistant Professor, Manipal University Jaipur (shtantika.mukherjee@jaipur.manipal.edu)
2 Assistant Professor, Manipal University Jaipur (hiteshi.agarwal@jaipur.manipal.edu)

REFERENCES

2 percent accuracy in Delhi police's facial recognition software: HC told. (2018, August 23). *Hindustan Times*. www.hindustantimes.com/cities/only-2-percent-accuracy-in-delhi-police-facial-recognition-software-high-court-told/story-D4d2oP3PAVn8OwyCqpA4FO.html

Aadhaar Act 2016 (India).

Anivar Aravind v. Ministry of Home Affairs, GM PIL WP (C) 7483 of 2020 (India, 2020).

Artificial Intelligence Act 2024 (EU).

Bharatiya Nagarik Suraksha Sanhita, *2023* (India)

Bureau of Police Research & Development. (2024). *Effectiveness Of CCTV surveillance systems for police – Comparative study.* https://bprd.nic.in/uploads/pdf/Effectiveness%20of%20CCTV%20Surveillance%20Systems%20for%20Police.pdf

Centre for AI and Digital Policy. (2023). *Artificial intelligence and democratic values 2022.* www.caidp.org/reports/aidv-2022/

Common Cause and Lokniti. (*2023*). *Status of policing in India report.* www.commoncause.in/wotadmin/upload/REPORT_2023.pdf

K.S. Puttaswamy (Retd.) v. Union of India, (2019) (1) SCC 1 (India).

Leslie, D. (2020). Understanding bias in facial recognition technologies. *SSRN Electronic Journal.* https://doi.org/10.2139/ssrn.3705658

Mann, M., & Smith, M. (2017). Automated facial recognition technology: Recent developments and approaches to oversight. *University of New South Wales Law Journal*, *40*(1). https://doi.org/10.53637/KAVV4291

Marda, V., & Narayan, S. (2020). Data in New Delhi's predictive policing system. In *Proceedings of the 2020 Conference on Fairness, Accountability, and Transparency* (pp. 317–324). https://doi.org/10.1145/3351095.3372865

Naren, N., & Mishra, A. (2025). Dissecting the regulatory landscape of facial recognition technology. In B. N. Mukherjee, R. Uduwerage-Perera, M. Mathew, & S. Kumar Tripathi (Eds.), *Rethinking the Police for a Better Future: Navigating Policing Challenges with Accountability and Trust* (pp. 131–147). Springer Nature Switzerland. https://doi.org/10.1007/978-3-031-83173-7_8

NITI Aayog. (2022). *Responsible AI for All.* www.niti.gov.in/sites/default/files/2022-11/Ai_for_All_2022_02112022_0.pdf

Parsheera, S. (2019, December). *Adoption and Regulation of Facial Recognition Technologies in India: Why and Why Not?* (Data Governance Network working paper no. 5). https://doi.org/10.2139/ssrn.3525324

Rawls, J. (1971). *A Theory of Justice.* Harvard University Press.

Selvi v. State of Karnataka (2010) 7 SCC 263

Simmler, M., & Canova, G. (2025). Facial recognition technology in law enforcement: Regulating data analysis of another kind. *Computer Law & Security Review*, *56*. https://doi.org/10.1016/j.clsr.2024.106092

Sinha, A. (2024, March 13). *The Landscape of Facial Recognition Technologies in India.* Tech Policy Press. https://techpolicy.press/the-landscape-of-facial-recognition-technologies-in-india

14 Artificial Intelligence and Product Liability

A Consumer Protection Act, 2019 Perspective

Monidipa Sengupta and Shreya Matilal

INTRODUCTION

While artificial intelligence is a largely benevolent technique, it is but a matter of time that these systems lead to situations where legal liability arises. The fundamental difference between a system using artificial intelligence and a system that uses a traditional computer programme is the ability of the artificial intelligence system to make decisions without human intervention, or making decisions with only human supervision and not intervention. In such circumstances, the question arises as to who should be made responsible when these systems make a decision that causes harm or damage to a human being. Certainly, the answer cannot be to blame the system employing the artificial intelligence technology itself, as it would provide a carte blanche for manufacturers and sellers to flood the market with faulty and harmful, even malicious, systems and escape the liability that should be ascribed to them. But due to the unique nature of these systems, one cannot treat them the way a traditional computer software is treated either. This brings us to the next part of this chapter, where the authors would analyse how the ascription of liability would be done when a product liability action is brought due to the damages or injury caused to a human being due to an interaction with an artificial intelligence system.

An examination of the product liability principles in the context of harms caused by interactions with artificial intelligence systems is necessary. Even though a vast majority of artificial intelligence-driven projects are safe and beneficial, there is a non-zero probability that at some point in time these systems would make a decision that causes harm to a human being. This is especially true as artificial intelligence systems become more common in high-risk sectors. The risk of serious injury is higher in sectors such as transport (for example, self-driving cars making an erratic decision can cause loss of life), healthcare (for example, surgical arms running on an artificial intelligence system may make a decision causing harm to a person that could have been preventable), facial recognition (for example, artificial intelligence systems used to track criminals relying of racially biased data leading to harassment and targeting of innocent people), deepfakes (for examples, systems that can produce fake videos of a person engaging in criminal activity such as robbery leading to police harassment), etc.

In such situations, it is imperative to ask who is to bear the blame or the liability of the damage or injury caused by an artificial intelligence system. The following section will deal in depth with the principles of product liability as applied to legal liability arising out of interaction with artificial intelligence systems.

Product liability laws provide a recourse to consumers against defective products sold to them or harmful services provided to them. This is based on the principle of *caveat venditor*, putting the burden on the seller or manufacturer of a product or provider of service to compensate for the injury

DOI: 10.1201/9781003629146-15

or loss caused by a defect in said product or service. The principles governing product liability laws derive both from contract law and tort law. Product liability principles evolved from the tort law of negligence and from the laws of contract, which dealt with warranty. Can tortious liability be contractually limited?

Product liability in its current form is a strict liability wrong, meaning that even if the manufacturer or seller took due care and had no intention of causing harm or injury to the plaintiff, they can be found liable for any damage caused to the plaintiff due to a defect in the product that they manufactured or sold to the plaintiff. This has made product liability a wrong without an intent on the part of the defendant to cause damage or injury.

The Indian legislature has included a Chapter on Product Liability in the Consumer Protection Act 2019. This Act has covered all required definitions and has made provisions that cover the liabilities of all stakeholders.

The advent of artificial intelligence as popular technique in software products has led to the question of who the liability would be ascribed to in an event where damage is caused by an interaction with such systems. In this chapter, the authors would explore the principles pertaining to product liability and analyse how they can be applied in instances where legal damages are incurred due to interaction with artificial intelligence systems.

This chapter is divided into two parts. In the first part of this chapter will explore the development of product liability laws. The first part studies the development of product liability in common law jurisdictions and then analyses how those principles were applied in India before the Consumer Protection Act 2019.

The second part analyses the provisions of the Consumer Protection Act 2019. This part is divided into two parts dealing with the liability of product manufacturers and product sellers, respectively, in matters where interactions with artificial intelligence systems lead to injury to a person.

GENESIS OF PRODUCT LIABILITY

The product liability law, as it stands today, combines the law of tort and contract. A leading authority commenting on the nature of product liability stated that product liability law has to be located in the hybrid of tort-contract-warranties. Be that as it may, the genesis of modern theories of product liability law revolves around negligence, breach of warranty, misrepresentation, and strict liability.

In the 19th century, the early case laws wherein manufacturers of a product were sued for causing injury to the plaintiffs, in general, were exempted from liability unless there were direct contractual relationships between the plaintiffs and the manufacturers. For example, in *Winterbottom v Wright*[1] the plaintiff suffered injury due to the collapse of a railway coach, and the court held that the manufacturer of the coach was not liable as there was no privity of contract.

This view of manufacturer's liability started changing following the famous New York Court of Appeals opinion by Judge Cardozo in the case of *MacPherson v. Buick Motor Co.*[2] In this 1916 opinion, the requirement of privity was relaxed for negligence actions. In the mentioned case, the plaintiff was injured due to the collapse of one of the wheels in his car manufactured by the defendant company. The defendant, despite not having manufactured the wheel itself, could have easily detected the defect in the wheel through reasonable inspection. The plaintiff had bought the car from a dealer and, as such did not have a contract with the defendant manufacturer company. Judge Cardozo opined that if the negligence was on the part of the defendant company, then it must be held liable even without having a privity of contract with the plaintiff. Further, in *Baxter v. Ford Motors Co.*[3] where the court had previously held that consumers should be able to recover damages for false advertising especially when the advertisement was aimed directly at the consumer. Also, in the case of *Jacob E. Decker & Sons Inc. v. Capps*,[4] the court explained that liability must be based on "the broad principle of public policy to protect human health and life."

By shifting to strict liability principles, the courts started to slowly but surely shift the burden of proof from the plaintiff to the defendant in matters related to product liability. In 1944, Judge Traynor opined that "In my opinion it should now be recognised that a manufacturer incurs an absolute liability when an article that he has placed on the market, knowing that it is to be used without inspection, proves to have a defect that causes injury to human beings."[5] With the idea of reducing the plaintiff's burden of proof, the courts eventually developed the concept of implied warranty and made the concept of strict liability on the manufacturer more well-defined.

The Ohio Supreme Court in *Rogers v. Toni Home Permanent Co.*,[6] abolished the privity bar in express warranty matters as express warranty action originally derived from tort of deceit and not contract.[7] This judgement was made relying on *Baxter v. Ford Motors Co.*,[8] which was discussed earlier in this chapter.

In 1960, in the case of *Henningsen v. Bloomfield Motors, Inc.*,[9] the plaintiff's wife suffered injury due to a malfunction with the car's steering wheel. The plaintiff had purchased the car from the defendant dealership. The court held that with every sale of a product, there was an implied warranty or guarantee of safety. Also, despite the plaintiff being the sole owner of the car, the implied warranty of safety extended to every reasonably foreseeable user of the car. This concept of implied warranty furthered the cause of reducing the plaintiff's burden of proof against manufacturers of defective products and held manufacturers of defective products more accountable for the safety and security of their products. In the words of Dean William Prosser, Henningsen marked the "fall of the citadel of privity."[10]

A few years later, in *Greenman v. Yuba Power Products, Inc.*,[11] where the plaintiff was injured while using a gadget, the Supreme Court of California held that the plaintiff could sue the manufacturer if they could show that they suffered an injury while using the product for its intended purpose due to a defect in the product's design or manufacture of which the plaintiff was not made aware.

It is a simple deduction that liability can only be attached to the defendant when a causal link has been established between the defect in the product and the plaintiff's injury. In other words, only the "actual cause" of injury is considered while attaching liability to a defendant.

For this determination, the court asks the question "if not for the defect in the product, would the injury of the plaintiff have occurred"? If the answer to that question is 'no', then the defendant is held liable.

In *Barnett v. Chelsea & Kensington Hospital Management Committee*,[12] the plaintiff's husband had gone to the defendant's hospital when he felt ill after drinking some tea. Despite the husband looking very sickly, the orderly (due to medical reasons of their own) turned him away and asked him to consult other doctors. The husband died in a few hours due to arsenic poisoning. In the action against the defendant hospital, the judge found that there was evidence of negligence but that this negligence could not cause injury or death to the plaintiff's husband. In the humble opinion of the author, a far better action may have been brought against the person who sold the plaintiff tea which had arsenic in it.

But despite its near-universal acceptance, this test suffers from some limitations. There is often a tenuous relation between actions. For example, if a person in the city of Kolkata had to take an alternate route to their workplace due to the construction of the flyover by the Kolkata Municipal Corporation, and they got robbed on this new route. They can probably claim that if the Kolkata Municipal Corporation had not started construction on the flyover, they would not have been robbed. And while this claim is factually accurate, the causal link between the action and injury is too slim to be of any impact. This brings us to the second issue with the but-for test. Because of the many tenuous relations of actions and outcomes, this test can be misused easily to add parties to a claim in a frivolous manner. In the previous example, this may even include the elected representative from that constituency in the claim if this test were strictly followed.

The courts in the USA had used the Consumer Expectation Test to determine the liability of the manufacturer or seller during the 1960s. According to the Second Restatement of Torts, the

Consumer Expectation Test is that "A product is defective when, at the time of sale or distribution... is defective in design. A product is defective in design when the foreseeable risks of harm posed by the product could have been reduced or avoided by the adoption of a reasonable alternative design by the seller or other distributor, or a predecessor in the commercial chain of distribution, and the omission of the alternative design renders the product not reasonably safe."[13]

But this test had evolved into the Risk-Utility test by the 1990s. This tries to do a cost-benefit analysis of whether the risk of using the product is greater than the utility of said product. If that is so, then the manufacturer or seller would be held liable for the damage or injury caused by the use of the product. This test is an evolution of the Hand Formula used to determine the calculus of negligence. It compares the risk of using the damaged product with the cost of manufacturing an alternative and presumably safer design. If the probability of injury and the gravity of injury are greater than the cost of an alternative safer design and the diminished utility of the product, then the manufacturer or seller would be held liable for the damage caused by the product.

While both the Consumer Utility and the Risk-Utility test have their own benefits and practical difficulties in application, they are both excellent tools in the determination of product liability of defective products and have been used individually and in combination by the Courts in the USA, for example, in *Tincher v. Omega Flex, Inc.*[14]

THE GENERAL PRINCIPLES OF PRODUCT LIABILITY

The development of product liability principles is a story of the coming together of tort and contract law principles in a manner to slowly transfer the burden of proof from the plaintiff to the manufacturer or vendor whose defective products or services cause damage to the plaintiff. A product liability claim could be based on negligence, breach of warranty, or strict liability. If the claim of the plaintiff was based on negligence of the manufacturer or any party in the chain of manufacturing or the seller, then the plaintiff had to prove that the manufacturer or the seller failed to meet the reasonable standard of care while manufacturing or selling the product. The higher the risk that a defective product could cause injury or damage, the higher the standard of care had to be met by the manufacturer or the seller to escape liability. If the claim is based on an implied or express warranty provided by the manufacturer or seller by way of a written guarantee as to the fitness of the product or oral guarantee by the seller while making the sale, then the plaintiff has the burden to prove that the product was not fit as per the warranty provided by the manufacturer or seller. Implied warranties will be discussed towards the end of this section while discussing the case of *Henningsen v. Bloomfield Motors, Inc.*[15] if the claim is based on strict liability then the burden of proof shifts from the plaintiff as they neither have to prove that the manufacturer or seller have not met a reasonable standard of care, nor do they have to prove that a product has not met the warranty provided by the manufacturer or seller.

POSITION IN INDIA

POSITION BEFORE CONSUMER PROTECTION ACT, 2019

Today, product liability refers to the liability of all parties in the manufacturing chain, starting from the manufacturer of parts to the retailer, for the injury caused by a defect in a product. In many jurisdictions, the definition of a product is extended to intangible products and even services as under the Consumer Protection Act 2019, of India.

However, till 2019, India too utilised this amalgamation of the tort law of negligence and the laws relating to the breach of contract to deal with claims of product liability. But with the enactment of the Consumer Protection Act 2019, that has changed. In the following section, the authors will explore and analyse the various provisions related to product liability introduced in the Act of 2019 before analysing their applicability in the instances where legal liability arises out of interactions with artificial intelligence systems.

India did not have a product liability regime enshrined in legislation till the enforcement of the Consumer Protection Act 2019. Before the Consumer Protection Act of 2019, plaintiffs had to rely on laws regarding negligence, warranty, strict liability or a combination thereof. Indian courts have, in the past, dealt with product liability claims based on the principles of negligence and strict liability.

As discussed in the previous section this put an unfair burden of proof on an injured plaintiff, except in matters of strict liability. With the shift in perspective in legal jurisprudence heralded by the courts of the United States of America, regarding the shift in the burden of proof from the plaintiff to the defendant in the evolving landscape of product liability laws. This was first reflected in the opinion of the Karnataka High Court in the case of *Airbus Industries vs Laura Howell Linton*,[16] which involved an aircraft crash that caused many casualties. The respondents claimed that courts in Texas would be a better forum due to the lack of product liability laws in India, to which the single judge bench had opined "*a mere fact that the Indian Courts does not have the strict product liability law, it is not wise to say that in such a situation and parties can go without any remedy. As it was done in Charan Lal Sahu v. Union of India (Bhopal Gas Disaster) that such antiquated acts can be drastically amended or fresh legislation should be enacted to save the situation.*" The Court effectively stressed the need to have the principles of product liability enshrined in the extensive legislative framework of India.

Even in the absence of legislation dealing directly and explicitly with product liability, India had drawn learnings from the common law jurisdictions regarding product liability. The major principles that India adopted were the dilution of privity of contract, introduction of strict liability and the reduction of the plaintiff's burden of proof. Indian courts initially largely relied on the Sale of Goods Act, 1930. The principles of product liability that now makes the manufacturer liable for injury caused by their product was severely constrained by the principle of privity of contract.

It was noted in *Eastern Mining Contractors (P) Ltd. v. Premier Automobiles Ltd.*[17] that no privity of contract existed between the consumer and manufacturer and therefore an action could not be brought against the manufacturer for an injury caused by their manufactured product. This position was diluted in *G. McKenzie & Co. Ltd. v. Nagendra Nath Mahalanabish,*[18] where the court came to the conclusion that two separate actions were available to the consumer- first, an action for breach of contract against the seller and second, an action in tort against the product manufacturer. Finally, the courts arrived at a conclusion that reflects the current standing of product liability law in India, where both product manufacturer and product seller can be ascribed liability, in *Eternit Everest Ltd. v. C.G Abraham,*[19] where the seller was held to be an agent of the manufacturers, and therefore the manufacturers were held liable under Section 16 of Sale of Goods Act 1930. This finally established a clear legal nexus between the consumer and the manufacturer that was previously shielded by the privity of contract.

Even though the Consumer Protection Act 1986 did not deal with product liability directly, it was a step forward from the Sale of Goods Act 1930, as courts started recognising the existence of strict product liability against product manufacturers based on an implied contract between product manufacturers and consumers.[20] Despite this, a certain amount of uncertainty and doubt remained in Indian law regarding the liability of manufacturers in product liability actions that was ultimately remedied with a comprehensive chapter in the Consumer Protection Act 2019.

Position after Consumer Protection Act, 2019 Analysed in Relation to Injuries Arising out of Interactions with Artificial Intelligence Systems

In time, India did include a chapter on product liability in its Consumer Protection Act of 2019. This Chapter and the Act deal with product liability in great detail and pave the way for the development of a product liability regime in India.

A brief look at the definition clause of the Consumer Protection Act 2019 shows that the legislature has provided definitions that are broad in scope and clearly intend to bring together all product liability claims under the umbrella of the Consumer Protection Act 2019.

The liability accrued from the potential injuries that may be caused due to interactions with artificial intelligence systems can be broadly studied under the sections dealing with the liability of product manufacturers and product sellers under the Consumer Protection Act, 2019. The European Union has recently introduced three regulatory Bills regarding artificial intelligence, and in all three, artificial intelligence systems have been concluded to be products and not services. Therefore, there is clearly no party that can be considered a service provider in the instances of injuries arising out of interactions with artificial intelligence systems. This rules out the application of Section 85 of the Consumer Protection Act 2019 in the ascription of liability that arises out of interaction with artificial intelligence systems.

While the product liability regime in India is very well defined, the governance norms for systems using artificial intelligence has not been analysed in depth. This is an unacceptable position for a growing economy, especially when much of India's economic growth is due to the fast-paced development in the software services sector.

With artificial intelligence techniques becoming a mainstay in the software industry, finding wide-ranged application in healthcare, education, transport, finance, cybersecurity, etc., it becomes extremely important to discuss how to deal with the instances of legal liability arising out of interactions with artificial intelligence systems.

ANALYSING MANUFACTURERS WITH RESPECT TO INJURIES ARISING OUT OF INTERACTIONS WITH AI SYSTEMS

The Consumer Protection Act, 2019 defines product manufacturer as a person who "(i) makes any product or parts thereof; or (ii) assembles parts thereof made by others; or (iii) puts or causes to be put his own mark on any products made by any other person; or(iv) makes a product and sells, distributes, leases, installs, prepares, packages, labels, markets, repairs, maintains such product or is otherwise involved in placing such product for commercial purpose; or (v) designs, produces, fabricates, constructs or re-manufactures any product before its sale; or (vi) being a product seller of a product, is also a manufacturer of such product."[21]

Section 84 of the Consumer Protection Act, 2019 deals with the liability of the product manufacturers. The manufacturer of a product would be found liable in a product liability action if any of the following five conditions are met. First, that the product manufactured by them has a manufacturing defect. Second, the product manufactured by them contains a defect in its design. Third, there were manufacturing specifications that the manufacturer did not follow. Fourth, the product manufactured fails to fulfil the express warranty provided by the manufacturer. It must be noted that in the case of a product liability claim brought against a manufacturer, the Indian Consumer Protection Act 2019 does not follow the concept of implied warranty. Fifth, that the manufacturer of the product either did not provide sufficient and proper instructions on how to use the product without incurring any harm or did not provide enough warning about the product being used in an improper, incorrect, or hazardous manner. If any of the above conditions are proved by the consumer, then the manufacturer of the product would be found liable in a product liability action, without the plaintiff having the burden to prove that the manufacturer was negligent regarding the product's manufacture or fraudulent regarding the express warranty provided.

In *Maruti Udyog v. Hasmukh Lakshmichand*,[22] the manufacturing defect is much more than an ordinary defect which can be cured by replacing the defective part. Manufacturing defect is fundamental basic defect which creeps in while manufacturing the machinery. To prove such a defect, the opinion of an expert is necessary. This opinion of the court must be read with Section 2(10) of the Consumer Protection Act 2019, which provides the definition for "defect." This sub-section defines the term 'defect' as any fault, imperfection or shortcoming in the quality, quantity, potency, purity or standard which is required to be maintained by or under any law for the time being in force or under any contract, express or implied or as is claimed by the trader in any manner whatsoever in relation to any goods or product and the expression "defective" shall be construed accordingly.

An artificial intelligence system comprises not only of the software that is employing artificial intelligence techniques but also the associated hardware that is crucial for the software to perform the task or tasks that it is designed to perform. In such a system, the hardware of the system is the machinery that undergoes a manufacturing process as is understood in the definition and opinion quoted earlier. It is, therefore, amply clear that the term 'manufacturing defect' applies to the hardware component attached to the artificial intelligence system concerned. For example, in a matter concerning an injury caused to a pedestrian by a self-driving car, the hardware unit is the car itself. The manufacturer of the car is the person or entity which bears the liability of a manufacturing defect

Another factor that must be considered is that of proximal cause. The simple existence of a manufacturing defect does not accrue liability. The manufacturing defect must also be the proximal cause of the injury. In the self-driving car example, the manufacturing defect could be in the tyres, which could be made of low-quality material, causing them to burst and injure a pedestrian. In this case, the proximal cause of injury would be the bursting of the tire due to the use of substandard material. In such a case, keeping in mind that the whole car is not manufactured by the same entity, the manufacturer of the tire would bear the liability of the injury. If the party which assembled all the manufactured parts into a car was responsible for inspection of quality (provided that the defect could have been detected by the inspection) then the liability of the injury would be shared by the manufacturer of the tire and the party which assembled the final product.

"Defect in design" is another key ingredient of Section 84. The term "design" is defined in relation to a product, means the intended or known physical and material characteristics of such product and includes any intended or known formulation or content of such product and the usual result of the intended manufacturing or other process used to produce such product.[23] Reading the definition of the terms 'design' and 'defect' as provided in the Consumer Protection Act, 2019, it can be assessed that the software component of an artificial intelligence system is a material characteristic of the system. Revisiting the self-driving car example, if the injury to the pedestrian was caused by a decision made by the artificial intelligence software, then it would be considered a 'fault' or 'shortcoming' in the software itself and would amount to a defect as defined under Section 2(10) of the Consumer Protection Act, 2019. In such a case, the developer of the software would bear liability of the injury.

A defect in design can also occur in the hardware component of the system. Consider, for example, a surgical arm operated with the aid of an artificial intelligence software that is not designed to provide maximum expected mobility of the surgical arm. This fault or shortcoming leads to an injury in a patient undergoing surgery. In such a situation, the manufacturer of the arm itself would be liable for the injury.

Although in cases of software, which would be the major and relevant component of the product in artificial intelligence systems, manufacturing and design defects might sound similar, there is a subtle difference. Manufacturing defect is invoked when one unit of a product manufactured by the manufacturer is defective in a manner such that it causes injury to a person. For example, a manufacturer produces an artificial intelligence system used in a surgical arm whose intended purpose is to assist a surgeon in medical procedures. One of these surgical arms gets equipped with a corrupted version of the artificial intelligence software and is sold to a hospital, where it causes preventable harm to a patient during a medical procedure. In such a case, the patient and the hospital may bring a product liability claim against the manufacturer of the surgical arm.

Design defects are defects found in a class of products. For example, the manufacturer of a CCTV-based security system that flags racial minorities as potential law-breakers will be held liable in a product liability claim in the event a person flagged by the faulty system is harassed by the security. The liability, again, will be on the manufacturer as under Section 84 of the Consumer Protection Act 2019. The only situation where the liability in a product liability action brought for an injury arising out of an interaction with an artificial intelligence system with a design defect would be on the seller of the artificial intelligence system, seller is when the identity of the manufacturer of said system is unknown, as per Section 86(d) of the Consumer Protection Act 2019.

A manufacturer of a product can also be made liable if they do not conform to the express warranty provided by them. The Consumer Protection Act, 2019, defines express warranty as any material statement, affirmation of fact, promise or description relating to a product or service warranting that it conforms to such material statement, affirmation, promise or description and includes any sample or model of a product warranting that the whole of such product conforms to such sample or model.[24] Such an express warranty can apply to both the software and hardware components of an artificial intelligence system. The liability for the injury caused by the artificial intelligence system's components not conforming to the express warranty made by the manufacturer would be borne by the person or persons who made the express warranty for the system. Should the manufacturer fail to provide sufficient and proper instructions on how to safely use the artificial intelligence systems or warnings on how not to misuse the artificial intelligence systems, then they would be found liable under Section 84(e) of the Consumer Protection Act 2019.

ANALYSING SELLER'S LIABILITY WITH RESPECT TO INJURIES ARISING OUT OF INTERACTIONS WITH AI SYSTEMS

Product seller, in relation to a product, means a "person who imports, sells, distributes, leases, installs, prepares, packages, labels, markets, repairs, maintains, or otherwise is involved in placing such product for commercial purpose and includes (i) a manufacturer who is also a product seller; or (ii) a service provider."[25] This provision puts India a step ahead of the corresponding law in United States where the Third Restatement of Tort states that "services, even when provided commercially, are not products."[26]

If a product liability action is brought by a plaintiff against a product seller, provided that the seller is not also the product manufacturer, the plaintiff will have the burden to prove at least one of the following conditions for the action to succeed. First, the product seller had significant control over the various manufacturing processes of the product. These can include designing, testing, packaging, labelling, and manufacturing of the product that caused the injury or damage to the plaintiff. Second, the product seller has modified or altered the product in some manner. The plaintiff would have to prove that this specific modification or alteration is the actual and proximate cause of the harm caused to the plaintiff. Third, the seller also made an express warranty, which was not dependent on the warranty made by the manufacturer. The plaintiff has to prove that the product failed to conform to the express warranty provided by the seller. Fourth, if the manufacturer of the product is unknown, the seller will be liable in a product liability claim. This will also be similar if the service of notice, process, or warrant cannot be effected on the manufacturer. If the manufacturer is not bound by the law currently in force in India, or an order cannot be enforced against them, then the seller will be liable in the product liability action. Fifth, if the seller does not take reasonable care in the assembly, inspection, and maintenance of the products, then they shall be found liable in the product liability action. Also, if at the time of sale, the seller doesn't convey instructions for proper use of the product or a warning about improper use of the product as received from the product manufacturer, and this omission is the cause of the injury or damages suffered by the plaintiff, then the product seller would be held liable in the product liability action.

One of the key factors for the ascription of liability to the product seller in a product liability action is that the product seller should have exercised substantial control over the various aspects of manufacturing the product. The concept of substantial control was elaborated upon in the case of

Short v. Henderson.[27] This was elaborated to include the ability to select employees and the power to decide pay. The ability to control the method of doing work and the authority to suspend services. If a product seller has similar control over the various steps in the manufacturing process, then they can be ascribed liability in a product liability action.

Another factor to be kept in mind is the alteration or modification of the product by the seller. The seller would only be found liable if the product in question was altered or modified at the time of sale. This concept of alteration or modification can be extended to the product being covertly dangerous for use (for example, a seller who has sold a seemingly undamaged bag knowing that the bag cannot carry the weight typically expected similar products and the bag subsequently tears due to a heavy object that results in physical injury to the buyer) even though the product did not seem defective at the time of purchase. This can be related to the product's longevity, sturdiness, or the risk of using it. Such alteration or modification by the product seller can push it into the ambit of 'defect' as defined under Section 2(10) of the Consumer Protection Act, 2019, as discussed in the previous section of this chapter.

A product is not considered defective if it is safe for use in a specific manner and the injury or damage is a result of some misuse, inappropriate use, or use in a manner other than for which the product is habitually used. For example, an instant noodles manufacturer cannot be held liable if a consumer suffers harm after consuming an exceptionally large amount of the manufacturer's product.

The defect in the product must make the product unreasonably dangerous. While most products available for consumption are dangerous under certain circumstances, and some are downright harmful to human beings, the concept of unreasonable danger applies to the danger that an average consumer of the product would not be able to anticipate due to a defect in the product. A good example of this would be the sale of cigarettes. While smoking cigarettes is by itself a severely harmful activity, a regular consumer of cigarettes assumes the risk. But consider a situation where the manufacturer of the cigarettes mixes sawdust in the tobacco resulting in lung damage due to it. An average consumer of cigarettes does not assume that risk, and the mixing of sawdust in the tobacco makes the cigarette unreasonably dangerous for consumption.

Similarly, the concepts of express warranty and the omission of conveying instructions or warnings, as may be the case, would apply to product sellers in a manner similar to their application to product manufacturers.

An amalgam of the consumer expectation test and the risk-utility test can bring to light some factors that can help determine liability in these matters. First, the usefulness of the artificial intelligence systems to the user and to the community, and whether the usefulness or desirability of the artificial intelligence systems is more than the potential harm or gravity of injury it can cause. If the answer is yes, then the manufacturer or seller would not be found liable in a product liability claim. Second, whether another product or artificial intelligence systems exist that can perform the same task with the same efficiency without sacrificing the safety aspects. If the answer is yes, then the product manufacturer or seller would be found liable in a product liability action because the manufacturer can feasibly remove the unsafe characteristics of the systems without compromising efficiency and functionality. Third, can the user avoid the harm or injury based on intuition, common knowledge, or through instructions provided by the manufacturer or seller. If the answer is yes, then the manufacturer or sellers are not to be found liable in a product liability claim.

CONCLUSION

The capacity of an artificial intelligence system to rewrite part or the whole of its software makes it unique and often gives rise to the notion that the current legal system does not contain the laws required to ascribe liability to injuries arising out of interactions with artificial intelligence systems. This is because the decision-making process of some artificial intelligence systems is assumed to be independent of human intervention or supervision. The authors would like to reiterate that this pseudo-sentience presumed of artificial intelligence systems is more akin to a small pet animal than an adult human being of sound mind. Therefore, despite its obvious capacity to cause harm to humans who interact with it, the legal liability arising out of any interaction with an artificial intelligence system must be ascribed to one or more of the persons in its ecosystem (manufacturer seller, developer, etc.).

As with many discussions related to artificial intelligence, it might be argued that the particular decision that was the proximate cause of the injury was the decision made by the system itself without any human intervention, implying that holding the manufacturer liable would be a mistake. This implication arises due to mass anthropomorphising of artificial intelligence systems, fuelling the assumption of human-like intelligence. As of right now, the state of the art in the field of artificial intelligence is such that if one has to imagine these systems as sentient it would be more accurate to imagine these systems are sentient in the manner of a small animal. Attaching any responsibility, liability, or requirement for transparency to these systems would simply provide a path for manufacturers and sellers of such systems to avoid being held liable. The manufacturers of artificial intelligence systems must be held strictly liable for harms and injuries caused by interactions with artificial intelligence systems manufactured by them.

A vast majority of all artificial intelligence systems are employed as tools for the performance of certain tasks. There is always a non-zero probability that such artificial intelligence systems may cause injury or harm to a human being interacting with it. The liability arising from such interaction with an artificial intelligence system can be addressed by the branch of law that deals with product liability. India addresses such legal claims under Sections 84 and 86 of Consumer Protection Act 2019.

In a majority of the product liability actions brought for injuries arising from interactions with artificial intelligence systems, the liability would be ascribed to the manufacturer of the artificial intelligence systems. Some exceptions to this are when the seller has either omitted from conveying the instructions and warnings by the manufacturer of the artificial intelligence systems to the buyer, or when they are intimately and significantly involved in and have control over processes such as designing, packaging, labelling, testing and manufacturing of the artificial intelligence systems.

Despite being a relatively new development in liability regimes, product liability has all the tools required to address injuries arising out of interactions with artificial intelligence systems and is an excellent method to address injuries due to defective artificial intelligence systems being floated to the market and users by manufacturers and sellers.

NOTES

1 (1842) 152 ER 402 (Exchequer of Pleas 1842).
2 217 N.Y. 382. (New York Court of Appeals 1916).
3 168 Wash. 456, 12 P.2d 409, 88 A.L.R. 521 (1932) (The Supreme Court of Washington 1932).
4 139 Tex. 609, 164 S.W.2d 828, 142 A.L.R. 1479 (1942) (Texas Supreme Court 1942).
5 Escola v. Coca-Cola Bottling Co., 24 Cal.2d 453 (Supreme Court of California 1944).
6 167 Ohio St. 244, 4 Ohio Op. 2d 291, 147 N.E.2d 612, 75 A.L.R.2d 103 (1958) (California Supreme Court 1958).
7 Rogers v. Toni Home Permanent Co., 147 N.E.2d at 614 (Ohio Supreme Court 1958).
8 168 Wash. 456, 12 P.2d 409, 88 A.L.R. 521 (1932) (Washington Supreme Court 1932).
9 32 N.J. 358. (New Jersey Supreme Court 1960).
10 Prosser (1962). The Fall of the Citadel (Strict Liability to the Consumer). *50 Minn. L. Rev. 79.* https://scholarship. law.umn.edu/cgi/viewcontent.cgi?article=3558&context=mlr
11 59 Cal.2d 57. (Supreme Court of California 1963).
12 1969 1 QB 428 (High Court of Justice, Queen's Bench Division 1968).
13 Restatement (Second) of Torts § 402A, cmt. b (1965).
14 180 A.3d 386. (Pennsylvania Superior Court 2018).
15 32 N.J. 358. (Supreme Court of New Jersey 1960).
16 ILR 1994 KAR 1370 (Karnataka High Court 1994).

17 1962 SCC OnLine Bom 63 (Bombay High Court 1962).
18 1945 SCC OnLine Cal 24 (Calcutta High Court 1945).
19 2003 SCC OnLine Ker 180 (Kerala High Court 2003).
20 Jagrut Nagrik v. Baroda Automobiles Sales and Service, 2010 SCC OnLine NCDRC 250 (National Consumer Disputes Redressal Commission India 2010); Tata Motors Jivan Tara Building v. Rajesh Tyagi, 2013 SCC OnLine NCDRC 1031 (National Consumer Disputes Redressal Commission India 2013).
21 Section 2 (36), Consumer Protection Act, 2019.
22 (2009) CPJ 229 (NC) (Delhi State Consumer Disputes Redressal Commission 2009).
23 Section 2(12), Consumer Protection Act, 2019.
24 Section 2(20), Consumer Protection Act, 2019.
25 Section 2 (37), Consumer Protection Act, 2019.
26 Restatements (Third) of Torts 19(b), cmt. b (1965).
27 (1946) 62 TLR 427 (House of Lords 1946).

15 Ethical Challenges in Using Artificial Intelligence for Evidence Generation in Criminal Investigations

Balancing Innovation and Justice

Harsh Mahaseth and Sadqua Khatoon

INTRODUCTION

Artificial intelligence (AI) has revolutionized criminal investigations through effective processing of data, pattern detection, and improved forensic analysis. Machine learning tools assist in suspect profiling through the analysis of crime statistics (McCue, 2018), while facial recognition matches videos captured from surveillance to databases of crimes (Garvie, 2019). Predictive analytics anticipate future crime based on previous patterns (Ferguson, 2017), and derives vital information from reports and online sites (Brantingham et al., 2018). AI also accelerates DNA, fingerprint, and ballistics processing, enhancing investigative results. Contrary to traditional techniques subject to delay and inaccuracy (Meijer & Wessels, 2019), AI facilitates real-time crime reactions and preventive policing (Ahmed et al., 2025). But its use brings with it serious ethical concerns—algorithmic discrimination, untrustworthy evidence, privacy intrusion, and accountability deficits jeopardize judicial impartiality (Meijer & Wessels, 2019). While AI minimizes human bias, its black-box approach to decision-making can perpetuate discrimination (Garvie, 2019).

The study promotes a strong ethical framework highlighting openness, legal accountability, and protection of civil rights. Properly regulated, AI can improve justice without undermining human dignity.

AI IN CRIMINAL INVESTIGATIONS: CAPABILITIES AND APPLICATIONS

AI is transforming criminal investigations by enhancing decision-making, speeding up processes, and improving the analysis of evidence. Predictive policing assists in resource allocation based on historical crime data (Brantingham et al., 2018), whereas facial recognition assists with suspect identification but incurs privacy and bias issues. AI enhances forensic reliability through DNA, fingerprint, and ballistics analysis and assists with cybercrime detection through behavior monitoring and anomaly detection.

In spite of these developments, ethical issues—transparency, overreach of surveillance, and bias in algorithms—require robust regulation. Technologies such as geospatial mapping predict crime hotspots, allowing targeted interventions (Brantingham et al., 2018). Finally, a value-driven framework is needed to balance technological innovation with justice and civil liberties.

DOI: 10.1201/9781003629146-16

Crime Prediction and Predictive Policing

AI is transforming criminal justice through the strengthening of predictive policing, automation of forensics, and surveillance. Predictive software examines crime patterns and social contexts to inform patrols and resource deployment (Ferguson, 2017), though it is criticized for inducing bias and inequity. In forensic science, AI contributes to automated data extraction and fraud detection, while NLP is used in threat analysis. Facial recognition improves accuracy in suspect identification at the risk of privacy invasions and misidentification (Garvie, 2019). This is while AI-driven surveillance systems enhance promptness in responses but raise ethical issues on mass data collection. They require robust ethical frameworks and regulation to ensure civil liberties and justice are protected.

Case Studies and Real-World Applications

Some nations have implemented AI-based technologies to maximize public safety and optimize policing, with bias and privacy concerns still looming. LAPD in Los Angeles employs PredPol, an AI-based platform that projects locations of likely crime using historical data to enable strategic patrol deployment (Ferguson, 2017). Critics suggest it can potentially serve to entrench racial profiling and necessitates strict control to prevent discriminatory effects (Meijer & Wessels, 2019). In London, the Metropolitan Police use facial recognition technology to match suspects in real time by scanning crowds and comparing faces with crime databases (Garvie, 2019). While useful, this technology has concerned people about false positives and intrusion into individual privacy, prompting calls for regulatory openness. Singapore uses AI-empowered CCTV systems to track public areas, study patterns, and identify unusual behavior to alert authorities of possible threats. These systems aid proactive security, but they raise controversy regarding mass surveillance, data security, and state intrusiveness.

These international examples highlight the double reality of AI in policing: major operational advantages with ethical challenges demanding solid regulation and accountability.

ETHICAL CHALLENGES IN AI-GENERATED EVIDENCE

Although AI improves police work, there are certain moral dilemmas that must be resolved.

Bias and Discrimination in Algorithms

AI systems need enormous datasets to operate efficiently, but the datasets tend to capture systemic social biases, causing discriminatory outcomes (Buolamwini, 2023). Systemic data discrimination, underrepresentation, and inherent disparities can cause discriminatory AI action, especially in facial recognition technology, which misclassifies individuals from marginalized groups at an increasing rate (Leslie, 2020; Bhardwaj, 2024). These inaccuracies lead to false arrests and discriminatory court rulings and perpetuate racial profiling, as in the case of the COMPAS algorithm wrongly tagging Black defendants as high-risk (Angwin et al., 2016). Errors in facial recognition have also resulted in arrests of innocent people, with trials ensuing concerning the admissibility of AI-generated evidence in the courtroom (Leslie, 2020).

Depending on biased AI instruments risks the right to a fair trial and equal protection under the law, so their uncontrolled usage is both unfair and illegal (Brożek et al., 2023).

Privacy and Watching

AI-powered surveillance networks gather huge amounts of personal information frequently without people s knowledge or consent. Facial recognition, biometrics, and predictive analytics are used to monitor people's whereabouts, behaviors, and interactions. Much-hyped for public safety, such surveillance can infringe on privacy rights and open the door to abuse by corporations and governments. Legal experts caution that it threatens authoritarianism and civil rights violations. Litigation has questioned the admissibility of evidence based on AI, particularly if it is obtained illegally.

Having Clarity and Comprehensibility

AI systems are often referred to as "black boxes," as it may be hard to understand how decisions are made. Due to the fact that how AI-generated evidence works is not well known, individuals fear being held accountable and trusting it. It is hard to tell whether AI-generated evidence can be presented in court because of the black box problem. Judges and lawyers might struggle to determine the legitimacy of AI-based decisions if the algorithms supporting them are not fully transparent (Brożek et al., 2023). The right to explanation, which protects those affected by AI decisions to understand the rationale behind them, is growing in legal systems. The aim of explainable AI (XAI) is to make AI decision-making more understandable in such a way that individuals are able to observe how they function. Two of the methods that contribute toward an understanding of AI are Shapley Additive Explanations (SHAP) and Local Interpretable Model-Agnostic Explanations (LIME).

Taking Responsibility and Accountability

It is difficult to assign blame for AI errors. Developers, organizations, and end users all have a role to play when it comes to implementing AI. But who should be held accountable for AI errors is frequently unclear under the law (Upmann, 2024).The increasing autonomy of AI systems raises concerns about accountability. Due to the lack of clear mechanisms for holding individuals accountable, victims of AI errors frequently struggle to obtain justice (Cheong, 2024). It is very difficult to get justice for those harmed by AI errors. People run the risk of making poor decisions based on AI in the absence of established channels for obtaining justice (Upmann, 2024).

LEGAL AND REGULATORY ENVIRONMENT

The acceptability of AI evidence in courts is being scrutinized worldwide, with judicial systems demanding the evidence to be reliable, transparent, and just. The EU AI Act presents one of the most formalized regulatory frameworks by categorizing AI into four levels of risk—low, limited, high, and unacceptable—and imposing oversight and explainability on high-risk systems. In comparison, the U.S. structure is sector-focused, with efforts such as the Blueprint for an AI Bill of Rights and legislation like the Colorado AI Act and NYC Bias Audit Law targeting transparency and impact assessments (Brookings Institution). China prioritizes national security, and India is developing AI regulations based on data protection and ethical deployment (Web Asha Technologies).

Yet, disjointed legal frameworks make cross-border collaboration complicated and challenge accountability for AI-mediated decisions (Sherman, 2025). Policymakers continue to argue over who is responsible when algorithms yield errors or biased results. As AI extends its activities into surveillance and investigation, setting uniform ethical standards is crucial to protect human rights and maintain legality (Engler, 2023).To overcome these challenges, it is imperative to achieve a transparent and fair legal system in the era of AI.

Framework for Ethical AI Use in Criminal Justice

Fairness, accountability, transparency, and privacy (FATP) must be guaranteed to ensure ethical AI application in criminal justice. Fairness entails removing algorithmic bias using diverse training data sets and regular auditing, particularly in sentencing and predictive policing systems (Bharati, 2024). Accountability requires transparent legal processes determining liability for AI-caused mistakes or unjust convictions. Legislators, coders, and law enforcement agencies need to establish who is responsible and how the decision can be appealed or rectified. Transparency is essential, as AI algorithms tend to be "black boxes." Applications such as XAI and LIME provide greater clarity on how the decisions were arrived at, making it easier for judges and lawyers to understand AI-generated evidence (Bharati, 2024). Privacy concerns arise from AI's reliance on large datasets. To protect individuals' rights, technologies like facial recognition and predictive analytics must comply with data protection laws, and strict regulations must prevent unauthorized data use (Bharati, 2024). All these principles together constitute the ethical basis for incorporating AI into the criminal justice system.

Proposed Model for Governance: Finding a Balance between Innovation and Justice

In order to have equitable and accountable use of AI in criminal justice, an integrated governance framework is necessary. This involves setting up autonomous watchdog institutions comprising lawyers, ethicists, technology specialists, and civil society representatives to inspect AI tools, look into grievances, and suggest reforms. AI systems need to be audited and certified prior to deployment to maintain transparency, precision, and justice (Bharati, 2024). Publicly available bias tests and reports regarding sources of data, decision processes, and rates of error are critically important for accountability (Bharati, 2024).

Interagency coordination of law enforcement, judiciary, developers, and civil society is vital. Police officers require ethical training for accountable use of AI; courts need to assess the transparency and admissibility of evidence produced by AI; and developers must develop explainable, bias-reduced systems. Civil society acts as a watchdog by keeping an eye on human rights effects and informing ethical deployment of AI. These AI technologies such as facial recognition and predictive policing augment investigations but threaten to erode due process, fairness, and privacy. The EU's AI Act is a promising approach by categorizing systems according to risk and requiring oversight—though critics caution overregulation can inhibit innovation (Wang & Wu, 2024). Finding the balance between innovation and legal protection is essential to making AI enhance, not undermine, justice.

RECOMMENDATIONS AND WAY AHEAD

Embedding AI in criminal justice requires a phased, responsible approach to align progress with ethical protection. Policymakers need to start with pilot schemes to test the effectiveness and mitigations against ethical issues prior to full implementation. Public consultation—particularly with civil rights organizations, legal professionals, and impacted communities—is crucial to determine potential risks and build trust (Wang & Wu, 2024). Judges' training and law enforcers' and developers' training must prioritize ethical literacy such as bias detection, data privacy, and accountability. Public trust is established through transparency in AI procurement and use when governments open up on how technologies are procured and utilized (Wang & Wu, 2024). Legal education needs to change by integrating AI ethics to equip future professionals in preserving justice and due process in an AI-led system. Interdisciplinary studies that bridge technology and law will empower experts to develop strategies for dealing with intricate AI applications.

Technological solutions such as XAI and LIME increase transparency by interpreting decision-making processes (Wang & Wu, 2024). Placing prior emphasis on these technologies guarantees that AI-based evidence will be subject to critical examination in court, assisting in aligning the utilization of AI with human rights principles and legal norms.

CONCLUSION

Integrating AI into the criminal justice system provides operational advantages but creates essential ethical issues. It enhances police and court efficiency but also risks algorithmic bias, accountability, privacy, and transparency. Marginalized groups can be harmed by biased results, and AI's unexplained decision-making makes it difficult to admit and interpret in court. Surveillance and data gathering also raise privacy concerns. For ethical application, strong governance systems are needed. Solutions range from mandatory bias audits, certification programs, and independent monitoring. There is a need for cooperation between developers, law enforcers, judges, civil society, and the public in order to establish standards that meet the requirement of both innovation and justice. Ethical training, public engagement, and open, cautious adoption of AI can ensure the requirements of both are maintained. AI has to uphold essential legal principles like due process, fairness, and human rights. Regulatory frameworks such as the EU AI Act provide direction, but there are gaps—particularly on cross-border responsibility and attributing liability to algorithms. Further commitment to ethical regulation is crucial. Prioritize XAI for enhancing transparency and building public trust. Legal ethics education, interdisciplinary conversation, and community engagement can serve to anticipate future issues. Embedding AI ethics in criminal justice education will equip future lawyers to use AI-based systems responsibly. Human-centered AI governance and interpretability ultimately determine that justice will not be undermined.

REFERENCES

Ahmed, S., Khan, M. F., Singh, B., Singh, N., & Sharma, B. (2025). Enhancing crime scene analysis. In *IGI global eBooks* (pp. 63–84). https://doi.org/10.4018/979-8-3693-9405-2.ch004

Angwin, J., Larson, J., Mattu, S., & Kirchner, L. (2016). *Machine bias*. ProPublica.

Bharati, R. K. (2024). Ethical implications of AI in criminal justice: Balancing efficiency and due process. *International Journal of Multidisciplinary, 9*(7), 93–105.

Bhardwaj, N. (2024). *Algorithmic bias in facial recognition technologies*. Towards AI.

Brantingham, P. J., Brantingham, P. L., & Taylor, W. (2018). Artificial intelligence and crime prediction: A new approach to crime mapping. *Crime Science, 7*(1), 1–9.

Brożek, B., Furman, M., Jakubiec, M., & Kucharzyk, B. (2023). The black box problem revisited. *Artificial Intelligence and Law, 32*, 427–440.

Buolamwini, J. (2023). *Unmasking the bias in facial recognition algorithms*. MIT Sloan.

Cheong, B. C. (2024). Transparency and accountability in AI systems. *Frontiers in Human Dynamics, 6*, 1421273.

Engler, A. (2023). *The EU and U.S. diverge on AI regulation*. Brookings Institution.

Ferguson, A. G. (2017). *The rise of big data policing: Surveillance, race, and the future of law enforcement*. NYU Press. https://nyupress.org/9781479892822/the-rise-of-big-data-policing/

Garvie, C. (2019). Facial recognition technology and law enforcement: Ethical and legal implications. *Georgetown Law Center on Privacy & Technology*. www.congress.gov/crs_external_products/R/PDF/R46541/R46541.2.pdf

Leslie, D. (2020). *Understanding bias in facial recognition technologies*. The Alan Turing Institute.

Meijer, A., & Wessels, M. (2019). Predictive policing: Review of benefits and drawbacks. *International Journal of Public Administration, 42*(12), 1031–1039. https://doi.org/10.1080/01900692.2019.1575664

Sherman, N. (2025). AI regulations around the world. *Mind Foundry*. www.mindfoundry.ai/blog/ai-regulations-around-the-world

Upmann, P. (2024). *Who is accountable when AI makes erroneous decisions?* AIGN.

Wang, X., & Wu, Y. C. (2024). Balancing innovation and regulation in the age of generative artificial intelligence. *Journal of Information Policy, 14*, 385–416.

16 Designing 'Legitimate' AI-Driven Evidence Mechanism from the Rule of Law Perspective

Akanksha Bisoyi

INTRODUCTION

Penal theorists observe AI to be a functional artifact,[1] which institutionalizes the 'AI-driven evidence mechanism'[2], with an aspiration to support the criminal justice system.[3] This mechanism can be seen to operate in two key spheres—first, it involves the evaluation of 'input' data to predict future conduct of an individual and inform judicial decision-making, and second, it generates 'output' or 'machine evidence' derived from this processed 'input' data.

However, these functions are not immune to tribulations. The first function prompts an 'input framing dilemma', which means that for an AI to function as a recommendation tool, it must be fed with case-specific information, a process that is complex and subjective by default. This complexity was acknowledged in the development of early computerized sentencing systems in the 1980s and 1990s (Schild, 1998). Schwarze and Roberts argue that 'the principal barrier to creating a functioning sentencing algorithm lies at the input stage' (Schwarze & Roberts, 2022, p. 211), where the accurate portrayal of crime details remains difficult and susceptible to oversights.[4]

The second function induces the admissibility of the 'machine evidence' hurdle. This raises questions such as 'Will AI be treated as an evidentiary mechanism?' 'Can AI-generated data serve as evidence in criminal proceedings?'[5] Could it be considered a type of 'machine'[6] evidence? Under the Bharatiya Sakshya Adhiniyan 2023 (hereinafter BSA), which governs the evidentiary rules, guiding the admission and exclusion of evidence in court, the 'legal' admissibility of such data must be scrutinized for its constitutionality and legitimacy.

Despite potential advantages, the integration of AI artifacts into India's 'human-centered' criminal justice institution, which is primarily adversarial in nature with limited inquisitorial elements, poses procedural and constitutional concerns for evidence evaluation and admissibility. The 'mixed-methods' fact-finding procedure, traditionally dependent on human reasoning, must evaluate to what extent this AI-generated 'machine evidence' can serve as a valid, transparent, and objective tool for judicial fact-finding.

AI IN CRIMINAL ADJUDICATION

India's 2018 National Strategy for AI defines AI as 'a constellation of technologies that enable machines to act with higher levels of intelligence and emulate the human capabilities of sense, comprehend, and act' (NITI Aayog, 2018, p. 12). In Europe, an AI system is defined as a machine-based system that operates with varying autonomy, adapts post-deployment, and infers outputs like predictions or recommendations based on inputs that influence environments (Artificial Intelligence Act, 2024, Article 3(1)).

DOI: 10.1201/9781003629146-17

In a criminal adjudication process, narrow AI systems are primarily used, which are built with 'rule-fetish' instructions that are 'mindlessly' executed with instantaneity to fulfill a 'rigid' purpose while remaining riddled with obscurantist features.[7] The primary functions of such systems are twofold: first, the 'input' data evaluative mechanism, and second, the output or 'machine evidence' generative mechanism.

Within the architecture of the 'input' data evaluative mechanism, defining what constitutes 'input data' is of prominence. 'Input data' comprises both 'manually' entered information, such as the individual's criminal record, and observational data autonomously gathered by the AI system,[8] representing its dual nature. According to Doob and Park, a criminal record constitutes six elements:[9]

'(1) the number of prior convictions, (2) the recency of the last conviction, (3) whether the past record includes violent offenses, (4) the length of time since the offender was first convicted, (5) whether the present offense was more serious than the most recent offense for which he had been sentenced, and (6) the nature or severity of the offender's most recent sentence' (Doob & Park, p. 61).

To fructify AI's functionalities like risk assessment or sentencing recommendations, these elements are fed into the system through human agency. The real-time data generated by IoT systems, such as sensors and connected devices, adds another layer of input data complementing the inputs from human interventions. AI can then automate the extraction and integration of this dynamic data through identifying the relevant data, preserving evidentiary values for legal proceedings, and compiling information from multiple, often geographically dispersed cloud-storage sources.

The input data, irrespective of the way it is derived, produces output that may serve as evidence within the justice system—a concept referred to as 'machine evidence'. The primordial configuration of machine evidence is in '0s' and '1s', which must be translated into an analog form to be useful (Kerr, 2007, pp. 238–239). The machine-generated evidence is qualified as third-generation forensic evidence,[10] distinct from the first[11] and second generations[12] that 'traditionally' require human intervention, as it relies on source code,[13] which facilitates the feature of obscurantism (Roth, Trial by Machine, 2016, pp. 1269–1276). This idea runs in parallel with the notion of 'machine testimony', which was introduced to differentiate between simple tools aiding human communication and intelligent machines, such as AI artifacts, that can independently analyze data and convey messages.[14]

Input 'Framing' Dilemma

The concept of 'framing' captures how information presentation shapes public understanding and engagement (Entman, 1993). Framing theory posits that information must be structured through emphasis, selection, and omission, which affect interpretation and response.[15] In AI systems used in criminal justice, the input data framing phase establishes the foundation for evidence generation, as it not only reflects but actively constructs a crime's narrative.

The input framing dilemma highlights the tension between accurately capturing the nuanced realities of criminal cases and the limitations of the input data 'frame' provided by humans or AI.[16] This dilemma manifests through performing the act of 'manual' data entry, especially when extensive information is required to describe a crime or when 'accurate' data input is challenging. Certain elements, such as the harm component of a crime, cannot be translated to an algorithmic 'fixed' input value, making it difficult to be represented in binary terms. Moreover, while attempting to input all parameters of a crime, each carrying different weights, there is a risk of oversimplification of the case complexities, which can hinder contextual interpretation and accurate representation of reality (Schwarze & Roberts, 2022, p. 212). Conversely, entering too little information can lead to coarse classifications and misgrouping of crimes (Schild, 1998, p. 160). These challenges illustrate how AI-generated evidence can only approximate the 'true' sentence, as the input data 'only imperfectly captures all the components' (Schwarze & Roberts, 2022, p. 213), potentially distorting case outcomes and undermining the principle of parity that underpins the rule of law.

The way AI systems autonomously gather data based on human behavioral observations also gives rise to the input framing dilemma. These systems are constrained by the quality, scope, and biases embedded in their training data. Machine learning models trained on historical datasets may encode and perpetuate existing societal biases,[17] influencing how the evidence is interpreted, collected, or authenticated, thereby compromising fairness and accuracy. Furthermore, as narrow AI systems often mine personal data from IoT devices, they risk capturing sensitive or irrelevant information, raising significant questions about consent, data protection, and the permissible boundaries of automated evidence collection.[18]

'Machine Evidence' under BSA

Section 39(2) of the BSA highlights the importance of information transmitted or stored in 'electronic or digital form'.[19] Although these terms are not explicitly defined in the Act, their context implies alignment with the notion of 'electronic form evidence'.[20] The explanation to Section 79 Information Technology Act (hereinafter IT Act) provides clarity by defining electronic form evidence as 'any information of probative value that is either stored or transmitted in electronic form', including computer data, audio, video, and cell phone.

Section 2(1)(e) of the BSA defines evidence to include both oral statements[21] and documentary evidence that explicitly includes electronic or digital records establishing their status as primary evidence admissible for court inspection, covering emails, server logs, and messages.[22] The IT Act supplements this by defining 'electronic record' under Section 2(1)(t),[23] which includes 'data', explained under Section 2(1)(o).[24] Section 63, BSA, affirms the admissibility of electronic records, granting them the same legal effect, validity, and enforceability as 'traditional' documents. Importantly, the admissibility pertains to the content embedded within the electronic medium, rather than the medium itself.

Scientific evidence[25] can be admitted through three main channels: first, expert testimony under Section 39(1) BSA[26]; second, the doctrine of judicial notice as described in Sections 51 and 52(2) BSA; and third, Section 141 BSA,[27] which mandates the *de facto* admission of relevant evidence. Within this evidentiary framework, machine evidence, proposed as third-generation forensic evidence, can be seen as straddling both electronic and scientific evidence. Although it may appear objective and data-driven, such evidence is susceptible to error and bias, necessitating expert elucidation. Like earlier forms of scientific evidence, machine evidence undergoes a lifecycle of initial skepticism (Aronson, 2007), rigorous testing, and eventual acceptance, sometimes to the point of 'blind trust'.[28] This makes the verification of both the evidence and the systems responsible for its storage, processing, or analysis essential (Mason & Seng, 2017).

The Arjun Panditrao decision[29] reaffirms that 'relevancy' remains the foundational criterion for admissibility.[30] As per Sections 3 to 50, BSA, evidence must first satisfy the threshold of relevance. Admissibility then represents the second stage of the evidential process, requiring legal conformity, such as the provision of a certificate for certain types of electronic records.[31] The third and final component is proof. Under Section 2(1)(j) BSA, evidence must establish the probability of a fact to the satisfaction of the court.[32] Reliability, therefore, is not just about admissibility but also concerns the court's appreciation of evidence, assessed holistically[33] to meet the standards of proof beyond a reasonable doubt.

The Daubert standard,[34] recognized by Indian courts, offers a systematic framework for evaluating the admissibility of scientific evidence. Under this framework, the factors to consider are the following: first, the existence of a known error rate associated with the methodology employed; second, the general acceptance of the methods within the relevant scientific or technical community familiar with the methodology; third, the extent to which the methodology has undergone peer review by experts in the relevant field; and fourth, the applicability of standard procedures or protocols to the employed methodology. These criteria are, particularly, instrumental in determining the reliability of evidence generated by AI artifacts.

However, applying traditional evidentiary standards to 'machine evidence' is not 'plain sailing'.[35] AI artifacts often exhibit a degree of obscurantism, operating in ways that are not easily comprehensible to legal actors. In response, certain jurisdictions like Singapore[36] have adopted a presumption of evidentiary reliability, which shifts the burden of disproving reliability to the opposing party. Nonetheless, the proponent of evidence is still obligated to produce concrete substantiating evidence, not merely assertions, demonstrating the robustness of the AI system (Ladkin, 2020), necessitating expert testimony and user validation.[37]

Machine Evidence as a 'fact-Finding' Tool

The primary goal of fact-finding in criminal proceedings is to establish the truth (Weigend, 2011), as judicial determinations of guilt or innocence depend on 'the verity' of facts (Turner & Weigend, 2019). However, machine evidence does not seamlessly integrate into the conventional evidentiary model, where (human) communication occurs in a formalized manner to pursue 'the verity'. It relies on experts to bring life to this 'verity' created, in terms of articulating how such data is generated, including the artifact's functioning, its assumptions, and its limitations. In adversarial proceedings, such expert testimony often lacks sufficient transparency regarding the AI's raw 'inputs' or operational mechanisms. This obscurantism complicates the judge's task of evaluating the reliability and relevance of the evidence. Despite these limitations, courts may still admit machine evidence, often through written expert reports, particularly if it can establish material facts more convincingly than its exclusion would allow. For example, facial recognition or GPS-based movement tracking evidence may be deemed probative, especially when corroborated by other forms of evidence.

India predominantly follows an adversarial model with limited inquisitorial features to promote justice in specific contexts. This procedural model shapes evidentiary rules, particularly how statements are evaluated, and is necessary for reasoned verdicts that can withstand an appeal. Although judges in India are not the primary fact-finding agents,[38] they do possess limited inquisitorial powers under Section 348 BNSS and Section 168 BSA[39] to summon experts or request relevant documentation.

Yet, a fundamental ambiguity persists: how much scrutiny must AI artifacts undergo to satisfy the requirement of 'the verity'? The role of experts is paramount here, not only to capture and present the machine evidence but also to contextualize and assess its probative value.[40] However, as AI artifacts grow increasingly complex, often surpassing human cognitive capabilities, even experts often struggle to articulate the 'totality' of their operational processes. This gap between technical obscurantism and legal expectation poses a critical concern in judicial settings, where decision-makers require clear, reasoned explanations to assess the reliability and admissibility of such evidence.

DESIGNING A 'LEGITIMATE' AI-DRIVEN EVIDENCE MECHANISM

The evidentiary value of AI artifacts in criminal justice fundamentally depends on the quality of data and algorithms engineered that govern their functioning. For AI-driven evidence mechanisms to be admissible, it is essential to clearly define the specific problem the artifact is designed to address. This clarity enables the court to assess the evidence's validity, reliability, and the potential for functional creep, where the AI's application extends beyond the 'prototypical' intents in ways that may be legally or ethically problematic.

In order to ensure the legitimacy of AI-driven evidence mechanisms, it is necessary to confront the core limitations that hinder their integration into legal fact-finding. These limitations can be broadly categorized into three interrelated challenges: obscurantism, bias, and lack of accountability. Obscurantism refers to the 'black box' nature of AI artifacts, wherein the computational processing that transforms 'input' data into 'output' evidence remains obscure. This 'enigmatic' feature can mislead courts into assuming that AI-generated outputs are 'by design' reliable and objective, simply because they are machine-produced. The Supreme Court of Canada, in *Ewert vs. Canada*,[41] explicitly rejected this assumption, holding that AI craftsmanship used in sentencing must be demonstrably accurate and transparent, reinforcing the need for algorithmic accountability as a prerequisite for evidentiary use.

Bias is another significant concern, often rooted in the data used to train AI artifacts. Incomplete, under-/un-representative, or inaccurate data can result in skewed outcomes that disproportionately affect certain groups. Such systemic biases threaten the fairness of judicial decisions.[42] For instance, the decision of the Dutch District Court[43] in 2020 to strike down the SyRI, an AI tool for a welfare fraud detection system, highlighted how algorithmic surveillance can disproportionately target marginalized communities. Similarly, in *EEOC v. iTutorGroup*,[44] the U.S. Equal Employment Opportunity Commission sanctioned an AI-driven hiring system for age discrimination, revealing how embedded prejudices in data and design can translate into unlawful practices.

The third limitation, lack of accountability, is compounded by the presence of obscurantism and bias. AI artifacts often operate autonomously or in obscure conjunction with human decisions, making it difficult to locate responsibility when errors occur. The distributed nature of AI design and deployment complicates efforts to hold specific actors accountable for evidentiary reliability or ethical implications of AI outputs (Logan & Ferguson, 2016, pp. 549–615). In legal proceedings, this lack of traceability poses a serious challenge, as courts require clear attribution of fault and rationale behind evidentiary claims.

Taken together, these limitations underscore the imperative of developing legitimately designed AI-driven evidence mechanisms—instruments that not only meet legal admissibility thresholds but also align with the rule of law.

LEGITIMACY

Legitimacy, in the context of AI-driven evidence mechanisms, refers to their alignment with the foundational principles of the rule of law, as articulated through the interpretive lens of the BSA. It is not merely a question of technological functionality or formal legal admissibility; rather, it embodies a composite standard encompassing legal validity, moral justifiability, procedural fairness, and social trust.

From a Kelsenian perspective, legitimacy begins with legal validity: AI evidentiary mechanisms must be grounded in a valid legal norm within the established constitutional hierarchy.[45] Yet, legal derivation alone does not suffice. Hart introduces an internal dimension, emphasizing that legitimacy also requires acceptance from within the judicial architecture. AI artifacts must resonate with the 'internal point of view'[46] of legal actors and conform to the shared rules of recognition.[47] Fuller, emphasizing the 'inner morality of law', insists that legal rules governing AI be statutorily anchored,[48] consistently applied, and accessible to judicial scrutiny, ensuring predictability and fairness.[49]

These formalist accounts must be complemented by normative standards. Drawing from Rawls, legitimacy further requires that AI artifacts be transparent, inclusive, and fair, that is, justifiable in terms that reasonable citizens can accept, even in conditions of moral pluralism.[50] Finnis furthers this by asserting that legitimacy is derived not only from procedural correctness but also from substantive orientation towards the common good,[51] promoting justice, truth, and human dignity.

Since legitimacy is also a function of public trust, efficacy alone cannot sustain legitimacy without normative endorsement by legal actors and society.[52] Tyler's research shows that perception of fairness, rather than coercion, fosters compliance,[53] while Zuboff warns that opaque, unaccountable algorithms threaten to erode democratic legitimacy and public confidence in systems.[54]

Within the Indian constitutional framework, this layered understanding of legitimacy imposes a dual burden on AI evidentiary mechanisms—they must not only comply with procedural rules but also uphold the legal guarantees enshrined in Article 14,[55] Article 20,[56] and Article 21.[57] When these layers are combined, they constitute what may be called 'the rule of law by design recipe'[58]—a model for embedding AI within the legal order in a manner that is substantively just and procedurally sound.

The Rule of Law by Design Recipe

The rule of law requires that all individuals, including the State, are subject to the law, ensuring fairness, transparency, and accountability as enshrined in Articles 14 and 21 of the CoI. Hence, AI artifacts must be designed and implemented in a 'legitimate' manner, adhering to these rule of law principles. To meet this standard, the rule of law by design recipe (hereinafter 'the RoL-bD-recipe') offers a normative and practical framework. The RoL-bD-recipe advocates embedding constitutional safeguards directly into the design and deployment of technological artifacts. This means operationalizing the principles of due process, non-discrimination, and transparency within the technical architecture of AI systems, ensuring that technology strengthens rather than undermines justice.

The RoL-bD-recipe draws from a constellation of design paradigms—legal by design, data protection by design, human dignity by design, legal protection by design, value-sensitive design, and compliance by design[59]—to ensure that the affordances within the technological environment do not override or dilute the legal protections but rather function as functions for enforcing them.[60] When applied to AI-driven evidence mechanisms, the RoL-bD-recipe ensures that guarantees under Articles 14, 20, and 21, CoI, are not winnowed out.

In practice, this means incorporating procedural and substantive safeguards, for example, affordances of due process, accountability, and transparency into the system architecture. The RoL-bD-recipe does not reject the use of AI per se; rather, it insists its application be fair, just, and reasonable under Article 21.[61] Similarly, Article 20(3), which protects against self-incrimination, remains central in evaluating machine evidence. As affirmed in *Selvi vs. State of Karnataka*, the use of technology in criminal proceedings must respect the principle of 'voluntariness' and adhere to standards of reliability.[62]

AI-driven evidence mechanisms that internalize these constitutional thresholds, both in design and deployment, may be admissible under Section 63 BSA. However, their legitimacy depends not just on technical accuracy or evidentiary value, but also on their ability to embody and operationalize the rule of law principles through design.

Recipe for nput 'Framing' Dilemma

Recognizing that algorithms depend on structured, quantifiable data, which by default involves a reductive process, the RoL-bD-recipe does not seek quick fixes. Instead, it emphasizes procedural safeguards and institutional involvement to ensure fairness and consistency in how information is framed and entered.

A central pillar of the RoL-bD-recipe is the embedding of constitutional values into system design. This underscores the necessity for AI artifacts to acknowledge the limitations of structured data[63] and to create institutional space for human oversight, contextual interpretation, and contestability. Rather than replacing judicial discretion, AI should serve as an advisory tool that supports judges, thereby ensuring that case outcomes are not dictated solely by pre-framed inputs and preserving human judgment in final decisions.

To better capture case-specific nuances, the RoL-bD-recipe advocates for standardized yet flexible protocols, such as incorporating narrative fields that allow for recording complex factors like emotional and cognitive responses or socio-economic backgrounds. These design features contribute to procedural fairness and consistency by reinforcing regular audits, validation mechanisms, and the inclusion of marginalized perspectives. Such measures reduce the risks of biased or incomplete data framing while promoting transparency and reviewability.[64]

The human-in-the-loop affordance is one of the key ingredients of the RoL-bD-recipe. Early judicial involvement in designing algorithms ensures data structures and interpretative parameters reflect real-world complexities. This collaboration fosters a context-aware system and helps reduce inconsistencies and unpredictability arising from input variation. Such an affordance can be implemented through the 'restricted application model', wherein judges first propose a decision independently, and the AI system offers an advisory recommendation only if it suggests a more lenient outcome.[65] This model preserves judicial authority while allowing AI to act as a secondary check against unduly decisions.

Finally, the RoL-bD-recipe promotes 'knowledge-sharing'[66] among judges and practitioners to standardize input practices, especially for difficult-to-quantify elements.[67] This collaborative approach enhances the reliability of AI outputs, minimizing the risk of distorted or biased recommendations and reinforcing the legitimacy of AI's role in criminal justice.

Recipe for 'Machine' Evidence in Fact-Finding

Given the inverse relationship between explainability and performance in AI artifacts,[68] especially in adversarial models, the RoL-bD-recipe emphasizes the critical role of human 'expert' oversight throughout the AI lifecycle. While AI systems may outperform human capabilities in data processing, their epilogue remains obscure and difficult for judges to deduce and interpret. To bridge this knowledge gap, the RoL-bD-recipe reinforces the inclusion of human experts as interpreters, who translate complex algorithmic outputs into legally intelligible narratives, even though their explanations may fail to demonstrate a clear chain of causality.

Accordingly, the RoL-bD-recipe advocates for *ex-ante* design principles that construct evidentiary traceability and interpretability into the AI artifacts rather than solely relying on *ex-post* explanations of human experts. Features such as audit trails,[69] metadata logs,[70] tamper-proof storage,[71] and version-controlled records act as 'evidentiary proxies', enabling legal actors to independently trace and evaluate AI outputs.[72] These mechanisms aspire to mimic the accountability 'indicators' found in human testimony,[73] thereby facilitating the admissibility and reliability of machine evidence.

To further strengthen procedural legitimacy, the RoL-bD-recipe promotes pre-trial institutional assessments, including certifications[74] or reliability indices,[75] that rigorously evaluate AI artifacts before they enter the courtroom. This shifts from mere *ex-post* human interpretation or 'outcome validation' towards anticipatory oversight, relocates important evidentiary scrutiny outside the court, easing the judiciary's burden and ensuring that machine evidence is not just accurate, but also intelligible and contestable.

CONCLUSION

The integration of AI artifacts within legal processes must be anchored in constitutional principles and evidentiary norms to preserve the integrity, reliability, and accountability of AI-generated evidence in judicial proceedings. The RoL-bD-recipe offers a constitutionally grounded and operationally pragmatic framework that addresses the input framing dilemma and admissibility of the 'machine evidence' hurdle by incorporating legal safeguards, accountability mechanisms, and transparency norms at the formative stages of AI system development. This proactive design strategy contrasts with the inadequate practice of retrofitting traditional evidentiary procedures onto obscurantist AI artifacts.

In a criminal justice system, where the consequences of error are profound, it is imperative that AI artifacts not merely fulfill technical standards of reliability or formal thresholds of admissibility but must also conform to the principles of democratic legitimacy to ensure they reinforce, rather than undermine, the foundational tenets of the rule of law. This necessitates the application of the RoL-bD-recipe, which would facilitate a rigorous examination of epistemic reliability and evidentiary robustness of AI-generated outputs, foregrounding the normative dimensions of technological integration into judicial decision-making.

NOTES

1 Labeling AI as 'AI artifacts' emphasizes their status as human-made constructs—not autonomous beings or neutral tools, but products of design, intention, and context. The term artifact foregrounds the fact that AI reflects the choices, assumptions, and values of its creators, including datasets used, design objectives, and deployment environments. Unlike terms like 'agent' or 'system', which can obscure human responsibility, artifact reinforces accountability, materiality, and social embeddedness. It also allows us to treat AI not as inherently intelligent or independent but as objects of critique and governance, much like legal texts, maps, or algorithms—constructed, situated, and modifiable.
2 This notion originates from the concept of AI-driven 'intelligent courts'. See Xu (2017) for more information.
3 . Ryberg, J., & Roberts, J. V. (Eds.). (2021). *Sentencing and Artificial Intelligence*. Oxford University Press. *Studies in Penal Theory and Philosophy*; Roberts, J. V., & Ryberg, J. (2023). *Sentencing the Self-Convicted: The Ethics of Pleading Guilty*. Hart Publishing; Ryberg, J. (2024). Criminal Justice and Artificial Intelligence: How Should We Assess the Performance of Sentencing Algorithms. *Philosophy & Technology, 37*(1), Article 9. https://doi.org/10.1007/s13347-024-00694-3.
4 . Ryberg, J., & Roberts, J. V. (Eds.). (2022). *Sentencing and Artificial Intelligence* (p. 211). Oxford University Press.
5 Hildebrandt, M. (2008). *A vision of ambient law*. In R. Brownsword & K. Yeung (Eds.), *Regulating technologies*
6 Roth, A. (2017). *Machine testimony. Yale Law Journal, 126*(1972), 1972–2053. Retrieved from Yale Law Journal website
7 Calo, R. (2015). *Robotics and the lessons of cyberlaw. California Law Review, 103*(3), 513–563. https://digitalcommons.law.uw.edu/faculty-articles/23/ Bryan Casey and Mark A. Lemley, *You Might be a Robot*, 105 Cornell L. Rev. 287 (2020). https://scholarship.law.cornell.edu/clr/vol105/iss2/2; Chesterman, S. (2021). *We, the Robots? Regulating artificial intelligence and the limits of the law* (Introduction) (NUS Law Working Paper No. 2022/015, pp. 1–12). Cambridge University Press. Available at SSRN: https://ssrn.com/abstract=4231363
8 Such observational data often extend beyond simple measurements of human behavior and capture extensive information about their environment.
9 These elements are nuanced, context-dependent, and often embedded in human judgment, raising questions about how accurately and consistently they can be translated into machine-readable formats. Consequently, the integrity of the evaluative mechanism depends heavily on both the precision of human input and the interpretive capacity of the AI system.
10 Machine evidence is generated by systems that operate based on AI's agency, which can automatically execute the input entered (without any human intervention) as well as monitor environments and assess human behavior. In 2007, Murphy proposed a taxonomy of forensic evidence, differentiating first-generation evidence from second-generation evidence, the latter of which is characterized by its greater complexity and scientifically robust design, emerging primarily from the limitations of the first generation. See Murphy (2007) for more information.
11 Typical examples include fingerprint analysis and ballistics.
12 Exemplified by DNA analysis and location tracking.
13 The opacity of source code creates significant trust issues in criminal fact-finding, as flaws may be hard to detect.
14 See Roth, Trial by Machine (2016) and Roth, Machine Testimony (2016) for more information on the term 'machine testimony'.
15 By highlighting certain elements while downplaying others, information guides perception, influences judgment, and steers decision-making. This influence relates to cognitive biases, like confirmation bias, where individuals accept information that aligns with their beliefs and disregard contradictory evidence. See Goffman (1974) for more information.
16 AI artifacts rely on structured, often reductive, case-specific inputs, which can skew interpretation and outcomes. This dilemma highlights the ethical and epistemological implications of data representation in AI-assisted decision-making, emphasizing how framing in both human and machine contexts affects perception and justice operationalization.
17 See Bagaric, Svilar, Bull, Hunter, & Stobbs (2022) for more information.
18 These challenges underscore the need for adaptive legal frameworks that can mediate the tensions between the efficiencies offered by AI-assisted tools and the imperative to safeguard individual rights. Ensuring accountability, transparency, and contextual sensitivity in both data curation and system deployment is essential for mitigating the risks posed by the input framing dilemma in AI-driven legal processes. See Sen (2024) for more information.
19 Section 39(2) of the The Bharatiya Sakshya Adhiniyam (2023) states 'When in a proceeding, the court has to form an opinion on any matter relating to any information transmitted or stored in any computer resource or any other electronic or digital form, the opinion of the Examiner of Electronic Evidence referred to in section 79A of (The Information Technology Act, 2000) (hereinafter IT Act) is a relevant fact'.
20 The term 'electronic form evidence' has not been statutorily defined under the BSA. Conversely, Section 94 of the The Bhartiya Nagarik Suraksha Sanhita (2023) (hereinafter BNSS) employs the term 'digital evidence', but neither BNSS nor BSA offers a definition for 'electronic evidence' or 'digital evidence'.

21 Section.2(1)(e) of BSA denotes that 'statements given electronically' refer specifically to live statements made through 'audio-video electronic means' as defined in the BNSS. It excludes previously recorded electronic statements. Section 2(1)(a) BSA stipulates that 'audio-video electronic means' shall include use of any communication device for the purposes of video conferencing, recording of processes of identification, search and seizure or evidence, transmission of electronic communication, and for such other purposes and by such other means as the State Government may, by rules, provide. This is on account of two reasons: first, the word statements given electronically is to be read along with the ensuing words 'which the court permits or requires to be made before it by witnesses in relation to matters of fact under inquiry'. Thus, the statements will have to be made before the court, and such statements should be either permitted or required to be made before the court. The phrase 'permits or requires to be made before it by witnesses' indicates an act done in presenti. When the statement is made, the person who made it should be a witness before the court. It cannot mean something that has already happened like in the case of a recorded message or a delayed live feed. And second, the moment an image or audio-video is recorded, it becomes an 'electronic record', and it gets converted into 'documentary evidence' mentioned in S.2 (1)(e)(ii) BSA.

22 Sec 2(d), illustration vi, BSA. Electronic records under BSA refer to 'records on emails, server logs, documents on computers, laptops, or smartphones, messages, websites, locational evidence, and voice mail messages'.

23 Section 2(1)(t) IT Act defines 'electronic record' exhaustively, including 'data, records, or data generated, images or sounds stored, received, or sent in electronic form, or microfilm or computer-generated microfiche'.

24 S. 2(1)(o) IT Act defines 'data' as a representation of information, knowledge, facts, concepts, or instructions that are being prepared or have been prepared in a formalized manner, and is intended to be processed, is being processed, or has been processed in a computer system or computer network, and may be in any form (including computer printouts, magnetic or optical storage media, punched cards, or punched tapes) or stored internally in the memory of the computer.

25 In criminal proceedings, this evidence is crucial for aiding judges in establishing the factual context of cases. It includes various elements such as polygraph tests, lie detection, DNA evidence, finger and footprints, voice identification and recognition, and autopsy reports. See McCormick (1981) and Hill (2016) for more information. Also see Selvi v. State of Karnataka.

26 See 'State of U.P vs Krishna Gopal & Anr', 'Siddheswar Prasad Singh vs Bhaba Sundari Pramanick Sha And Anr', 'Malay Kumar Ganguly vs Sukumar Mukherjee & Ors', and 'Ramesh Chandra Agrawal vs Regency Hospital Ltd. & Ors'.

27 Section 141 BSA reads as 'When either party proposes to give evidence of any fact, the Judge may ask the party proposing to give the evidence in what manner the alleged fact, if proved, would be relevant; and the Judge shall admit the evidence if he thinks that the fact, if proved would be relevant, and not otherwise'.

28 This observation has been made by Richard Myers at the Data, Technology and Criminal Law Workshop at Duke University (April 5-6, 2019).

29 Arjun Panditrao Khotkar vs. Kailash Kushanrao Gorantyal, AIR 2020 SC 4908, AIRONLINE 2020 SC 641

30 The judges in Arjun Panditrao note that what may be relevant may not be admissible. What may be relevant and admissible, may not be proved. What may be relevant, admissible and proved may not be reliable. This insinuates that relevancy is the first step in deciding whether evidence can be considered at all.

31 See Section 63 BSA.

32 Defined as the efficacy of admissible evidence in substantiating the alleged facts.

33 This facet is integral to the culmination of trial proceedings, during which the court rigorously examines each established fact against the benchmark of reliability to reach a comprehensive conclusion. Following the proof, the court arrives at a conclusion through a holistic assessment of the totality of evidence. Each piece of evidence is meticulously evaluated against others to uphold the principle of reliability. Reliability, in the context of evidentiary standards, pertains to the extent to which evidence is deemed credible and trustworthy. This methodology aligns with the overarching framework of the BSA, which permeates the entire scope of the statute, both historically and contemporaneously. The process through which reliability is discerned is termed 'appreciation of evidence', involving the critical assessment of the reliability and credibility of evidence presented. It is posited that criminal cases hinge upon the standard of proof beyond a reasonable doubt; it frames the underlying ethos governing evidentiary standards.

34 See Daubert v. Merrell Dow Pharmaceuticals, Inc., para, 579, 593–94 for more information.

35 The question of who bears the responsibility for demonstrating or contesting the validity of evidence generated or assisted by AI systems presents a significant challenge. Moreover, with regard to the rationale for requiring a declarant's presence in court to assess demeanor and credibility, application to AI-generated evidence faces a fundamental challenge. Unlike human witnesses, AI systems cannot be cross-examined, observed, or psychologically evaluated. Nor can their creators serve as adequate substitutes, since the development and operation of AI typically involve numerous contributors, none of whom can fully account for the system's autonomous decision-making, especially when machine learning programming is utilized. This lack of a vetting mechanism undermines the procedural safeguards that are central to fair adjudication. While efforts in explainable AI are ongoing, current technologies fall short of providing the kind of transparent, causal reasoning that courts require to evaluate credibility and reliability. See Chessman (2017) and Park et al. (2018) for more information.

36 See Section 4(2) of the The Statutes of the Republic of Singapore, Evidence Act, Chapter 97 (1990).

37 The authenticity and trustworthiness of such systems may be corroborated by testimonies from the users who have interacted with them. A person using the system must be sufficiently knowledgeable about how it works.
38 In the Indian criminal justice system, the role of the judge is generally that of a neutral arbiter between the prosecution and the defense.
39 Section 348, BNSS, grants courts broad authority to summon any person as a witness or to recall and re-examine witnesses already presented, should the court consider their testimony crucial to the 'just' decision of the case. This provision includes expert witnesses, such as forensic and technical specialists. Similarly, Section 168, BSA confers upon judges the ability to pose questions to any witness or to mandate the production of relevant documents to discover adequate proof of pertinent facts. This reflects a limited inquisitorial aspect, permitting judges to transcend their traditionally passive roles under certain circumstances.
40 When assessments or other data produced by AI systems are presented as evidence, they function in many respects as a form of expert testimony.
41 Ewert v. Canada (2018)
42 See Roth, Trial by Machine (2016, pp. 1245–1306, 1269–1270) for more information.
43 SyRI legislation in violation of European Convention on Human Rights (2020).
44 See U.S. Equal Employment Opportunity Commission (2023).
45 See Kelsen (1941) for more information.
46 See Hart (2012, pp. 206–212) for more information.
47 Machine evidence becomes part of a legitimate legal system only when its use is recognized as valid under the system's shared rule of recognition and not merely imposed through external enforcement or administrative decree.
48 It means that AI tools used for generating evidence must be clearly and formally authorized by law; for example, either mentioned or regulated under a statute like the BSA or other laws governing digital evidence, surveillance, or data protection. This ensures that their use is not arbitrary or based only on administrative discretion or private agreements but instead has a clear legal basis that can be reviewed and challenged in court.
49 See Fuller (1964, pp. 33–94) for more information.
50 See Rawls (1993, p. 137) for more information.
51 See Finnis (2011, pp. 273–276) for more information.
52 Hart distinguishes between efficacy (whether rules are obeyed) and legitimacy (whether rules are accepted as binding). A functioning AI tool may be effective, but not legitimate unless the legal community endorses its use under accepted norms and principles.
53 See Tyler (1990) for more information.
54 See Zuboff (2019) for more information.
55 Article 14, Constitution of India (hereinafter CoI) guarantees equality before the law. It states that 'The State shall not deny to any person equality before the law or the equal protection of the laws within the territory of India'.
56 Article 20 CoI guarantees protection in respect of conviction for offences. It states that '(1) No person shall be convicted of any offence except for violation of a law in force at the time of the commission of the Act charged as an offence, nor be subjected to a penalty greater than that which might have been inflicted under the law in force at the time of the commission of the offence. (2) No person shall be prosecuted and punished for the same offence more than once. (3) No person accused of any offence shall be compelled to be a witness against himself'.
57 Article 21 CoI guarantees protection of life and personal liberty. It states that 'No person shall be deprived of his life or personal liberty except according to procedure established by law'.
58 'The rule of law by design recipe' captures the idea that embedding the rule of law into technological systems is not just about following a rigid framework; it is about deliberate construction, contextual adaptation, and creative iteration. The word 'recipe' aligns with design thinking, conveying a sense of guided practice: a flexible, step-by-step process involving key 'ingredients' like transparency, accountability, and procedural fairness, which can be adjusted based on institutional or technological contexts. It emphasizes that the rule of law is not just a static ideal, but a co-created, operational reality that is something that must be thoughtfully assembled and tested—like a dish crafted for a specific setting.
59 These notions aim to translate 'values' and 'legal requirements' into technical specifications, ultimately guiding the design of socio-technical systems.
60 Hagan posits that the 'by design' approach serves as a valuable complement to traditional legal methodologies such as empirical legal studies, while Perry-Kessaris advocates for the integration of design methodologies within socio-legal research. In contemporary academic discourse, the 'by design' concept resides at the intersection of law, philosophy, and technology. See Hagan (2020, p. 3) and Perry-Kessaris (2020, p. 1427) for more information.
61 The mere existence of illegally collected evidence does not automatically render it inadmissible in courts, indicating that while the right to privacy under Article 21 is a serious concern in the digitized era, it is not absolute in nature and must comply with public interest. Moreover, in instances where conflicts arise between the right to privacy and the right to a fair trial across all phases of the judicial process, including investigation, inquiry, trial, appeal, revision, and retrial, the right to privacy may, at times, have to yield to the right to a fair trial, which is also protected under Article 21. See Ritesh Sinha vs State Of Uttar Pradesh and Justice K.S. Puttaswamy (Retd) And Anr. vs Union Of India And Ors, pp. 95, para. 47.

62 In Selvi vs. State of Karnataka, the court held that 'various evidence-gathering techniques such as Narcoanalysis, brain mapping, lie detection, and polygraphy tests are violative of Article 20 (3) case and Article 21 of the Constitution. These tests cannot be regarded as completely truthful and reliable; hence, there are chances of false results and a scope of errors. It comes in conflict with the standard of proof 'beyond reasonable proof', which is an essential element of criminal trials'.

63 The structured data may not fully capture the richness of a case.

64 Decisions about data input ought to be transparent and reviewable, allowing judges, lawyers, and defendants to trace and challenge how specific inputs influence algorithmic outcomes. This prevents AI tools from becoming unaccountable decision-makers and supports the right to an effective remedy. Finally, the RoL-bD-recipe demands that these systems remain reflexive and adaptable—capable of evolving in response to new legal interpretations, user feedback, and social concerns—so that they do not entrench outdated practices but continue to align with constitutional and ethical norms.

65 Under this model, the sentencing process begins with the judge independently proposing an appropriate sentence. The case-specific sentencing factors and the judge's preliminary recommendation are then entered into the AI system. If the judge's proposed sentence is more severe than the algorithm's suggestion, the AI generates an advisory recommendation based on prior comparable cases. If not, the algorithm simply confirms the judge's decision. This approach ensures that algorithms act as a secondary check, potentially counterbalancing overly harsh sentences, while leaving judicial discretion fully intact.

66 This 'early involvement' factor is related to the second measure, that is, the 'knowledge sharing' strategy.

67 The RoL-bD-recipe calls for uniform data input practices once the algorithm is operational.

68 Research indicates a trade-off between AI system performance and explainability: as accuracy increases, interpretability often decreases. See Doshi-Velez, et al. (2017, p. 2) for more information.

69 Audit trails record how data was acquired, processed, and evaluated.

70 Metadata logs identify changes made by the system during its operation.

71 Tamper-proof storage are standardized protocols for preserving machine evidence in its original form—to safeguard the integrity of machine evidence during collection, storage, and presentation, the RoL-bD-recipe advocates for the integration of tamper-proof systems, cryptographic seals, and version-controlled logs within AI infrastructures. These mechanisms serve to preserve the original state of the evidence and protect against undetected alterations, either by the system itself or external manipulation.

72 The RoL-bD-recipe proposes the AI systems to embed a 'version-controlled record system', which means that the artifact is built to generate explainable outputs, evidentiary documentation, and process-level disclosures that can be evaluated independently.

73 This RoL-bD-recipe provides a basis for constructing a functional equivalence to the traditional mechanisms of evaluating human testimonial accountability for the AI system.

74 Includes certifications or institutional reviews that scrutinize the AI's source code, training data, learning behavior, and performance metrics prior to its use as evidentiary material. See Perel & Elkin-Koren (2017, pp. 186–198) for more information.

75 The resulting certification or reliability index could then serve to aid the trier of fact without overburdening the adversarial process with technical disputes.

REFERENCES

Aronson, J. (2007). *Genetic witness: Science, law, and controversy in the making of DNA profiling*. Rutgers University Press.

Bagaric, M., Svilar, J., Bull, M., Hunter, D., & Stobbs, N. (2022). The solution to the pervasive bias and discrimination in the criminal justice system: transparent and fair artificial intelligence. *American Criminal Law Review, 59*(1), 95–148.

Bharatiya Sakshya Adhiniyam, 2023, No. 47 of 2023 (India). Legislative Department, Ministry of Law and Justice.

Calo, R. (2015). Robotics and the lessons of Cyberlaw. *California Law Review, 103*(3), 513–564.

Casey, B., & Lemley, M. (2020). You might be a robot. *Cornell Law Review, 105*(2), 287–362.

Chessman, C. (2017). A" source" of error: Computer code, criminal defendants, and the constitution. *California Law Review, 105*(1), 179–228.

Chesterman, S. (2021). Through a glass, darkly: Artificial intelligence and the problem of opacity. *The American Journal of Comparative Law, 69*(2), 271–294.

Doshi-Velez, F., Kortz, M., Budish, R., Bavitz, C., Gershman, S., O'Brien, D., . . . Weller, A. (2017, November 3). *Accountability of AI under the law: The role of explanation* (Berkman Klein Centre Working Group on Explanation and the Law, Berkman Klein Centre for Internet & Society, working paper.) Harvard University. ssrn_id3162237_code2640331.pdf.

Entman, R. M. (1993). Framing: Toward clarification of a fractured paradigm. *Journal of communication, 43*(4), 51–58. https://doi.org/10.1111/j.1460-2466.1993.tb01304.x.
Ewert v. Canada, 2018 SCC 30, [2018] 2 S.C.R. 165 (S.C.C. 2018 June 13).
Finnis, J. (2011). *Natural law and natural rights* (2nd ed.). Oxford University Press.
Fuller, L. L. (1964). *The morality of law*. Yale University Press.
Goffman, E. (1974). *Frame analysis: An essay on the organization of experience*. Northeastern University Press.
Hagan, M. (2020). Legal design as a thing: A theory of change and a set of methods to craft a human-centered legal system. *Design Issues, 36*(3), 3–15. https://doi.org/10.1162/desi_a_00600
Hart, H. L. A. (2012). *The concept of law* (3rd ed.; J. Raz & P. A. Bulloch, Eds.; Clarendon law series). Oxford University Press.
Hildebrandt, M. (2008). Ambient intelligence, criminal liability and democracy. *Criminal Law and Philosophy, 2*, 163–180. https://doi.org/10.1007/s11572-007-9042-1
Hill, K. D. (2016). The crisis in scientific publishing and its effect on the admissibility of technical and scientific evidence. *John Marshall Law Review, 49*(3), 727–750.
Justice K.S. Puttaswamy (Retd) And Anr. vs Union Of India And Ors, AIR 2017 SC 4161, (2017) 6 BOM CR 78 (India, Sup. Ct., Aug. 24, 2017).
Kelsen, H. (1941). The Pure Theory of Law and Analytical Jurisprudence. *Harvard Law Review, 55*(1), 44–70.
Kerr, O. S. (2007). 11. Digital evidence and the new criminal procedure. In J. Balkin, J. Grimmelmann, N. Kozlovski, E. Katz, S. Wagman, & T. Zarsky, *Cybercrime: Digital cops in a networked environment* (pp. 221–246). New York University Press. https://doi.org/10.18574/nyu/9780814739334.003.0013
Ladkin, P. B. (2020). Robustness of software. *Digital Evidence and Electronic Signature Law Review, 17* 15–24.
Logan, W. A., & Ferguson, A. G. (2016). Policing criminal justice data. *Minnesota Law Review, 101*(2), 541–616.
Malay Kumar Ganguly vs Sukumar Mukherjee & Ors, AIR 2010 SC 1162, 2010 AIR SCW 769 (India).
Mason, S., & Seng, D. (2017). *Electronic evidence* (4th ed.). Institute of Advanced Legal Studies. University of London Press. Electronic Evidence and Electronic Signatures – University of London Press.
McCormick, M. (1981). Scientific evidence: Defining a new approach to admissibility. *Iowa Law Review, 67*(5), 879–916.
Murphy, E. (2007). The new forensics: Criminal justice, false certainty, and the second generation of scientific evidence. *California Law Review, 95*(3), 721–798.
NITI Aayog. (2018). *National strategy for artificial intelligence*. Government of India. www.niti.gov.in/sites/default/files/2023-03/National-Strategy-for-Artificial-Intelligence.pdf
Park, D., Hendricks, L. A., Akata, Z., Rohrbach, A., Schiele, B., Darrell, T., & Rohrbach, M. (2018). Multimodal explanations: Justifying decisions and pointing to the evidence. In *Proceedings of the IEEE conference on computer vision and pattern recognition, ((CVPR)* (pp. 8779–8788). Multimodal Explanations: Justifying Decisions and Pointing to the Evidence | IEEE Conference Publication | IEEE Xplore.
Perel, M., & Elkin-Koren, N. (2017). Black box tinkering: Beyond disclosure in algorithmic enforcement. *Florida Law Review, 69*(1), 181–222. https://scholarship.law.ufl.edu/flr/vol69/iss1/5?utm_source=chatgpt.com
Perry-Kessaris, A. (2020). Making socio-legal research more social by design: Anglo-German roots rewards, and risks. *German Law Journal, 21*(7), 1427–1445. https://doi.org/10.1017/glj.2020.77
Ramesh Chandra Agrawal vs Regency Hospital Ltd. & Ors, AIR 2010 SC 806, 2009 AIR SCW 7308 (India)
Rawls, J. (1993). *Political liberalism*. Columbia University Press.
Rechtbank Den Haag. (2020, February 5). *SyRI legislation in violation of European Convention on Human Rights*, C-09-550982-HA ZA 18-388.
Regulation (EU) 2024/1689 of the European Parliament and of the Council of 13 June 2024 laying down harmonised rules on artificial intelligence (Artificial Intelligence Act). (2024). Official Journal of the European Union, L, 202, 1–108.
Ritesh Sinha vs State Of Uttar Pradesh, AIR 2019 SC 3592, AIRONLINE 2019 SC 740 (India).
Roth, A. (2016). Machine testimony. *Yale Law Journal, 126*(7), 1972–2053.
Roth, A. (2016). Trial by Machine. *The Georgetown Law Journal, 104*(5), 1245–1305.
Ryberg, J., & Roberts, J. V. (2022). *Sentencing and artificial intelligence*. Oxford University Press.

Ryberg, J., & Roberts, J. V. (Eds.). (2023). *Sentencing the self-convicted: The ethics of pleading guilty*. Hart Publishing.

Schild, U. J. (1998). Criminal sentencing and intelligent decision support. In G. Sartor, & K. Branting, *Judicial applications of artificial intelligence* (pp. 47–98). Springer Netherlands. https://doi.org/10.1007/978-94-015-9010-5_3

Schwarze, M., & Roberts, J. V. (2022). Reconciling artificial and human intelligence: Supplementing not supplanting the sentencing judge. *Georgetown Law Journal, 104*(5), 1245–1305. www.researchgate.net/publication/368722325_Reconciling_Artificial_and_Human_Intelligence_Supplementing_Not_Supplanting_the_Sentencing_JudgeMathis_Schwarze_and_Julian_V_

Sen, P. (2024). Balancing Act: Navigating artificial intelligence, data privacy, and legal challenges in the digital age. *International Journal of Law Management & Humanities, 7*(2), 3062–3073.

Siddheswar Prasad Singh vs Bhaba Sundari Pramanick Sha And Anr, AIR 1978 CAL 4 (India).

State of Karnataka, AIR 2010 SC 1974, (2010) 7 SCC 263 (India).

State Of U.P vs Krishna Gopal & Anr, AIR 1988 SC 2154, 1988 SCR SUPL. (2) 391(India).

The Information Technology Act, 2000, *No. 21 of 2000*. (India) Legislative Department, Ministry of Law, Justice and Company Affairs.

The Statutes of the Republic of Singapore, Evidence Act, Chapter 97. (1990). The Government Printer, Singapore 1990.

Turner, J. I., & Weigend, T. (2019). The purposes and functions of exclusionary rules: A comparative overview. In S. Gless, & T. Richter (Eds.), *Do exclusionary rules ensure a fair trial?. Ius Gentium: Comparative Perspectives on Law and Justice* (Vol. 74). Springer.

Tyler, T. R. (1990). *Why people obey the law*. Yale University Press.

U.S. Equal Employment Opportunity Commission. (2023, November 4). *iTutorGroup to pay $365,000 to settle EEOC discriminatory hiring suit*. U.S. Equal Employment Opportunity Commission. www.eeoc.gov/newsroom/itutorgroup-pay-365000-settle-eeoc-discriminatory-hiring-suit

Weigend, T. (2011). Should we search for the truth, and who should do it. *North Carolina Journal of International Law and Commercial Regulation, 36*(2), 389–416.

Xu, A. (2017). Chinese judicial justice on the cloud: a future call or a Pandora's box? An analysis of the 'intelligent court system' of China. *Information & Communications Technology Law, 26*(1), 59–71.

Zuboff, S. (2019). *The age of surveillance capitalism*. PublicAffairs.

17 Honour Killings and Digital Justice

The Role of AI in Modernising Legal Evidence in India

Shikha Vasishta

INTRODUCTION

Honour killings, in which women are often killed by members of their own family to uphold perceived family honour, continue to be a prevalent and distressing occurrence in India. Honour killings most often arise out of resistance to inter-caste or inter-faith marriages and are motivated by deeply rooted patriarchal and caste-based social norms (Jaiswal & Mishra, 2023). Though such types of crimes have been most prevalent in northern states such as Uttar Pradesh, Haryana, and Punjab, in recent years, there has been an increasing number of reported cases even from southern states (The New Indian Express, 2023). Official reports by the National Crime Records Bureau (NCRB) reported 25 honour killings in 2019–2020 and 33 in 2021, although analysts opine that the actual numbers would have been much higher, considering they are underreported (The Indian Express, 2024).

Notwithstanding sustained legal and judicial effort in the guise of the Supreme Court's historical ruling in Shakti Vahini v. Union of India (2018) reiterating the right to personal liberty and de-emphasising community intrusiveness in personal relationships, honour killings remain a challenge to the effectiveness of India's justice system (Shakti Vahini v. Union of India, 2018). The repetition of these offences is also fuelled by social complicity, tampering with evidence, and intimidation of victims and witnesses that tend to hamper effective investigation and prosecution (Jaiswal & Mishra, 2023).

As a counter to these issues, increased focus can be seen on whether digital technologies and artificial intelligence (AI) could benefit the criminal justice system (Das & Bhattacharyya, 2023). New initiatives like Maharashtra's MARVEL (Maharashtra Research and Vigilance for Enhanced Law Enforcement) are only examples of attempts to use AI for law enforcement operations with the aims of augmented crime forecasting, collection of evidence, and investigation efficiency (Indian Express, 2024). Concurrently, the implementation of the Bharatiya Sakshya Adhiniyam, 2023, is a landmark in the modernisation of India's evidence law, unequivocally accepting electronic and digital evidence (Ratanlal & Dhirajlal, 2025). Nevertheless, the application of AI to criminal law poses considerable legal and ethical concerns, largely on privacy, algorithmic bias, and safeguarding fundamental rights as explicated under Justice K.S. Puttaswamy v. Union of India (2017).

This chapter critically analyses the nexus between honour killings, digital justice, and AI in India. It attempts to assess whether AI technologies can help alleviate evidentiary and procedural burdens in honour killing cases while simultaneously raising questions over legal, ethical, and cultural stakes involved. By analysing recent judicial verdicts, law reform, and technology-oriented policing strategies, the chapter tries to add substance to the debate on how to make India respond more effectively to honour killings and achieve justice.

DOI: 10.1201/9781003629146-18

LITERATURE REVIEW

Indian honour killings are a persistent and intricate phenomenon that has continued to attract relentless attention from sociologists, legal experts, and human rights activists. The violence of homicide, as is mostly perpetrated against women who violate patriarchal or caste rules, is embedded in society and is normally rationalised as justified calls for family honour and social norms. Researchers such as Chowdhry (2016) have indicated how honour killings are themselves not isolated events but part of an organised system of social management that legitimates the control of women's autonomy, particularly in marriage and sex. It is maintained by opaque community webs, like the khap panchayats, that historically sanctioned or legitimised such violence.

Scholarship in law has identified huge loopholes within India's criminal justice system with regard to honour crimes. While murder in itself is criminalised under the Indian Penal Code, not having a specific legal category of honour killings tends to lead to prosecution issues, such as evidence collection and witness harassment (Jaiswal & Mishra, 2023). In Shakti Vahini v. Union of India (2018), the Supreme Court ruling was historic, calling on authorities to safeguard vulnerable couples and decrying extrajudicial actions by community groups. To date, however, implementation is patchy, and the dynamic between social complicity and institutional reluctance to act continues to invade justice (Shakti Vahini v. Union of India, 2018).

Over the past decade, scholarship has come to look more and more to technological innovation's potential, most notably AI, to solve long-standing evidentiary and procedural problems. Das and Bhattacharyya (2023) contend that AI-based instruments, including predictive policing software and forensic digital analysis, have the ability to transform detection and prevention of honour-based violence by allowing police to detect trends and intervene ahead of time. Maharashtra's MARVEL programme, for instance, has been praised as a trailblazing attempt to combine AI with crime analysis and prevention, using big data to produce actionable intelligence for the police (The Indian Express, 2024). Innovations of this kind are not, however, without dispute. Academics warn that the use of AI in policing and evidence handling raises fundamental issues related to privacy, data security, and the possibility of algorithmic bias concerns that are especially urgent for a society characterised by extreme social and economic inequalities (Jaiswal & Mishra, 2023; Rao, 2023).

The legal framework is also changing to align with these technological changes. The Bharatiya Sakshya Adhiniyam, 2023, is an important legislative step towards clearly enacting the admissibility of electronic and digital evidence in Indian courts (Ratanlal & Dhirajlal, 2025). However, there remains concern about authenticating AI-created evidence and its compatibility with constitutional privacy and due process protections, as explicated in Justice K.S. Puttaswamy v. Union of India (2017).

In addition, literature offers an active context in which legal reform, emerging technologies, and previous social arrangements intersect. While as much as digital and AI tools offer promising avenues for improving the response to honour killings, applications must be well-tuned in such a way that progress towards justice is not made at the expense of individual rights or on the back of exacerbating current inequalities. The challenge, as this literature review illustrates, is how to release the maximum potential of technology without eliminating its threats and limitations altogether.

METHODOLOGY

This chapter utilises a qualitative legal research design, integrating doctrinal analysis with an empirical case study approach to thoroughly examine the nexus of honour killings, digital evidence, and AI in India. Doctrinal analysis is utilised to critically examine statutory provisions, judicial decisions, and legislative modifications, particularly in the domain of the Bharatiya Sakshya Adhiniyam, 2023, and landmark cases such as Shakti Vahini v. Union of India (2018). To this end, case study research permits close scrutiny of selected incidents, i.e., the 2023 Amethi honour killing and the

MARVEL programme, with assistance from primary evidence such as court hearings, government reports, and policy briefs, supplemented by secondary sources culled from peer-reviewed journals and established media. Thematic analysis and qualitative data are drawn on to identify rigorously and make sense of evidentiary concerns, technology interventions, and socio-legal implications. The mixed approach is warranted by its ability to capture both the doctrinal basis and the everyday realities of legal reform, making for a rich and contextually informed analysis. The blended approach is legitimised by the ability of the same to grasp both the doctrinal underpinnings and the lived experiences of legal reform so that nuanced and contextualised examination is achieved.

CONTEXTUALISING HONOUR KILLINGS IN CONTEMPORARY INDIA

Honour killings today in India continue to be a serious human rights abuse, deeply embedded in patriarchal, caste, and traditional social norms. Although traditionally found in northern states like Haryana, Punjab, and Uttar Pradesh, recent crime statistics and case studies indicate that honour-based violence is now reported across a geographically broader set of states—Tamil Nadu, Telangana, Maharashtra, and Kerala—dispelling the belief that honour crimes occur only in rural or northern areas (Tomar & Sharma, 2025). The National Crime Records Bureau recorded honour killings in no less than a dozen states and union territories in 2018, with Punjab, Uttar Pradesh, and Haryana still being hotspots, but cases are on the rise in southern and urban regions (IRB, 2020).

The honour killings' sociocultural drivers are multifaceted and include perceived shame due to inter-caste, inter-religious, or same-gotra unions, along with disruptions in traditional gender roles and authority patterns (Patwardhan et al., 2023). Community institutions like khap panchayats, particularly in Haryana and western Uttar Pradesh, have traditionally condoned or plotted such violence, like the infamous Manoj–Babli case, where a couple of young people were killed on khap orders for marrying in the same gotra (Tomar & Sharma, 2025). Some recent high-profile incidents, like the 2015 murder of Dalit teenager Gokulraj in Tamil Nadu and the 2013 death of Dalit man Ilavarasan in Dharmapuri, bring to focus that honour-based violence and caste violence are common in southern India too (Seshadri, 2023).

India's legal action has reformed but is still unfinished. The Indian Penal Code and the revised Bharatiya Nyaya Sanhita criminalise murder and conspiracy, yet fail to address the collective and conspiratorial character of honour killings (Tomar & Sharma, 2025). Landmark Supreme Court judgements like Lata Singh v. State of Uttar Pradesh (2006), Bhagwan Dass v. State (2011), and Shakti Vahini v. Union of India (2018) have decried honour killings, instructed states to create safeguarding mechanisms for vulnerable couples, and advocated for severe punishments. Despite this, implementation is uneven, and conviction rates are not high; even where there are convictions, perpetrators are frequently released on bail within months.

THE PROMISE AND PERILS OF DIGITAL JUSTICE IN INDIA

The fast-paced digital revolution of India's justice system has brought with it a new age of promise as well as danger. AI, digital forensics, and sophisticated data analytics now form the core of India's attempts to transform law enforcement, judicial administration, and evidence management (Press Information Bureau [PIB], 2025; Indian Express, 2024). While these innovations bring unparalleled potential for efficiency, transparency, and accessibility, they also create new legal, ethical, and procedural issues that need to be carefully managed in order to ensure the protection of fundamental rights and safeguard justice.

AI integration with the Indian police is especially conspicuous for its potential for transforming crime investigation and prevention. The Maharashtra Research and Vigilance for Enhanced Law Enforcement (MARVEL) programme is an exemplary case in point: India's first autonomous, state-run organisation with the objective of using AI for law enforcement (Indian Express, 2024).

MARVEL modules support police in the analysis of mass data, forecasting crime hotspots, and following up on suspects based on AI-driven analysis of CCTV and digital communications. The use of the platform's partnership with academic and technological partners provides customised AI solutions for difficult investigations, ranging from missing persons to organised crime. At the national level, the Vimarsh 2023 5G Hackathon, held by the Department of Telecommunications and the Bureau of Police Research & Development, featured technologies like AI-based FIR filing with voice recognition, predictive policing, and real-time monitoring, all aimed at making law enforcement more responsive and agile. These advancements are supplemented by Phase III of the e-Courts Project, which utilises AI for the management of cases, legal translation, and citizen-facing chatbots, further simplifying judicial processes (PIB, 2025).

Yet, the use of AI in justice and policing also poses substantial threats. Fears regarding privacy of data, bias in algorithms, and surveillance overreach become more relevant as predictive policing and facial recognition technologies increasingly permeate (Dixit et al., 2025). Effective AI deployment calls for strong regulatory systems, evident ethical standards, and regular training for policing officials in order to ensure technological advancement does not come at the cost of civil liberties.

The application of digital evidence in honour killing cases is a classic example of the promise and intricacy of digital justice. Digital forensics, including the recovery and analysis of information from mobile phones, computers, and CCTV systems, has emerged as an important tool for investigators and prosecutors (Deepali & Verma, 2024). In recent high-profile cases, WhatsApp messages, call logs, and location information have furnished decisive evidence of conspiracy, intent, and multiple actor involvement, frequently overcoming obstacles caused by witness intimidation or community silence (Indian Express, 2024). The Bharatiya Sakshya Adhiniyam, 2023, strengthened the legal system further by making digital and AI-created evidence formally admissible, establishing new levels of authentication and chain of custody.

But there are still challenges. Authentication of electronic evidence, susceptibility to tampering, and the need for expert forensic services can complicate prosecutions, particularly in rural or low-resource jurisdictions. Additionally, the greater reliance on AI-generated insights and digital footprints means transparency and explainability of evidence introduced into a court can be challenged, potentially leading to wrongful convictions if the systems have not been tested to the highest available standards. Therefore, as much potential as digital justice has in aiding the resolution of honour killing cases' evidentiary and investigative challenges, its pitfalls are subject to ongoing scrutiny, regulatory supervision, and dedication towards maintaining due process and human rights.

NAVIGATING LEGAL, ETHICAL, AND SOCIETAL CHALLENGES

The inclusion of AI in India's justice system is both an opportunity and a deep challenge, especially with regard to algorithmic bias, privacy, and equity. AI-enabled policing and welfare technologies like facial recognition and predictive policing have consistently shown systematic bias against already marginalised groups—Dalits, Muslims, Adivasis, and trans people—because of biased historical data and under-representation in data sets (Context, 2023). These biases can result in over-policing, false arrests, and exclusion from critical services for vulnerable communities, thereby reinforcing current social hierarchies instead of deconstructing them. India's Digital Personal Data Protection Act, 2023, though promoting privacy protection, does not require algorithmic equity or anti-discrimination audits, which create important gaps in accountability (Pandey & Shukla, 2025). Conversely, the European Union's AI Act mandates robust algorithmic audits and dataset examination to protect fundamental rights, and comparable legislative proposals across North America focus on anti-discrimination and transparency (Kaushal, 2024). Indian policymakers, such as at the 2023 G20 Summit, have recognised these shortcomings and urged a holistic framework to respond to algorithmic accountability and ensure constitutional protections of equality and privacy (Kaushal, 2024). Ultimately, digital justice in India needs not only technological advancement but also strong legal protection, participatory data practices, and a social justice commitment that guarantees AI works to empower, not exclude, society's vulnerable (DEF, 2024).

TOWARDS A RIGHTS-BASED AND DIGITALLY RESPONSIVE JUSTICE FRAMEWORK

The confluence of honour killings and digital justice in India requires a rights-oriented legal response that unifies constitutional principles and technological innovation. While AI-based technologies can potentially facilitate the collection of evidence and accelerate investigations, they need to be balanced with protection against surveillance abuse and algorithmic bias. Policy change must feature the enactment of a general national law addressing honour killings in precise terms, such as provisions for the handling of digital evidence, as well as measures for implementing controls on police use of AI. Also noteworthy is the provision of legal support, digital literacy, and protection of marginalised groups opposing caste or religious hierarchies. Empirical constraints do exist, however, due to underreporting, the lack of disaggregated statistics, and restricted access to audits of AI applications. Subsequent research needs to examine the socio-legal aspects of algorithmic justice, assess the effectiveness of state-level legal reforms, and develop ethics guidelines such that technology enhances, not derails, access to justice and human dignity.

CONCLUSION

In conclusion, the struggle against honour killings in India stands at a crossroads shaped by both deep-seated social custom and broad advances in digital justice. While technology and legal reform have offered new methods of detection, investigation, and prosecution, honour-based violence reveals the entrenched power of patriarchy, caste, and communal complicity. The introduction of AI and digital evidence promises to transform the dispensation of justice more effectively and with wider access. However, these innovations raise new ethical and procedural challenges, particularly in relation to privacy, algorithmic bias, and equitable access to justice. Making substantial progress involves more than technical solutions or legislative reforms; it requires a holistic approach that restricts social mindsets, empowers vulnerable groups, and offers robust protection for individual rights. The future of digital justice in India hinges on rising to the challenge of finding an equilibrium between innovation and accountability, transparency, and inclusiveness. It is only by combining legal, technological, and social methods that India can hope to eradicate honour killings and build a justice system that truly protects the dignity and rights of all Indians.

REFERENCES

Chandran, R. (2023, September 11). *Racist, sexist, casteist: Is AI bad news for India?* Context by Thomson Reuters Foundation. www.context.news/digital-rights/racist-sexist-casteist-is-ai-bad-news-for-india.

Chowdhry, P. (2016). *Contentious marriages, eloping couples: Gender, caste, and patriarchy in northern India.* Oxford University Press. https://archive.org/details/contentiousmarri0000chow.

Das, D., & Bhattacharyya, P. (2023). Artificial Intelligence and criminal justice system in India. *NUJS Journal of Regulatory Studies, 8*(4),1–22. www.nujs.edu/wp-content/uploads/2024/01/vol-8-iss-4-1.pdf.

Deepali, & Verma, R. D. (2024). Role of digital forensics and criminal investigation in India. *International Journal of Research Publication and Reviews, 5*(11), 1–8. https://ijrpr.com/uploads/V5ISSUE11/IJRPR34611.pdf.

Digital Empowerment Foundation. (2024, February 19). *Just AI – No digital justice without social justice.* Digital Empowerment Foundation. www.defindia.org/just-ai-no-digital-justice-without-social-justice/.

Dixit, S., Tripathi, T., & Singh, R. (2025). Incorporating artificial intelligence into India's judicial and law enforcement systems. *International Journal of Forensic Medicine and Research, 5*(2), 1–12. www.ijfmr.com/papers/2025/2/41822.pdf.

Immigration and Refugee Board of Canada. (2020, June 4). *Responses to information requests (RIRs)* [Research report no. 458113]. www.irb-cisr.gc.ca/en/country-information/rir/Pages/index.aspx?doc=458113.

Jaiswal, A., & Mishra, P. C. (2023). Artificial Intelligence (AI) and criminal justice system: Potential benefits and risks. *ShodhKosh: Journal of Visual and Performing Arts*, 4(2), 3693–3698. https://doi.org/10.29121/shodhkosh.v4.i2.2023.4143.

Justice K.S.Puttaswamy(Retd) And Anr. v. Union Of India And Ors. (2017) 10 SCC 1 Kaushal, T. (2024, September 10). *Algorithms, biases, and the Constitution: A threat to the Golden Triangle? Student Law Journal (SLJ), Volume III*. Dharmashastra National Law University. .

Pandey, A., & Shukla, U. (2025, June 4). *Algorithms of oppression: Addressing AI bias in India. Cell for Law & Technology*.https://clt.nliu.ac.in/?p=1144.

Patwardhan, K., Sharma, S., & Gupta, A. (2023). The Evidence Act's role in honour killings in India. *Kuey, 30*(1), 8967–8975. https://kuey.net/index.php/kuey/article/download/8967/6791/17181.

Press Information Bureau. (2025, February 25). *Integrating AI in India's judiciary and law enforcement*. www.pib.gov.in/PressReleasePage.aspx?PRID=2106239.

Rao, S (2023). Perspective on the immorality of honor killings – A review article. *Medico Legal Update, 23*(1), 327–332. https://ijop.net/index.php/mlu/article/download/327/2933/6873.

Ratanlal, & Dhirajlal. (2025). *The Bharatiya Sakshya Adhiniyam, 2023 (28th ed.)*. LexisNexis.

Seshadri, S. (2023). Comparative analysis on honour killing prevalent in India and other countries. *SSRN*. https://papers.ssrn.com/sol3/papers.cfm?abstract_id=4520199.

Shakti Vahini v. Union of India. (2018) 7 SCC 192 (Supreme Court of India).

Sripad A. M. (2023, September 4). *Killing honour in the name of 'honour killings'. The New Indian Express*. www.newindianexpress.com/states/karnataka/2023/Sep/04/killing-honour-in-the-name-of-honour-killings-2611437.html.

The Indian Express. (2024, July 18). To fight crime using AI, Maharashtra Police create MARVEL. *The Indian Express*. https://indianexpress.com/article/cities/mumbai/to-fight-crime-using-ai-maharashtra-police-create-marvel-9460472/.

Tomar R., & Sharma, N. (2025). Indian framework against honour killing. *International Journal of Law, 11*(4), 26–29. www.lawjournals.org/assets/archives/2025/vol11issue4/11054.pdf.

18 The Future of Due Diligence

Integrating Retrieval-Augmented Generation into Corporate Legal Workflows

Shouvik Kumar Guha and Vivasvan Gautam

INTRODUCTION

In the legal field, language is as important as currency (Katz et al., 2023, p. 1). Institutions, judges, legislators, lawyers, and law firms produce and function on interpretation of a massive corpus of legal texts. Due diligence is the process of ascertaining whether a deal or commercial transaction between an Acquirer and a Target is sound from legal, commercial, and financial points of view. The scope and application of due diligence within the legal field are contingent upon the subject and purpose of the assessment. Due diligence processes are tailored to the specific circumstances of each transaction or business deal, reflecting the requirements of all participants. The norms and decision-making processes guiding discovery vary widely depending on the specific context, influencing everything from data collection to interpretation. From a purely commercial and economic perspective, due diligence involves a comprehensive assessment of the target company's market and sector and an evaluation of customer perception. A commercial due diligence process involves evaluating a firm's capital structure, accurately determining the value of vendor assets, analyzing balance sheets, assessing cash flows, reviewing corporate governance, and examining engineering operations.[1] In legal due diligence, the party that intends to enter as a purchaser would like to have information regarding:

1. Assets: These may be both tangible or intangible assets that may include buildings, computers, machinery, furniture, trademarks, goodwill, business plans, equipment, and facilities (Spedding, 2009).
2. Customers: It is important to identify who forms part of the customer base for the company. Traditionally, there were only two criteria that were considered of paramount importance for customers, i.e., to identify "who are the customers" and "where are they located." The rise of big data has led to a greater emphasis on analytical thinking within companies and investment circles, fostering a wider application of statistical analysis, quantitative methods, and machine learning. These algorithms utilize datasets encompassing customer location, behavior, and physiological characteristics to develop predictive models, facilitating decision-making by identifying patterns undetectable through conventional due diligence (Kastrup et al., 2025; Xie et al., 2016).

Traditionally, due diligence projects have involved lawyers meticulously reviewing large quantities of documents—often stored in a physical data room—resulting in a laborious process filled with the shuffling of papers and intense focus. The due diligence team conducts a thorough review of relevant materials over a period of weeks or months to ascertain potential liabilities for a buyer

DOI: 10.1201/9781003629146-19

involved in mergers and acquisitions (M&A). This process requires a meticulous approach to scrutinize, assess, structure, and analyze the existing or standing obligations as well as potential associated risks that may arise from an entity or a transaction. Each M&A transaction has its own unique characteristics; however, the due diligence process generally involves some common steps (Spedding, 2009, p. 6):

1. Asset transfer from one party to the other.
2. Determining existence of risk that can adversely affect future value of assets in consideration or obligations that are associated with the transaction.
3. Coming up with an arrangement to proportionally allocate or distribute risk between parties.

Legal professionals must conduct due diligence that goes beyond awareness of statutes, bylaws, and circulars; it demands a thorough determination of relevant factors. A part of the reason to conduct due diligence is also about gaining "reasonable foresight." A well-trained transaction lawyer is expected to protect their client or customer from everything that can go wrong in a business transaction, however remote. Therefore, due diligence is fundamentally about having prudence, recognizing the possibility that losses can arise and a deal may not generate expected profits. However, traditional methods of performing due diligence are also fraught with their own set of challenges. The sheer volume of information that a legal team has to parse demands a significant amount of time and resources to cull out and identify critical pieces of information, akin to searching for needles in a haystack. Moreover, such critical pieces of information then have to be organized and assembled and need to be established in such a manner that enables the transaction lawyers to find intricate links and connections that may not become visible from isolated scrutiny of documents. This inherent complexity and tediousness of the due diligence process for a transacting party has given rise to considerable demand among legal practitioners and law firms for automated techniques that are accurate in conducting due diligence.

NATURAL LANGUAGE PROCESSING, LEGAL TEXTS, AND CHALLENGES IN LEGAL INTERPRETATION

How Do Large Language Models Function?

The history of neural networks goes as far back as 1986, the year in which Geoffrey Hinton, David Rumelhart, and Ronald Williams put forward key concepts in machine learning, including "backpropagation" which eventually became fundamental knowledge within the field (Rumelhart et al., 1986). Several other methodologies such as Support Vector Machines, Conditional Random Fields, Deep Learning, Deep Neural Networks, and Advances in computing, particularly GPU and TPU infrastructure, eventually allowed large language models (LLMs) to process massive datasets. The field of natural language processing has seen considerable advancements through LLMs in recent years. Originally, such systems were rudimentary and rule-based. With time, "supervised" and "unsupervised" approaches for learning techniques in neural networks were proposed. In contrast to supervised learning, which relies on human intervention, unsupervised learning allows systems to independently acquire problem-solving rules through self-directed learning. In contemporary applications, ChatGPT, where GPT stands for Generative Pre-Trained Transformer model, has gained significant traction with the publication of a pathbreaking paper titled "Attention is all you need" (Vaswani et al., 2017). This allowed the LLMs to achieve a breakthrough in performance by utilizing "next token prediction," which in simple terms means "collecting a dataset of training examples demonstrating correct behaviour for a desired task and train system to imitate these behaviours" allowing LLMs to become "unsupervised multitask learners" (Radford et al., 2019, p. 1). In essence, LLMs function by predicting the next word in a sequence based on the words that came before it. For example, consider the sentence: "Bob is baking a chocolate ______." LLMs determine the conditional probabilities of subsequent tokens (e.g., "pizza," "bicycle," "cake") from their vocabulary by processing the complete input sequence. This prediction is based on "transformer architecture" by learning complex relationships within a massive corpus of the dataset (Radford et al., 2019; Vaswani et al., 2017). Using a self-attention mechanism, the model considers the relationships between all tokens to predict the most likely next word. This allows the model to recognize chocolate as food. The model selects the next word based on a probability distribution across the entire vocabulary. The token with the highest probability, "cake" in this instance, is selected. Because LLMs handle tokens probabilistically and stochastically, their output to some degree is inherently random and not predictable.

Training Corpus of Large Language Models and Legalese

The internet is the "wealth of knowledge" that has been used to train most of the leading LLMs that exist today (Kandpal et al., 2023, p. 1). It contains all the information regarding names, birthdays of historical figures, codes of several projects, and plenty of conversations that happen on social media sites and microblogging sites. LLMs can capture semantic information from large-scale unlabeled text (Mikolov et al., 2013). LLMs are trained using a variety of data sources, including web pages, books, academic papers, Wikipedia, code from sites like Stack Overflow and BigQuery, and other diverse datasets (Zhao et al., 2025, pp. 13–14). However, training LLMs on vast amounts of general internet data also leaves much to be desired when it comes to processing legal documents. Legal texts are considerably more complex and harder to understand than typical internet content (Friedrich, 2021). Context significantly impacts the understanding and interpretation of certain words within legal documents. The word "security," for instance, has multiple meanings in legal contexts, depending on its usage. According to Black's Law Dictionary, the term "security" encompasses at least four distinct meanings ("Security," 2004, p. 1504):

1. An extension of funds or credit in exchange for collateral;
2. A state of being safe from harm;
3. A guarantor or surety to a contract;
4. An instrument representing ownership in a business entity such as stocks, debentures, trusts, or investment contracts.

Certain legal terminology may still be unfamiliar to the average citizen who has been fortunate to receive an education based on English (Mertz, 2007, p. 43). Gaining functional proficiency in the usage of legalese requires years of academic study coupled with a decent amount of practical experience. Many words in legal language—for example, "herein," "hereof," "estoppel," "lien," and the Latin terms "habeas corpus," "ab initio," "ad hoc," and "ad idem"—are not typically found in everyday conversation or writing. This semantic usage and its depth can be challenging for individuals who are not familiar with the legal lexicon or legalese. LLMs, much like humans learning legal jargon, benefit from targeted training and fine-tuning on relevant data to perform well in specialized fields. Furthermore, merely bridging the linguistic chasm between legalese and plain English is insufficient to fulfill the requirements of effective legal services. Understanding and interpreting legal language presents a significant challenge for both humans and LLMs. This domain-specific nature of legalese presents as a significant challenge when we attempt to utilize LLMs for complex legal tasks.

Problem of Hallucination

LLMs acquire grammar, language syntax, and world facts from the vast amounts of text and data used in their training. Existing literature predominantly ascribes the achievements of LLMs to their method of storing training data as parameters in their internal memory (Petroni et al., 2019).

Remember from the earlier section that LLMs operate as probabilistic systems. It has been noted that the innate tendency of LLMs to produce outputs that deviate from factual accuracy or that contain nonsensical information is a key feature often described as the production of "hallucinations." This concept of hallucination has been borrowed from the psychological literature that defines it as "perception of an entity or event that is absent in reality" (Macpherson & Platchias, 2013). Given the probabilistic and stochastic nature of token prediction, LLMs are susceptible to generating inaccurate text and spurious references, some potentially entirely fictional. Readers, especially from the domain of law, should be aware that hallucinations can be deceptively realistic upon cursory review yet a thorough investigation invariably exposes their fabricated origins. There have been a few instances where lawyers have "mistakenly" cited AI-generated, non-existent cases, highlighting the dangers of relying on fabricated content by LLMs (Brodkin, 2023; Merken, 2025).

Types of Hallucinations

In a survey by Huang et al. (2025), hallucinations were classified into two primary categories: "factuality hallucination" and "faithfulness hallucinations." Under the factuality hallucination, especially in the legal domain, the LLM can either produce a "factual contradiction" or a "factual fabrication" (J. Li et al., 2023). In the category of factual contradictions, the LLM's generation is demonstrably false, such as LLM can generate output in which it ascribes the theory of relativity to Newton rather than its true author, Einstein. In instances of "factual fabrication," the LLM may produce inaccurate information that cannot be corroborated with established real-world data. An example of such situation "factual fabrication" is to ask an LLM to give us the adverse environmental impact of constructing the Taj Mahal, and the LLM fabricates facts such as that the construction of the Taj Mahal led to the extinction of the Asiatic Lion in Uttar Pradesh (Huang et al., 2025, p. 1:6). Research also shows that a neural network's activation patterns during output generation reflect its internal assessment of a statement's truthfulness, which may allow an LLM to cross-check the validity of statements provided by a user by comparing them to information or knowledge within their parameters (Azaria & Mitchell, 2023; Burns et al., 2024).

"Faithful hallucinations," the second major category, result from the LLM's training methods (Gekhman et al., 2024). Both supervised fine-tuning and reinforcement learning using human feedback can contribute to this type of hallucination (Ouyang et al., 2022; Zhang et al., 2024). Studies have shown that LLMs become prone to hallucination during supervised fine-tuning because training the annotated dataset given by the user exceeds pre-existing and pre-defined boundaries within the parameters. LLMs, therefore, need to fit the training data that exists beyond the actual knowledge boundary within the parameters. This creates a mismatch, resulting in the model's failure to reject input and a subsequent tendency to generate fabricated content. So, outputs may contain hallucinations if the prompts provided by the user were not sufficiently clear, which gives rise to the following three types of faithful hallucinations (Adlakha et al., 2024):

1. Instruction Inconsistency—in which the user's instructions lacked clarity, resulting in misaligned LLM output.
2. Context Inconsistency—Sometimes, users give instructions that the LLM ignores, resulting in an output that contradicts the prompt's context.
3. Logical Inconsistency—A type of LLM hallucination occurs when the model's reasoning process is flawed, producing an erroneous conclusion.

Knowledge Boundary Limitations

Another significant limitation of most foundational LLMs is their "knowledge boundary," which is a consequence of the boundaries of their training data, which often excludes information from rapidly changing or regularly updated fields (Kasai et al., 2023). As a result, these LLMs also come up with a "cut-off" date, which essentially means that they store information up to a certain point in time (Cheng et al., 2024). Now, knowledge boundaries within the computer science literature have been classified primarily into five types (M. Li et al., 2024):

1. Parametric knowledge: A type of knowledge residing within the defined parameters of an LLM is readily verifiable through the use of a single query expression. This often can be understood by the example of a "cut-off" date in which LLMs are not able to answer to prompts seeking factual information such as "Which party won the majority in the State of New Delhi in 2025?"
2. Universal knowledge boundary: This encompasses the complete collection of all knowledge presently known to humankind, representing the sum total of human understanding.
3. Prompt-agnostic known knowledge: This is inherently independent from the specific query expression inputted into the LLM, implying a foundational level of understanding separate from immediate prompts. For example, if you were to ask an LLM a question such as, "Is the earth flat?" the response you would invariably receive is "No."
4. Prompt-sensitive knowledge: This type of knowledge within LLMs is dependent on the information given through prompts.
5. Model specific unknown knowledge: This type of knowledge simply does not exist within the parameters of LLMs and cannot be verified by a query expression.

A limited knowledge boundary can lead to undesirable LLM behavior. Insufficient training and a lack of domain-specific knowledge (like legal expertise) cause LLMs to generate outputs based on outdated information and be constrained by temporal limitations. Then, in other cases, LLMs can also generate answers with

1. Overconfidence: LLMs can often display overconfidence while generating outputs to unknown or less known subjects, which mostly happens due to their limited generalization abilities and overfitting of unfamiliar data due to reward systems
2. Lack of contextual clarity: In the domain of law, context is considered paramount, and lack of context can also misalign output in numerous ways:
   a. Untruthful responses by misled context: Extending the example that we had discussed earlier, if a user provides an LLM with the prompt "The earth is actually flat *because* [false and misleading content]." Depending on the model's training and type, it might begin responding with "Yes" to the same question if asked again, exhibiting a learned response pattern. False responses can also arise when the LLM considers irrelevant information, even if the user's query is accurate.
   b. Random and biased responses: Such responses by LLMs mainly occur because LLMs are unable to recognize ambiguities or their training data was skewed, leading to partiality in responses.

This limitation of knowledge within parameters presents a unique challenge for legal professionals because, under common law, judges constantly shape the law through their rulings. Factuality errors in LLM responses are what lawyers should be most concerned about. Verifying the output is the only way to identify AI hallucinations; although LLMs offer potential for streamlining traditional methods, complete reliance still remains premature. Within the paradigm of Reinforcement Learning from Human Feedback, where human supervisors provide feedback to LLMs, a strange phenomenon has been observed: LLMs may prioritize appeasing human overseers, even when factual knowledge is retained within their parameters, resulting in a tendency towards pandering to user opinions. In such types of situations, careful prompting with clear instructions and providing correct context may turn out to be helpful. Therefore, one of the contemporary challenges in the domain of natural language processing in LLMs is to focus on coming up with strategies that can address the challenge of hallucination and provide LLMs with capabilities to access sources of knowledge or information that lie beyond their parameters. There are several methodologies that exist that have been proposed for mitigation for hallucination, and among them, one such method is to use Retrieval-Augmented Generation (RAG).

RETRIEVAL-AUGMENTED GENERATION

Historically, automating the intricate reasoning processes involved in legal matters has presented significant challenges. However, advancements in natural language processing offer hope for automating some parts of the due diligence process. Moreover, the current training approach for LLMs, based on size and scaling, produces unpredictable emergent properties that might prove valuable when dealing with legal documents (Wei et al., 2022). While LLMs perform impressively on tasks requiring everyday English, their lack of access to specialized knowledge and vocabulary in the domain of law creates a roadblock in their success in the field of Law. The recent trends in natural language processing within the domain of law are focusing on relation extraction, named entity recognition, entity linking, and coreference resolution. These techniques, and their various combinations, find further application in text classification, summarization, and Q&A generation (Krasadakis et al., 2024, p. 3). Even though LLMs at the time of writing this are fully capable of passing or clearing bar exams of various jurisdictions, they still have a long way to go before they can become reliable and trustworthy in the domain of Law (Chalkidis, 2023). The parameterized form of knowledge also makes the LLMs behave like a "black box" in which a user does not have the ability to determine why, on giving a particular input, a certain output was provided. Recall that LLMs are stochastic and probabilistic in nature, so asking such LLMs a question multiple times can generate multiple variations of answers. This only adds to the problem of generation of inaccurate information by LLMs, which is frequently observed when dealing with queries concerning post-cut-off world events or specialized fields such as Law, where model training is insufficient. The cost of fine-tuning neural networks to handle specialized or proprietary information, for example, in legal contexts, has traditionally been substantial (Gao et al., 2024). Therefore, one of the proposed approaches to enable LLMs is to link them with a data pipeline to external knowledge sources to generate output. This is also known as RAG. RAG was first introduced by Fabio Petroni, Aleksandra Piktus, Vladimir Karpukhin, Naman Goyal, Heinrich Küttler, Mike Lewis, Wen-tau Yih, Tim Rocktäschell, Sebastian Riedel, and Douwe Kiela at Facebook's (now Meta) AI research lab (Lewis et al., 2021). This method enabled the integration of the pre-existing parameterized implicit knowledge base within LLMs and non-parametric retrieval-based systems, thereby mitigating (at least to some extent if not removing) the inherent limitations of LLM hallucinations.

We can also illustrate RAG with an analogy: imagine students taking an exam. During closed-book examinations, the use of external resources is strictly forbidden. Conversely, in open-book examinations, students are granted permission to access and incorporate relevant information within their answers. RAG works in a similar manner, in which LLMs are integrated with external knowledge sources and can generate output by referring to or retrieving information from external knowledge sources. In simple words, RAG allows us to connect the LLMs to retrieve information in real time, either from the internet or from a database that may be stored privately as well as locally with us. The LLMs for such locally deployed systems would not require the internet to function. Establishing data pipelines between LLMs and external knowledge sources will allow the LLMs to tap into data, information, or knowledge that may not exist within its parameters or, that with the passage of time, becomes outdated or obsolete (Tonmoy et al., 2024, p. 2). This also mitigates the issue of hallucinations to some extent that we have seen in the previous sections, as the output now becomes grounded in the contextual information being provided via documents or external sources rather than being solely produced from LLMs' internal parameters. Knowledge derived solely from large datasets, lacking inherent adaptability, cannot be dynamically updated. In addition, the computational cost of expanding or updating the knowledge's parametric form has been high for both training and inference (Gao et al., 2024, pp. 2–3). Therefore, utilizing RAG also enables the model to stay updated with the current landscape or latest information without engaging in extensive retraining to update the parameters. RAG has already been effectively applied for the purpose of legal document drafting (Pipitone & Alami, 2024). However, the literature relating to the creation of benchmarks for RAG systems is rather limited.

We have to also note that most of the legal documents exist in PDF, Word, Excel, or even image-based formats with unique structures, terminologies, and nuances. The data within the majority of legal documents is presented in a raw, unstructured format, lacking a consistent organizational structure. In contrast to the structured format of Excel data, unstructured data from the point of view of machine learning algorithms is a chaotic jumble of information without a clear organizational scheme. The unstructured nature of this data presents significant challenges in developing and implementing downstream applications for RAG systems. Driven by the need for standardized evaluation, researchers have been developing a comprehensive framework and assessment system for testing retrieval algorithms, incorporating various performance indicators.

How Does an RAG System Function?

In the most basic form of implementation of RAG, a set of documents is converted into vector embeddings via various text processing techniques such as chunking, embedding, and indexing (Figure 18.1). After processing, these vector embeddings are subsequently indexed and stored in a scalable vector database for efficient retrieval. In a functional RAG system, a user provides a query to an LLM, initiating a semantic similarity search within the stored vector database. If the search

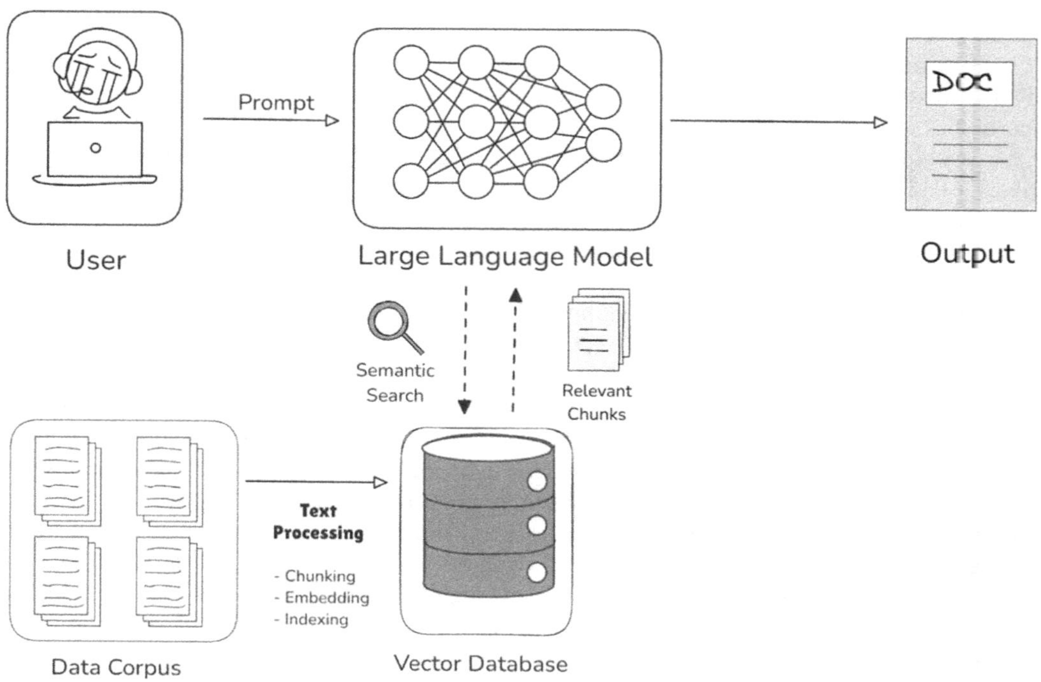

FIGURE 18.1 The diagram depicts the manner in which an RAG system functions.

function finds relevant information in the vector database, that information is also sent to the LLM. Finally, having retrieved relevant information from its document corpus, the LLM provided the user with output.

Application of RAG Systems in Due Diligence and Evidence Evaluation

RAG allows the LLMs to pinpoint highly relevant textual snippets from a given corpus of data. A well-designed and implemented RAG system can enable legal professionals to extract critical information from vast repositories of unstructured documents. For example, in contract review analysis, RAG can expedite the process of searching, locating, and extracting key terms, clauses, and obligation as well as potential risks that may be associated with an M&A transaction. Since the information generated by the RAG system will be grounded, they also may be able to highlight or locate clauses like termination, indemnification, and limitation of liabilities within the relevant corpus of data. Further, in the domain of compliance monitoring, RAG systems can enable real-time monitoring of the transaction documents. When potentially problematic information emerges that can have an impact on existing agreements or create new risks, an RAG system theoretically should be able to flag such changes or modifications within the updated corpus of documents, enabling the legal due diligence teams to address or mitigate emerging issues. By leveraging such capabilities, RAG systems allow us to move beyond traditional keyword searches and introduce the ability to conduct sophisticated context-aware and context-specific evaluation of document repositories because we have seen in the previous section how words are transformed into vector embeddings in the RAG systems. The above illustration is not merely theoretical in nature. Indeed, proof-of-concept systems already automate due diligence using such NLP techniques. For example, companies like Kira Systems and Luminence have deployed RAG systems to speed up the review process in due diligence (Filipsson, 2024).

Persistent Challenges and Limitations of RAG Systems

RAG systems, if implemented optimally, can automate a crucial part of due diligence, i.e., reducing time for searching relevant documents. Despite the clear potential of RAG systems, their application within law firms in the literature is still unexplored, particularly regarding the usage of open-source enterprise solutions. Licensing proprietary software solutions while being extremely powerful can also be explored, but there will be risk of data leakage and breach of confidentiality. It cannot be said with certainty how open the Law firms will be to exploring solutions that would do computation on the cloud. The vast processing of data that is stored within the private networks of law firms will require further research and optimizations in retrieval settings for robust, cost-effective, reliable, and scalable solutions (B & Purwar, 2024). Moreover, it cannot be stressed enough how important the reliability of retrieval algorithms and sources will determine the efficacy of RAG systems in the legal domain. Effective retrieval techniques will depend upon the quality and comprehensiveness of the sources from which the information is being extracted. Not only will the quality of sources from which information is being retrieved but also the retrieval mechanism itself will be dependent upon chunking and embedding practices utilized by the RAG system. The optimal granularity (page, paragraph, or sentence level) for chunking and embedding algorithms will need to be determined by the researchers on a case-by-case basis. The content's semantic integrity may be compromised if the granularity is not appropriate. A key component will be the vector embedding model, converting chunked text into vector representations to systematically organize data as key–value pairs. This will dramatically improve the speed of text retrieval from the vector database because the model's numerical vectors allow for rapid searching and indexing. Poorly designed embedding models will negatively affect the accuracy of similarity comparisons between queries and embedded content, potentially resulting in inaccurate and misleading LLM outputs. A very recent publication by

Google that has implemented an RAG system on its Gemini 1.5 model has found that LLMs tend to achieve higher accuracy when the context provided to them is "sufficient" (Joren et al., 2025). While it may be possible for LLMs to "know" certain answers based on their parametric knowledge from pre-training, any additional context removes ambiguity and works to bridge the gap between knowledge to answer a query. To pitch an enterprise solution in this area, results with and without the retrieval mechanism must be published. However, well-designed and maintained RAG systems should be able to endow LLMs with source attribution capabilities in which LLMs can identify and utilize information being provided to them within their generation process, subverting the "black-box" phenomenon. To enable LLMs to effectively pair user query tokens with retrieved information, researchers may also utilize reasoning models that can perform methods like "plan then generate," "generate then reflect," and "self-attribution," which facilitate the identification, evaluation, and reflection upon context-sensitive aspects of the query; this sophisticated approach helps ensure that retrieved data precisely aligns with user intent.

CONCLUSION

While RAG presents today a significant advantage in leveraging LLMs for legal tasks such as due diligence by providing grounded, accurate, verifiable information, we also need to remain aware of the current limitations and potential pitfalls that are associated with utilization of RAG. The language used in the legal system has its own specialized vocabulary, syntax, and nuances driven by context that general-purpose LLMs may struggle to understand and grasp the meaning and implication of. Again, with the risk of repeating ourselves, the utility of RAG is highly dependent upon the quality of sources from which the information is being retrieved and also on the quality of the retrieval mechanisms that have been relied upon to identify the most pertinent or relevant information within the document corpus. Ongoing research and developments are actively attempting to address the challenges that the current paradigm of RAG systems faces. With the rapid advancement of AI models, including RAG, the legal community faces a crucial task: establishing systematic, data-driven methods for evaluating AI capabilities in legal contexts, a process demanding careful consideration of ethical and practical implications. The practical, real-world uses of RAG systems are significantly under-researched outside of academic computer science publications; their potential impact in diverse fields remains largely unknown. The tech industry's breakneck speed contrasts sharply with the slower pace of adoption in fields like law, where the cautious nature of the profession creates a significant hurdle. Successful integration of AI's performance and capabilities presents a considerable hurdle for the legal profession, requiring lawyers to learn new skills and re-evaluate existing methods.

NOTE

1 There are several indicators that one can look for conducting commercial due diligence. For example, growth, price, margin assumptions, customer requirements, market capitalization, relative market strength, customer retention, strength of management of the company, system integration, scalability, sustainability, threat by competitors, retention of key staff or employees, sales and logistic operations, value drivers in the business plan, opportunities and risks.

REFERENCES

Adlakha, V., BehnamGhader, P., Lu, X. H., Meade, N., & Reddy, S. (2024). Evaluating Correctness and Faithfulness of Instruction-Following Models for Question Answering. *Transactions of the Association for Computational Linguistics*, *12*, 681–699. https://doi.org/10.1162/tacl_a_00667.

Azaria, A., & Mitchell, T. (2023). *The Internal State of an LLM Knows When It's Lying* (No. arXiv:2304.13734). arXiv. https://doi.org/10.48550/arXiv.2304.13734.

Brodkin, J. (2023, December 13). *Michael Cohen's lawyer cited three fake cases in possible AI-fueled screwup*. Ars Technica. https://arstechnica.com/tech-policy/2023/12/michael-cohens-lawyer-cited-three-fake-cases-in-possible-ai-fueled-screwup/.

Burns, C., Ye, H., Klein, D., & Steinhardt, J. (2024). *Discovering Latent Knowledge in Language Models Without Supervision* (No. arXiv:2212.03827). arXiv. https://doi.org/10.48550/arXiv.2212.03827.

Chalkidis, I. (2023). *ChatGPT may Pass the Bar Exam soon, but has a Long Way to Go for the LexGLUE benchmark* (No. arXiv:2304.12202; Issue arXiv:2304.12202). arXiv. https://doi.org/10.48550/arXiv.2304.12202.

Cheng, J., Marone, M., Weller, O., Lawrie, D., Khashabi, D., & Durme, B. V. (2024). *Dated Data: Tracing Knowledge Cutoffs in Large Language Models* (No. arXiv:2403.12958). arXiv. https://doi.org/10.48550/arXiv.2403.12958.

Filipsson, F. (2024, March 26). *NLP Tools in the Legal Industry – AI-Enabled Legal Professionals*. https://redresscompliance.com/nlp-tools-in-the-legal-industry-ai-enabled-legal-professionals/.

Friedrich, R. (2021). Complexity and Entropy in Legal Language. *Frontiers in Physics*, *9*, 671882. https://doi.org/10.3389/fphy.2021.671882.

Gao, Y., Xiong, Y., Gao, X., Jia, K., Pan, J., Bi, Y., Dai, Y., Sun, J., Wang, M., & Wang, H. (2024). *Retrieval-Augmented Generation for Large Language Models: A Survey* (No. arXiv:2312.10997). arXiv. https://doi.org/10.48550/arXiv.2312.10997.

Gautam, B., & Purwar, A. (2024). *Evaluating the Efficacy of Open-Source LLMs in Enterprise-Specific RAG Systems: A Comparative Study of Performance and Scalability* (No. arXiv:2406.11424). arXiv. https://doi.org/10.48550/arXiv.2406.11424.

Gekhman, Z., Yona, G., Aharoni, R., Eyal, M., Feder, A., Reichart, R., & Herzig, J. (2024). *Does Fine-Tuning LLMs on New Knowledge Encourage Hallucinations?* (No. arXiv:2405.05904). arXiv. https://doi.org/10.48550/arXiv.2405.05904.

Huang, L., Yu, W., Ma, W., Zhong, W., Feng, Z., Wang, H., Chen, Q., Peng, W., Feng, X., Qin, B., & Liu, T. (2025). A Survey on Hallucination in Large Language Models: Principles, Taxonomy, Challenges, and Open Questions. *ACM Transactions on Information Systems*, *43*(2), :1-42:55. https://doi.org/10.1145/3703155.

Joren, H., Zhang, J., Ferng, C.-S., Juan, D.-C., Taly, A., & Rashtchian, C. (2025). *Sufficient Context: A New Lens on Retrieval Augmented Generation Systems* (No. arXiv:2411.06037). arXiv. https://doi.org/10.48550/arXiv.2411.06037.

Kandpal, N., Deng, H., Roberts, A., Wallace, E., & Raffel, C. (2023). Large Language Models Struggle to Learn Long-Tail Knowledge. *Proceedings of the 40th International Conference on Machine Learning*, 15696–15707. https://proceedings.mlr.press/v202/kandpal23a.html.

Kasai, J., Sakaguchi, K., Takahashi, Y., Bras, R. L., Asai, A., Yu, X. V., Radev, D., Smith, N. A., Choi, Y., & Inui, K. (2023). *REALTIME QA: What's the Answer Right Now?*.

Kastrup, T., Grant, M., & Nilsson, F. (2025). Data Analytics use in Financial due Diligence: The Influence of Accounting and Commercial Logic. *Qualitative Research in Accounting & Management*, *22*(2), 158–185. https://doi.org/10.1108/QRAM-10-2023-0188.

Katz, D. M., Hartung, D., Gerlach, L., Jana, A., & II, M. J. B. (2023). *Natural Language Processing in the Legal Domain* (No. arXiv:2302.12039). arXiv. https://doi.org/10.48550/arXiv.2302.12039.

Krasadakis, P., Sakkopoulos, E., & Verykios, V. S. (2024). A Survey on Challenges and Advances in Natural Language Processing with a Focus on Legal Informatics and Low-Resource Languages. *Electronics*, *13*(3), 648. https://doi.org/10.3390/electronics13030648.

Lewis, P., Perez, E., Piktus, A., Petroni, F., Karpukhin, V., Goyal, N., Küttler, H., Lewis, M., Yih, W., Rocktäschel, T., Riedel, S., & Kiela, D. (2021). *Retrieval-Augmented Generation for Knowledge-Intensive NLP Tasks* (No. arXiv:2005.11401). arXiv. https://doi.org/10.48550/arXiv.2005.11401.

Li, J., Cheng, X., Zhao, W. X., Nie, J.-Y., & Wen, J.-R. (2023). *HaluEval: A Large-Scale Hallucination Evaluation Benchmark for Large Language Models* (No. arXiv:2305.11747). arXiv. https://doi.org/10.48550/arXiv.2305.11747.

Li, M., Zhao, Y., Deng, Y., Zhang, W., Li, S., Xie, W., Ng, S.-K., & Chua, T.-S. (2024). *Knowledge Boundary of Large Language Models: A Survey* (No. arXiv:2412.12472). arXiv. https://doi.org/10.48550/arXiv.2412.12472.

Macpherson, F., & Platchias, D. (2013). *Hallucination: Philosophy and psychology*. MIT Press.

Merken, S. (2025, February 18). AI 'hallucinations' in court papers spell trouble for lawyers. *Reuters*. https://www.reuters.com/technology/artificial-intelligence/ai-hallucinations-court-papers-spell-trouble-lawyers-2025-02-18/.

Mertz, E. (2007). *The language of law school: Learning to 'think like a lawyer'*. Oxford University Press.

Mikolov, T., Sutskever, I., Chen, K., Corrado, G. S., & Dean, J. (2013). Distributed Representations of Words and Phrases and their Compositionality. *Advances in Neural Information Processing Systems*, *26*. https://proceedings.neurips.cc/paper/2013/hash/9aa42b31882ec039965f3c4923ce901b-Abstract.html.

Ouyang, L., Wu, J., Jiang, X., Almeida, D., Wainwright, C., Mishkin, P., Zhang, C., Agarwal, S., Slama, K., Ray, A., Schulman, J., Hilton, J., Kelton, F., Miller, L., Simens, M., Askell, A., Welinder, P., Christiano, P. F., Leike, J., & Lowe, R. (2022). Training Language Models to follow Instructions with Human Feedback. *Advances in Neural Information Processing Systems*, *35*, 27730–27744.

Petroni, F., Rocktäschel, T., Lewis, P., Bakhtin, A., Wu, Y., Miller, A. H., & Riedel, S. (2019). *Language Models as Knowledge Bases?* (No. arXiv:1909.01066). arXiv. https://doi.org/10.48550/arXiv.1909.01066.

Pipitone, N., & Alami, G. H. (2024). *LegalBench-RAG: A Benchmark for Retrieval-Augmented Generation in the Legal Domain* (No. arXiv:2408.10343). arXiv. https://doi.org/10.48550/arXiv.2408.10343.

Radford, A., Wu, J., Child, R., Luan, D., Amodei, D., & Sutskever, I. (2019). *Language Models are Unsupervised Multitask Learners*.

Rumelhart, D. E., Hinton, G. E., & Williams, R. J. (1986). Learning Representations by Back-Propagating Errors. *Nature*, *323*(6088), 533–536.

Security. (2004). In B. A. Garner (Ed.), *Black's Law Dictionary* (9th ed., p. 1504). West, Thomson Reuters.

Spedding, L. S. (2009). *The due diligence handbook: Corporate governance, risk management and business planning* (1st ed). Elsevier CIMA.

Tonmoy, S. M. T. I., Zaman, S. M. M., Jain, V., Rani, A., Rawte, V., Chadha, A., & Das, A. (2024). *A Comprehensive Survey of Hallucination Mitigation Techniques in Large Language Models* (No. arXiv:2401.01313). arXiv. https://doi.org/10.48550/arXiv.2401.01313.

Vaswani, A., Shazeer, N., Parmar, N., Uszkoreit, J., Jones, L., Gomez, A. N., Kaiser, Ł., & Polosukhin, I. (2017). Attention is All you Need. *Advances in Neural Information Processing Systems*.

Wei, J., Tay, Y., Bommasani, R., Raffel, C., Zoph, B., Borgeaud, S., Yogatama, D., Bosma, M., Zhou, D., Metzler, D., Chi, E. H., Hashimoto, T., Vinyals, O., Liang, P., Dean, J., & Fedus, W. (2022). *Emergent Abilities of Large Language Models* (No. arXiv:2206.07682). arXiv. https://doi.org/10.48550/arXiv.2206.07682.

Xie, K., Wu, Y., Xiao, J., & Hu, Q. (2016). Value Co-Creation between Firms and Customers: The Role of Big Data-Based Cooperative Assets. *Information & Management*, *53*(8), 1034–1048. https://doi.org/10.1016/j.im.2016.06.003.

Zhang, S., Dong, L., Li, X., Zhang, S., Sun, X., Wang, S., Li, J., Hu, R., Zhang, T., Wu, F., & Wang, G. (2024). *Instruction Tuning for Large Language Models: A Survey* (No. arXiv:2308.10792). arXiv. https://doi.org/10.48550/arXiv.2308.10792.

Zhao, W. X., Zhou, K., Li, J., Tang, T., Wang, X., Hou, Y., Min, Y., Zhang, B., Zhang, J., Dong, Z., Du, Y., Yang, C., Chen, Y., Chen, Z., Jiang, J., Ren, R., Li, Y., Tang, X., Liu, Z., … Wen, J.-R. (2025). *A Survey of Large Language Models* (No. arXiv:2303.18223). arXiv. https://doi.org/10.48550/arXiv.2303.18223.

19 Redefining "Worker" in the Age of AI

Challenges and Legal Reforms for Labor Laws in India

Suman Dinesh Jain

INTRODUCTION

The rapid integration of artificial intelligence (AI) in various industries has redefined traditional employment structures, creating a complex legal challenge for India's labor framework. AI-driven automation, algorithmic decision-making, and the rise of the gig economy have blurred the lines between conventional employees and independent workers, making it imperative to reconsider the legal definition of a "worker."[1] Traditional labor laws, such as the *Industrial Disputes Act, 1947*,[2] and the *Code on Social Security, 2020*,[3] primarily focus on employer–employee relationships in structured workplaces, leaving a significant gap in protections for gig workers, freelancers, and AI-managed workers.

For instance, platforms like Zomato, Uber, and Swiggy operate through AI-powered algorithms that allocate tasks, monitor worker performance, and even determine wages.[4] However, the individuals engaged in these tasks are often classified as independent contractors, thereby excluding them from critical labor rights such as minimum wages, social security, health benefits, and protection against wrongful termination.[5] Similar issues arise in AI-driven workplaces, where automated systems make hiring and firing decisions, raising concerns about fairness, bias, and accountability.[6]

Globally, countries like the UK and the EU have introduced measures to recognize gig workers under labor protection frameworks.[7] India, too, must modernize its legal approach by adopting a broader and more inclusive definition of "worker," ensuring that AI-driven employment structures do not exploit the workforce.[8] This paper explores the challenges posed by AI in labor law, examines international best practices, and proposes key legal reforms to create a balanced framework that fosters innovation while safeguarding worker rights.

EVOLUTION OF THE DEFINITION OF "WORKER" IN INDIA

The definition of "worker" in India has undergone significant evolution, shaped by industrialization, socio-economic changes, and technological advancements. The legal interpretation of a worker has expanded over time to accommodate emerging work structures, yet it remains largely rooted in traditional employer–employee relationships. With the advent of AI and digital platforms, this definition faces new challenges that demand urgent legal reforms.

EARLY INDUSTRIAL ERA: THE TRADITIONAL WORKER

During British rule and the early years of India's independence, the concept of a worker was primarily associated with industrial and factory-based employment. The **Factories Act, 1948**, and

DOI: 10.1201/9781003629146-20

the **Industrial Disputes Act, 1947**, defined a "worker" as a person engaged in manual, skilled, or unskilled labor for wages under an employer's control. This definition focused on structured employment relationships in factories and industrial establishments, leaving out agricultural workers, domestic workers, and informal laborers.

Inclusion of Contract and Informal Workers

Over time, India's workforce expanded beyond factory-based employment. The **Contract Labor (Regulation and Abolition) Act, 1970**, brought contract workers under legal protection, ensuring basic rights such as wages and working conditions. Similarly, the **Unorganized Workers' Social Security Act, 2008**, aimed to provide a social security net for informal sector workers, acknowledging the growing number of non-traditional employment forms.

Gig Economy and Platform-Based Work

The rise of digital platforms like Uber, Swiggy, and Zomato has further challenged the traditional understanding of a worker. These platforms classify individuals as "partners" or "independent contractors" rather than employees, thereby excluding them from labor protections.[9] The **Code on Social Security, 2020**, was a step toward recognizing gig and platform workers, but it did not fully equate them with traditional employees, leaving significant gaps in their rights and benefits.

AI-Driven Work and Algorithmic Management

With AI increasingly playing a role in recruitment, task allocation, performance monitoring, and even terminations, a new category of AI-managed workers has emerged.[10] Automated decision-making systems blur the line between employment and freelancing, raising concerns about worker rights, algorithmic bias, and accountability.[11] Existing labor laws do not explicitly address these issues, creating a legal vacuum.

The Need for a Modern, Inclusive Definition

India must now redefine "worker" to include AI-managed employees, gig workers, and freelancers under legal protection. Drawing from global examples like the **UK's Employment Tribunal rulings**[12] and the **European Union's Directive on Platform Work**, India can establish a more inclusive framework ensuring social security, fair wages, and algorithmic transparency.

The evolution of the worker's definition in India reflects changing work dynamics, but current laws remain inadequate for AI-driven employment. A forward-looking legal reform is necessary to balance technological innovation with fair labor protections.

RELEVANT CASE LAWS

Indian Cases

Uber India Systems Pvt. Ltd. v. Competition Commission of India (2022)

- **Issue:** Whether Uber drivers should be considered employees or independent contractors.
- **Relevance:** This case highlights how ride-hailing services operate through AI-driven algorithms that assign work and determine earnings, challenging the traditional employer–employee relationship. The decision emphasized the need for better labor protection for gig workers.[13]

Pavan Hans Limited v. Aviation Karmachari Sanghatana (2020)

- **Issue:** Whether contractual employees were entitled to provident fund benefits.
- **Relevance:** This case can be linked to gig and platform workers who lack access to social security benefits. The Supreme Court ruled in favor of providing financial security to contract workers, supporting arguments for extending similar benefits to gig workers.[14]

Peoples Union for Democratic Rights v. Union of India (1982) (Asiad Workers Case)

- **Issue:** Whether workers employed through contractors were entitled to minimum wages and other labor protections.
- **Relevance:** This landmark judgment expanded the interpretation of "worker" under Article 21 of the Indian Constitution. It supports the argument that gig and AI-managed workers deserve basic labor rights.[15]

Nitisha v. Union of India (2021)

- **Issue:** Bias in selection and promotion criteria in employment.
- **Relevance:** This case is important for AI-driven employment, where automated decision-making can lead to biased hiring, promotions, or terminations. The Supreme Court recognized systemic discrimination, supporting the need for algorithmic accountability in AI-driven workplaces.[16]

International Cases

Aslam v. Uber BV (UK Supreme Court, 2021)

- **Issue:** Whether Uber drivers are employees or independent contractors.
- **Ruling:** The UK Supreme Court ruled that Uber drivers are "workers" and entitled to minimum wage, holiday pay, and other employment benefits.
- **Relevance:** This case provides a strong precedent for India to reconsider the status of gig workers and introduce legal reforms ensuring fair labor rights.[17]

National Labor Relations Board v. Google (USA, 2023)

- **Issue:** AI-driven workplace monitoring and worker rights.
- **Relevance:** This case examined how AI and data-driven surveillance impact employees' rights to privacy, fair treatment, and collective bargaining, raising concerns about AI regulation in labor laws.[18]

Glovo Case (Spain, 2020)

- **Issue:** Whether gig workers of food delivery platform Glovo were employees.
- **Ruling:** The Spanish court ruled that Glovo riders are employees, requiring the company to provide labor protections.
- **Relevance:** This case strengthens the argument that AI-managed gig workers should be given employee status and legal benefits.[19]

These cases highlight the evolving nature of employment relationships due to AI and automation. Drawing from both Indian and international case laws, the research can argue for necessary legal reforms to **define "worker" inclusively**, ensuring fair wages, social security, and algorithmic transparency in AI-driven work environments.

COMPARATIVE STUDY: ENHANCEMENTS FROM INTERNATIONAL LAWS FOR DEFINING "WORKER"

The traditional definition of "worker" is evolving globally due to the rise of AI-driven employment, gig economy jobs, and remote work structures. Many countries have redefined their legal frameworks to accommodate these changes. A comparative study of international labor laws can provide valuable insights for India to **modernize its legal definition of "worker"** and extend labor protections to new-age employment models.

United Kingdom: Expanding the Definition of Worker

- **Key Features:**
  - The UK distinguishes between "employees," "workers," and "independent contractors," with **workers** having certain rights like minimum wage and holiday pay, even if they are not traditional employees.
  - **Case Law:** *Aslam v. Uber BV (2021)*—The UK Supreme Court ruled that Uber drivers were "workers" and entitled to benefits like paid holidays and minimum wage.
- **Lesson for India:**
  - India can introduce a **third category of workers** beyond "employees" and "self-employed" to include gig, AI-managed, and platform workers with essential rights.

European Union: Platform Work Directive and Algorithmic Management

- **Key Features:**
  - The **EU Platform Work Directive (2023)** grants gig workers the presumption of employment unless proven otherwise.
  - It mandates **transparency in AI-driven employment decisions**, ensuring that workers have the right to challenge algorithmic decisions on wages, work hours, and dismissals.
- **Lesson for India:**
  - Introducing **presumption of employment** for gig and AI-managed workers to prevent misclassification as independent contractors.
  - Regulating **AI-based work assignment and monitoring** to ensure fair treatment of AI-managed workers.

United States: Worker Classification Tests and AI in Employment

- **Key Features:**
  - The **Economic Realities Test** and **ABC Test** are used to determine whether a worker is an employee or independent contractor.
  - The **National Labor Relations Board (NLRB)** and the **Equal Employment Opportunity Commission (EEOC)** are reviewing cases where AI-based hiring and termination systems have led to unfair employment decisions.
- **Lesson for India:**
  - Implementing a **structured test for defining workers** based on economic dependence and control rather than just contract terms.
  - Establishing **AI fairness and accountability policies** in hiring and employment practices.

Australia: Gig Economy Protections Under Fair Work Laws

- **Key Features:**
  - The **Fair Work Commission** has recognized some gig workers as employees based on work conditions.

- Laws are being developed to ensure **minimum standards for gig workers** in terms of pay, work hours, and dispute resolution.[20]
- **Lesson for India:**
  - Establishing **minimum wage and welfare protections** for gig and platform workers.
  - Creating an **independent body** to review cases of worker misclassification.

Canada: Expanding Labor Protections to Gig Workers

- **Key Features:**
  - Some Canadian provinces have expanded **labor protections to gig workers**, ensuring access to social security benefits.
  - The **British Columbia Supreme Court (2023)** ruled that AI-managed workers deserve the same labor protections as traditional employees.
- **Lesson for India:**
  - Expanding **social security coverage** to gig, freelance, and AI-managed workers.
  - Strengthening **legal recognition of digital and remote work models** in labor laws.

RECOMMENDATIONS FOR INDIA

1. **Introduce a Third Category of Workers**—Recognize "platform workers" or "AI-managed workers" with rights to minimum wage and dispute resolution.
2. **Implement an Employment Classification Test**—A structured test (similar to the ABC Test) to prevent worker misclassification.
3. **Regulate Algorithmic Management**—Ensure AI-driven employment decisions are **transparent, explainable, and challengeable**.
4. **Extend Social Security Benefits**—Expand **EPF, ESI, and pension schemes** to gig and platform workers.
5. **Create a National Gig & AI Workforce Policy**—Establish a framework to **define, protect, and regulate AI-driven work models**.

International best practices show that **labor laws must adapt to AI-driven and gig-based employment.** India has the opportunity to redefine "worker" in a way that balances **economic flexibility with essential protections**, ensuring **fair treatment for all types of workers in the digital economy**.

FINDINGS

1. **Outdated Legal Definitions**: Indian labor legislation such as the **Industrial Disputes Act, 1947**, and even the more recent **Code on Social Security, 2020**, is rooted in industrial-era employment structures and do not sufficiently address the complexities of gig economy, AI-managed, or platform-based work.
2. **Legal Vacuum for AI-Managed Workers**: There is no express mention or legal clarity regarding employees who work under **algorithmic control**, where AI assigns tasks, monitors performance, and takes decisions like hiring or termination. This legal vacuum makes such workers vulnerable to exploitation without redressal.
3. **Exclusion from Social Security Benefits**: Gig and platform workers—although partially recognized under the **Social Security Code**—do not enjoy the full range of protections available to traditional employees, including provident fund, health insurance, maternity benefits, and grievance mechanisms.[21]
4. **Prevalence of Misclassification**: Many digital platforms categorize workers as **independent contractors** to avoid statutory obligations like minimum wages, working hours, or

termination safeguards. This practice amounts to **misclassification**, denying workers their rightful entitlements.

5. **Algorithmic Bias and Opacity**: AI systems used in recruitment and employment decisions often operate as black boxes, with little transparency. Biased algorithms can reinforce inequality (e.g., gender, caste, region), yet workers have limited legal recourse to challenge such decisions.
6. **International Trends Offer Valuable Models**: Jurisdictions like the **UK, EU, Australia, and Canada** have initiated reforms by introducing broader worker classifications, mandatory algorithmic transparency, and a presumption of employment in digital platform contexts.

RECOMMENDATIONS

1. **Redefine "Worker" in Indian Labor Laws**: Amend the definition of "worker" across all major labor codes to **include gig workers, platform workers, and AI-managed employees**. Introduce a **tiered classification system**, similar to the UK model, distinguishing between employees, workers, and contractors with corresponding rights.
2. **Implement Structured Employment Classification Tests**: Introduce a formal employment test, such as the **ABC Test** used in the US, to reduce misclassification of workers. The test should be based on criteria like **control, dependency, and nature of work**, rather than labels or contract terms alone.
3. **Ensure Access to Social Security and Benefits**: Mandate **EPF, ESI, maternity benefits, and pension coverage** for all gig and platform workers. This could be financed through **shared contributions** from platforms, government, and the workers themselves.
4. **Create Legal Safeguards for Algorithmic Management**: Enact rules that ensure **algorithmic transparency**, the **right to explanation**, and the **right to challenge automated decisions**. Require companies to **audit and report** AI decisions impacting workers.
5. **Strengthen Dispute Resolution Mechanisms**: Establish **dedicated tribunals** or fast-track forums for gig and AI-managed workers to address labor disputes efficiently. Promote **Online Dispute Resolution (ODR)** for accessibility and efficiency.
6. **Introduce a National Gig and AI Labor Policy**: India should adopt a **comprehensive policy** that governs the rights, responsibilities, benefits, and protections for digital and AI-driven workforces, incorporating ethical AI use and fairness in labor practices.
7. **Promote Reskilling and Job Transition Schemes**: Government and private sectors must collaborate on **AI literacy, reskilling, and upskilling programs** to help workers transition into AI-augmented roles or new sectors.

CONCLUSION

The definition of "worker" in India is currently inadequate to meet the needs of a rapidly transforming labor market shaped by AI and digital platforms. As AI redefines employment structures—shifting power from human managers to algorithms—labor laws must evolve to protect the rights, dignity, and livelihoods of all working individuals, regardless of how their work is organized or delivered.

Gig and platform workers, as well as those employed under algorithmic supervision, face a precarious situation where they contribute significantly to the economy but remain outside the protective umbrella of the law. International practices offer useful guidance, but India's solution must be tailored to its socio-economic and legal landscape.

Reform is not just a legal necessity but a **constitutional imperative**—ensuring the right to livelihood under **Article 21**, the right to equality under **Article 14**, and the directive principles advocating just and humane working conditions. The future of work in India must be **inclusive, equitable, and legally secure**, and redefining "worker" is the foundational step toward that future.

NOTES

1 Valerio De Stefano (2016). The Rise of the "Just-in-Time Workforce": On-Demand Work, Crowdwork, and Labour Protection in the "Gig Economy." *Comparative Labor Law & Policy Journal*, 37(3), 471–504. http://dx.doi.org/10.2139/ssrn.2682602
2 The Industrial Disputes Act 1947, INDIA CODE
3 The Industrial Disputes Act, No. 14 of 1947, INDIA CODE
4 Ghosh, S. (2022). Algorithmic Management in India's Gig Economy: A Legal Black Hole. *NLSIR (National Law School of India Review).*
5 Ministry of Labour and Employment India (2021). *Draft Rules under Code on Social Security.* https://labour.gov.in/sites/default/files/pre_published_draft_rules_on_employees_compensation.pdf
6 Bales, K., Stone, K., & Blackham, A. (2018). Algorithmic Management and the Future of Work. *Oxford Internet Institute Working Paper.*
7 *Uber BV v. Aslam*, [2021] UKSC 5 (U.K. Supreme Court 2021); European Commission (2023). *Directive on Improving Working Conditions in Platform Work.* https://eur-lex.europa.eu/legal-content/EN/TXT/PDF/?uri=CELEX:52021PC0762
8 International Labour Organization (2021). *World Employment and Social Outlook 2021: The Role of Digital Labour Platforms in Transforming the World of Work.* www.ilo.org/publications/flagship-reports/role-digital-labour-platforms-transforming-world-work
9 Valerio De Stefano (2016). The Rise of the "Just-in-Time Workforce": On-Demand Work, Crowdwork, and Labour Protection in the "Gig Economy." *Comparative Labor Law & Policy Journal*, 37(3), 471–504. http://dx.doi.org/10.2139/ssrn.2682602
10 Bales, K., Stone, K., & Blackham, A. (2018). Algorithmic Management and the Future of Work. *Oxford Internet Institute Working Paper.*
11 Ghosh, S. (2022). Algorithmic Management in India's Gig Economy: A Legal Black Hole. *NLSIR (National Law School of India Review).*
12 *Uber BV v. Aslam*, [2021] UKSC 5 (U.K. Supreme Court 2021).
13 *Uber India Systems Pvt. Ltd. v. Competition Commission of India*, 2022 SCC OnLine Del 2583 (Supreme Court of India 2022).
14 *Pavan Hans Ltd. v. Aviation Karmachari Sanghatana*, (2020) 13 SCC 85 (Supreme Court of India 2020).
15 *People's Union for Democratic Rights v. Union of India*, AIR 1982 SC 1473 (Supreme Court of India 1982).
16 *Nitisha v. Union of India*, (2021) 2 SCC 740 (Supreme Court of India 2021).
17 *Uber BV v. Aslam*, [2021] UKSC 5 (U.K. Supreme Court 2021).
18 *Nat'l Lab. Rels. Bd. v. Google LLC*, Case No. 32-CA-271966, Decision and Order (2023) (National Labour Relations Board USA 2023).
19 *Tribunal Supremo*, Sala de lo Social, Sentencia 805/2020, STS 805/2020 (Supreme Court of Spain 2020).
20 *Klooger v. Foodora Australia Pty Ltd.*, [2018] FWC 6836 (Fair Work Commission Australia 2018).
21 Ministry of Labour and Employment India (2021). *Draft Rules under Code on Social Security.* https://labour.gov.in/sites/default/files/pre_published_draft_rules_on_employees_compensation.pdf

BIBLIOGRAPHY

PRIMARY LEGISLATIONS AND LEGAL DOCUMENTS (INDIA)

Code on Social Security, 2020.
Contract Labour (Regulation and Abolition) Act, 1970.
Industrial Disputes Act, 1947.
The Constitution of India – Articles 14, 21, and 43.
Unorganised Workers' Social Security Act, 2008.

CASE LAWS (INDIA & INTERNATIONAL)

Aslam v. Uber BV, UKSC 5 [2021] (UK Supreme Court 2021).
Klooger v. Foodora Australia Pty Ltd., [2018] FWC 6836 (Fair Work Commission Australia 2018).
Nat'l Lab. Rels. Bd. v. Google LLC, Case No. 32-CA-271966, Decision and Order (2023) (National Labour Relations Board USA 2023).
Nitisha v. Union of India, (2021) 2 SCC 740 (Supreme Court of India 2021).
Pavan Hans Ltd. v. Aviation Karmachari Sanghatana, (2020) 13 SCC 85 (Supreme Court of India 2020).

Peoples Union for Democratic Rights v. Union of India, AIR 1982 SC 1473 (Supreme Court of India 1982).
Tribunal Supremo, Sala de lo Social, Sentencia 805/2020, STS 805/2020 (Supreme Court of Spain 2020).
Uber BV v. Aslam, [2021] UKSC 5 (U.K. Supreme Court 2021).
Uber India Systems Pvt. Ltd. v. Competition Commission of India, 2022 SCC OnLine Del 2583 (Supreme Court of India 2022).

International Laws & Policies

European Union Platform Work Directive, 2023 (European Union).
Fair Work Act, 2009 (Australia).
General Data Protection Regulation (GDPR), 2016 (European Union).
National Labor Relations Act, 1935 (USA).
UK Employment Rights Act, 1996 (United Kingdom).

Academic & Policy Sources

Bales, K., Stone, K., & Blackham, A. (2018). *Algorithmic Management and the Future of Work*. Working Paper. Oxford Internet Institute.
De Stefano, V. (2016). The Rise of the "Just-in-Time Workforce": On-Demand Work, Crowdwork, and Labour Protection in the "Gig-Economy". *Comparative Labour Law & Policy Journal*, 37(3), 471–504.
Ghosh, S. (2022). *Algorithmic Management in India's Gig Economy: A Legal Black Hole*. NLSIR (National Law School of India Review).
ILO. (2021). *World Employment and Social Outlook: The Role of Digital Labour Platforms in Transforming the World of Work*. ILO.
Ministry of Labour and Employment India. (2021). *Code on Social Security Draft Rules*. Ministry of Labour and Employment India.

Name- Suman Dinesh Jain, Advocate (BBA, LLB, LLM)

Socially Handling – "Project Uncarbon"

City- Surat, Gujarat

Occupation – IP and Labour Lawyer

Contact No. – 9898871096

Mail Id. – advsumanjain95@gmail.com

20 The Future of Legal Evidence with the Help of Artificial Intelligence and e-Discovery

Riya Banerjee, Sarfaraz Ahmed Khan, and Anik Bhattacharya

INTRODUCTION

The combination of artificial intelligence (AI) with e-discovery in evidence management is radically altering the legal landscape. AI-powered tools are transforming how legal practitioners collect, handle, and analyze evidence, increasing efficiency and accuracy. E-discovery, or the identification, gathering, and production of electronically stored information (ESI), has become a critical component of modern litigation. This study investigates the future of legal evidence using AI and e-discovery, focusing on breakthroughs, obstacles, and ethical implications.

THE ROLE OF ARTIFICIAL INTELLIGENCE IN LEGAL EVIDENCE

AI-Powered Legal Research and Document Review

AI is redefining the legal industry by changing the way legal research and document review are handled. Traditionally, conducting legal research involved hours of physical labor, combing through case law, laws, and legal commentaries. Today, AI technologies armed with advanced natural language processing (NLP) can parse legal text, locate relevant precedents, and provide informative legal summaries with extraordinary efficiency and accuracy (Katz et al., 2017).

According to McGinnis & Pearce (2014), AI-powered platforms can do legal research activities at 30%–60% faster than human lawyers. For example, technologies like ROSS Intelligence and Westlaw Edge use machine learning algorithms to not only retrieve legal texts but also predict key citations and indicate contradicting rulings. This enables legal practitioners to make educated choices faster.

AI-powered tools are also revolutionizing document review, a critical step in litigation and due diligence. These systems use predictive coding and machine learning to examine and categorize massive amounts of documents, emails, and data depending on their relevance, privilege, and secrecy. According to research, AI-assisted document review can achieve up to 94% accuracy against 88% for human reviewers (Grossman & Cormack, 2011). Furthermore, this reduces the risk of human error and significantly lowers legal costs.

Furthermore, AI can identify patterns, detect abnormalities, and recommend legal strategies based on precedent and statistical analysis, which aids in legal forecasting and risk management (Surden, 2019). As AI advances, its integration into legal research and document review promises to improve both the speed and quality of legal services.

DOI: 10.1201/9781003629146-21

Predictive Analytics in Legal Decision-Making

Predictive analytics, powered by AI and machine learning, is becoming an increasingly important tool in the legal profession, particularly in decision-making processes. AI algorithms can predict the outcomes of legal conflicts by evaluating massive databases of historical legal cases, judicial decisions, and procedural records. This enables lawyers, judges, and legal teams to make informed, data-driven strategic decisions even before a case enters the courtroom.

Machine learning algorithms detect trends and connections by using categorization models built on previous judicial decisions. Tools such as Lex Machina and Premonition, for example, examine massive amounts of court data to assess how individual judges have previously ruled, the success rates of specific law firms, and the impact of case variables on results (Surden, 2019). These tools are especially useful for litigation strategy, as they can predict the likelihood of winning or losing a lawsuit, estimate potential damages, and propose best timing for settlement offers.

A remarkable application of predictive analytics in real-world legal practice happened in the United States, when a machine learning model correctly predicted 70.2% of Supreme Court judgments over nearly two centuries (Katz et al., 2017). This model revealed not only AI's ability to discover legal patterns but also its potential to reduce uncertainty in high-stakes cases.

Predictive tools are also utilized in criminal justice to make decisions about punishment and bail. For example, the Public Safety Assessment (PSA) tool, which is utilized in various US jurisdictions, estimates the likelihood of a prisoner reoffending or failing to appear in court, allowing judges to make more uniform and unbiased bail decisions (Brennan et al., 2009). While these applications boost efficiency, they have prompted arguments about fairness, transparency, and bias in algorithmic decision-making (Angwin et al., 2016).

Furthermore, predictive analytics improves case priority and resource allocation. Law firms can utilize outcome prediction to decide which cases to pursue, how to devote time and resources, and when to suggest alternate dispute settlement techniques.

As AI learns from increasingly complex legal datasets, its role in shaping legal strategy, lowering litigation costs, and enhancing access to justice is projected to rise considerably.

AI in Forensic Evidence Analysis

AI is rapidly altering forensic science by improving the speed, accuracy, and reliability of evidence analysis in criminal investigations. AI-powered technologies enable law enforcement and forensic professionals to recognize trends, authenticate evidence, and identify suspects with remarkable precision.

Deep learning-powered face recognition technologies are routinely employed to identify individuals in surveillance footage, matching facial traits against vast databases in seconds. For example, the Federal Bureau of Investigation (FBI) in the United States uses the Next Generation Identification (NGI) system, which includes facial recognition, to aid in criminal investigations. According to the US Government Accountability Office (GAO), in 2016, NGI's facial recognition section could search more than 30 million photographs.

AI also plays an important role in voice analysis. AI can identify speakers from audio recordings using speech pattern recognition and voice biometrics, even in noisy or distorted surroundings. These skills are critical in situations involving ransomware, threats, or covert recordings. Police departments and intelligence agencies around the world already employ tools like Nuance Communications' forensic voice analysis software.

In digital forensics, AI aids in the analysis of massive volumes of data, such as emails, chat logs, metadata, and hard drive contents, in order to spot anomalies, extract essential information, and rebuild timelines. Machine learning models are especially beneficial for detecting cybercrime signatures like phishing schemes and malware behavior, as well as detecting deepfake media using pixel pattern inconsistencies and temporal discrepancies (Nguyen et al., 2019). These solutions not only accelerate investigations but also increase the reliability of digital evidence in court.

Furthermore, AI systems may evaluate the integrity of digital content, warning any potential tampering or manipulation. In one famous case, forensic AI helped validate metadata differences in altered surveillance footage used in a corporate fraud prosecution, resulting in a conviction (Goodson et al., 2015).

While AI significantly improves forensic capabilities, it also raises questions about accuracy, bias, and misuse. For example, facial recognition algorithms have been criticized for making more mistakes when identifying people with darker skin tones (Buolamwini & Gebru, 2018). AI forensic technologies must be continuously validated, transparent, and regulated to ensure ethical usage.

THE ADVANCEMENTS IN E-DISCOVERY

E-discovery, also known as electronic discovery, is the act of finding, gathering, and producing ESI for use in legal proceedings. With the exponential growth of digital data, AI-driven and blockchain-enabled e-discovery solutions have changed traditional litigation and investigative workflows, automating evidence retrieval, enhancing accuracy, and ensuring digital integrity.

AUTOMATED E-DISCOVERY TOOLS

AI-powered e-discovery tools have significantly increased the efficiency of legal document review by automating the identification and categorization of important digital content. These platforms use machine learning algorithms to scan huge amounts of unstructured data—such as emails, papers, audio recordings, and chat logs—and rank their relevance to a legal situation.

One of the most important advancements in this sector is Technology-Assisted Review (TAR), which employs predictive coding to iteratively train algorithms to spot patterns and judge document relevancy. This method has proven to be faster and more accurate than typical manual reviews. For example, in *Moore v. Publicis Groupe* (2012), the Southern District of New York permitted the use of TAR in discovery, setting a legal precedence for AI-driven review processes in court (Losey, 2016).

Advanced solutions such as Relativity, Everlaw, and Logikcull include AI-enhanced search capabilities, automatic redaction tools, and sentiment analysis, drastically lowering costs and review durations. AI solutions can reduce e-discovery costs by as much as 80% while raising overall document review accuracy by approximately 86%.

BLOCKCHAIN AND SMART CONTRACTS IN EVIDENCE INTEGRITY

Blockchain technology is revolutionizing the integrity of digital evidence through immutability and transparent traceability. By timestamping and cryptographically linking data blocks, blockchain ensures that once data is recorded, it cannot be altered without leaving a trace—crucial for maintaining a secure **chain of custody** in legal investigations.

Blockchain technology is improving the integrity of digital evidence by ensuring immutability and transparent traceability. Blockchain assures that once data is stored, it cannot be altered without leaving a trail, which is critical for establishing a secure chain of custody in legal investigations (Zhang et al., 2019).

LegalTech businesses such as ChronoLogic and OpenLaw have created blockchain-powered legal applications that are gaining popularity in corporate litigation, intellectual property protection, and government evidence management systems. In high-profile cybercrime investigations, a blockchain-based chain of custody has been important in defending the admissibility of digital evidence.

Cloud-Based e-Discovery Solutions

Cloud computing has introduced scalable and secure infrastructure for modern e-discovery systems. Cloud-based technologies allow for real-time cooperation across geographically dispersed legal teams, providing seamless access to evidence while preserving compliance with jurisdictional privacy and security laws, such as GDPR and HIPAA.

These systems are especially effective for multi-party litigation, internal business investigations, and international legal issues. For example, Microsoft Azure Purview and Amazon Web Services CloudTrail provide compliance-ready e-discovery capabilities that are linked with enterprise technologies. Cloud platforms also allow for rapid expansion during litigation spikes, enabling thousands of concurrent users and enormous databases.

According to Jones (2018), cloud-based legal solutions enhance discovery response times by 30%–50% while lowering infrastructure costs by eliminating the requirement for on-premise hardware. Furthermore, when combined with AI algorithms, cloud platforms improve document culling, information extraction, and predictive analysis, expediting the entire litigation support process.

CHALLENGES AND ETHICAL CONSIDERATIONS

Data Privacy and Confidentiality Concerns

The use of AI and e-discovery in legal processes raises substantial data privacy concerns. AI systems frequently handle large volumes of sensitive data, needing stringent adherence to data privacy standards such as the General Data Protection Regulation (GDPR) and the California Consumer Privacy Act (CCPA). These regulations require transparency in data processing and give people control over their personal data.

Furthermore, the possibility for AI systems to mistakenly leak confidential information emphasizes the importance of strong security measures. Law companies and legal departments must ensure that AI technologies comply with data privacy regulations and include encryption and access controls to preserve client information.

Bias and Fairness in AI Algorithms

AI systems can unintentionally perpetuate existing biases in training data, resulting in unfair outcomes in legal decision-making. For example, skewed datasets can lead to discriminatory practices in areas such as bail and punishment. The COMPAS algorithm, employed in the United States for calculating recidivism risk, has been challenged for its racial prejudice (AI Now Institute, 2019).

To mitigate such risks, it's essential to implement bias detection and correction mechanisms in AI systems. Regular audits, diverse training datasets, and transparency in algorithmic decision-making processes are crucial steps toward ensuring fairness and equity in AI applications within the legal domain.

Ethical Implications of AI in Evidence Handling

The use of AI in legal evidence handling creates ethical concerns, such as over-reliance on automated methods and the potential loss of human judgment. While AI can improve efficiency, it should not replace human oversight in key legal decisions. Ensuring that AI tools are utilized to supplement rather than substitute human expertise is crucial for safeguarding the integrity of legal proceedings (Surden, 2020).

Furthermore, the "black box" aspect of some AI systems, where decision-making processes are opaque, raises concerns about accountability and transparency. Legal professionals must advocate for understandable AI models that provide explicit rationale for their outputs, enabling scrutiny and promoting trust in AI-assisted legal processes (AI Now Institute, 2019).

FUTURE TRENDS AND IMPLICATIONS

AI-Driven Legal Assistants and Virtual Judges

The introduction of AI-powered legal assistants promises to transform legal research and case analysis. These tools can quickly evaluate legal papers, discover important precedents, and help you create legal arguments. In some jurisdictions, AI is being researched for adjudicating small disputes, increasing access to justice, and minimizing court backlogs (Susskind, 2019).

However, the idea of AI-powered virtual judges calls into question the role of human judgment in legal decision-making. Ensuring that AI technologies are utilized to help rather than replace human adjudicators is critical for sustaining the concepts of justice and fairness.

Quantum Computing in Legal Evidence Processing

Quantum computing has the potential to transform legal evidence processing by allowing for quick examination of complicated datasets. Its unique processing capabilities may speed up e-discovery and forensic investigations, allowing for more efficient handling of enormous volumes of electronic data (Cambridge University Press, 2025).

Nonetheless, incorporating quantum computing into judicial processes needs a thorough examination of data security and ethical concerns. As quantum technologies progress, developing regulatory frameworks to oversee their usage in the legal sphere will be necessary to prevent misuse and assure conformity with legal requirements (Cambridge University Press, 2025).

Regulatory Frameworks for AI in Legal Evidence

The rapid growth of AI technology emphasizes the need for robust regulatory frameworks to oversee their use in legal evidence. These frameworks should cover topics like data privacy, algorithmic transparency, and accountability. International initiatives are underway to set rules that balance innovation and the protection of fundamental rights (Alfiani & Santiago, 2025).

In India, the NITI Aayog has issued guidelines for responsible AI, emphasizing the relevance of ethical issues in AI deployment. As AI is increasingly integrated into legal procedures, establishing explicit regulations will be crucial in ensuring that technology improvements correspond with legal and ethical standards (Mohanty & Sahu, 2024).

AI IN INDIAN LEGAL EVIDENCE

Current Applications and Developments

In India, the legal profession is starting to adopt AI technologies to improve efficiency and accuracy. The Supreme Court's launch of the Supreme Court Portal for Assistance in Court Efficiency (SUPACE) demonstrates this trend. SUPACE helps judges by summarizing case files and locating relevant legal precedents, which streamlines court processes.

AI is also making advances into forensic science in India. Advanced algorithms are used for activities such as fingerprint analysis, facial recognition, and voice identification, assisting law enforcement agencies with evidence validation and criminal investigations.

Challenges and Ethical Concerns

Despite these advances, various obstacles prevent wider application of AI in India's judicial system. The Indian Evidence Act of 1872 lacks explicit provisions for AI-generated evidence, requiring legislative modifications to accommodate evolving technologies (Dasgupta, 2023).

Ethical concerns remain, including the risk of algorithmic prejudice, a lack of transparency in AI decision-making, and possible abuses of privacy rights. Addressing these concerns demands the creation of solid ethical principles and the installation of supervision mechanisms to ensure that AI applications in the legal realm maintain justice and fairness (Kapoor, 2021).

The Future of AI and E-Discovery in India

Looking ahead, AI and e-discovery are poised to revolutionize India's legal scene. Integrating blockchain technology could improve the integrity of digital evidence by offering immutable recordings, while AI-driven dispute resolution platforms may offer efficient alternatives for settling minor legal concerns (Mukherjee, 2024).

Establishing robust regulatory frameworks and investing in capacity-building efforts will ensure that AI's integration into India's legal system increases access to justice and maintains the rule of law.

CONCLUSION

The changing environment of AI in the legal profession offers both enormous opportunities and considerable obstacles. As shown throughout this essay, AI has the ability to alter legal procedures by increasing efficiency, reducing human error, and allowing for more exact legal research and predictive analysis. However, moving forward, it is critical to address the ethical concerns, privacy issues, and potential biases inherent in AI systems. AI application in judicial systems must be undertaken with prudence, with the goal of complementing rather than replacing human judgment.

The potential of AI in law, from automating ordinary operations to assisting in complicated disputes, highlights its importance in determining the future of legal practice. Nonetheless, stakeholders must address the implications of AI for access to justice, specifically how to ensure that AI technologies do not perpetuate inequality or exclude vulnerable populations. Transparency, accountability, and a strong legal framework will be essential for building trust in AI systems and maximizing their positive impact.

In conclusion, while AI's promise in law is apparent, its implementation must be carefully regulated. By emphasizing ethical norms, regulatory monitoring, and ongoing communication among legal professionals, technologists, and legislators, AI can play a transformative role in the legal profession, leading to a fairer, more efficient judicial system.

This essay examined the integration of AI in the legal profession, noting both its transformative potential and the obstacles it poses. The article's primary results are as follows:

Productivity Improvements: AI has demonstrated tremendous potential in automating mundane legal operations, boosting research accuracy, and enabling predictive analytics, all of which contribute to more efficient legal practices.

Ethical Questions: While AI can increase efficiency, there are questions regarding prejudice, privacy, and justice in legal decision-making procedures. Biased algorithms have the potential to perpetuate societal imbalances, which must be addressed.

Impact on Legal Employment: While AI has the potential to improve the legal profession, it also raises worries about employment displacement. Legal professionals must adapt to new technology, and ongoing education will be critical in sustaining their jobs alongside AI.

Access to Justice: AI has the ability to democratize legal services, making them more accessible to underprivileged communities. However, the cost of technology and lack of regulation may restrict its advantages to those who need them the most.

Based on these findings, numerous recommendations are made to ensure the good influence of AI in law:

- Ethical Framework Development: It is critical to create thorough ethical guidelines for AI usage in the legal area that ensure algorithms are transparent, responsible, and bias-free. Regular audits and supervision measures must be in place.
- Regulatory Oversight: Governments and legal authorities should provide clear regulatory frameworks for AI technology in the legal industry. This will assist in resolving issues about privacy, prejudice, and maintaining human oversight in decision-making systems.
- AI Training for Legal Practitioners: Legal practitioners should undergo continual training in AI and its consequences to guarantee they can successfully employ technology in their practice while maintaining ethical standards.
- Encourage Inclusivity: AI developers and legal institutions should work to produce solutions that emphasize access to justice, particularly for marginalized populations that would otherwise be excluded from the advantages of AI technology.

REFERENCES

AI Now Institute. (2019). AI Now 2019 Report. https://ainowinstitute.org/wp-content/uploads/2023/04/AI_Now_2019_Report.pdf.

Alfiani, F. R. N., & Santiago, F. (2025). A comparative analysis of artificial intelligence regulatory law in Asia, Europe, and America. *ResearchGate*. www.researchgate.net/publication/386107722.

Angwin et al. (2016). *Machine bias: There's software used across the country to predict future criminals.* And it's biased against blacks. ProPublica. www.propublica.org/article/machine-bias-risk-assessments-in-criminal-sentencing.

Brennan et al. (2009). Evaluating the predictive validity of the COMPAS Risk and Needs Assessment System. *Criminal Justice and Behavior*, 36(1), 21–40. https://doi.org/10.1177/0093854808326545.

Buolamwini, J., & Gebru, T. (2018). Gender shades: Intersectional accuracy disparities in commercial gender classification. *Proceedings of Machine Learning Research*, 81, 1–15. http://proceedings.mlr.press/v81/buolamwini18a/buolamwini18a.pdf.

Cambridge University Press. (2025). Quantum computing and the law: Navigating the legal implications of a quantum leap. *European Journal of Risk Regulation.*

Dasgupta, R. (2023). AI and legal frameworks in India: The need for reform. *Indian Journal of Law and Technology*, 15(2), 112–128.

GAO (U.S. Government Accountability Office). (2016). Face recognition technology: FBI should better ensure privacy and accuracy. GAO-16-267. www.gao.gov/products/gao-16-267.

Goodison et al. (2015). *Digital evidence and the U.S. criminal justice system: Identifying technology and other needs to more effectively acquire and utilize digital evidence.* RAND Corporation.

Grossman, M. R., & Cormack, G. V. (2011). Technology-assisted review in e-discovery can be more effective and more efficient than exhaustive manual review. *Richmond Journal of Law and Technology*, 17(3), 1–48. https://jolt.richmond.edu/.

Jones, I. (2018). Cloud computing and e-discovery: Challenges and opportunities. *Journal of Legal Technology*, 15(2), 78–95.

Kapoor, S. (2021). Ethical implications of AI in the legal sector. *Technology & Law Review*, 8(4), 233–249.

Katz, D. M., Bommarito, M. J., & Blackman, J. (2017). A general approach for predicting the behavior of the Supreme Court of the United States. *PLoS ONE*, 12(4), e0174698. https://doi.org/10.1371/journal.pone.0174698.

Losey, R. (2016). *E-discovery for the legal professional.* American Bar Association.

McGinnis, J. O., & Pearce, R. G. (2014). The great disruption: How machine intelligence will transform the role of lawyers in the delivery of legal services. *Fordham Law Review*, 82(6), 3041–3066. https://ir.lawnet.fordham.edu/flr/vol82/iss6/15.

Mukherjee, A. (2024). The future of e-discovery in Indian litigation. *International Journal of Digital Law*, 19(2), 101–119.

Nguyen et al. (2019). Deep learning for deepfakes creation and detection: A survey. *arXiv preprint arXiv:1909.11573*. https://doi.org/10.48550/arXiv.1909.11573.

Surden, H. (2019). Artificial intelligence and law: An overview. *Georgia State University Law Review*, 35(4), 1305–1339. https://readingroom.law.gsu.edu/gsulr/vol35/iss4/6/.

Surden, H. (2020). *Artificial intelligence and legal reasoning*. Cambridge University Press.

Susskind, R. (2019). *Online courts and the future of justice*. Oxford University Press.

Zhang et al. (2019). Blockchain and digital evidence: An emerging legal paradigm. *International Journal of Law and Information Technology*, 27(2), 140–160.

21 Beyond a Reasonable Bot

Preserving Judicial Discretion in AI-Augmented Adjudication

Sanjeeb K. Panigrahi,[1] *Siddharth Anand Panda,*[2] *and Nishtha Mahapatra*[3]

ALGORITHMS AT THE GATES OF JUSTICE

In 2023, a US attorney used ChatGPT to draft a court filing in a personal injury case against Avianca Airlines. Unbeknownst to him, he cited six fictitious cases that were generated out of thin air by the AI. Relying on the information furnished by the AI, the attorney submitted fabricated precedents replete with fake quotes and gibberish citations. This error came to light when Avianca's lawyers failed to verify the cases, prompting Judge P. Kevin Castel to flag the matter as "unprecedented." The attorney admitted he was unaware of the tool's limitations and insisted there was no malafide. The case marked one of the earliest real-world examples of AI infiltrating the courtroom, highlighting the risks of uncritical reliance on generative tools in legal practice and the urgent need for digital literacy in the profession.

Undeniably, AI promises efficiency for its prowess of rapid legal research and data-driven insights. With nearly 60 lakh cases pending in India's high courts as of 2024, AI tools could offer substantial relief by instantly summarizing precedents and identifying relevant statutes to make expediency effective. AI tools like ChatGPT and Gemini offer a tantalizing solution for procedural delays, potentially expediting routine tasks and freeing judges to focus on core judicial functions. Nevertheless, the unease is squarely palpable. Integrating AI into judging touches the very nerve of judicial integrity. Critics worry that mechanizing any part of the decision-making process may undermine the human qualities essential to justice and thus advocate the discretion status quo (Roth, 2015).

The prospect of algorithmic influence in verdicts raises profound questions: Can a machine appreciate the texture of justice? Can code account for the conscience and contextual judgment that judges are sworn to exercise? Even though GenAI holds promise of increased efficiency, it is warned that it could introduce concerns of bias and opacity, potentially undermining judicial discretion and the rule of law (Socol de la Osa & Remolina, 2024). If decisions start being informed or even made by algorithms, the fear is that the "soul" of judgment in its careful weighing of evidence and equitable application of law to unique facts could be lost in favor of automated uniformity.

We argue that while AI and predictive analytics can indeed augment the judicial process, their indiscriminate adoption poses a serious threat to the human element of judging. The allure of AI, thus, must not overshadow the need for judicial prudence.

JUDICIAL DISCRETION'S INNATE NEED FOR A HUMAN ELEMENT

Judicial discretion is often misunderstood as antithetical to the rule of law when, in fact, it is what gives spirit to the letter of law, lest it become dead and bland. H.L.A. Hart tried to unravel the "open

DOI: 10.1201/9781003629146-22

texture" of law such that even the most precisely crafted rules will eventually encounter situations that legislators did not foresee (Zipursky, 2008). In this "penumbra" of uncertainty (Zipursky, 2008), judges must exercise discretion to bridge the gap between abstract rules and concrete reality. Far from undermining the law, such discretion breathes life into it by allowing justice to be responsive to nuances as they present themselves. Kenneth C. Davis (1969) advocated "discretion" as an "indispensable necessity" in any legal system, especially in adjudication such that no legal rule can dictate outcomes for *all* cases without some measure of flexibility. In India, the importance of judicial discretion finds express recognition in both constitutional and statutory provisions.

Article 142 of the Constitution of India empowers its Supreme Court to "*pass such decree or make such order as is necessary for doing complete justice*" in any matter before it. This is a breathtaking grant of equitable power; a recognition that "complete justice" may at times require the Court to depart from strictly procedural or substantive rules in order to grant appropriate relief.

This has enabled some of the most landmark and innovative judgments in Indian history, precisely because the Court could go beyond black-letter law to meet the demands of justice. In the aftermath of the Bhopal gas tragedy, the Supreme Court invoked Article 142 to approve a settlement and devise a relief package for thousands of victims, even though procedural and substantive laws at the time were inadequate for such mass tort resolution (*Union Carbide Corporation v. Union of India*, 1989). In 2017, the Court invoked its extraordinary power to ban liquor sales within 500 meters of national highways to curb drunk driving (*State of Tamil Nadu v. K. Balu*, 2017). A Constitution Bench granted divorce on grounds of "irretrievable breakdown" of marriage, even though no such ground exists in Hindu marriage law, thus delivering speedy justice in a dead marriage. Recently, the Supreme Court asserted its constitutional authority by setting clear timelines for Governors and the President to assent/dissent or return state bills (*State of T.N. v. Governor of T.N.*, 2025). These cases illustrate the Apex Court's potent use of discretion to fill legal gaps where rigid application of the law would have denied appropriate remedy.

Similarly, Section 165 of the Indian Evidence Act, 1872 explicitly granted judges the power to actively put questions to witnesses or parties at any stage of a trial "*in order to discover or to obtain proper proof of relevant facts*." This provision liberates judges from the passivity of the adversarial system whenever necessary, allowing them to dig deeper with their own questions. The law recognizes that truth-seeking may demand judicial intervention beyond the rules of evidence, and it entrusts judges with that discretion for the sake of justice (Chin, 1979).

Judicial discretion also facilitated the rise of public interest litigation in India, one of the world's unique judicial innovations. It was through judicial discretion that the courts expanded concepts of *locus standi* and justiciability to admit these cases. This eventually led to transformative decisions on prisoners' rights, environmental protection, bonded labor, sexual harassment guidelines, recognition of LGBTQ+ rights, and many other socio-economic rights.

The culture of Indian courtroom practice, especially in the lower courts, often expects judges to interject with tough questions to pin down elusive facts or clarify ambiguous testimony (Berti, 2011). An AI, by contrast, cannot depart from a script to follow the trail of truth as a human judge can. It doesn't have the ability to flexibly respond to, *inter alia*, a witness's evasive demeanor or a sudden revelation in testimony.

Judicial discretion is also central to sentencing jurisprudence. Perhaps the most vivid example is the "rarest of rare" principle (*Bachan Singh v. State of Punjab*, 1980). which elucidates that murder convicts be assessed individually, not treated identically, by weighing factors like the aggravating and mitigating factors. Likewise, in *State of Punjab v. Prem Sagar* (2008), the Supreme Court lamented the lack of consistent sentencing guidelines in India but reaffirmed the need for individualized sentencing. It has been clearly insinuated that uniformity must not become the goal unto itself at the cost of proportionality and contextual appropriateness.

Now, judicial discretion is not a free-for-all or personal whim. It is bounded by precedent, guided by legal principles, and subject to appellate review. Judges must give reasoned decisions explaining how they exercised their discretion, which provides accountability. Discretion operates not in defiance of legal norms but in service of them. It is the mechanism by which law remains in "particulars" and not just in "generalities" (Del Mar, 2025). Upendra Baxi (1985) describes "humane governance" as the idea that law should respond to real human suffering and complex situations, not just apply abstract rules.

To hand over significant aspects of adjudication to AI tools would, therefore, not just be a neutral technological shift. It could amount to a constitutional regression in the Indian context. It would mean replacing the locally grown and equity-driven approach of Indian judgment with a one-size-fits-all decision model, likely based on foreign data or generic parameters. It might sacrifice the creative remedies and empathetic interventions that Indian judges have used to fill policy gaps in favor of "playing by the data," ironically at a time when the Indian judiciary's distinctive contribution has been its flexibility in the face of crisis.

THE STANDARDIZATION RISK OF AI AND THE DISPLACEMENT OF DISCRETION

Machine learning algorithms can ingest vast databases of past cases, relevant statutes, and facts to predict legal outcomes or suggest decisions (Sourdin, 2018). For example, risk-assessment tools can now predict recidivism and match cases to precedents, while decision-support systems can suggest sentencing ranges based on past trends (Zeleznikow, 2023). In the United States, software like COMPAS (Correctional Offender Management Profiling for Alternative Sanctions) has been used to assess defendants' risk of re-offending, ostensibly to guide bail and sentencing decisions. China has gone even further with its introduction of "smart courts," where AI systems automatically screen case filings, suggest applicable laws, and, in some instances, draft verdicts for judges' approval (Cousineau, 2021). In India, the Supreme Court, in 2021, launched an AI portal called SUPACE (Supreme Court Portal for Assistance in Court Efficiency) designed to help judges by sifting through case documents and summarizing legal research (PIB, 2025). These innovations portend a future where much of the drudgery of legal analysis is outsourced to the machines, allowing judges to make quick and consistent decisions. But then, why are so many jurists wary that artificial intelligence could displace judicial discretion?

Predictive analytics introduce a subtle but critical danger i.e., "the over-standardization of justice" (Mizaras, 2025). By design, machine-learning models look to the past to predict the future. They detect patterns in historical data and assume those patterns should guide new decisions (Greenstein, 2022). In a reform-oriented legal system like India, dominant reliance on historical data (read: biased) can make AI not only reinforce old injustices but also legitimize them under the guise of scientific objectivity. In 2016, a ProPublica investigation revealed that the COMPAS algorithm tends to exhibit significant racial bias, flagging African American defendants as "high risk" for future crime at almost twice the rate of white defendants (ProPublica, 2016). Such disparities typically stem from the historical data used to train the model, in this case, data reflecting racial inequalities in arrests and convictions (Jackson & Mendoza, 2020). If a similar algorithm were naively transplanted into the Indian context, one could easily imagine analogous biases emerging along lines of caste, religion, class, region, etc. from the data ambiguously reflective of socio-economic disparities.

Another concern is automation bias, a well-documented cognitive bias where humans tend to favor suggestions from an automated system even when they have reason to doubt it (Ajunwa, 2019). Judges are not immune to the tendency to subconsciously defer to a computer's output simply because it carries a masquerade of technological objectivity (Tatiana, K., and Tomlinson, J., 2023). If an AI tool recommends denying bail or suggests a harsh sentence, a judge might attach undue weight to it at the expense of the judge's own independent analysis. Legal technologists thus warn against unconditional reliance on AI-generated content and caution against unqualified approval of automation. Without proper training and safeguards, introducing AI advice into the courtroom could skew human decision-making, effectively diminishing the role of discretion even if, formally, a judge still signs off on the outcome (Sourdin, 2018).

These dangers are compounded as algorithms of such AI tools that operate as "black boxes" for their proprietary systems' internal logic that is opaque to judges, lawyers, and litigants alike (Deeks, 2019). Unlike a human judge, who must articulate reasons for a decision that can be scrutinized, many AI models provide conclusions without clear explanations. The COMPAS tool and its developer, Equivant, do not publicly disclose the formula by which it calculates risk scores. In *State v. Loomis* (2016), a defendant argued that his due process rights were violated because he was sentenced based on a COMPAS risk score that neither he nor the court could scrutinize or challenge. The Wisconsin Supreme Court ultimately allowed COMPAS to be used, but such scores must never solely determine incarceration or sentencing. Pre-sentence reports must clearly state that the algorithm works on averages assessing population groups and not individual risk (Liu et. al, 2019). The very fact that a Supreme Court had to append footnotes of caution shows how problematic automation is in a domain that demands transparency.

Finally, and perhaps most importantly, AI lacks the human faculties essential to discretionary adjudication. No matter how sophisticated, a machine learning model has no moral intuition or empathy. It cannot feel the anguish of a victim or the anxiety of an accused. Put simply, an algorithm cannot imbibe law with fairness, nor can it recognize when justice demands due adherence or deviation from the norm. These are not bugs in the system of human judgment; they are features of a justice system that aims to do right by individuals. AI, by contrast, is fundamentally about aggregating and normalizing. But as any judge knows, many cases are not average. Turning over too much decision-making to AI risks a dystopia of "over-standardized justice," where like cases are treated alike but no one is treated well.

HARMONIZING AI WITH DISCRETION

Inevitably, AI is here to stay in the legal domain, and thus, we must design and deploy it in ways that respect and reinforce judicial discretion, rather than displacing it. How can we achieve the benefits of AI without sacrificing the human touch? We outline a multi-pronged strategy:

1. **AI as Assistive, Not Authoritative:** The foremost principle should be that any AI system in the courtroom serves as an aid to human judges, *not* a replacement or an oracle. In practical terms, this means AI outputs must be treated as non-binding suggestions or insights. The U.S. Sedona Conference's 2023 guidance on AI for judges emphasizes that "*while technological advances offer new tools to assist the judiciary, judicial officers must remain faithful to their core obligations of maintaining professional competence, upholding the rule of law, promoting justice, and adhering to applicable Canons of Judicial Conduct*" (Hon. Dixon Jr. et al., 2025). Therefore, judges must remain in control, and any tendency to defer blindly to the AI must be consciously resisted.
2. **Explainability and Transparency:** Given the dangers of black-box algorithms, it should be a strict requirement that AI tools used in judicial settings are explainable (Lim, 2021). The current trend of secret proprietary models is inimical to the justice system. Judges cannot be expected to trust or rely on a process they don't understand. Moreover, the parties to a case have a right to know the basis of decisions affecting them. The system should provide, along with any recommendation, a transparent account of the factors it considered. Explainable AI (XAI) techniques (Deeks, 2019) such as decision trees, rule-based models, logic-based frameworks, or interpretable machine learning should be prioritized for any courtroom use. The ultimate goal is to mirror the transparency that human judges must show. A transparent AI audit framework for any GenAI used in courts would greatly increase not only interpretability but also public trust.

3. **Bias Audits and Inclusive Design**: Any AI system deployed in courts should undergo rigorous bias auditing before and during its use. This involves testing the system with hypothetical scenarios to see if it yields systematically different outcomes for different demographic groups, e.g., based on race, caste, gender, etc. (Krištofík, 2025). If biases are detected, the tool must be corrected or scrapped. Furthermore, the training data for legal AI should be as representative as possible of the society it serves. For India, this means including data from diverse jurisdictions and accounting for socio-cultural context in model development. Importantly, these audits and their results should be public. Some jurisdictions, like the EU and Colorado State (Levi et. al., 2024), have rolled out mandatory bias and impact assessments for high-risk AI systems, and judicial tools should certainly qualify as high-risk given their potential effect on life and liberty.
4. **Contextual and Localized AI Solutions:** Indian legal institutions must resist the one-size-fits-all allure of importing foreign AI models or software without customization. The legal culture and ground realities in India differ markedly from those in, say, the United States or China. A risk assessment calibrated to U.S. criminal data might utterly misfire if applied to Indian accused persons due to different crime patterns, policing biases, etc. Therefore, any AI introduced should be locally developed or at least locally trained on Indian data, with Indian legal priorities in mind. Also, the values embodied in the Indian Constitution, such as the emphasis on reformative justice and social justice, should guide the design.
5. **Evolving Procedural Law for AI:** As AI tools become part of the judicial process, procedural laws and evidentiary standards will need updating. For instance, if a judge uses an AI response in arriving at a decision, should that be disclosed to the parties? One could argue yes, it's akin to relying on a piece of evidence not formally submitted by the parties, so perhaps the parties should have a chance to respond to the AI's suggestion. Rules might be developed requiring that any facts or case law an AI tool brings up must be entered into the court record if they influence the outcome. We might also see guidelines on citing AI in judgments. Crucially, evidentiary doctrines such as those governing the admissibility of scientific evidence could be invoked to challenge algorithmic outputs (Sallavaci, 2025); for example, a litigant might demand an adversarial testing of AI's inputs and the algorithm within in a given case.

The legal community must proactively engage with these questions so that the procedure adapts in tandem with technology, always keeping in focus the rights to fair trial and natural justice.

CONCLUSION

AI can analyze extensive datasets and spot patterns imperceptible to the naked human eye. It can certainly predict outcomes in a statistical sense and draft impressive legal prose. However, AI lacks the capacity to render justice as a normative and individualized exercise, which inherently requires human discernment. It cannot feel remorse or indignation, yet these emotions often underlie why a punishment is harsh or lenient or why a right is read expansively or narrowly. It cannot interpret silence or nuance the way a judge might perceive a witness hesitating and infer something unsaid. It cannot recognize irony or absurdity, qualities that sometimes make the difference in statutory interpretation or in assessing whether enforcing a law strictly would lead to unjust results. No machine can yet (or perhaps ever) feel the moral weight of sending someone to prison or appreciate the societal significance of extending a right to a marginalized group against entrenched norms. In such moments, calculation must yield to conscience. This is why entrusting justice entirely to machines is perilous, for it may yield a system that is efficient yet blind to fairness, deaf to nuance, and mute to the human condition.

NOTES

1 Judge, High Court of Orissa.
2 Research Assistant-cum-Judicial Clerk, High Court of Orissa.
3 Research Assistant-cum-Judicial Clerk, High Court of Orissa.

REFERENCES

Ajunwa, I. (2019). The paradox of automation as anti-bias intervention. *Cardozo Law Review, 41*, 1671. https://par.nsf.gov/servlets/purl/10267581.

Angwin, A., Larson, J., Mattu S., & Kirchner, L., ProPublica. (2016, Mar 23). *Machine Bias*. ProPublica. www.propublica.org/article/machine-bias-risk-assessments-in-criminal-sentencing.

Bachan Singh v. State of Punjab, (1980) 2 SCC 684.

Baxi, U. (1985). Taking suffering seriously: Social action litigation in the Supreme Court of India. *Third World Legal Studies, 4*(6). https://scholar.valpo.edu/twls/vol4/iss1/6

Berti, D. (2011). Courts of law and legal practice. In I. Clark-Decès (ed.), *A Companion to the Anthropology of India* (pp. 353–370). Chichester: Wiley-Blackwell. https://shs.hal.science/halshs-02335114/document

Chin, T.Y. (1979). Documents on affairs of state as evidence: Bringing a legal porcupine into judicial custody. *Malaya Law Review, 17*, 24.

Cousineau, C. (2021, Apr 15). *Smart Courts and the Push for Technological Innovation in China's Judicial System*. Centre for Strategic and International Studies. https://www.csis.org/blogs/new-perspectives-asia/smart-courts-and-push-technological-innovation-chinas-judicial-system

Davis, C.K. (1969). *Discretionary Justice: A Preliminary Inquiry*. Louisiana State University Press. Baton Rouge, 233.

Deeks, A. (2019). The judicial demand for explainable artificial intelligence. *Columbia Law Review, 119*(7), 1829–1850.

Del Mar, M. (2025). The relational life of institutional legal theory. In *Neil MacCormick: A Life in Politics, Philosophy, and Law*(pp. 420–496). Cambridge University Press.

Greenstein, S. (2022). Preserving the rule of law in the era of artificial intelligence (AI). *Artificial Intelligence and Law, 30*, 291–323. https://doi.org/10.1007/s10506-021-09294-4

Hon. Dixon Jr., H.B., Hon. Goddard, A.H., Grossman, M.R., Hon. Rodriguez, X., Hon. Schlegel, S.U., & Hon. Thumma, S.A. (2025). Navigating AI in the judiciary: New guidelines for judges and their chambers. *The Sedona Conference Journal, 26*(1), 3.

Jackson, E. & Mendoza, C. (2020). Setting the record straight: What the COMPAS core risk and need assessment is and is not. *Harvard Data Science Review*. https://hdsr.mitpress.mit.edu/pub/hzwo7ax4/release/7

Krištofík, A. (2025). Bias in AI (supported) decision aking: Old problems, new technologies. *International Journal for Court Administration,* 16(1).

Levi, S.D., Kumayama, K.D., Ridgway, W.E., Ghaemmaghami, M., & Neal, M.M. (2024, June 24). *Skadden*. www.skadden.com/insights/publications/2024/06/colorados-landmark-ai-act.

Lim, S. (2021). Judicial decision-making and explainable artificial intelligence: A reckoning from first principles. *Singapore Academy of Law Journal, 33*, 280–314.

Liu, H.W., Lin, C.F., & Chen, Y.J. (2019). Beyond State v Loomis: Artificial intelligence, government algorithmization and accountability. *International Journal of Law and Information Technology*, 27(2), 122–141.

Ministry of Law and Justice. (2025, Mar 20). *Use of AI in Supreme Court Case Management*. PIB. www.pib.gov.in/PressReleasePage.aspx?PRID=2113224.

Mizaras, V., Dwivedi, Y.K., Earp, B.D., Fenwick, M., Jurcys, P., Kozuka, S., & Porsdam Mann, S. (2025). Artificial intelligence, the right to a fair trial & the forthcoming. In *The Cambridge handbook of AI and technologies in courts*. Cambridge University Press.

Roth, A. (2015). Trial by machine. *Georgetown Law Journal, 104*, 1245.

Sallavaci, O. (2025). Algorithms on trial: Does evaluative probabilistic reporting of forensic evidence infringe the presumption of innocence? *Forensic Science International: Synergy, 11*. https://www.sciencedirect.com/science/article/pii/S2589871X25000208.

Socol de la Osa, D.U., & Remolina, N. (2024). Artificial intelligence at the bench: Legal and ethical challenges of informing—or misinforming—judicial decision-making through generative AI. *Data & Policy,* 6, e59. https://www.cambridge.org/core/journals/data-and-policy/article/artificial-intelligence-at-the-bench-legal-and-ethical-challenges-of-informingor-misinformingjudicial-decisionmaking-through-generative-ai/D1989AC5C81FB67A5FABB552D3831E46.

Sourdin, T. (2018). Judge v Robot?: Artificial intelligence and judicial decision-making. *University of New South Wales Law Journal,* 41(4), 1114–1133.

State of Punjab v. Prem Sagar, (2008) 7 SCC 550.

State of T.N. v. Governor of T.N., 2025 SCC OnLine SC 770.

State of Tamil Nadu v. K. Balu and Anr., (2017) 2 SCC 281.

State v. Loomis, 881 N.W.2d 749 (Wis. 2016).

Tatiana, K. & Tomlinson, J. (2023). Automation bias and the principles of judicial review. *Judicial Review, 28*(1), 9–16.

Union Carbide Corporation v. Union of India, 1989 SCC (2) 540.

Zeleznikow, J. (2023). The benefits and dangers of using machine learning to support making legal predictions. *Wiley Interdisciplinary Reviews: Data Mining and Knowledge Discovery,* 13(4), e1505.

Zipursky, B.C. (2008, Oct). Practical positivism versus practical perfectionism: The hart-fuller debate at fifty. *New York University School of Law, 83*(4), 1175. https://nyulawreview.org/issues/volume-83-number-4/practical-positivism-versus-practical-perfectionism-the-hart-fuller-debate-at-fifty/.

Index

W

For Product Safety Concerns and Information please contact our EU
representative GPSR@taylorandfrancis.com
Taylor & Francis Verlag GmbH, Kaufingerstraße 24, 80331 München, Germany

www.ingramcontent.com/pod-product-compliance
Lightning Source LLC
LaVergne TN
LVHW062124200926
848484LV00007B/1753

* 9 7 8 1 0 4 1 0 4 6 2 4 0 *